Merrimack College

Library

North Andover, Massachusetts

LUTHER'S WORKS

LUTHER'S WORKS

VOLUME 2

LECTURES ON GENESIS
Chapters 6—14

JAROSLAV PELIKAN
Editor

DANIEL E. POELLOT
Assistant Editor

CONCORDIA PUBLISHING HOUSE · SAINT LOUIS

Copyright 1960 by
CONCORDIA PUBLISHING HOUSE
Saint Louis, Missouri

Library of Congress Catalog Card No. 55-9893

MANUFACTURED IN THE UNITED STATES OF AMERICA

Contents

General Introduction	vii
Introduction to Volume 2	ix
CHAPTER SIX	3
CHAPTER SEVEN	81
CHAPTER EIGHT	103
CHAPTER NINE	131
CHAPTER TEN	187
CHAPTER ELEVEN	210
CHAPTER TWELVE	245
CHAPTER THIRTEEN	324
CHAPTER FOURTEEN	364
Index	401

General Introduction

THE first editions of Luther's collected works appeared in the sixteenth century, and so did the first efforts to make him "speak English." In America serious attempts in these directions were made for the first time in the nineteenth century. The Saint Louis edition of Luther was the first endeavor on American soil to publish a collected edition of his works, and the Henkel Press in Newmarket, Virginia, was the first to publish some of Luther's writings in an English translation. During the first decade of the twentieth century, J. N. Lenker produced translations of Luther's sermons and commentaries in thirteen volumes. A few years later the first of the six volumes in the Philadelphia (or Holman) edition of the *Works of Martin Luther* appeared. Miscellaneous other works were published at one time or another. But a growing recognition of the need for more of Luther's works in English has resulted in this American edition of Luther's works.

The edition is intended primarily for the reader whose knowledge of late medieval Latin and sixteenth-century German is too small to permit him to work with Luther in the original languages. Those who can, will continue to read Luther in his original words as these have been assembled in the monumental Weimar edition (*D. Martin Luthers Werke*. Kritische Gesamtausgabe; Weimar, 1883 ff.). Its texts and helps have formed a basis for this edition, though in certain places we have felt constrained to depart from its readings and findings. We have tried throughout to translate Luther as he thought translating should be done. That is, we have striven for faithfulness on the basis of the best lexicographical materials available. But where literal accuracy and clarity have conflicted, it is clarity that we have preferred, so that sometimes paraphrase seemed more faithful than literal fidelity. We have proceeded in a similar way in the matter of Bible versions, translating Luther's translations. Where this could be done by the use of an existing English version — King James, Douay, or Revised Standard — we have done so. Where it could not, we have supplied our own. To indicate this in each specific instance would have been pedantic; to adopt a uniform procedure would have been artificial — especially in view of Luther's own inconsistency in this regard. In each volume the translator will be responsible primarily for matters of text and language, while the responsibility of the editor will extend principally to the historical and theological matters reflected in the introductions and notes.

Although the edition as planned will include fifty-five volumes, Luther's writings are not being translated in their entirety. Nor should they be. As he was the first to insist, much of what he wrote and said was not that important. Thus the edition is a selection of works that have proved their importance for the faith, life, and history of the Christian Church. The first thirty volumes contain Luther's expositions of various Biblical books, while the remaining volumes include what are usually called his "Reformation writings" and other occasional pieces. The final volume of the set will be an index volume; in addition to an index of quotations, proper names, and topics, and a list of corrections and changes, it will contain a glossary of many of the technical terms that recur in Luther's works and that cannot be defined each time they appear. Obviously Luther cannot be forced into any neat set of rubrics. He can provide his reader with bits of autobiography or with political observations as he expounds a psalm, and he can speak tenderly about the meaning of the faith in the midst of polemics against his opponents. It is the hope of publishers, editors, and translators that through this edition the message of Luther's faith will speak more clearly to the modern church.

J. P.
H. L.

Introduction to Volume 2

IN the portion of his *Lectures on Genesis* presented in this volume (Weimar, XLII, 264–549; St. Louis, I, 436–921), Luther expounds the main body of the story of Noah, begun in Volume 1, and the accounts of the Flood and the Tower of Babel. He discusses also the first chapters in the story of Abraham, which will occupy all of Volume 3 of *Luther's Works* and part of Volume 4. The material set forth here, therefore, contains Luther's comments on the conclusion of the "general history" in Genesis and his description of the origins of the "special history," which begins with the call to Abraham. Thus the Book of Genesis is "the book of beginnings" in at least two senses for Luther: the beginnings of the history of the world, of the human race, its sin, God's promises, and His covenant with all humanity after the Flood; and the beginning of Israel, His chosen nation, the church, of His particular promises to it, and of His special covenant with it "in the loins of Abraham."

Luther's method of exposition remains that of the chapters translated in Volume 1. He bases his theological commentary on a grammatical and historical analysis of the Hebrew text and of translations. In these accounts of the eponymous ancestors of Israel such an analysis often consists of philological inquiry into the names of men and of places, together with a refutation of the fanciful and farfetched etymologies by which previous exegetes, both Jewish and Christian, have sought to explain these names. To amplify his knowledge of these etymologies and of other portions of the exegetical tradition as well, Luther depends on the works of Lyra and Burgensis (cf. *Luther's Works*, 1, Introduction, p. xi). Once more we have attempted to identify all the explicit and implicit references to Lyra, as well as to trace the many other references, citations, and allusions to Scripture, Christian writers, and classical authors in these *Lectures* — many of them not identified at all or erroneously labeled in other editions, including the Weimar edition. (In a few places, indeed, we have even had to question the reading of the transmitted text and to conjecture another reading in its place; cf. p. 336, note 19; p. 288, note 46.) Often this grammatical and historical analysis leads Luther into a polemical and homiletical excursus, suggested by certain parallels between the experience of the patriarchs and the situation of the church. Despite his continuing strictures on allegorical methods of Scriptural exposition, this volume of *Luther's Works*, like many of the other volumes of his exegetical works on the Old Testament, contains allegory as well.

This volume likewise contains further evidence of the editorial manipulation apparent in the earlier chapters of Luther's *Lectures on Genesis*. As the Introduction to Volume 1 has pointed out, present-day historical scholarship has raised serious doubts about the integrity of the materials collected in these *Lectures*, and with good reason. Our second volume contains the last part of the first volume in the original edition and the first part of the second (see p. 235). The editor, Veit Dietrich, is clearly responsible for the present state of the *Lectures*, even though Luther's name is attached to them. One should not be surprised, therefore, to discover Luther referring to events that had not yet happened when he was delivering these lectures in his classroom, but did happen between the time of the delivery of the lectures and the time of their appearance in print (e. g., p. 136). As in Volume 1, there are occasional asides to "the reader" (e. g., p. 259), a minor indication, but a significant one, that Luther's *Lectures on Genesis* are removed from the status of a verbatim transcript by at least two stages: students took down lecture notes, with a characteristic fluctuation in accuracy; editors compiled these notes, with a greater editorial liberty than current canons of scholarship would allow. In addition, there are passages here in Volume 2, as there are in Volume 1, where the very language and conceptual framework suggest the influence of Dietrich on the formulation of Luther's thoughts (e. g., p. 207 f., p. 242).

On the other hand, a careful study of this volume confirms the impression that the main body of this commentary on Noah and Abraham could have come from no one but Martin Luther. To mention only one example: when Noah's enemies taunt him for his opposition to the established church (see p. 50), or when the inner doubts in the heart of Abraham rise up to ask whether it is possible that he is the only one about whom God cares (see p. 293), this is Luther speaking out of his own fightings and fears as the Reformer and as the expositor of the Sacred Scriptures. J. P.

LECTURES ON GENESIS

Chapters 6–14

Translated by
GEORGE V. SCHICK

CHAPTER SIX

In the first five chapters Moses has described the human family as it was in the original world, and has set before our eyes the marvelous grandeur of the holy patriarchs who ruled the primitive world. In these five chapters, as in a first book, he sums up the story of the happiest portion of the entire human race and of the original world before the Flood. At this point we shall begin the second book of Genesis, which contains the story of the Flood and points out that all the descendants of Cain were destroyed, but that the family of the righteous endures through the ages. For when everything was perishing by the Flood, the family of the righteous was nevertheless preserved like an everlasting world.

But it is appalling for the entire human race to be destroyed down to eight souls, even though that age was truly a golden one. Later generations have never matched the excellence, the magnificence, and the splendor of the original world. And yet what God had created as most excellent and most outstanding among the human race He destroyed, for the sake of frightening us thoroughly, as it should be.

Nevertheless, even in this punishment God remained consistent. Whatever is most eminent God is wont to cast down and to humble. Peter, therefore, purposely declares (2 Peter 2:5) that God did not spare the first world. He wants to point out that in comparison with the succeeding world it was like a paradise. Similarly, God did not spare His most outstanding creation, the very angels, or the kings among His people, or the first-born of all times; but in the measure that men were endowed with greater gifts He also punished them the more severely when they began to misuse His gifts.

Thus in the second psalm the Spirit declares concerning kings (2:9): "Thou wilt rule them with an iron rod, and like a potter's vessel Thou wilt break them in pieces." Is He not Himself the Lord, who has established kings and wants everyone to honor and obey them? So He condemns and rejects the wisdom of the wise and the righteousness of the righteous (1 Cor. 1:19). It is the characteristic and continuing work of God that He condemns the most eminent, casts down the most powerful, and shakes the most brave, even though they are His creatures. But He does this to frighten the ungodly and to awaken us with many awe-inspiring examples of His wrath, that we may learn to despair of ourselves and to put our trust in His grace alone.

Therefore either men must live under the shadow of God's wings and with trust in His mercy, or they must perish. But now, after the Fall, the situation among men has become such that the more numerous the gifts with which one is endowed, the greater one's pride is. This was the sin of the angels who fell. This was the sin of the first and original world, in which the most excellent part of the human race lived. But because they acted arrogantly as a result of their wisdom and other gifts, they perished. This was the sin of the greatest kings. This was the sin of almost all the first-born.[1] What need is there of many words? This is the original sin, that we have neither the knowledge nor the capability to use God's great and excellent gifts properly.

When men in very high positions disgrace themselves, not the gifts or the material goods but those who possess them are at fault. But God is the kind of dialectician who convicts by association[2] and destroys the possessor along with the material gift or possession.

It is profitable to observe and note such examples diligently. They are intended to frighten the proud and to humble us, that we may learn that our lives and all that we have depend on God's approval, who is disposed to give grace to the humble but to destroy the proud (1 Peter 5:5). But because the world neither understands nor does this, the kings, the mighty, and the righteous constantly fall, one after the other, until there are abundant examples everywhere of God's wrath and judgment. Thus also the Blessed Virgin sings (Luke 1:51): "He scatters the proud in the imagination of their hearts; He puts down the mighty from their thrones; the rich He sends away empty."

All times, all courts, and all countries abound with such examples. And yet, thanks to the holy devil, the prince of the world, we have such hard hearts that we are not in the least affected by all this but boldly disregard it, even though we feel and see that we, too, must perish. Blessed, therefore, are those who take note of such things and,

[1] Cf. *Luther the Expositor*, pp. 97—98.

[2] Here Luther uses the technical term *arguere a coniugatis* from medieval logic and rhetoric.

admonished by the examples of wrath, humble themselves and live in the fear of God.

Therefore let us think of that original world, which perished in the Flood, as something outstanding; for in outward appearance it had the best, the holiest, and the most honorable men, compared with whom we are like the dregs of the earth. Scripture does not state that they were unjust and evil among themselves, but rather before God. God, it says, saw that they were evil. But God's eyes see and judge far differently from the eyes of men. "My ways," He says in Is. 55:8, "are not like your ways. But as the heaven is higher than the earth, so are My ways higher than your ways, and My thoughts than your thoughts."

Among themselves, therefore, these tyrants and giants were regarded as, and appeared to be, exceedingly wise and righteous, just as today our kings, princes, popes, bishops, theologians, doctors, jurists, and noblemen form the uppermost rank and are highly esteemed as the jewels and lights of the human race. The sons of God in the first world were like this, not because they were considered to be, but because their ability and their gifts made them superior by far. But because they mingled pride and contempt of God with these gifts, God cast them aside and destroyed them together with their gifts, as though they were the dregs and the dung of mankind.

This is a common fault of our nature. Unless it is restrained by the Holy Spirit, it cannot keep from becoming puffed up by the gifts that God has bestowed upon it. Therefore I have often said: "Man has no enemy deadlier than himself."[3] This I learn from my own experience, that I do not have so great a cause for fear outside myself as I have within myself. It is the gifts we have within ourselves that puff up our nature.

But just as God, who is by His nature most benevolent, cannot fail to endow us with sundry gifts and heap them upon us — such as a sound and healthy body, possessions, wisdom, industry, a knowledge of Scripture, and so forth — so we on our part cannot fail to become haughty and arrogant because of these gifts. Our life is very wretched if we must do without the gifts of God; but it is twice as wretched when we do have them, for we become twice as evil. So great is the mischief of original sin. Nevertheless, all men except the

---

[3] Luther may be referring to the Latin proverb, *Homo homini, aut sibi ipsi hostis*, or to some similar saying in German.

believers are either unaware of original sin or disregard it, as though it were something insignificant.

We observe this mischief not only individually in ourselves but also in others. How wealth does puff one up, even though it occupies the lowest position among the gifts of God! Accordingly, the wealthy, be they noblemen or burghers or peasants, regard all others as flies. Even greater is the misuse of other and more excellent gifts, namely, of wisdom and justice. Since these gifts are found among men, both results occur: God cannot put up with this pride, and we cannot give it up.

This was the sin of the original world. Among the descendants of Cain there were very fine and wise men; but before God they were very evil, since they were haughty because of their gifts and despised God the Giver. This mischief the world does not understand and does not condemn; God alone condemns it.

Now where these spiritual vices exist and flourish, it is easy to fall into the sins of the flesh. "For to fall away from God is the beginning of sin," as Sirach says (Ecclus. 10:13). Thus the first fall of the devil is from heaven into hell, that is, from the First Table into the Second.[4] After men begin to be ungodly, that is, do not fear God and do not believe God, but despise God, His Word, and His ministers, the result is that they fall from the true doctrine into heretical ideas, which they teach, defend, and adorn. Moreover, the world regards such sins as the height of piety; those who perpetrate them are praised as the only religious, godly, and righteous men, as the church and the children of God. Men are incapable of passing judgment on sins against the First Table. Afterwards those despisers of God fall into awful sins like adultery, theft, murder, and other sins that come under the Second Table.

I recount these facts to make us realize not merely that the original world was addicted to the sins against the Second Table, but that it sinned chiefly against the First Table. That is, it had wisdom, godliness, worship, and religion superb in appearance but adulterated and false. Therefore since wickedness contrary to the First Table was aboil, there followed the depravity of which Moses is going to speak

---

[4] As his catechetical explanations of the Decalog showed, Luther interpreted the First Commandment as the major premise of each of the subsequent Commandments; hence the fall into sin was always from the First Table to the Second, not vice versa.

in this chapter, namely, that men first polluted themselves with their lusts and then filled the world with tyranny, bloodshed, and injustice.

Accordingly, when the ungodly world has scorned both tables in this way, God, who is a consuming fire and jealous (Deut. 4:24), comes to inflict judgment. He punishes ungodliness in such a way that everything turns to ruin and neither king nor subject remains. Therefore we may assume that the closer the world was to Adam's Fall, the better it was; but it has deteriorated from day to day until our times, in which live the dregs and, as it were, the ultimate dung of the human race.

But if God did not spare that world, which was endowed with so many great gifts, what shall we σκύβαλα (Phil. 3:8) hope for when we are overwhelmed by even more misfortunes and evils? Nevertheless, if it please God, the Roman pontiff and his holy bishops, who do not believe these things, are an exception to this rule! But now I am coming to the text.

1. *And when men had begun to multiply on the face of the ground and daughters were born to them,*

2. *the sons of God saw that the daughters of men were fair; and they took to wife such of them as they chose.*

A very brief account, but it covers much ground. It is not to be understood in such a way that the population of the world did not begin to increase until Noah was five hundred years old, but it includes the earlier patriarchs. This is proved by the fact that Noah had no daughters. But because the account mentions daughters, it must certainly have reference also to the earlier times of Lamech, Methuselah, Enoch, and others. The world, therefore, was corrupt and wicked even before Noah's birth; and especially after the death of Adam, the first patriarch, many who had stood in awe of their first parent began to live more licentiously.

Moreover, just as we stated above that Noah is a virgin above all virgins,[5] so here we also observe that he was a martyr above all martyrs. The situation of our so-called martyrs is most fortunate; for, strengthened by the Holy Spirit, they overcome death in one hour and surmount all perils and temptations. Noah, however, lived among the ungodly a full six hundred years, amid many serious temptations and dangers, just as Lot did in Sodom.

[5] Cf. *Luther's Works*, 1, p. 355.

Perhaps this was also why Lamech, Noah's father, gave him this name at his birth. When the saintly father observed how prevalent wickedness was becoming in the world, he conceived the hope that his son would comfort the godly, namely, that he would combat sin and Satan, its author, and would restore the lost righteousness. But the wickedness then in its beginning not only did not subside at Noah's time but raged even more. Therefore Noah is a martyr above all martyrs. How much easier it is to surmount all perils in one hour than to observe the great wickedness of the world for so many centuries!

I hold the opinion, as I said above,[6] that Noah refrained from marriage so long to keep from being compelled to observe and experience the same troubles he observed among the descendants of other saints. The contemplation of human wickednes was a very great cross. Similarly Peter, in 2 Peter 2:8, states about Lot: "By what that righteous man saw and heard as he lived among them, he was vexed in his righteous soul day after day with their lawless deeds."

So the increase of men of which Moses speaks refers not only to the times of Noah but also to the age of the earlier patriarchs. It was then that the transgression of the First Table, namely, contempt of God and of His Word, had its beginnings. After this followed the flagrant sins: the injustice, tyranny, and lusts, of which Moses makes particular mention here and from which he starts out as from the source of evil. Consult all the historical accounts, look at the Greek tragedies, the barbarian and Latin history of all times; you will discover that every sort of trouble had its origin in lust. Where the Word is not present or is disregarded, men cannot avoid falling into lusts.

Lust brings with it countless other evils: haughtiness, injustice, perjury, etc. These sins cannot be curbed in any other manner than by the First Table, when men begin to fear God and to put their trust in Him. Then they will follow the Word like a lamp going before them in darkness and will not engage in those offenses but will beware of them. But when the First Table is set aside, it becomes possible for shameful deeds and sins of all sorts to prevail.

It may seem odd that among the sins Moses appears to be counting the begetting of daughters, even though he had praised the fathers for it earlier and even though it is a blessing of God also in the ungodly. Why, then, does he count it among the sins?

[6] Cf. *Luther's Works*, 1, p. 356.

My answer is: He does not condemn the begetting of children in itself; he condemns its abuse, which stems from original sin. Royal rank, wisdom, riches, and physical strength are good things; having them is also something good, for they are bestowed upon men by God.

But when men who have these gifts break away from the First Table and, equipped with these gifts, contend against the First Table and then offend more flagrantly against the Second Table also — that is damnable wickedness. For this reason Moses makes use of unusual expressions here. He says: "The sons of God saw that the daughters of men were fair; and they took to wife such of them as they chose," namely, without any regard for God or for natural and positive law.

After the First Table has been cast aside, the Second Table, too, is cast aside, and lust takes over the first or principal position. Lust becomes utterly bestial and looks down upon the procreation of children, but God has established marriage as an aid for our weak nature and especially as a means for begetting children. When lust becomes supreme in this way, the preceding and the following Commandments [7] are undermined and lose their power. Respect for parents is violated, murder is committed, the property of others is seized, false testimony is given, and so forth.

The word יִרְאוּ, "they saw," denotes not simply "to look at" but "to observe with satisfaction and pleasure." In the psalms the expression often occurs: "My eye has looked upon my enemies," that is, "with satisfaction have I seen the punishment of my enemies." [8]

In this passage, therefore, it means that after they had turned their eyes away from God and His Word, they turned them lustfully toward the daughters of men. There follows the unfailing result: from the infraction of the First Table men go on to violate the Second. When they despised God, they also despised the laws of nature and, according to their pleasure, took to wife whomever they chose. These are indeed harsh words; yet it is my opinion that their lust still stayed within bounds, because they neither committed incest with their mothers, as happened among the Canaanites in the world that followed, nor polluted themselves with the disgrace of the Sodomites.

---

[7] That is, violation of the Commandment, "You shall not commit adultery" (the sixth according to the medieval and the Lutheran reckoning), leads to violation of the Commandments against disobedience and murder (the fourth and fifth) and against stealing (the seventh).

[8] Luther is thinking of passages like Ps. 54:7 and Ps. 92:11.

Moses brings only this charge, that they discarded the laws of the fathers and followed no definite marriage law but simply their own lust and abducted the woman they loved, against the will of her parents.

Moreover, the fathers appear to have been unusually stern in forbidding any marriage with the Cainites. Later on, in fact, there was a law forbidding the Jews to intermarry with the Canaanites.[9] There are some who state that there were incestuous marriages before the Flood, since no regard was paid to blood relationship. But because Peter praises the first world,[10] I still believe that those hideous instances of incest had not yet happened, but that the sin of the first world consisted in this, that men despised the authority of their fathers and took their wives from the Cainites, as many as they pleased and whomever they chose, obviously under the dominating influence of lust. It is a harsh statement which declares: "Such as they chose."

But I have pointed out above more than once that those two races or churches, namely, that of Adam and that of Cain, were separated.[11] As Moses clearly bears witness, Adam banished the murderer from his company. And so Adam undoubtedly urged his descendants also to beware of the church of the evildoers and not to intermarry with the accursed race of Cain. For a time his descendants obeyed this advice or command.

But when Adam had died and the respect for the remaining patriarchs declined, the sons of God (that is, those who had the promise of the blessed Seed and belonged to the blessed Seed) also yearned for marriages and affinity with the ungodly race. Moses simply calls the sons of the patriarchs, to whom the promise of the Seed was given, "sons of God"; they were the true church. When they yielded to the seductions of the Cainite church, they also proceeded to gratify the desires of the flesh and to take wives from the Cainite race, likewise concubines, as many as they wanted and whomever they chose. Lamech and Noah observed this with grief; and for this reason, perhaps, they married rather late.

Here, too, the Jews come up with a variety of foolish ideas.[12] They

---

[9] This is a reference either to Gen. 24:3 or to Deut. 20:17.
[10] This seems to be an inference drawn from the statement in 2 Peter 2:5.
[11] Cf. *Luther the Expositor*, pp. 95—99.
[12] This material comes from Lyra on Gen. 6:1-2, sec. d.

describe the sons of God as incubi [13] from which that notorious and ungodly race was begotten; they further maintain that the sons of God are given this name because of their spiritual nature. The less extreme among them, on the other hand, prove these foolish ideas to be false and describe the "sons of God" as the sons of the mighty. Lyra neatly disposes also of this idea by pointing out that the punishment of the Flood was not a punishment upon the mighty alone, but upon all flesh, just as the punishment of the Last Day will be.

So far as incubi and succubi are concerned, I do not deny, but believe, that the devil may happen to be either a succubus or an incubus; for I have heard many relate their very own experiences.[14] Augustine, too, declares that he heard the same sort of story from trustworthy people whom he felt compelled to believe.[15] It delights Satan if he can delude us by taking on the appearance either of a young man or of a woman. But that anything can be born from the union of a devil and a human being is simply untrue. Such an assertion is sometimes made about hideous infants that resemble demons very much. I have seen some of these. But I am convinced either that these were deformed, but not begotten, by the devil, or that they are actual devils with flesh that they have either counterfeited or stolen from somewhere else. If with God's permission the devil can take possession of an entire human being and change his disposition, what would be so remarkable about his misshaping the body and bringing about the birth of either blind or crippled children?

Thus he is able to delude people who are irreligious and who live without the fear of God; when the devil is in the bed, the young man imagines he has a girl, and the girl that she has a young man. But that anything could be born from this cohabitation, this I do not believe. Yet in many places sorceresses have been consigned to the pyre and burned for having had commerce with a devil. If he is able to delude the eyes and ears to have you believe that you are seeing and hearing something that is not really there, how much easier it is for him to delude the sense of touch, which is the most obtuse in our nature! But I break off here; for these matters contribute nothing to

---

[13] Not only popular superstition but the *Vitae patrum*, with which Luther was acquainted, contained many accounts of evil spirits who had sexual intercourse with human beings; cf. also *Luther's Works*, 22, p. 266.

[14] See Luther's remarks in *The Ten Commandments Preached to the People of Wittenberg* (1518), W, I, 410.

[15] Augustine, *The City of God*, Book XV, ch. 23.

the passage before us. We got into this discussion because of the silly ideas of the Jews.

The true meaning of the passage is that Moses designates as sons of God those people who had the promise of the blessed Seed. It is a term of the New Testament and designates the believers, who call God Father and whom God, in turn, calls sons. The Flood came, not because the Cainite race had become corrupt, but because the race of the righteous who had believed God, obeyed His Word, and observed true worship had fallen into idolatry, disobedience of parents, sensual pleasures, and the practice of oppression. Similarly, the coming of the Last Day will be hastened, not because the heathen, the Turks, and the Jews are ungodly, but because through the pope and the fanatics the church itself has become filled with error and because even those who occupy the leading positions in the church are licentious, lustful, and tyrannical.

This is intended to produce dread in all of us, because even those who were born of the most excellent patriarchs began to be conceited and depart from the Word. They gloried in their wisdom and righteousness, just as the Jews did in their circumcision and in their father Abraham. Similarly, after the popes had abandoned the knowledge of God, His Word, and His worship, they proceeded to turn their ecclesiastical distinction into carnal luxury. Once the Roman Church was truly holy and adorned with most outstanding martyrs, but today we see to what depths it has fallen.

Therefore let no one glory in his gifts, however great they may be; the greatest gift is to be a member of the true church. But beware of becoming haughty on this account; for you may fall, just as Lucifer fell from heaven (Is. 14:12) and as we hear in this text that the sons of God fell into carnal pleasures. Therefore they are sons of God no longer; they are sons of the devil, who have fallen from both the First and the Second Table at the same time. Similarly, in former times the popes and bishops were good and holy men; but today they are the worst of all human beings and the dregs, as it were, of all society.

In this conglomeration of people who were becoming progressively worse and were departing from the godliness and virtue of their ancestors, saintly Noah lived, utterly despised and hated by all. How could he approve of this lust of the decadent generation? But they on their part were most intolerant of any censure.

While his example shines brightly and his saintliness fills all the lands, the world becomes worse day by day; the greater Noah's saintliness and chastity is, the greater the world's madness becomes through lust. These are the initial stages that always precede destruction. When God raises up holy men full of the Holy Spirit, to instruct and reprove the world, the world, intolerant of sound doctrine, indulges in sins with greater zeal and continues in them even more persistently. This was what happened at the beginning of the world, and we see that the same thing is happening now at the end of the world.

3. *Then the Lord said: My Spirit shall not continually judge in man, for he is flesh, but his days shall be a hundred and twenty years.*

Here Moses begins to describe Noah himself as a supreme pontiff and priest or, as Peter calls him, a "herald of righteousness" (2 Peter 2:5). But this text has been abused in various ways, for it is impossible for natural man to understand these spiritual matters. Accordingly, when interpreters with unwashed feet and hands leap into the Holy Scriptures and bring with them their human inclination and, as they themselves express it, "let reason rule," [16] they inevitably fall into all kinds of errors. Besides, it usually happens that the more excellent and the more spiritual the texts are, the more execrably they are perverted. Thus they have abused this text in such a variety of ways that if you follow the interpreters, you do not know what to believe.

The Jews are the first to crucify Moses in this passage.[17] This is their explanation: "My Spirit, that is, My displeasure and anger, will not continue upon mankind. I do not intend to be angry with men, but I shall spare them; for they are flesh, that is, they are prone to sin as a consequence of the sin that burdens them." Jerome agrees with this opinion and holds that this passage treats only the sin of lust, toward which we are all inclined by nature.[18] In the first place, however, he errs when he interprets "Spirit" as anger. Moses is speaking here of the Holy Spirit, as the antithesis, "for man is flesh," also

[16] It seems that this polemic is aimed both at the medieval scholastics and at some of the other reformers; Luther accused both groups of rationalistic exegesis. Cf. *Luther the Expositor*, p. 141.

[17] *Spiritus meus, id est, indignatio.* Lyra on Gen. 6:3, sec. g.

[18] In his comments on this verse Jerome cites Hos. 4:14: "I will not punish your daughters when they play the harlot, nor your brides when they commit adultery." *Liber hebraicarum quaestionum in Genesim, Patrologia, Series Latina,* XXIII, 997.

shows. Hence he is pointing out that the flesh is not only prone to sin but also hostile to God (Rom. 8:7).

In the second place, the idea itself is inconsistent; for what could be devised that would be more absurd? They see before their eyes God's boundless anger consuming the entire human race by the Flood; and yet they explain that God does not want to be angry with men, but wants to have compassion on them — and to do so after a hundred and twenty years, namely, at the very time of the Flood!

Rabbi Solomon offers this explanation:[19] The Spirit, which is in God, will no longer debate and wrangle. Just as though in His divine majesty God had debated and wrangled with Himself about what He wanted to do with man, whether He wanted to destroy him or spare him, and yet, wearied at last by the wickedness of the human race, had decided that He wanted to destroy man utterly.

Others apply the words to the created spirit:[20] "My spirit, namely, the one I breathed into the face of man, that is, the human soul, will not debate and contend any longer with the flesh, which follows lust. For I shall take away that spirit and free it from the flesh, so that when the flesh is destroyed, it will no longer give the spirit anything to do." This is Origen's opinion; it differs little from the Manichaean error, which ascribed sin, not to the entire human being but only to a part of him. Augustine states that it pleased him most in the doctrine of the Manichaeans to hear that his wickedness was not entirely his own but belonged to a part of his body that was evil from the beginning.[21] For the Manichaeans assumed two principles, a good one and an evil one, just as certain philosophers speak about strife and friendship. In this way men not only stray from the goal but also lapse into godless opinions.

Sanctes quotes Rabbi David and derives the verb יָדוֹן from נָדָן, "a sheath."[22] Moreover, just as the meaning is most unsuitable, so he also translates it with a most unsuitable word: "My Spirit will not be sheathed in man." Has anything more monstrous ever been heard? But the Jews make fools of these modern Hebraists by convincing them that Holy Scripture cannot be understood except by means of grammatical rules and their minute system of pointing. Therefore no

---

[19] Lyra on Gen. 6:3, sec. k.

[20] This is a reference to Origen, as Luther indicates a little later.

[21] Augustine, *Confessions*, Book III, chs. 6—7.

[22] Cf. *Luther's Works*, 1, p. 297, note 55, on Santes Pagninus.

meaning is so preposterous that they would not defend and garnish it with their fusty rules of grammar.²³

But tell me, what language has there ever been that men have successfully learned to speak as a result of grammatical rules? Are not rather those languages that adhere most closely to rules, such as Greek and Latin, nevertheless learned by using them? Therefore how great a folly it is in the instance of the sacred language, where theological and spiritual matters are treated, to disregard the particular character of the subject matter and to arrive at the sense on the basis of grammatical rules! Nevertheless, the rabbis and their pupils do this almost everywhere. Many nouns and verbs for which no use is seen in the language can be inflected. While they are engaged in these matters and search minutely everywhere for the derivation of a word, they hit upon some astounding notions.

Thus because in this passage the verb can be derived from the noun נָדָן, they come upon a monstrous meaning for it. They say: "My Spirit will not be confined as in a sheath." They have in mind the spirit of man, which is kept in the body as in a sheath. "I shall not leave it in the sheath," they say, "but I shall take it out and destroy the sheath." This preposterous idea has its origin in the fusty rules of the grammarians. But prime consideration ought to be given to usage, for from it the grammarian derives his knowledge.

I dwell on these matters at such great length in order to warn you not to follow such silly interpreters when you come across them and not to admire their ideas as some sort of extraordinary wisdom. Sometimes even great men take delight in these absurdities of the rabbis. They are no different from the sacramentarians, who do not deny the words of Christ, "This is My body," but explain them in this way: "Bread is bread, and nevertheless the body of Christ, that is, His creature."²⁴ "This is My blood," that is: "It is My wine." No one in his right mind would put up with this inclination to distort the meaning in the case of the stories of Terence or the eclogues of Vergil. Are we going to tolerate it in the church?

To understand the meaning of Scripture the Spirit of Christ is

---

²³ This statement must be seen in the context of Luther's high praise and gratitude for the work of grammarians, which he regarded as indispensable to sound study of the Scriptures. He is arguing merely against a reliance on the positivistic study of grammar and philology.

²⁴ Cf. *Luther the Expositor,* pp. 137—156, on the interpretation of these words.

needed. But we know that until the end of the world this is the same Spirit who was before all things. Through God's mercy we boast of having this Spirit; and through Him we have faith, a modest understanding of the Scriptures, and a knowledge of the other things that are necessary for godliness. And so we do not invent any new understanding, but we adhere to the analogy both of Holy Scripture and of the faith.[25]

Now throughout the Holy Scriptures the verb "to judge," דִּין, regularly denotes a public function in the church, or preaching by which we are convicted, reproved, instructed, and taught to distinguish good from evil, etc. Thus we read in Ps. 110:6: יָדִין בַּגּוֹיִם, "He will judge among the nations," that is, He will preach among the heathen. The verb is clearly the same as in our present passage. Furthermore, in the New Testament this expression, which is taken from the Hebrew, is very common, especially in the writings of Paul, who follows the Hebrew manner of speech more than the others.[26]

Hence I understand this passage in such a way that these words were spoken either by Lamech himself or by Noah as a new discourse addressed to the entire world. It was a public discourse or a declaration put forward in a public convocation. After Methuselah, Lamech, and Noah saw that by its sins the world was hastening straight to its destruction, they came to a close with this declaration: "My Spirit will no longer judge among men. That is, we are teaching in vain; we are warning in vain; the world does not want to be improved."

It is just as though amid the great waywardness of the present times someone were to say: "We teach, and we exert ourselves to recall the world to moderation and godliness; but we are ridiculed. We suffer persecution; we are killed. Yet in the end all men rush to their destruction, with blind eyes and deaf ears. Therefore we have to cease." Such are the words of a heart that is considering what ought to be done and is fearful, in a supreme crisis of the whole human race, that mankind cannot be brought to its senses.

This interpretation is in agreement with the analogy of the faith and of Holy Scripture. For when the Word is revealed from heaven, we see that some are converted and freed from condemnation. The

---

[25] Luther's words, *analogiam tum Scripturae sacrae tum etiam fidei sequimur*, appear to place Scripture and "the faith" (probably the Apostles' Creed) into a co-ordinate relationship; see also p. 333, note 16.

[26] Perhaps Luther has in mind a passage like 2 Cor. 5:14.

remaining mass despises it and unconcernedly indulges in greed, lust, and other vices, just as Jeremiah states about Babylon (51:9): "We have healed Babylon, but she was not healed. Forsake her, and let us go, each to his own country."

Similarly, the more diligently Moses and Aaron urged and instructed Pharaoh, the more unyielding he became. The Jews were not changed for the better by the very preaching of Christ and of the apostles. The same thing happens to us who are preaching today. What shall we do? We can deplore the blindness and obstinacy of people, but we cannot bring about a change for the better. Who would rejoice at the everlasting damnation of the popes and of their followers? Who would not prefer to have them receive the Word and come to their senses?

Methuselah, Lamech, and Noah witnessed a similar obstinacy in their time. Hence that utterance of despair burst forth from them: "My spirit, that is, sound doctrine, will no longer judge among men. Because you are unwilling to receive the Word and to give your assent to sound doctrine, you shall perish."

Thus these are the words of a troubled heart and, as Scripture expresses it, "God is troubled," that is, the heart of Noah, Lamech, Methuselah, and of the other holy men who are full of love toward all. As they see the wickedness of men, they are troubled and grieved.

This grief is particularly the grief of the Holy Spirit, as St. Paul states in Eph. 4:30: "Do not grieve the Holy Spirit of God, in whom you were sealed for the day of redemption." It means that the Holy Spirit is grieved when we wretched men are bewildered and tormented by the wickedness of the world, which despises the Word we preach in the Holy Spirit. Similarly, Lot was perplexed in Sodom (2 Peter 2:8); the godly Jews in Babylon under the wicked king Belshazzar; Jeremiah, when he preached to the ungodly Jews and cried out (Jer. 15:10): "Woe is me, my mother, that you bore me," and Micah in chapter seven: "Woe is me! I have become like one who is seeking a cluster in a vineyard and does not find one."

Furthermore, this anger of God is most terrible when He withdraws His Word. Who would not prefer physical afflictions like pestilence, famine, or the sword to a famine of the Word, which is always coupled with eternal damnation? The heathen, who are without the Word, provide an example of the terrible darkness into which Satan can bring men when God remains silent and does not speak to them. Who would not be appalled that the Romans, a people who excelled in wisdom and were famed above other nations for their strict decency, followed the custom that honorable matrons worshiped and crowned the abominable idol Priapus and brought espoused virgins to him?[27] What is more ludicrous than that the Egyptians paid divine honor to the calf Apis as a supreme divinity?[28]

The *Historia tripartita* asserts that the hideous custom of making prostitutes of virgins before their marriage was not abolished in Phoenicia and other adjacent regions until the rule of Constantine the Great.[29] These hideous practices — in fact, infamous actions — were regarded as piety and as righteousness among the heathen. There is nothing so ludicrous, stupid, obscene, or foreign to all decency that it could not be foisted as an act of sublime worship on men who lack the Word of God.

This is, therefore, the utmost punishment that the Lord threatens by the mouth of His holy patriarchs in this passage, namely, that He will no longer judge men through His Spirit, that is, that after this He is unwilling to grant His Word to men, since all teaching is in vain.

Our times will also bring this punishment upon Germany. We see how Satan is making haste, how restless he is, and how he tries every means to obstruct the Word of God. How many sects he has stirred up in our lifetime while we exerted ourselves with all diligence to maintain purity of doctrine! What will happen when we are dead? He will surely lead forth whole packs of sacramentarians, Anabaptists, antinomians, followers of Servetus and Campanus, and other heretics, who now are in hiding after being routed for the moment by the purity of the Word and the diligence of godly teachers, but who are eagerly waiting for any opportunity to establish their doctrines.[30]

Therefore let those who have the pure Word learn to receive it and to give thanks to the Lord for it, and let them seek the Lord while He may be found (Is. 55:6). When the Spirit of doctrine has

[27] Priapus was the deity of male sexuality, originating at Lampsacus.

[28] Apis was the sacred bull of the Egyptians at Memphis.

[29] Luther is referring to the story of the destruction of the temple of Venus at Aphaca on Mount Libanus, taken over by the *Historia tripartita* from Socrates Scholasticus, *The Ecclesiastical History,* Book I, ch. 18.

[30] Michael Servetus (d. 1553) attacked the traditional doctrine of the Trinity; so did John Campanus (d. ca. 1578), who had been present at the Marburg Colloquy in 1529. Even the Weimar editors regard it as probable that this is an editorial interpolation (see Introduction).

been taken away, the Spirit of prayer will also be taken away, as Zechariah calls Him (12:10). For the Spirit of prayer is joined with the Spirit of grace. But it is the Spirit of grace who convinces one of sin (John 16:8) and gives instruction about the forgiveness of sins, who condemns idolatry and gives instruction about the true worship of God, and who condemns greed, lust, and oppression and teaches chastity, patience, and charitableness. The Lord threatens in this passage that the Spirit will no longer judge, because men are unwilling to listen and cannot be improved. But when this Spirit has been taken away, the Spirit of prayer also has been taken away. For one who does not have the Word cannot pray.

Consequently, the duty of a priest is twofold: in the first place, to turn to God and pray for himself and for his people; in the second place, to turn from God to men by means of doctrine and the Word. Thus Samuel states in 1 Sam. 12:23: "Far be it from me not to pray for you and not to lead you to the good and the right way." He acknowledges that this is essential to his office.

It is proper, therefore, that the ministry be praised and esteemed for the great benefits it brings. When it is abolished or corrupted, it is not only impossible for men to pray; but they are utterly in the power of the devil, they do nothing but grieve the Holy Spirit by all their action, and thus they fall into the sin unto death for which one may not pray (1 John 5:16). Other lapses that happen to men are light, for the way of return remains open and a hope for pardon is left. But when the Holy Spirit is grieved and men are unwilling to be judged and convicted by the Holy Spirit, this is a desperate and incurable wound.

Yet how common this sin is today among all classes! Princes, nobles, even commoners and peasants, refuse to be reproved; they themselves rather reprove the Holy Spirit and judge Him in His ministers. They judge the ministry by the lowliness of the person. These are their thoughts: "This minister is poor and unimportant. Why, then, should he reprove me; for I am a prince, a nobleman, a magistrate?" Therefore, rather than put up with it, they despise the ministers together with the ministry itself and the Word. Must we not fear judgment of God like the one He pronounces here upon the first world?

These are the words of a father who is disinheriting his son, or of a merciless teacher who is expelling a pupil in anger, because without further ado He fixed a period of a hundred and twenty years to see whether they would repent within this space of time. If not, He threatens that His Spirit will no longer reprove and no longer dispute with them.

And so this word properly pertains to the ministry and in a manner depicts it. Every preacher or minister of the Word is a man of strife and of judgment, and because of his office he is compelled to reprove whatever is wrong, without regard for either person or office among his hearers. When Jeremiah did this with diligence, he encountered not only hatred but even grave danger (Jer. 20:2). He himself became so impatient that he wished he had never been born (Jer. 20:14-15).

If I had not been extraordinarily strengthened by God, I, too, would long since have been worn out and discouraged by this stubbornness of the unrepentant world. The ungodly grieve the Holy Spirit in us to such an extent that with Jeremiah we sometimes wish we had never undertaken anything. Therefore I often pray God that He would permit our generation to die together with us, because after our passing most perilous times will follow.

For this reason the wicked king Ahab called Elijah, too, a troubler of Israel (1 Kings 18:17), evidently because he reproved the idolatry, tyranny, and lust of his times.

And we also are regarded as troublers of Germany today. But it is a good sign when men condemn us and call us agitators. The Spirit of God is one who strives with men, reproves them, and condemns them. But men are so constituted that they want to have preached what pleases them, just as they frankly state (Micah 2:6): "Do not preach down to us; for disgrace will not overtake us, says the house of Jacob." This latter statement is given as the reason; for because they realize that they are the house of Jacob and the people of God, they do not want to be taken to task, nor do they want punishments and threats to apply to them.

Similarly, today the pope and his associates place their reliance on this one argument that they are the church, and they maintain that the church cannot err. But look at this text, and it will become clear how worthless this reasoning is.

Is it not the very "sons of God" whom God threatens here, saying that He no longer wants to judge them by His Spirit? What can be more excellent than this name? Moreover, without a doubt they gloried in this name and opposed the fathers who threatened them; or at least they despised their preaching. It does not seem likely that

God would vent His rage on the entire human race because of a few sins. But that grand title did not save them, nor was there any advantage in their being powerful and countless in number.

Six hundred thousand men came out of Egypt, and only two entered the land of Canaan; on account of their sins death prevented all the rest from entering.

Accordingly, it is obvious that God will not concern Himself with grand titles like "church," "pope," and "bishop." If they want to escape the wrath of God, they will need some other testimonial than their boast that they are the church. For thus it is written in Matt. 7:20-21: "You will know them by their fruits." Likewise: "Not everyone who says to Me, 'Lord, Lord,' shall enter the kingdom of heaven."

If a council ever takes place — which I doubt [31] — no one will be able to strip our adversaries of this title "church"; and, supported by this one fact, they will condemn and suppress us. But the verdict will be different when the Son of Man appears in His glory. Then it will be revealed that the holy martyr of God, John Hus, and Jerome of Prague were true and holy members of the holy church; [32] but that the pope, the bishops, the doctors, the monks, and the priests all were the church of the malevolent in the pestilential chair, [33] the true slaves of Satan who helped their father lie and murder.

Such a judgment of God we see also in this passage. It does not deny that the descendants of the saints were sons of God. God leaves them this grand title, by which they became puffed up and continued to sin without concern; and yet He threatens these very sons of God, who were taking the daughters of men to wife, that He will not only remove the Word from their minds and hearts but will also remove from their eyes and ears His officiating Spirit, who preaches, prays, reproves, teaches, and sighs in His holy ministers. This He will do because these sons of God are unwilling to be taken to task and reproved; because they are aware that they are the sons of God, they

---

[31] In a letter dated "the Friday after the Assumption of Mary 1535" (i. e., August 20, 1535) Luther wrote to Elector John Frederick: "I wish and pray that God will still give them [his Roman Catholic opponents] enough sense to convoke a council that is free and Christian. But on this question I am like doubting Thomas. I must put my hands and fingers into the sides and the wounds; otherwise I will not believe it. Nevertheless, God can do even more than that; in His hand are the hearts of all men." W, *Briefe*, VII, 238.

[32] Executed at the Council of Constance in 1415, John Hus and Jerome of Prague figured prominently in Luther's polemics.

[33] Apparently this is an allusion to the Latin of Ps. 1:2.

despise the Word and its teachers. Yet they do not escape punishment because of their title. The same thing will happen to the papists and to all enemies of the Word.

Thus it is my conviction that in this passage the emotions of the godly men are assigned to God Himself, in keeping with the common practice of Holy Scripture. So in Mal. 3:8 the Lord says that He was being pierced, or, as the Hebrew has it, that violence was being done to Him when the people were unfaithful in bringing the first fruits and tithes to the priests.

But what need, someone will say, has God of such a complaint? Can He not suddenly destroy the entire world when He wants to do so? Certainly He can, but He does not do it gladly, as He says (Ezek. 33:11): "I have no pleasure in the death of the wicked, but that the wicked turn from his way and live." This disposition proves that God is ready to pardon, to forbear, and to forgive sins if only people were willing to come to their senses. But because they continue to be stubborn and to reject every remedy, He is tortured, as it were, by their wickedness.

I therefore assign the words "God said" to the holy fathers who bore witness by public pronouncement that God was being compelled to inflict punishment, for they taught by divine authority. Accordingly, when Noah and his ancestors had preached for nearly a thousand years and yet the world was steadily becoming worse, they announced to the ungrateful world the verdict of God as one who reflected: "What good does it do for Me to preach endlessly and to permit My preachers everlastingly to cry out in vain? The more preachers I send and the longer I put off My wrath, the worse they become. Therefore I must put an end to preaching and bring on punishment. I shall not let My Spirit, that is, My Word, judge and preach forever while putting up with the wickedness of men; I am compelled to punish their sins."

"For man is flesh," that is: "Man is hostile toward Me. He is a physical being, but I am a Spirit. Man persists in his carnal ways, he ridicules the Word, he persecutes and hates My Spirit in the patriarchs. 'To the deaf the story is told.' [34] Therefore I must cease and let the man, who is so perverse, go his own ways." This is the contrast He wants to indicate when He declares: "For he is flesh."

Noah, Lamech, and Methuselah were very holy men full of the

---

[34] A proverbial expression common in Latin literature; cf., for example, Horace, *Epistles,* Book II, I, ll. 199—200.

Spirit of God. Accordingly, they performed their duties by teaching, admonishing, entreating, and insisting in season and out of season, as Paul says in 2 Tim. 4:2. But they were reproving "flesh," and therefore they were engaged in a futile task; for the flesh did not assent to sound doctrine. "Shall I," says He, "forever put up with this contempt of the Word?"

Therefore this statement contains a public complaint of the Holy Spirit through the holy patriarchs Noah, Lamech, Methuselah, and others, whom God took away before the Flood that they might not be eyewitnesses of His wrath as it raged over so wide an area. With one voice and mouth they all exhorted the giants and tyrants to repentance and added the threat that God would not forever bear with this contempt of His Word. But the flesh reacted in its customary way. In their carnal smugness and unconcern they treated the godly exhortations with contempt and regarded the holy patriarchs as feebleminded and foolish old men for threatening that God would also rage against His church, that is, against the descendants who had the promise of the future Seed.

As to the added clause, "and his days shall be a hundred and twenty years," Jerome also declares that it must not be understood of the years of human life or of the life span of individual persons.[35] It is a fact that after the Flood many lived to be more than two hundred years old. If one should refer it to the years of each individual person, it would be a promise that each individual would live so many years; but this is not in accord with fact. Therefore the text is speaking of the respite that was granted to the world for repentance before the Flood would come.

Furthermore, this meaning is in harmony with what precedes. God indicates His displeasure at this perversity of men. He is distressed and would gladly spare them; unwillingly, as it were, He permits the Flood to rage. Therefore He fixes a definite and adequate time for repentance, that men may come to their senses and escape the punishment. During that entire period Noah exhorted men to repentance, saying that God would no longer put up with their ungodliness and yet was so kind that He was granting adequate time for repentance, etc.

Thus the words and the thoughts agree beautifully. The preceding thought contains a threat. The Lord says in this passage: "I am

[35] Jerome, *Liber hebraicarum quaestionum in Genesim, Patrologia, Series Latina,* XXIII, 997.

unable to bear the contempt of My Word any longer. Through their boundless effort My preachers and priests achieve nothing but scorn. Therefore just as a father or a good judge would gladly spare a son, but the son's wickedness compels him to be severe, so I do not enjoy destroying the entire human race. I shall grant them a hundred and twenty years, during which they may come to their senses and I may spare them."

It was an awful affliction that neither the brothers nor the sisters of Noah were saved. For this reason it was necessary for the most earnest threats to precede, in the hope that they could be called back to repentance. Jonah foretold to the Ninevites that they would be destroyed within forty days; and they repented and were saved (Jonah 3:4-5).

Thus it is clear that the smugness of the first world was exceedingly great. Although it had a hundred and twenty years, it stubbornly persisted in its lusts and even laughed at its pontiff, the herald of righteousness, Noah (2 Peter 2:5).

Today, when the day of the Lord is drawing near, the situation is almost the same. We urge the papists to repent. We urge and warn our noblemen, burghers, and peasants not to continue to despise the Word; for God will not leave this unavenged. But we are spending our strength in vain, as Scripture says.[36] Few faithful are edified; these are gradually taken away before the calamity, and "no one understands," as is stated in Is. 57:1.[37] But after the Lord has thus beaten out the wheat and has gathered the grain in its place, what do you think will happen to the chaff? It will inevitably be burned with unquenchable fire (Matt. 3:12). This will be the lot of the world.

The world does not realize that this is being done now, that through the preaching of the Gospel the wheat is being separated from the chaff and is being gathered into the granary, so that later on the chaff, that is, the mass of the unbelievers, who live in darkness and idolatry, may be consigned to the fire, as is written in Is. 49:8: "In a day of salvation I have helped you; I have kept you." Those who allow this day of salvation to pass will have God as their punisher. For He is not inclined to take upon Himself the useless task of threshing empty chaff.

[36] Luther is probably thinking of Is. 49:4.
[37] The original has "Is. 56."

But the world is flesh; it does not yield. In fact, the closer it is to disaster, the smugger it is, and the more unrestrainedly it despises all godly exhortations. Even though this offense dismays the godly, we must still maintain that God does not reprove the world through His Spirit in vain and that the Holy Spirit is not grieved in vain in the godly. Christ makes use of this very example when He foretells the ungodliness and unconcern of our age: "They will be," says He, "as in the days of Noah and Lot" (Matt. 24:37).

Here we must note something with which St. Jerome also struggles: that the Flood came in the one hundredth year after the birth of Shem, Ham, and Japheth; but in this passage one hundred and twenty years are stated as the time of the Flood.[38]

This passage shows that Noah began his preaching about the coming punishment of the Flood before he had married, since up to that time he had lived in celibacy. Now consider at this juncture how he must have amused the smug and ungodly world. He foretells the destruction of the whole world by the Flood, and he himself marries. "Why?[39] Is it not enough that he alone perishes? Why does he take a companion along in the disaster? Oh, what a stupid old man! If he firmly believed that the world would perish by the Flood, he would rather perish alone than marry and engage in begetting children. But if he is going to be preserved, we, too, will be preserved."

Thus on account of Noah's marriage they began to disregard his preaching about the Flood with even greater assurance, unaware of the counsels of God, who acts in such a way that the world is completely at a loss to understand. How absurd it is that He promises Abraham descendants through Isaac and yet commands him to sacrifice Isaac!

St. Jerome, therefore, answers in this manner: God had indeed predetermined the time for the Flood at a hundred and twenty years; but since wickedness increased, He was compelled to shorten that time.

But we shall not make a liar out of God. No, we shall maintain this: While still unmarried, Noah proclaimed that the world had to be destroyed by the Flood. At God's command he later married a girl, a small branch, as it were, of the entire female race, and begot

[38] Cf. p. 23, note 35.
[39] These words are put into the mouth of the world.

three sons. It is written below (v. 8) that he found favor in the eyes of God. Otherwise he who had refrained from marriage for so long a time could have refrained even longer. But God wanted to leave a nursery of the human race, in order that there might be some restraint upon His anger; therefore He ordered Noah to marry. The ungodly regarded this as a sign that the world would not perish. Consequently, they lived in smugness and despised the preacher Noah. But God's plan was different. He would destroy the entire world, and through this righteous Noah He would leave a nursery for the coming world.

Thus Noah was the greatest prophet, whose like the world has not had. In the first place, he preached for the longest time; in the second place, he preached about the universal punishment of the entire world and even designated the year in which it would occur. Christ also prophesies concerning the Last Judgment, at which all flesh will perish. However, He says (Mark 13:32): "But of that hour no one knows besides the Father, who has reserved this for Himself." Jonah foretells to the Ninevites the forty days; Jeremiah, the seventy years of the captivity; Daniel, the seventy weeks till the advent of Christ. These are outstanding prophecies; they designate a definite time, the place, and the persons.

But this prophecy of Noah surpasses all the others because through the Holy Spirit he foretells a definite number of years when the entire human race will perish. He is worthy to be called the second Adam and the prince of the human race, through whose mouth God speaks and calls the entire world to repentance.

But it is a horrible fact that his preaching was despised with such unconcern that no one, not only among the Cainites but even among the descendants of Adam, mended his way. Accordingly, Noah was forced to witness the destruction of his brothers, sisters, and countless relatives by blood and marriage, all of whom derided the godly old man and his preaching as an old wives' tale.

This awful situation is presented for our consideration, to keep us from persisting in sin. If God did not spare the original world, which was the best, the very flower and youth of the world, in which so many holy men lived, but, as the psalm has it (81:12), "let them go according to the desires of their heart," and cast them away as though they had no part in the promise given to the church, how much less will He spare us, who have no such advantages?

In other words, the sentence reported in this passage — that God wants to grant the human race a hundred and twenty years for repentance — was pronounced and formally proclaimed before Noah begot any children.

About the family of the Cainites and who their patriarchs were at the time of the Flood, nothing is recorded, for Moses does not regard them as worthy of mention. Above he traced their family as far as Lamech, but whether his sons or his grandsons were living at the time of Noah is uncertain. It is certain that Cain's descendants were in existence up to that time. Indeed, they were so influential that they misled the sons of God into disgraceful acts; for the descendants of the holy patriarchs also perished in the Flood.

Therefore the holy patriarchs, as rulers of the true church, had warned their people to beware of the accursed race. But since the Cainites were displeased because they were being condemned, they tried every sort of evil trick to destroy the godly. The church of Satan is everlastingly at war with the church of God.

Now when the godly were gradually disappearing and ungodliness was on the increase, God stirred up Noah to exhort to repentance and to be an everlasting example for his descendants, one whose faith, persistence, and diligence in preaching his descendants might admire and imitate. This was a great miracle and an outstanding act of faith: upon hearing this decree through Methuselah and Lamech, that after a hundred and twenty years the world would perish in the Flood, Noah did not doubt that it was true.

Yet after nearly twenty years had passed, Noah took a wife and begot children. He should rather have thought: "If the whole human race is to perish, why shall I marry? Why shall I beget children? If I refrained for so many years, I shall also refrain in the future." But Noah does not do this. No, after the verdict has been rendered about the destruction of the world, he obeys God, who calls upon him to marry, and believes God, that even if the entire world should perish, he himself will be saved together with his children. This is an outstanding faith, one worthy of our reflection.

In the first place, he had that common faith about the Seed who would crush the head of the serpent, a faith which the other patriarchs also had. Moreover, it was a rare virtue to maintain this confidence in the face of so many corrupting influences and not to depart from God. Added to this faith there was, in the second place, particular faith, namely that he believed God both when He threatened destruction to all the rest of the world and when He promised deliverance to Noah himself and his sons. Without a doubt his grandfather Methuselah and his father Lamech earnestly urged him on to this faith. For this was difficult to believe, just as difficult as it was for the Virgin Mary to believe that she alone would be the mother of the Son of God.

This faith taught him to disdain the smugness of the world, which scoffed at him as at a deranged old man. This faith urged him to keep busy with the building of the ark, a structure which those notorious giants undoubtedly ridiculed as the utmost stupidity. This faith strengthened Noah to such an extent that he stood alone in the face of so many examples of the world and courageously despised the opinions of all people.

Accordingly, this is an almost inexpressible and miraculous faith, burdened as it was with unprecedented and indeed very serious points. Yet the Holy Spirit refers to this faith only in passing and does not go into detail, obviously in order that we may give more careful thought to all the circumstances. In the first place, consider that very corrupt age. In addition, before this time the church had very many saintly patriarchs; but now it is deprived of such leaders. Adam, Seth, Enos, Kenan, Mahalaleel, Jared, and Enoch — they all have died, and their number has been reduced to three: Methuselah, Lamech, and Noah. They are the only survivors when the judgment concerning the destruction of the world through the Flood is pronounced. These three see and must put up with the incredible wickedness of men, their idolatry, blasphemy, rash violence, and disgusting lusts, until finally Methuselah and Lamech are called out of this life. Then Noah alone pitted himself against a world rushing to its destruction, in the hope that perhaps he could preserve righteousness and check unrighteousnes. But what he achieved was so utterly nothing that he saw even the sons of God deteriorate into ungodliness.

This collapse and destruction of the church troubled and almost broke the heart of the righteous man, just as Peter states about Lot in Sodom (2 Peter 2:8). But if Lot was so tormented and distressed by the wicked works in one city, what shall we think of Noah, against whom not only the family of Cain raged, but whom even the deteriorating family of patriarchs opposed, even his own house, his brothers, his sisters, the children of his uncles and aunts, etc.? They were all corrupted and were drawn away from the faith by the daughters of men, as the text states: "They saw the daughters of men."

But, I ask you, why does it not also complain about the males? Or why does it not also complain about the daughters of God? It merely states: "They saw the daughters of men." The reason obviously is that after the Cainites had been shut out of the true church, the holy family of Seth had the special directive to beware even of marrying into that family, of becoming amalgamated with them either in respect to the state through marriage or in respect to the church through worship. The godly must beware of all opportunities for stumbling.

When the godly fathers forbade marriages with the Cainites, it was their chief concern to preserve their family uncontaminated. For into the homes of their husbands daughters bring the thoughts and even the ways of their own parents. Thus one reads in the history of the kings that Solomon was led astray by a foreign woman (1 Kings 11:1-8). Similarly, Jezebel introduced the wickedness of the Syrians into the kingdom of Israel (1 Kings 16:31-33).

The holy fathers saw that the same thing would happen in their own family. Therefore after the separation of the Cainites had been brought about by divine command, they decreed that the sons of the holy family should not marry the daughters of men. The daughters in the holy family could more readily be prevented from marrying Cainites, but the sons were less restrained and more unruly.

In this way Moses wanted to show that the beginning of all evil stemmed from the alliance of the sons of God with the daughters of men, whom they saw to be shapely. Since they were proud and powerful, and ardently sought after pleasures, the sons of men undoubtedly looked down upon the pitiable girls of the holy family, whom the holy fathers had not brought up in luxury but in simplicity and modesty and in poor circumstances. Therefore it was unnecessary to pass such a law for the girls, who were usually disregarded by the aristocratic Cainites.

If you reflect on the history of nations, you will find that even the greatest kingdoms have been destroyed because of women. Familiar is the shameful conduct of Helen. Moreover, the Holy Scriptures reveal that through the fault of a woman the entire human race fell.

Nevertheless, these facts must be mentioned without any reflection on the sex; for we have the command: "Honor your father and your mother," (Ex. 20:12) and likewise, "You men, love your wives" (Eph.

5:25). It is true that Eve picked the fruit first; but before she did this, she sinned through her idolatry and fell from the faith. As long as faith is in the heart, it rules and directs the body; but when it has departed from the heart, the body is the servant of sin. Therefore the fault does not lie in the sex but in the weakness common to both woman and man.

Thus in this passage Moses mentions the wrongs and the lusts. He leaves it to the reader to reflect that before they sinned against the Second Table, they sinned against the First and despised the Word of God. Otherwise the sons of God would have obeyed the wish of their godly parents, who forbade marriage with those outside the church.

Moses draws the conclusion that the descendants of the patriarchs first abandoned the worship and Word of God and departed from the commandments of their parents. Next they fell into sensuality and lust, and took to wife whomever they wished. They also became tyrants, made inroads on the possessions of others, etc. The world is unable to do otherwise: after it has turned away from God, it worships the devil. After it has despised the Word and has lapsed into idolatry, it plunges into all the vices of concupiscence. These vices rouse illicit desire and then wrath, so that in this way there is the utmost loss of discipline [40] in all the appetites. When the godly reprove this, there follow acts of violence and tyranny against the godly.

Thus the sin of the age of the Flood comprises the sum total of what can be called sin both against the First and against the Second Table, namely, that the ungodly first forsake God and despise His Word through their unbelief and then also depart from obedience to their parents, become murderers, adulterers, etc.

I mention this to keep you from thinking that either sex or marriage in itself is being blamed. It is the transgression of the commands of God and the disobedience toward parents that is particularly condemned, because, since the Cainites had no part in the true church, the godly parents wanted their offspring to be separate from the Cainites also in civil life, in order that they might not be led astray through association with ungodly spouses. But when their descendants disregarded God's command and ignored the authority of parents, they fell into the sin of unbridled covetousness and wrath. Thus the integrity of sex and the dignity of matrimony are preserved; ungod-

---

[40] Here Luther uses the Greek word ἀταξία, which means a lack or loss of discipline.

liness alone is reproved, which first forsakes God and then is also the source of violence against the saints.

This is what the words themselves convey: "The sons of God saw that the daughters of men were fair." Why did they not see the daughters of God too and desire those who were in the church and had the promise of the Seed? Are they not proved guilty of holding in contempt a sex of their own family, that is, of the true church, and of commingling with the worldly and godless family of the Cainites? They disdain the artlessness and the dignity of their own women and prefer the flattering, bedecked, and voluptuous women of the Cainite family — these they desire and cherish, but the former they either completely disregard or treat in a disgraceful manner.

With the same kind of eyes with which Eve looked at the fruit when she was about to sin in a moment, the sons of God look at the daughters of men. Eve had seen the forbidden tree even before that time, but with eyes of a faith that kept in mind God's command; therefore she had no desire for it but rather fled from it. But when the eyes of her faith had been blinded and she looked at the tree merely with the eyes of the flesh, she stretched out her hand with pleasure and encouraged her husband Adam to do the same thing.

Likewise the descendants of the patriarchs had seen before this time that the daughters of the Cainites excelled in beauty, dress, and polish. Still they did not marry them. The eye of faith kept in mind God's command and the promise about the Seed who was to be born from the family of the godly. But when they had lost these eyes of faith, they no longer saw either God's command or His promise but simply followed the desire of the flesh, disdained the artless, good, and respectable girls of their own family, and married Cainite women whom they found dainty, attractive, and witty.

Therefore it is no sin that they take wives; sex itself is not condemned. But this is condemned, that they disregard God's command and marry women they should not have married. They allow themselves to be drawn by their wives from the true worship to the ungodly worship of the false church; and after the manner of the Cainites they disregard the authority of their parents, commit acts of violence, tyrannize, etc.

This sin Moses points out clearly when he states: "They took to wife such of them as they chose." It is as though he were saying: "To take a wife is nothing evil; if it is done properly, it is something good. But those men were sinning in this respect, that without discretion and contrary to the will and judgment of the fathers they married whomever they themselves wished, as many as they wished, and without distinction took married women as well as unmarried ones."

This is a harsh statement. With it Moses indicates the great sins that they promiscuously took two or more wives, exchanged wives, or took them away from others by force the way Herod took possession of his brother Philip's wife (Mark 6:17). This boundless dissoluteness of their lusts Moses points out and condemns.

Berosus writes that there also were incestuous marriages among them and that they married their sisters and mothers.[41] But I doubt that they were as wicked as that. It is sinful enough that when marrying wives they gave no consideration to sound judgment, to the authority of their parents, or even to the Word of God, but simply followed their lust and illicit desire. They carried off whomever they wished and could, and thus through their passionate lust they disorganized both the home and the state, and, let me add, the church as well.

Therefore the sin of the original world was the disorganization of all classes of men. The church was undermined by the idolatrous and ungodly forms of worship as well as by the tyrants who cruelly persecuted the godly teachers and holy men; government was destroyed through their tyranny and acts of violence; and the home was ruined by their perverse lusts. This world-wide corruption was the unavoidable result of the downfall of godliness and decency. Men were not only evil; they were utterly incorrigible.

4. *Moreover, there were giants upon the earth in those days.*

Moses continues his description of the sin and the guilt which led to the coming of the Flood. There was, in the first place, the fact that the sons of God fell away from the worship and Word of God and became entirely worldly, with the result that they corrupted not only the church but also the state and the home.

Now he adds that wickedness had increased to such an extent that there were giants on the earth. Moreover, he explicitly states that from the cohabitation of the sons of God with the daughters of men there were born, not sons of God but giants, that is, arrogant men who usurped both the government and the priesthood.

---

[41] Berosus, the Babylonian historian, is quoted by Josephus to substantiate his account of the Flood; he is mentioned also by several church fathers.

The pope does the same thing when he usurps both spiritual and temporal power. However, the chief evil would not lie in this if he made use of this usurped power only for the preservation of the state and the church. This is his greatest sin, that he misuses his power for the support of idolatry, for attacks on sound doctrine, and for tyranny even in the state. When the papists are reproved with the Word of God, they refuse to be reproved; they say that they are the church and cannot err, and they also rage against the godly with colossal brutality. Moses calls such men "giants," who usurp powers, both of the state and that of the church, and sin without the least restraint.

The Book of Wisdom depicts such men. They say (Wisd. of Sol. 2:11): "Let our might be our law of right." And in Ps. 12:4: "With our tongue we will prevail, our lips are with us; who is our master?" And in Ps. 73:4 ff.: "They are arrogant with unconcern, and when they use force on others, they boast of it." Giants were such men as boldly opposed the Holy Spirit when He warned, entreated, taught, and reproved through Lamech, Noah, and the sons of Noah.

There is some argument about the origin of the word, and there are those who derive it from נָפַל, which means "to fall." [42] But they understand it in what is practically a passive meaning, namely, that when other men saw their huge bodies and their unusual size, they collapsed from fear. Let the rabbis make it their business to see whether this is true, for it is ridiculous to call them נְפִלִים because others fell. Others present this etymology: they were so called because they had fallen off from the common height of human beings. They appeal to the passage in Num. 13:34, from which it is clear that the נְפִלִים, or giants, had rather large bodies just as the עֲנָקִים and the רְפָאִים did. I am not judging who holds the more correct view, especially since it is an established fact that it is impossible to give an account of every word and to point out its origin.

Here another question turns up. Why did only those men who were born from the sons of God and the daughters of men deviate from the normal stature of human beings? But I have nothing in reply to this question except that in this passage the text states nothing about their stature. In Num. 13:34 it is stated: "We saw giants, the sons of עֲנָק from the giants; and we seemed to ourselves like grasshoppers." There the hugeness of their bodies is pointed out,

[42] For these philological observations Luther seems to have drawn not only on Lyra but also on humanistic scholarship.

but not in this passage. Therefore they may be called giants for some other reason than the size of their bodies.

To give my own opinion about the word, I believe that it should be explained neither in a neutral nor in a passive sense, but in an active sense; for although the verb נָפַל does not belong to the third conjugation, which is generally the proper one for transitive verbs, it is often used in the active sense.[43] Thus in Joshua 11:7: "And Joshua and all his people of war came upon them by the waters of Merom וַיִּפְּלוּ בָּהֶם, and they fell upon them." If you explain the verb יִפְּלוּ in a neutral sense, as though Joshua and his men had fallen before the enemy, the account will contradict this; for the meaning is that they fell upon them and suddenly overwhelmed them.

Therefore this passage — and any like it — induces me to conclude that they were not called נְפִלִים because of the large size of their bodies, as the rabbis believe, but because of their tyranny and oppression. They raged violently, without any consideration for laws and decency, but exclusively in pursuit of their own pleasures and desires. Those who rule rightfully Scripture calls shepherds and princes.[44] But those who rule through injustice and violence are properly called נְפִלִים, because they fall upon and oppress those who are beneath them.

Similarly, Ps. 10:9 says: "He oppresses, he lays low, וְנָפַל בַּעֲצוּמָיו חֵלְכָּאִים, and with his mighty ones falls upon the assembly of the poor." There the Holy Spirit is speaking of the rule of Antichrist, who, He states, will rage in such a manner as to annihilate what he can; and if there is something he cannot annihilate, he will at least beat it down and later on with all his power crush what has been beaten down. For it is immaterial whether you render בַּעֲצוּמָיו "with his might" or "with his mighty ones." This power, says the Holy Spirit, he uses only against those who are חֵלְכָּאִים, that is, poor and already victims of oppression. The others, who have a reputation because of their power, he worships, in order to win them for his side.

Such is my explanation of the giants or נְפִלִים in this passage, as being not men of huge mass of body, as in the passage in Numbers, but unruly and mischievous men, the way the poets depict the Cyclopes, who fear neither God nor men but pursue only their own desires and rely on their own power and strength. They sit in the

[43] Luther's knowledge of Hebrew grammar came from several sources, including John Reuchlin's *First Principles;* cf. *Luther's Works,* 14, p. 335, note 54.

[44] It seems that a passage like Is. 44:28 is in Luther's mind here.

place of supreme authority and have control over empires and kingdoms. They even arrogate spiritual power to themselves. Moreover, they employ that power against the church and against the Word of God as they please, etc.

At this point one should take note of the strange counsel of God, who directs us to respect the government, to obey it, to serve it, and to give it honor. Yet whenever they are threats and awful scoldings, these we see directed almost entirely against rulers, against kings and princes, as though God pursued them with a special hatred. Scripture commands us to honor the government, but it itself does not honor the government. Scripture overthrows it by threatening the most severe punishments. Scripture commands us to respect the government, but it itself appears to despise governments, inasmuch as it does not flatter but threatens them.

Did not Mary in her hymn sternly inveigh against princes (Luke 1:51-53): "He scatters the proud in the imagination of their hearts, He puts down the mighty from their thrones, and He sends the rich away empty"? If we believe that these statements are true, who would wish to be found among such men? For them certain destruction is ready and imminent. Who would not prefer to be of lowly station and to go hungry?

The second psalm likewise charges governments with a grave offense when it declares that with united forces and efforts they resist the Lord and His Christ and harass His kingdom (Ps. 2:1-2). Similarly Isaiah (25:2): "The city of the mighty He has turned into a ruin." The whole Bible is full of statements of this kind.

Accordingly, Scripture does not bestow honor on the governments but threatens them with destruction and, as it were, makes them an object of open contempt. Nevertheless, it commands us most painstakingly to respect them, to give them honor, and to accord them every kind of service. Why is this?

Undoubtedly it is because the Lord Himself wants to be the only one to punish them, has reserved vengeance for Himself, and has not granted it to their subjects. Jeremiah, in chapter twelve (12:1),[45] discusses how it happens that when the Lord is righteous, the way of the ungodly meets with success. But later he concludes (12:3): "Thou, O Lord, dost fatten them and prepare them for the slaughter."

Accordingly, you may say that ungodly governments are like God's

[45] The original has "chapter thirteen."

swine. He fattens them; He gives them wealth, power, honors, and the obedience of their subjects. Therefore they are not molested, but they themselves molest and oppress others. They do not suffer violence; they inflict it on others. They do not give, but they take away from others until the hour comes when they are slaughtered like swine that have been fattened for a long time. Hence the German proverb which says that a prince is a rare bird in the kingdom of heaven: *Fursten sind wildbrett im Himel.*

Accordingly, those men whom Moses designates in this passage by the detestable and ugly name נְפִלִים without a doubt held positions in the lawful government of the church and of the state. But because they do not make use of their office as they were bound, God brands them with the hateful word and disgraces them. Just as we in the corrupt state of our nature cannot make use of even the slightest gift without haughtiness, so God is most intolerant of haughtiness and puts down the mighty from their thrones, sends the rich away empty, etc.

Thus I take the word נְפִלִים in an active meaning, in the sense of tyrants, oppressors, and brigands. But I believe that here, as happens also in other languages, Moses transferred this word from the usage of his time to the time before the Flood, with a slight change in meaning; for just as those Anakim were tyrants who relied on their physical power, so these degraded descendants of the sons of God misused their power and prestige to oppress good men, as Moses will now explain.

When the sons of God came in to the daughters of men, they bore children to them. These were the mighty men that were of old, the men of renown.

Jerome translates: These are the mighty men *a seculo;* but in this passage the noun *seculum* does not denote duration of time, nor is it in the category of quantity. These giants did not exist from the beginning of the world; they were born only after the sons of God had deteriorated. But *seculum* has a meaning in the category of substance. Thus Moses is explaining the kind of power on which they relied, namely, secular or worldly power. They despised the ministry of the Word as a worthless occupation. Therefore they seized upon a worldly occupation, just as our papists have done. They preferred the possession of abundant revenues and of secular realms to the hatred of all men because of the Gospel.

So far as Moses is concerned, the word עוֹלָם denotes the world itself and an age of time. One must, therefore, note carefully when it has the meaning "age" or "duration of time," in Scripture and when it means "world." In this passage it must have the meaning "world," for these men were not in existence from the beginning of time.

Therefore this clause presents a description of the power they received, not from the church or from the Holy Spirit but from the devil and the world. As a result, it is, as it were, the antithesis of what Christ says before Pilate: "My kingdom is not of this world" (John 18:36). The ministers of the Word contend with hunger and are troubled by the hatred of all classes. Therefore they cannot practice tyranny; but those who wield authority, who rule states, and who have castles and villages — they are the men who are capable of tyranny.

This clause also serves to describe the small church [46] with its few souls. These are cross-bearers who have neither prestige nor wealth but do have the Word. This is their only wealth, but it is wealth that the world both despises and persecutes. By contrast the נְפִלִים, or giants, not only usurp the glorious name of the church on the grounds that they are descended from the patriarchs, but they also wield authority. They are the lords, and with their power they oppress the wretched church. Therefore Moses calls them מֵעוֹלָם נְפִלִים, the mighty men of the world or in the world, or worldlings and temporally mighty men.

What Jerome renders by "renowned men" appears in the Hebrew as "men of name," that is, men renowned and distinguished in the world. But here, too, Moses touches upon the sin of those Cyclopes: when they had possession of everything in the world, they also had an excellent reputation and were renowned throughout the whole world, and this to such a degree that by contrast the true sons of God, namely, Noah with his children, were in the utmost disgrace and were considered heretics, children of the devil, and people who lowered the prestige of both the church and the state. The same thing is now happening to us. In Matt. 24:37 Christ Himself bears witness that there will be a similarity between the last times and the times of Noah.

Moses has already declared that the Holy Spirit was taken away

---

[46] Here Luther uses the word *ecclesiola*.

from the ungodly and that they were abandoned to the ways of their own desires. They were scoundrels, as the pope with his cardinals [47] and bishops are today, who not only are addressed as princes and wield authority, but also lay such claim to the name "church" that they can put us under a curse as heretics and condemn us with the utmost smugness. They do not allow themselves to be called tyrants, ungodly, and irreligious; they want to be called most gracious, most holy, and most honorable.

Therefore the meaning is not the one which Lyra adopts when he explains "famous" as "notorious." [48] For the world does not call the pope Antichrist but gives him the name "most holy one" and admires him as one who, together with his carnal [49] creatures, is completely filled with the Holy Spirit and cannot err. For this reason it humbly worships him, no matter what he commands and directs.

Thus the giants stood in high repute and enjoyed the extraordinary admiration of the whole world. Noah, on the contrary, together with his people, was condemned as a rebel, a heretic, and an enemy of the sovereignty of both the state and the church. We who affirm our faith in the Gospel are regarded similarly today by the popes and the bishops.

Thus this passage presents a description of the sins besetting that age, namely, that they were men alienated from the Word and given over to their lusts and reprobate minds, men who sinned against the Holy Spirit with persistent impenitence, the defense of ungodly acts, and assaults on the acknowledged truth. Nevertheless, in the midst of all their blasphemous conduct they retained a reputation and distinction not only as secular government but also as church, as though they had been elevated by God to the position of angels. But when things had come to such a pass, when Noah and Lamech, together with their forefather Methuselah, were teaching in vain, God gave these people over to the desires of their own hearts (Ps. 81:12) and kept silence until they would face the Flood in which they were refusing to believe.

This is what it means to desert God and the church, and to marry forbidden wives. One sin, if it is not immediately checked, leads to

---

[47] It seems that Luther is punning on the basis of the similarity between *carnalibus* and *cardinalibus*.

[48] Lyra on Gen. 6:4, sec. o, interprets *famosi* as *malae famae*.

[49] See note 47 above.

another sin, and from there again to another, in endless sequence, until one arrives at the stage which Solomon describes in Prov. 18:3: "When the ungodly man arrives at the bottom of sin, he views it with contempt." Even if, later on, you should warn such people, they pay no heed whatever. They think they need no teacher, and they are sure that they are in the right; they do not believe in a life after this life, nor do they hope for salvation even in their manifest sins. But disgrace and reproach overtake them in the end. This persistent impenitence and utmost contempt for the Word impelled God to bring on the universal destruction of all flesh by the Flood.

5. *The Lord saw that the wickedness of man was great in the earth, and that every imagination of the thoughts of his heart was only evil continually.*

6. *And the Lord was sorry that He had made man on the earth.*

This is the passage of which we made use against free will, about which Augustine writes that without grace or the Holy Spirit it is incapable of anything but sin.[50] The scholastics, who are patrons of free will, are hard pressed not only by the clarity of this passage but also by the authority of Augustine, and they sweat over it. Concerning Augustine they maintain that he is speaking in exaggerated terms and is following a practice of the farmers. Thus Basilius writes of someone who went too far in refuting the opposition. When farmers try to make crooked branches grow straight, they bend them a little more in the opposite direction. The scholastics maintain that in order to check the Pelagians in his defense of grace, Augustine similarly expressed himself more rigorously against free will than was proper.[51]

But so far as this passage is concerned, they misapply it when they maintain that the text speaks only of the evil generation before the Flood, and that people are better now, at least some, who make good use of their free will. The poor fellows do not see that it is speaking of the human heart in general and that there is expressly added the little word, רַק, "only." In the third place, they are not aware of this either, that later, in the eighth chapter (v. 21), the

---

[50] Cf. Luther's *The Bondage of the Will* (1525), W, XVIII, 736.

[51] Actually, Augustine battled on two fronts. Against the Pelagians he defended the inevitability of sin, but against the Manicheans he defended responsibility for sin; statements taken from either controversy require those from the other controversy for completeness.

same statement is repeated after the Flood in almost identical words. For God declares that the imagination of man's heart is evil from his youth. There He is surely not speaking only of those who were in existence before the Flood, but of those to whom He makes the promise that after this there will never come another general destruction by water, that is, of all the descendants of Noah. These words, "The imagination of the human heart is evil," apply universally.

Hence we draw the universal conclusion that without the Holy Spirit and without grace man can do nothing but sin and so goes on endlessly from sin to sin. But when there is also this added element that he does not uphold sound doctrine, rejects the Word of salvation, and resists the Holy Spirit, then, with the support of his free will, he also becomes an enemy of God, blasphemes the Holy Spirit, and completely follows the evil desires of his heart. Witnesses of this are the example of the Jews at the time of the prophets, of Christ, and of the apostles; the example of the first world at the time of the preacher Noah; and also the example of our adversaries today, who cannot be persuaded by any means that they are sinning, that they are in error, and that their forms of worship are wicked.

Other statements of Holy Scripture prove the same thing. Or is not Ps. 14:2-3 general enough when it says: "The Lord looks down from heaven upon the children of men, to see if there are any that act wisely, that seek after God. They have all gone astray." Paul repeats this in Rom. 3:10. Likewise Ps. 116:11 states in general: "Every human being is a liar"; and Paul (Rom. 11:32): "God has shut up all under sin." All these passages are very general and most emphatically conclude in our favor that without the Holy Spirit, whom Christ alone bestows, man can do nothing else than err and sin. For this reason Christ also declares in the Gospel (John 15:5): "I am the vine, you are the branches; apart from Me you can do nothing. Without Me you are like branches that are cut off, dry, dead, and ready for the fire."

This is also the reason why it is the office of the Holy Spirit to reprove the world (John 16:8), namely, that He might recall the world to repentance and to a recognition of this fault. But the world remains the same; even when it is reprimanded by means of the Word of God, it does not listen. It assumes that the forms of worship it has chosen for itself, although they lack the Word of God, are pleasing to God nevertheless; and it does not allow itself to be moved from this conviction.

If there is ever a council, the final verdict and outcome regarding this very doctrine of free will will be that one must abide by what the pope and the fathers have decided.[52] Even if we should shout ourselves hoarse saying that of himself and without the Holy Spirit man is evil and that whatever he does without the Holy Spirit, or without faith, is condemned before God, for the heart of man and even his thoughts are corrupt — we shall achieve nothing.

Therefore we must fortify ourselves and hold firmly to this doctrine, which sets before us our sin and condemnation. This knowledge of our sin is the beginning of our salvation, that we completely despair of ourselves and give to God alone the glory for our righteousness. Otherwise why does Paul lament in Rom. 7:18 and freely confess that there is nothing good in him? Moreover, for the same reason he states plainly, "in my flesh," that we may realize that our defect is healed by the Spirit of God alone. When this fact is firmly established in our hearts, a large portion of the foundation for our salvation has been laid. Thereafter we have the clear assurance that God does not cast aside sinners, that is, those who recognize their sin and desire to come to their senses, who thirst for righteousness (Matt. 5:6) or the forgiveness of their sins through Christ.

We must, therefore, beware diligently of being found among those Cyclopes, who oppose the Word of God and boast of their own free will and of their own powers. Though we often go astray, though we stumble and sin, nevertheless, if we yield to the Holy Spirit by a humble confession of our wickedness when He reproves us, the Holy Spirit Himself will be with us. He will not only not impute to us the sins we have acknowledged but through the grace of Christ will cover them and will grant us a full measure of the other gifts we need for this life as well as for that which is to come.

But the very words of Moses should be noted carefully. In this passage he has employed an unusual expression with a definite design. He does not simply state that the *thoughts* of the human being are evil, but the very *imagination* of his thoughts. He applies this term to every capacity of human thought or of human reason and free will, even though it may be of the highest quality. He calls it imagination because man devises it with the utmost effort, selects, and fashions it as a potter does, and regards it as something very beautiful.

[52] See p. 21, note 31.

But this, says Moses, is evil, and not just once, but continually and at all times; for without the Holy Spirit reason is entirely devoid of any knowledge of God. Furthermore, to be devoid of any knowledge of God means to be completely ungodly; it means to live in darkness and to regard as best those things that are worst. I am speaking about things that are good in a theological sense, for in this instance a difference must be made between civil affairs and theology. God gives His approval to the governments of the ungodly; He honors and rewards excellence even in the ungodly. Yet He does this so far as this present life comes into consideration, not the future life. And reason does have an understanding of what things are good as far as the state is concerned.

But when we discuss free will, we ask what its powers are from the theological point of view, not in civil affairs or in matters within the realm of reason. We maintain, however, that man without the Holy Spirit is completely ungodly before God, even if he were adorned with all the virtues of all the heathen. In the historical accounts of the heathen there are certainly outstanding instances of self-control; of generosity; of love toward fatherland, parents, and children; of bravery; and of philanthropy. Yet we maintain that the loftiest thoughts about God, about the worship of God, and about the will of God are a darkness more than Cimmerian.[53] The light of reason, which has been granted to man alone, has insight only into what benefits the body. This is the perverted love of carnal desire.

Therefore this statement is not to be understood in a trivial sense, the way the Jews and the sophists understand it; they suppose that it is speaking only of the lower part of man, which is brutish, but that "reason strives toward the highest good." [54] Accordingly, they confine "the imagination of his thoughts" to the Second Table, as did the Pharisee who disapproved of the tax collector and declared that he was not like the others (Luke 18:11). He spoke fine words, for it is not something evil to thank God for His gifts. But we declare that even this very act is something evil and ungodly, because it has its origin in the utmost lack of knowledge about God and is truly a prayer turned into sin; for it serves neither the glory of God nor the welfare of man.

You may likewise be aware that in some of their writings the

[53] Homer, *Odyssey,* Book XI, l. 14.
[54] Luther is citing the scholastic axiom *rationem deprecari ad optima.*

philosophers have clever discussions about God and about the providence by which God controls everything. Some people find these statements so pious that they make all but prophets out of Socrates, Xenophon, and Plato.[55] But because such discussions do not realize that God sent His Son Christ for the salvation of sinners, these superb discussions themselves represent the utmost lack of the knowledge of God and are nothing but blasphemies, according to the statement in this passage, which declares directly that all the imagination, every endeavor of the human heart, is only evil.

This applies, therefore, not only to the sins before the Flood but to man's entire nature — to his heart, his reason, and his intellect, even when man feigns righteousness and wants to be most holy. This the Anabaptists do today when they get the idea into their heads that they can live without sin, and when they are intent on attaining what appear to be outstanding virtues. The rule is: When hearts are without the Holy Spirit, they do not only have no knowledge of God but even hate Him by nature. How can something that has its origin in a lack of knowledge of God and in a hatred of God be anything else than evil?

But here another question is raised. Moses says: "God saw that all the thoughts of man were evil." Likewise: "and He was sorry that He had made man." Now if God foresees everything, why does Moses say that God saw only now? If God is wise, how can it happen that He repents of something He did? Why did He not see this sin or this corrupt nature of man from the beginning of the world? Why does Scripture attribute to God a temporal will, vision, and counsel in this manner? Are not God's counsels eternal and ἀμετανόητα (Rom. 2:5), so that He cannot repent of them? Similar statements occur in the prophets, where God threatens punishments, as in the case of the Ninevites. Nevertheless, He pardons those who repent.[56]

To this question the scholastics have nothing else to reply than that Scripture is speaking in human fashion, and therefore such actions are attributed to God by some figure of speech. They carry

---

[55] This may be aimed at Zwingli, whose statements about the possible salvation of Socrates had aroused Luther's ire; cf. Luther's *Short Confession on the Blessed Sacrament* (1544), W, LIV, 143.

[56] Luther seems to be thinking of the contrast between Jonah 1:2 and Jonah 3:10.

on discussions about a twofold will of God: "the will of His sign" and "the will of His good pleasure." [57] They maintain that "the will of His good pleasure" is uniform and unchangeable, but that "the will of His sign" is changeable; for He changes the signs when He wishes. Thus He did away with circumcision, instituted Baptism, etc., although the same "will of good pleasure," which had been predetermined from eternity, continued in force.

I do not condemn this opinion; [58] but it seems to me that there is a less complicated explanation, namely, that Holy Scripture is describing the thinking of those men who are in the ministry. When Moses says that God sees and repents, these actions really occur in the hearts of the men who carry on the ministry of the Word. Similarly, when he said above: "My Spirit will not judge among men," he is not speaking directly of the Holy Spirit as He is in His own essential nature or of the Divine Majesty but of the Holy Spirit in the heart of Noah, Methuselah, and Lamech, that is, of the Spirit of God as He is carrying on His office and administering the Word through His saints.

It is in this manner that God saw human wickedness and repented. That is, Noah, who had the Holy Spirit and was a minister of the Word, saw the wickedness of men and through the Holy Spirit was moved to grief when he observed this situation. Paul also similarly declares (Eph. 4:30) that the Holy Spirit is grieved in the godly by the ungodliness and wickedness of the ungodly. Because Noah is a faithful minister of the Word and the mouthpiece of the Holy Spirit, Moses correctly states that the Holy Spirit is grieving when Noah grieves and wishes that man would rather not be in existence than be so evil.

Therefore the meaning is not that God from eternity had not seen these conditions; He sees everything from eternity. But since this wickedness of man now manifests itself with the utmost violence,

[57] "There is this difference between will and anger, that anger is never attributed to God properly, since in its proper meaning it includes passion; whereas will is attributed to Him properly. Therefore in God there are distinguished will in its proper sense and will as attributed to Him by metaphor. Will in its proper sense is called the 'will of good pleasure' *(voluntas beneplaciti)*, and will metaphorically taken is the 'will of sign' *(voluntas signi)*, inasmuch as the sign itself of will is called will." Thomas Aquinas, *Summa theologica*, I, Q. 19, Art. 11.

[58] Luther could not very well disapprove of this distinction, having himself used it against Erasmus in *The Bondage of the Will* (1525), W, XVIII, 715.

God now discloses this wickedness in the hearts of His ministers and prophets.

Thus God is immutable and unchanging in His counsel from eternity. He sees and knows all things; but He does not reveal them to the godly except at His own fixed time, so that they themselves may see them too. This seems to me to be the simplest meaning of this passage, and Augustine's interpretation differs little from it.[59]

I follow this general rule: to avoid as much as possible any questions that carry us to the throne of the Supreme Majesty. It is better and safer to stay at the manger of Christ the Man.[60] For there is very great danger in involving oneself in the mazes of the Divine Being.

To this passage belong others that are similar; in them God is depicted as though He had eyes, ears, a mouth, a nose, hands, and feet, the way Isaiah, Daniel, and the other prophets saw Him in their visions. In such passages Scripture speaks about God no differently from the way it speaks about a human being. Because the Anthropomorphites assigned human form to the Divine Being they were found guilty of heresy.[61]

If the Anthropomorphites had so crude a conception, they deserved to be found guilty; for they were manifestly in error. As Christ states (Luke 24:39), a spirit has no flesh and bones. I rather incline to the opinion that the Anthropomorphites had in mind some method of imparting doctrine to the simple. God in His essence is altogether unknowable; nor is it possible to define or put into words what He is, though we burst in the effort.

It is for this reason that God lowers Himself to the level of our weak comprehension and presents Himself to us in images, in coverings, as it were, in simplicity adapted to a child, that in some measure it may be possible for Him to be known by us. Thus the Holy Spirit appeared in the form of a dove (Matt. 3:16), not because He is a dove. Yet in that simple form He wanted to be known, received, and worshiped; for He was truly the Holy Spirit. Likewise, in the same passages, even though no one will maintain that God the Father was the voice sounding from heaven, He nevertheless had to be received and worshiped in this simple image.

[59] Cf., for one example, Augustine, *De catechizandis rudibus*, ch. 19.

[60] This counsel came from Luther's own personal experience; cf. his comments on Gen. 26:9, W, XLIII, 461.

[61] Cf. *Luther's Works*, 1, pp. 14—15.

That Scripture thus assigns to God the form, voice, actions, emotions, etc., of a human being not only serves to show consideration for the uneducated and the weak; but we great and learned men, who are versed in the Scriptures, are also obliged to adopt these simple images, because God has presented them to us and has revealed Himself to us through them. Similarly, the angels also appear in human form, although it is an established fact that they are altogether spirits. But we are unable to recognize spirits when they present themselves as spirits; images, however, we recognize.

This is the simplest procedure for dealing with passages of this kind, for we cannot define what God is in His nature. Yet we can define what He is not, namely, that He is not a voice, not a dove, not water, not bread, and not wine. Nevertheless, He presents Himself to us in these visible forms, deals with us, and puts these forms before us to keep us from degenerating into erratic and vagabond spirits [62] who indeed carry on discussions about God but are profoundly ignorant of Him as of One who cannot be comprehended in His unveiled majesty. God sees that this way of knowing God is impossible for us; for, as Scripture states (1 Tim. 6:16), He dwells in unapproachable light, and He has made known what we can grasp and understand. Those who adhere to this truly understand God; while those who boast of visions, revelations, and enlightenments and follow them are either overwhelmed by God's majesty or remain in utter ignorance of God.

The Jews likewise had their own images by which God showed Himself to them: the mercy seat, the ark, the tabernacle, the pillars of cloud and fire, etc. In Exodus (33:20) He says: "Man shall not see Me and live." Therefore He puts before us an image of Himself, because He shows Himself to us in such a manner that we can grasp Him. In the New Testament we have Baptism, the Lord's Supper, absolution, and the ministry of the Word.

These, in the terminology of the scholastics, are "the will of the sign," and these we must consider when we want to know God's will. The other is His "will of good pleasure," the essential will of God or His unveiled majesty, which is God Himself. From this the eyes must turn away, for it cannot be grasped. In God there is sheer Deity, and the essence of God is His transcendent wisdom and omnipotent power. These attributes are altogether beyond the grasp of reason;

---

[62] Apparently a reference to the "fanatics" of the left wing.

and whatever God has purposed by this "will of His good pleasure" He has seen from eternity.

An investigation of this essential and divine will, or of the Divine Majesty, must not be pursued but altogether avoided. This will is unsearchable, and God did not want to give us an insight into it in this life. He merely wanted to indicate it by means of some coverings: Baptism, the Word, the Sacrament of the Altar. These are the divine images and "the will of the sign." Through them God deals with us within the range of our comprehension. Therefore these alone must engage our attention. "The will of His good pleasure" must be completely discarded from consideration unless you are a Moses, a David, or some similar perfect man, although these men, too, viewed "the will of His good pleasure" without ever diverting their eyes from "the will of the sign."

Now the operation of God is called "the will of the sign"; for He comes out toward us to deal with us through some sort of covering and external object that we can grasp, such as the Word of God and the ceremonies He has instituted. This will, they say, is not almighty. For example, even though in the Ten Commandments God prescribes what He wants done, it is not done. Thus Christ instituted the Lord's Supper to strengthen our trust in His mercy; and yet many partake of it to their judgment (1 Cor. 11:29), that is, without faith.

But I return to Moses. He states that God sees the wickedness of men and repents. The scholastics have this explanation: "He sees and repents, namely, with 'the will of the sign,' not with 'the will of His good pleasure' or with His essential will." We maintain that Noah's heart was moved by the Holy Spirit, so that he realized that God was angry with man and wanted to destroy him. Moreover, this is an understandable interpretation, one that does not involve us in discussions about the absolute power or majesty of God, which are fraught with very great dangers, as I have seen in the instance of many men. Such spirits are first puffed up by the devil to believe that they have the Holy Spirit; they disregard the Word; yes, they even blaspheme, and they boast of nothing but the Spirit and visions.

This is the first stage of error, when men disregard God as He has enveloped Himself and become incarnate, and seek to scrutinize the unveiled God.[63] Later on, when the hour of judgment arrives and they feel the wrath of God, when God is judging and investigating

---

[63] Cf. *Luther the Expositor,* pp. 102—107.

their hearts, then the devil ceases to puff them up, and they despair and die. For they are walking unsheltered in the sun and are abandoning the shade, which gives relief from the heat (Is. 4:6).

Let no one, therefore, contemplate the unveiled Divinity, but let him flee from these contemplations as from hell and the veritable temptations of Satan. Let it be the concern of each of us to abide by the signs by which God has revealed Himself to us, namely, His Son, born of the Virgin Mary and lying in His manger among the cattle; the Word; Baptism; the Lord's Supper; and absolution. In these images we see and meet a God whom we can bear, one who comforts us, lifts us up into hope, and saves us. The other ideas about "the will of His good pleasure," or the essential and eternal will, slay and condemn.

And yet they use the term "will of His good pleasure" in an improper sense. The name "will of His good pleasure" ought to be given to that will which the Gospel reveals and of which Paul states in Rom. 12:2: "That you may prove what is the good will of God." And Christ (John 6:40): "This is the will of God that everyone who sees the Son should have eternal life." Likewise (Matt. 12:50): "My brother is he who does the will of My Father." Likewise (Matt. 3:17): "This is My Son, with whom I am well pleased."

This will of grace is correctly and precisely designated as "the will of His good pleasure"; and it is the one and only antidote and remedy against what is termed either "the will of the sign" or "the will of His good pleasure," about which the scholastics carry on their discussions in connection with the Flood and the destruction of Sodom.

In both these events there is manifested a terrible wrath against which hearts cannot find any protection except through the will of grace, namely, by keeping in mind that the Son of God was sent into the flesh to free us from sin, death, and the tyranny of Satan.

This will of the divine good pleasure was ordained from eternity and was revealed and displayed in Christ. It is a life-giving, pleasant, and lovely will. For this reason it alone deserves to be called "the will of His good pleasure." But the good fathers usually passed over the promises and do not lay stress on them, even though these can properly be called "the will of good pleasure."

When they bid us direct our view to "the will of the sign," they are indeed doing well; but that alone is not enough. When we look at the Ten Commandments, are we not terrified by the sight of our sins? If to these you should add those awful examples of wrath, which are likewise "the will of the sign," it is impossible for the heart to take courage unless it considers what we call "the will of good pleasure," that is, the Son of God, who portrays for us the heart and will of His Father, namely, that He does not want to be angry with sinners but wants to show them mercy through His Son, as the latter says (John 14:9): "Philip, he who has seen Me has seen the Father."

The incarnate Son of God is, therefore, the covering in which the Divine Majesty presents Himself to us with all His gifts, and does so in such a manner that there is no sinner too wretched to be able to approach Him with the firm assurance of obtaining pardon. This is the one and only view of the Divinity that is available and possible in this life. But on the Last Day those who have died in this faith will be so enlightened by heavenly power that they will see even the Divine Majesty Itself. Meanwhile we must come to the Father by that way which is Christ Himself; He will lead us safely, and we shall not be deceived.

The addition in the text — "The Lord was sorry that He had made man on the earth" — I regard as an antithetical statement. God is thinking, not of man on the earth, who is subject to sin and death, but of the heavenly being who is the lord of sin and death. God is indicating that He loves this man, but the earthly one He hates and contemplates destroying.

6. *And it grieved Him to His heart.*

God grieved so much that He was sorely troubled in His heart. The verb is עָצַב, which He employed above when He said: "In sorrow you will bring forth" (Gen. 3:16). It occurs also in Ps. 127:2: "The bread of sorrow." This expression must be understood in accordance with the usage of Scripture. One should not imagine that God has a heart or that He can grieve. But when the spirit of Noah, of Lamech, and of Methuselah is grieved, God Himself is said to be grieved. Thus we should understand this grief to refer to its effect, not to the divine essence. When, by revelation of the Holy Spirit, Noah and his father and grandfather perceived in their hearts that God hated the world because of its sins and intended to destroy it, they were grieved by its impenitence.

This is the simple and true meaning. If you refer these words to the will of the divine essence, that God had determined this from eternity, such a discussion is fraught with peril and cannot be carried on except by spiritual men and such as have been well trained by their trials, men like Paul, who dared carry on a discussion about predestination. We shall take our position on a lower level, one which brings less peril with it, namely, that Noah and the other fathers were filled with grief when the Spirit revealed His wrath to them. The inexpressible groanings of these outstanding men are assigned to God Himself because they proceed from His Spirit.

Of these groanings we shall encounter another example in Abraham, who, like a wall, put himself in the way of the danger threatening Sodom and did not give up his pleading until he had arrived at five [64] righteous men (Gen. 18:23-32). In this instance the Holy Spirit undoubtedly filled the heart of Abraham with countless groanings of all sorts in His effort to gain deliverance for the wretched people.

Likewise, what does Samuel not do for Saul? He cries and wails so long that God is compelled to restrain him (1 Sam 16:1): "How long will you grieve over Saul when I have rejected him from being king over Israel?"

And Christ, too, when He gazed at Jerusalem, which was to be laid waste within a few years on account of its sin, was most deeply moved and troubled in His heart (Matt. 23:37-39).

Such emotion the Holy Spirit stirs up in the hearts of the godly. Wherever He is, He is touched by the afflictions of others. He teaches, He trains, He spares no effort, He prays, He moans, He groans, etc. Moses and Paul similarly long to be accursed for the benefit of their people.[65]

Thus the very holy man Noah, together with his father and his grandfather, wastes away with grief when he sees the dreadful wrath of God. Noah takes no pleasure in the ruin of the entire human race but is worried and greatly troubled. Meanwhile the sons of men are living in the utmost smugness. They laugh and rejoice; they even scoff at him. Ps. 109:4 describes a similar situation: "In return for my love they accuse me, even as I make prayer for them." Paul says in Phil. 3:18: "I tell you with tears." What else can holy men do when the world absolutely refuses to mend its ways?

This is the perpetual characteristic of the true church: it not only experiences suffering and is dishonored and held in contempt, but

---

[64] This appears to be Luther's own gloss on Gen. 18:32.

[65] Luther is pointing to the parallel between Ex. 32:32 and Rom. 9:3.

it also prays for those who afflict it and is gravely concerned about their perils. In contrast, the closer the ungodly are to their condemnation, the greater is the smugness with which they indulge in amusements and pleasures. Therefore when the hour of judgment arrives, God, on the other hand, closes His ears to such an extent that He does not even hear His beloved children as they pray and beg for mercy for the ungodly. Ezekiel (13:5) complains that no one is found to set himself up as a wall in Israel's behalf, a function that properly belongs to the prophets, according to him.

But it is impossible for the ungodly to pray. Let no one, therefore, hope for any prayer from our adversaries, the papists. We are praying for them and setting ourselves up like a wall against the wrath of God; and if by any chance they were to come to repentance, they would, without a doubt, be saved through our tears and groanings.

It is an awful example that God did not spare the first world when Noah, Lamech, and Methuselah set themselves up like a wall. What shall we suppose will happen when there are no such walls, that is, when there is no church at all? The church is always a wall against the wrath of God. It grieves, it agonizes, it prays, it pleads, it teaches, it preaches, it admonishes, as long as the hour of judgment has not yet arrived but is impending. When it sees that these activities are of no avail, what else can it do than grieve deeply over the destruction of impenitent people? Seeing a large number of their kinsmen and relatives about to perish increased the grief of the godly fathers.

This grief Moses was unable to portray in a better and clearer manner than to state that the Lord was sorry that He had made man. When he describes man's nature, which was fashioned according to the image of God, he states that God saw everything that He had made, and that it was very good (Gen. 1:31). Thus the Lord delights and rejoices in His creatures. In this passage He changes His opinion completely and states the opposite, namely, that He grieves and is sorry that He ever made man.

By the Holy Spirit's revelation Noah and the other fathers shared these sentiments; otherwise they would have persisted in their former happy thoughts, and in accordance with the earlier promise they would have had the conviction that God was pleased with all His works. They would not have thought that God's wrath was so intense that He intended to destroy not only the whole human race but all the animals of heaven and earth, though they certainly had committed no sin, and even the earth itself, which, because of men's sins, did not keep its former excellence after the Flood. Lyra cites certain writers who have maintained that the surface of the earth was worn away by the Flood to the extent of about three handbreadths. Paradise certainly was completely laid waste and ruined by the Flood.[66] Therefore we have an earth today that is obviously more cursed than the one in existence before the Flood and after Adam's sin. Yet the earth that existed then was nothing in comparison with the excellence of the first earth, before sin.

Through the revelation of the Holy Spirit the holy fathers saw these disasters a hundred and twenty years in advance. But the wickedness of the world was so great that men compelled the Holy Spirit to keep silence. For fear of the gravest dangers Noah did not dare disclose these threats; but he carried on discussions about God's great wrath with his father, his grandfather, his children, and his wife. It was no less bearable for the sons of men to hear these facts than it is today for the papists when they hear it stated that they are the church of Satan, not of Christ. They prided themselves on their ancestry, and over against Noah's preaching they laid stress on the promise of the Seed. They supposed it was impossible that God would destroy the entire human race this way.

In like manner, the Jews did not believe the prophets and Christ Himself when He called them to repentance; for they maintained that they were the people of God, because they had the temple and its worship.

Today the Turks are puffed up by their victories, which they regard as a reward for their faith and religion, because they believe in one God; but us they regard as heathen, as though we believed in three gods. They say: "God would not give us so many victories and kingdoms if He were not favorably inclined toward us and did not approve of our religion."

It is this very thought that blinds the papists too. They see themselves in the highest position. Therefore they maintain that they are the church, and for this reason they do not fear any threats of divine judgment. It is a devilish line of thought when men seek to get support for their sins through the name of the Lord.

But if God did not spare the first world, the generation of the

[66] Cf. p. 204, note 43.

holy patriarchs, who possessed the promise concerning the Seed, and if He preserved only very small remnants, then the Turks, the Jews, and the papists boast of the name of God in vain. According to Micah (2:7), the words of God promise good to those who walk uprightly. Hence there are evils in store for those who do not walk uprightly; these men God threatens, and these He destroys without any regard for the title "church" and without any consideration for their large numbers. It is the remnants who walk uprightly that He preserves. But you will never convince the world of this.

Undoubtedly the descendants of the patriarchs who perished in the Flood vastly overstated their argument about the prestige of the church. They charged Noah himself with blasphemy and lies. "Stating that God is about to destroy the whole world by the Flood," they maintained, "is the same as saying that God is not compassionate and not a father, but a cruel tyrant. Noah, you are preaching the wrath of God! Has not God promised deliverance from sin and death through the Seed of the woman? God's wrath will not swallow up the entire earth. We are God's people, and we have outstanding gifts of God. God would never have granted us these gifts if He had decided to proceed against us in such a hostile manner." In this manner the ungodly are wont to apply the promises to themselves, and because of their reliance on them they disregard and laugh at all threats.

The careful consideration of all this is profitable to fortify us against being offended by the smugness of the ungodly. For the same things that happened to Noah happen to us. Our adversaries attribute to themselves the name "people of God" as well as the worship, grace, and everything else that goes with it; to us, on the contrary, they attribute everything that is demonic. When we reprove them for their blasphemy and say that they are the church of Satan, they rage against us with every kind of cruelty. Therefore we lament with Noah and commit our cause to the Lord, just as Christ did on the cross; for what else are we to do? We wait for God to sit in judgment on the earth and to make it clear that He loves the remnant of those who fear Him and hates the mass of the unrepentant sinners, even though they boast that they are the church, that they have the promises, and that they have the worship of God. Thus He destroyed the entire original world and made His promise concerning the Seed come true for that wretched and tiny remnant, Noah and his sons.

8. *But Noah found favor in the eyes of the Lord.*

These are words that restored Noah's courage and life. Such great wrath of the Divine Majesty would have slain him if God had not added the promise to preserve him. Nevertheless, it is likely that his faith was still troubled even though he heard this promise. It is unbelievable how much the contemplation of the wrath of God depresses the heart.

Furthermore, here there is a new expression of the Holy Spirit — an expression which the heavenly messenger Gabriel also employs when addressing the Blessed Virgin (Luke 1:30): "You have found favor with God." This expression very clearly rules out any merit and gives praise to faith, by which alone we are justified before God, that is, are acceptable to God and please Him.

9. *These are the generations of Noah. Noah was a righteous man, blameless in his generation; Noah walked with God.*

10. *And Noah had three sons, Shem, Ham, and Japheth.*

With this passage the Jews begin not only a new chapter but also a new lection.[67] This is a very short historical account, but one that gives outstanding praise to this patriarch Noah, namely, that he alone continued to be righteous and faultless when the rest of the sons of God were deteriorating.

We must keep in mind that there were many excellent men among the sons of God. Some of them lived with Noah as long as five hundred years. The age before the Flood was very long-lived, not only so far as the sons of God were concerned, but also so far as the sons of men were concerned. The experience they gathered in the course of so many years was extraordinary. Much they learned from their forefathers; much they themselves saw and experienced.

When all these people became corrupt, Noah alone remained steadfast, a truly amazing man. He turned aside neither to the left nor to the right; he retained the true worship of God; he kept the pure doctrine and lived in the fear of God. There is, therefore, no doubt that the perverse generation hated him intensely and harassed him in various ways while exposing him to ridicule: "Is it you alone who is wise? Is it you alone who pleases God? Are all the rest of us in error? Shall we all be condemned? Is it you alone who is not

---

[67] A reference to what seemed to be the liturgical divisions of the Old Testament text.

in error? Is it you alone who will not be condemned?" Therefore the righteous and holy man had to determine by himself that all the others were in error and should be condemned, but that only he, together with his descendants, would be saved. Even though he reached this correct conclusion, it was very difficult. Thus the holy man wrestled with various thoughts like these.

The wretched papists assail us today with this one argument, saying: "Do you think that all the fathers were in error?" It is indeed painful to maintain this, especially about the better ones — Augustine, Ambrose, Bernard, and that entire company of excellent men who ruled the church by the Word, who have been adorned with the distinction and lofty name "church," and for whose labors we have both praise and admiration.

But surely Noah himself encountered a hardship no smaller in the fact that although he alone was declared to be righteous and blameless, the sons of men claimed the name "church" for themselves too. After the sons of the patriarchs had united with them by marriage, then indeed they considered it insanity on the part of Noah and his family to follow another doctrine and other forms of worship.

Today our life is very short, and yet the extent to which human minds are advancing is quite clear. What do you suppose happened in those very long lives, when the keenness and vigor of the human mind was also greater? Our nature today is duller and more stupid by far. Nevertheless, although men were endowed with so many gifts, they rushed blindly into ungodliness, as is stated later on (v. 12): "All flesh has corrupted their way. But Noah alone is righteous and perfect."

One may differentiate between these two words in such a manner as to observe that Noah is declared "righteous" in relation to the First Table and "perfect" in relation to the Second Table. He is declared righteous through his faith in God, because he believed first the universal promise about the Seed of the woman and later on also the special one about the destruction of the world by the Flood and about the preservation of his descendants. He is declared perfect because he walked in the fear of God and carefully avoided murder and the other sins with which the ungodly were polluting themselves in violation of their conscience; and he was in no way influenced by the many offenses of the most distinguished, the wisest, and, in appearance, the holiest men.

This was an outstanding virtue. To us today it seems impossible that one man should defy the entire world and condemn as evil all the rest, who glory in the church, the Word, and the worship of God, and that he should maintain that he alone is a son of God and acceptable to God. Noah, accordingly, is truly an amazing man. Moses bestows praise on this great courage by adding explicitly: "In his generation," or "in his age," as though he were to say that it was indeed the worst and the most depraved.

Above, in the story of Enoch, we gave the meaning of "to walk with God," namely, to carry on the business of God in public.[68] To be righteous and perfect is evidence of personal excellence; but to walk with God is something public, namely, to carry on God's business before the world, to occupy oneself with His Word, and to teach His worship. Noah was not only righteous and holy so far as his own person was concerned, but he was also a confessor. He informed others of the promises and threats of God, and in that most wicked and depraved age he carried out and suffered everything that is the obligation of a person in a public position.

If I had been aware that so many men in the generation of the wicked were opposing me, I surely would have given up the ministry in despair. No one believes how difficult it is for one man to oppose the common opinion of all other churches, to contend against the views of very good men and very good friends, to condemn them, and to teach, live, and do everything in opposition to them. Noah did this because he was gifted with marvelous steadfastness. Blameless as he was before men, he not only did not leave God's business undone but carried it on courageously and with determination among the most wicked men until he was told: "My spirit will not argue with man any longer." The verb "argue" perfectly describes Noah's frame of mind when the ungodly heard him preaching.

Peter (2 Peter 2:5) gives an excellent explanation of "walking with God" when he calls Noah a preacher, not of man's righteousness but of God's, that is, of faith in the promised Seed. Moses does not indicate what sort of reward he received from the ungodly for this preaching. It is enough for him to state that he preached righteousness and gave instruction in the true worship of God in opposition to the whole world, that is, in opposition to the most excellent, most devout, and wisest men. More than one miracle was

[68] See *Luther's Works*, 1, pp. 344—345.

necessary to prevent the ungodly from surrounding and killing him. We observe and experience today how much wrath, hatred, and envy one sermon addressed to the people generates. To what, then, shall we suppose that Noah was subjected? He preached not a hundred, not two hundred, but even more years, up to the final hundred years, during which God did not want the ungodly to be instructed any longer, because they would only become more infuriated and more wicked.

From the character and nature of the world and of the devil, from the experiences of the apostles and prophets, and from our own experience we can infer how great an example of patience and of all virtues Noah was. He was righteous and blameless in that wicked generation and walked before God; that is, he ruled the churches by the Word. And after the awful threat had been pronounced and one hundred twenty years had been fixed as the period after which the world would perish by the Flood, he married and begot children.

Moreover, it is likely that he traveled over the entire world and preached everywhere, giving instructions concerning the true worship of God. His strenuous efforts restrained him from marriage because of his extreme distress, for he was waiting for a better and more God-fearing age. But when he realized that this was a mistaken hope and the divine voice indicated to him the definite time when the world would perish, then he was prompted by the Holy Spirit to turn his mind to marriage, in order that he might leave at least a seed for the new age. In this way the holy man preserved the human race not only spiritually in the true Word and worship but also physically through procreation.

Just as before the Flood a new church begins in Paradise through Adam and Eve, who believed the promise,[69] so at this point also a new world and a new church take their beginning from Noah's marriage; it is the seedbed, as it were, of that world which is to endure until the end of the world.

I stated above that this marriage was a great offense for the ungodly and that they turned it into a big joke.[70] "How is it that the world is to perish in so short a time and yet Noah begets children when he is already five hundred years old?" They regarded this as reliable evidence that the world would not perish by the Flood.

[69] See *Luther's Works*, 1, p. 247.
[70] Cf. p. 25.

Accordingly, they began to live even more dissolutely and to despise all threats with the utmost smugness, as Christ says (Matt. 24:38): "In the days of Noah they drank, they ate, etc." For the world does not understand the counsels of God.

About the order of the sons of Noah I have spoken above.[71] Japheth was the first-born, Shem was born two years after Noah had begun to build the ark, and Ham two years later. Although these facts are not expressed in detail, yet they are carefully noted by Moses.

11. *Now the earth was corrupt in God's sight, and the earth was filled with violence.*

Lyra comments on this passage — perhaps because of the opinion of the rabbis — that the birds and the rest of the animals had also departed from their nature and crossbred with various kinds.[72] But I do not believe this. Among the beasts the creation or nature stayed the way it was created. They did not fall by sinning, as man did. No, they were created merely for this physical life. Therefore they do not hear the Word, and the Word does not concern itself with them; they are altogether without the Law of the First and the Second Table. Hence these words must be applied only to man.

That even the animals bore the punishment of sin and perished by the Flood, together with mankind, happened because God wanted to destroy man completely, not only in body and soul but also with his possessions and the dominion with which he had been created. Examples of similar punishments occur in the Old Testament. In the sixth chapter of Daniel the enemies of Daniel are thrown into the lions' pit, together with their wives, children, and their entire household (Dan. 6:24). The same thing happened in Num. 16, when Korah, Dathan, and Abiram perished (16:32). Something similar is also what Christ states in the Gospel (Matt. 18:25) of the king who commands his servant to be sold, together with his wife, his children, and all his possessions.

In this very same manner not only the human beings but also all their possessions were destroyed by the Flood, that there might be full and complete punishment for sin. The beasts of the field and the birds of the heaven were created for mankind; these are the

---

[71] See *Luther's Works*, 1, pp. 357—358.
[72] Lyra on Gen. 6:11, sec. f.

wealth and the possessions of men. Accordingly, the animals perished, not because they sinned but because God wanted man to perish among and together with all those things that he had on the earth.

Here Moses expressly adds the clause, "The earth was corrupt in God's sight," in order to indicate that in the sight of his age Noah was treated and regarded as a stupid and worthless person. In contrast, the world appeared to itself most holy and most righteous; it assumed that it had adequate reasons for persecuting Noah, especially so far as the First Table and the worship of God were concerned. To be sure, the Second Table likewise gives rise to pretense and hypocrisy; but there is no comparison with the First. An adulterer, a thief, and a murderer can remain hidden for a time, but not forever. But the sins against the First Table usually remain hidden under the guise of saintliness until God reveals them. Ungodliness never wants to be considered and actually to be ungodliness; it strives to be praised for piety and godliness. It embellishes its forms of worship to such a degree that in comparison with them the true forms of worship and true godliness are filthy.

The verb שָׁחַת is very common in Holy Scripture, and it is striking. Moses also employs it in Deut. 31:29: "I know that after my death you will surely act corruptly; and turn aside from the way"; and David, in Ps. 14:3: "All are corrupt and have become detestable." Furthermore, both passages are really speaking of sins against the First Table; that is, they charge those who are saintliest in appearance with false worship of God and with false doctrine. It is impossible for an ungodly life not to follow in the wake of false doctrine.

When Moses states that the earth was corrupt in the sight of God, he clearly points out the contrast, namely, that the hypocrites and tyrants were of the opinion that what Noah taught and did was wrong, but that they taught and did everything in the saintliest manner. But, says Moses, the opposite was true. The earth, that is, the entire world, or all human beings, was corrupt, namely, so far as the First Table is concerned, they did not have the true Word or the true worship. This distinction in regard to the First and Second Table is very much to my liking and has undoubtedly been pointed out by the Holy Spirit.

Moreover, by his addition — "And the earth was filled with violence" — he indicates that this is the unvarying sequence of events: after the Word has been lost, and faith has ceased to exist, and tradition and ἐθελοθρησκεῖαι, as Paul calls them (Col. 2:23), flourish in place of the true forms of worship, acts of violence and a shameful life follow.

The word חָמָס properly denotes violence, force, and harm, with disregard of all law and equity, when anyone may do what he pleases, and whatever things are done are done not by law but by force. If this was their kind of life, someone may say, how could they maintain an outward reputation for saintliness and righteousness? As though indeed one did not have similar examples before one's eyes today! What has the world ever seen that is crueler than the Turks? Nevertheless, they adorn all their brutality with the name of God and godliness.

Thus the popes have not only seized for themselves the wealth of the world, but they have filled the church itself with endless errors and blasphemous doctrines. They live in unspeakable voluptuousness; and when they wish, they sow dissension in the hearts of kings and give ample occasion for war and bloodshed. Nevertheless, in the midst of these very blasphemies and infamous deeds they claim the right to the name and designation "the saintliest"; they boast that they are the vicars of Christ, the successors of Peter, etc.

Accordingly, the greatest wrongs are associated with the designation of holiness, church, true religions, etc. If anyone should express disapproval, he is immediately clubbed with the curse of excommunication and is condemned as a heretic and an enemy of God and the church. Next to the Roman popes and their confederates there is no people that prides itself more on its godliness and righteousness than the Turks, who despise Christians as idolaters but regard themselves as the saintliest and wisest of men. And yet what else is their life and godliness than endless murder, robbery, depredation, and other awful crimes?

The examples of the present time, therefore, show how those two incompatibles can exist side by side: the utmost godliness is paired with the greatest abominations, the utmost violence with the appearance of righteousness. This is also the reason why men become so hardened and smug, and do not look for the punishment they have deserved because of their sins.

12. *And God saw the earth, and behold, it was corrupt; for all flesh had corrupted their way upon the earth.*

Because God's wrath is so dreadful and because the destruction of all flesh, with the exception of eight souls, is already imminent, the language of Moses is somewhat richer in this passage and makes use of repetitions, which, nevertheless, are not purposeless but have their special emphasis. He stated previously that the earth was corrupt; now, as in the orderly progress of a trial, he states that God saw this and gave thought to the punishment. In this manner he depicts the order, as it were, according to which God customarily proceeds.

Today spiritual-minded people are right in their conviction that the pope is the Antichrist and rages madly against the Word and the kingdom of Christ. But the very people who have this conviction are unable to bring about an improvement in this ungodliness. Ungodliness grows daily, and the contempt of godliness becomes greater from day to day. It is then that they reflect: "What is God doing? Why does He not punish His enemies? Is He asleep and not interested at all in human affairs?" The delay of the judgment is torture for the godly. They themselves are unable to bring aid to religion in its distress; and they see that God, who is able to do so, connives at the raging of the popes, who are smugly sinning against both the First and the Second Table.

Thus Noah, too, sees that the earth is filled with acts of violence. Therefore he groans and sighs toward heaven, in order to rouse God to judgment, as from a sleep. Such cries occur frequently in the Psalms: "Why dost Thou stand afar off?" (10:11); "Lord, how long?" (13:2); "Regard us, O Lord, and behold our affliction" (9:13); "Arise, judge my cause" (7:6); etc.

What Moses points out in this passage finally happens. God, too, sees these things and hears the cry of the godly, who can judge the world — for the spiritual man judges everything (1 Cor. 2:15) — but cannot improve it. Ungodliness is altogether incorrigible when it is adorned with the appearance of godliness. The same thing is true of tyranny when it is adorned with the appearance of righteousness and provident care. It is nothing new that those who seize other men's wives, daughters, houses, fields, and wealth nevertheless want to be righteous and holy men, just as we pointed out above in the instance of the papacy.

Therefore the second step is that God sees the wickedness of the world after the saints have seen and judged it, as He states below about Sodom (Gen. 18:20-21): "The outcry against Sodom has come to Me," and above (Gen. 4:10): "The voice of your brother's blood is crying to Me." But the sobs and groanings of the godly always come before God sees. By them God is roused as though from sleep.

This is what Moses wanted to indicate in this passage by the verb "He saw," namely, that at last God saw the afflictions of the godly and heard their cries, which finally filled the heavens, so that God, who thus far had paid no attention to anything and had appeared to support the efforts of the ungodly by giving them success, is awakened as though from sleep. Indeed, He saw everything far more quickly than Noah, for He is the searcher of hearts and cannot be deceived by a pretense of godliness as we can; but only when he is thinking of the punishment does Noah realize that He sees.

We are afflicted similarly today by excessive and unheard-of wickedness. Out of sheer wantonness our adversaries condemn the acknowledged and confessed truth. They aim at our throats, and out of devilish rage they cause the blood of the godly to flow. Those blasphemous, sacrilegious, and murderous acts against the kingdom and the name of God are so well known that they cannot be denied. Nevertheless, our adversaries defend those acts as the height of justice. While they are battling to preserve their tyranny, they even claim for themselves the name "church." What else can we do in these circumstances than cry to God that He hallow His name and not permit His kingdom to be destroyed and His fatherly will to be obstructed?

But the Lord is still sleeping and does not yet see the great ungodliness, because as yet He does not indicate that He sees it. He permits us to be tortured by those distressing sights. Accordingly, we are still in the first stage, and the verse which states that the whole earth was corrupt is applicable to our age. But the second stage will arrive when the time comes. Then we shall be able to maintain with utter confidence that not only we but God, too, sees and hates such great ungodliness. Although God in His longsuffering lets many things go unnoticed for a long time, nevertheless He will live up to His motto (Ps. 98:9): "He will judge the world with righteousness."

The laments of Jeremiah in chapters 12 and 20 reveal how distressing and hard this delay is for the godly. There the holy man all but resorts to blasphemies, until he is finally told that the king of Babylon will come and punish the unbelieving scoffers. Then Jeremiah sees that God pays attention to the earth and is the Judge on the earth.

The universal verdict which follows is intensely dreadful, namely, that all flesh on the earth had corrupted its way and that after God had begun to survey the children of men, He had not found any, from the highest down to the lowest, from the greatest to the least of the fathers, whom He could save from destruction.

But it is far more dreadful to hear this if one gives closer consideration to the first world and does not appraise it on the basis of the wretched remnants we have today. Just as everything the earth brought forth at that time was better and more excellent, so we must also think that the majesty and pomp of our princes and the pretense of holiness and wisdom of the popes is as nothing compared with that pretense of godliness, righteousness, and wisdom that existed in the first world among those eminent men.

Nevertheless, the text states that all flesh had corrupted its way except Noah alone, with his descendants; that is, all men were ungodly, lived in idolatry and false religion, hated the true worship of God together with the promises of the Seed, and persecuted Noah for proclaiming forgiveness of sins through the Seed and for threatening with eternal doom anyone who did not believe that there was forgiveness.

13. *And God said to Noah: I have determined to make an end of all flesh; for the earth is filled with violence through them; behold, I will destroy them with the earth.*

After Noah and his people had cried for a long time and had blamed the wickedness of the world, the Lord finally indicated that He, too, saw the wickedness and intended to punish it. This second stage we are waiting for today; and there is no doubt that there will be some to whom the coming destruction of the world will be revealed, unless perhaps that destruction will be the Last Day and the Last Judgment, something that I would indeed wish for.[73] We have seen enough wickedness in these few and evil days of ours. Just as at the time of Noah, godless men adorn their misdeeds with the name of holiness and righteousness. Accordingly, there can be no hope for penitence or reformation. When that stage was reached at the time of Noah, the decisive verdict was pronounced at last, as the Lord had indicated above when He gave orders to refrain from discussions and said that He was sorry He had made man.

[73] It is not clear how Luther distinguishes this destruction from the Last Judgment, which he expected to come during his lifetime or shortly thereafter.

Reason cannot believe there can be such wrath. Nor can reason understand it adequately. See how different these words are from the former! Above we heard that God saw everything He had made, and it was very good (Gen. 1:31). He also bestowed upon man and beast the blessing of increase. He placed the earth and all the riches of the earth under the rule of man (Gen. 1:28). He added — and this is most important — the promise concerning the Seed of the woman and of eternal life. He established not only the household and the state but also the church (Gen. 3:15). How, then, does it happen that the first world, which, as Peter expresses it, was established by the Word in this manner, perishes by water (2 Peter 3:5-6)?

There is no doubt that the children of the world cited all these objections to Noah when he was preaching about the coming total destruction, and that they openly charged him with lying; since the household, the state, and the church were established by God, God would not utterly destroy what He had established. They maintained that man was created in order to procreate and to have dominion over the earth, and therefore that water would not overwhelm and destroy him.

The papists beset us similarly with this one argument: Christ will be with His church until the end of the world, and the gates of hell will not prevail against it (Matt. 16:18). Of this they boast extravagantly; they believe it is impossible for them to perish. Peter's boat, they say, may be tossed about by the waves; but it cannot be overwhelmed by them. The smugness and assurance before the Flood was similar, and yet we see that the whole earth perished. They indeed continued to boast that God's institutions were everlasting, and that God had never abolished or completely changed anything He had once created. But consider the outcome, and you will realize that they were wrong, while Noah alone was right.

Unless he is enlightened by the Holy Spirit, it is impossible for man not to be convinced by this argument. To maintain that God is about to destroy completely what He created — is this not the same as making God capricious and changeable? Yet God reveals to Noah himself that He intends to bring on the end, not of one part of the flesh or the earth but of all flesh and the whole earth. Since they divide the earth into three parts, would it not be awful enough to threaten one third with destruction? But to rage against the entire earth and against all mankind — this seems to conflict with the order and the intention of God, who said that everything was very good. Accordingly, these matters are too lofty to be understood or grasped by human reason.

What is the reason for this great wrath? Certainly, as the text states here, it is to be found in the fact that the earth is filled with violence. An amazing reason! The text says nothing about the First Table; it stresses only the Second Table, as though God intended to say: "About Myself I shall say nothing. I shall not say that they hate, blaspheme, and persecute My name and Word. How disgracefully they live among themselves! Neither the household nor the state is properly managed; everything is done with violence, nothing with reason and law. Therefore I shall destroy both mankind and the earth."

Thus we see that in our age God leaves the desecration of the Mass unnoticed, the desecration which has been an awful abomination and has filled the whole world. He also leaves the godless doctrines unnoticed, and the rest of the sins that have had a place in our religion. But since men live among themselves in such a manner that no consideration is given either to the state or to the household, and since such great greed, such varied forms of perfidy, and finally such manifold wickedness have become prevalent, who does not see that God is compelled, as it were, to punish, yes, even to destroy Germany?

It is the abundance of His compassion and love that causes God to complain more about the wrongs with which His members are oppressed than about those that are inflicted on Him. We see that He is silent about the latter in this passage when He threatens destruction not only for mankind but also for the earth.

There were two results of the Flood: the powers of man were diminished; and his wealth, together with that of the earth, was reduced. The fruits that the trees produced were utterly unlike those they bore before the Flood. Before the Flood turnips were better than melons, oranges, or pomegranates were afterwards.[74] Pears were more delicious than spices are today. The strength in a man's finger was probably greater than it is today in his entire arm. In like manner, his reason and wisdom were far superior. But God inflicted punishment because of sin not only on man but also on his possessions

---

[74] Cf. *Luther's Works*, 1, pp. 203—207, where Luther describes with similar vividness the contrast between the state of the world before the Fall and its condition after the Fall.

and dominion, in order that His wrath might also be a lesson for his descendants.

How does He bring about the destruction? It is obvious that He takes the element water and destroys everything. The force with which this element is wont to rage is well known. Even though the air may be pestilential, it does not always contaminate trees and roots. But water not only demolishes everything and not only tears out trees and roots, but it carries away the very surface of the earth and alters the soil, so that even the most fertile fields are ruined by the saltiness of the earth and by the sand. This, then, was the destruction of the first world.

But for the present world there will be a different punishment, as the color of the rainbow indicates.[75] The lowest color, whose area is defined, is that of water. The water in the case of the Flood raged in such a way that the measure of the punishment was still fixed and, after the sinners had been destroyed, the earth was given back to the godly remnant, to be inhabited. But the outer arc of the rainbow, which is indefinite in extent, has the color of fire, namely, of that element by which the entire world will burn. But after this destruction there will follow a better world, one that will last forever and will serve the godly. This is what God seems to have portrayed in the rainbow.

14. *Make yourself an ark of gopher wood, make rooms in the ark, and cover it inside and out with bitumen.*

The Lord first concerns Himself with the preservation of the remnants from that small seed, the three sons of Noah; for Noah did not beget any more children. This is a significant indication of the mercy of God toward those who walk in His ways.

Some take גֹּפֶר to be fir; others, pine; and still others, cedar. Therefore it is difficult to tell what it means. Nevertheless, it appears to have been chosen because of its lightness and also because of its resinous character, so that it might float more readily on the water, and the water would be less able to seep through it.

קִנִּים denotes nests or small chambers, places set apart in view of the different kinds of animals. Bears, sheep, deer, and horses did not occupy one area, but each kind had its own special quarters.

But what "bitumen" was I do not know. Among us the ships are pitched and caulked with oakum. And indeed pitch is suitable for

[75] See p. 149.

keeping out water, but it is also likely to cause fires. But we have no "bitumen" that would last in water. Accordingly, I have no objection if some understand "bitumen" to be pitch.

Someone may ask: Why does God give such detailed directions about everything? The command about getting the ark ready was enough. So far as space and the method of construction are concerned, reason itself sees what must be done, as many outstanding works of craftsmen prove. Why, then, does God instruct Noah so carefully about the length, the width, and the height of the ark, and about covering it with bitumen? Surely in order that Noah, after preparing everything in accordance with God's direction (just as Moses patterned the tabernacle after the original on the mountain), might believe with greater confidence that he and his people would be preserved, and that he might not become distrustful of the task that God Himself had assigned and had given him orders how to perform. This is the reason why God gives such careful directions about everything.

15. *This is how you are to make it: the length of the ark three hundred cubits, its breadth fifty cubits, and its height thirty cubits.*

This passage presents a neat problem in geometry and mathematics about the form and bulk of the ark. The opinions of writers vary.[76] Some maintain that it was square; others, that it was pointed, something like our houses in Europe. I myself believe that it was square, for Eastern people were not familiar with gabled houses. Those they lived in were square. It is clear from the Gospel that they walked about on the roofs (Mark 2:4). The shape of the temple was similar.

Then there is also some discussion about the difference of the chambers — about the upper, the middle, and the lower part (for the text makes mention of these parts) — and about which animals occupied which part. But this question cannot be settled. It is likely that Noah and the birds occupied the uppermost part, the clean animals the middle part, and the unclean animals the lowest, although the rabbis would maintain that the lowest was used for putting away the manure. I myself believe that the manure was thrown out, perhaps through the window. Since there were so many animals in the ark for more than a year, it was necessary to get rid of the manure.

---

[76] In his discussion of this question Lyra presents diagrams of the ark.

Augustine, writing against Faustus, quotes from Philo that, according to geometrical computation, the ark had the proportions of the human body.[77] When a human being lies on the ground, his body is ten times longer than it is high and six times longer than it is wide. Thus three hundred cubits are equal to six times fifty and ten times thirty.

These facts are later applied to the body of Christ, that is, to the church, which has an entrance, namely Baptism, through which the clean and the unclean enter without distinction. Even though the church is small, it is nevertheless the ruler of the world; and the world is preserved on its account, in the same way as the unclean animals were preserved in the ark. Others have applied them also to the body of Christ, which had a wound in its side, just as the ark had a window. These allegories, if not actually scholarly, are nevertheless harmless, inasmuch as they contain no error; and one may use them — except in debates — for the sake of embellishment.[78]

16. *Make a window for the ark, and finish it to a cubit above; and set the door of the ark in its side; make it with lower, second, and third decks.*

See how careful an architect God is, and how carefully He considers and assigns all parts of the building. The word צֹהַר, however, does not actually denote a window, but the light of midday.

The question is raised here whether the ark had only one window or several. It is a common method of expression in the Hebrew language to use a singular for a plural, or a collective for a distributive, as in "I shall destroy man from the earth." Here the text is certainly speaking, not of one man but of many. But it seems to me that there was only one window to admit light to the people's quarters.

The Latin translator is so extraordinarily obscure that one cannot know what his intention is.[79] I am fully convinced that he had his mind fixed on a form of ship such as we have today, where passengers are usually carried in the lower part. Nor can one understand fully what He is saying about the door, since it is certain that there was

---

[77] Augustine, *Reply to Faustus the Manichean,* Book XII, ch. 16.

[78] This allegory comes from the passage of Augustine quoted in the preceding note.

[79] The Latin translation to which Luther is objecting reads: *Fenestram in arca facies, et in cubito consummabis summitatem ejus.*

both a window of a cubit's width in the upper part of the ark and a door in the middle of its side, in its navel, as it were. Similarly, Eve was made from the middle part of the man. The entire structure had three stories, an upper one, a middle one, and a lower one; and in my opinion the upper one was illuminated by the light of day through the window.

But you will ask: What sort of window was that, and how could it last in rains of such great frequency and violence? For it was not raining in the usual way if the water increased so much in forty days that it rose fifteen ells above all the mountains. The Jews maintain that the window was closed with crystal, which permitted the light to pass through.[80] But to me it seems useless to pursue these inquiries too inquisitively; for godliness or the kingdom of Christ is not imperiled if we have no knowledge of some features of this structure, whose architect was God.

Still I do not see in what respect this matter is not clear, provided you agree that there was a window in the upper story, on the side. Concerning the door it is certain that it was about thirteen or fourteen cubits above the earth; for the ark had a draught of about ten cubits, inasmuch as it was carrying a heavy cargo: animals of every kind and supplies for more than a year. Let these statements suffice to give a vague idea of the ark; for besides the height and length Moses gives no further indication, except that it had three stories, an entrance, and a window.

We shall put aside countless other questions. What was the nature of the air in the ark, since that mass of water, especially when it went down, gave off a great and pestilential stench? Where did they get the water they drank? For water cannot be kept uncontaminated for an entire year. It is for this reason that mariners often look for nearby harbors, in order to take on sweet water. Furthermore, how could the malodorous bilge water be removed?

Let us put aside these and other unessentials which the procedure of mariners suggests (otherwise there will be no end of questions) and be satisfied with this simple explanation: in the lowest part of the ark bears, lions, tigers, and other wild animals were probably kept; in the middle part, the tame and manageable animals, together with the supplies that cannot be stored in places without ventilation; and in the upper part were the human beings with the domestic animals and the birds. Let this be enough for us.

[80] The source of this information is Lyra on Gen. 6:16, sec. o.

17. *For behold, I, I will bring a flood of waters upon the earth, to destroy all flesh in which is the breath of life from under heaven; everything that is on the earth shall die.*

Previously God threatened the human race with general destruction. Here He indicates the method, namely, that He intends to make use of a novel kind of punishment and destroy everything by the Flood. Such a punishment the world had not known until that time. As appears from the prophets (Ezek. 6:12), the usual punishments are plague, famine, war, and savage beasts. Human beings and animals perish by the plague. By war even the earth is ruined, for it is deprived of its tillers. The sufferings resulting from famine, even though they appear to be connected with less cruelty, are nevertheless the most distressing by far. With the fourth kind of punishment our regions have almost no experience. But even though each one of these would be adequate to afflict the human race, God wanted to make use of a novel kind of punishment against the first world, a punishment by which all flesh that has breath would be destroyed.

Because this form of punishment was unheard of in former ages, the ungodly had little faith in it. This was their thinking: "If God is angry at all, is He not able to discipline the disobedient by war and plague? The Flood would destroy the rest of the creatures too, even though they have committed no sin. God will surely not give thought to anything like this in regard to the world."

To keep this sort of unbelief out of the heart of Noah and of the godly, God emphatically repeats the pronoun: "I, I will bring." Then He adds clearly that He will destroy the flesh that is under the heaven and on the earth. Here He excepts the fish, whose domain grows larger from the rising water.

Accordingly, this sentence serves to indicate the vastness of God's wrath, through which men lose not only their bodies and their lives but even their universal dominion throughout the world.

18. *But I will establish My covenant with you; and you shall come into the ark, you, your sons, your wife, and your sons' wives with you.*

This consolation Moses had already indicated above, when he said that Noah had found favor. There was need of this, not only to keep Noah from despairing before such a terrible wrath but also in order that his faith might be strengthened amid the punishment that was about to rage. It was not easy to believe that the entire human race would perish. The world regarded Noah as exceedingly stupid for believing such things; it derided him and without a doubt also made his structure the object of ridicule. In order to encourage him in such trying circumstances, God speaks with him several times and now reminds him of the covenant.

The question is raised among the interpreters: What sort of covenant was this? Lyra explains it as the promise that God would defend him against ungodly men who had threatened him with death; Burgensis maintains that this covenant must be referred to protection against danger on the water.[81] Others assume that it denotes the covenant of the rainbow, the covenant which the Lord established with Noah later on.

In my opinion, however, the text speaks of the spiritual covenant or of the promise of the Seed who would crush the head of the serpent. That covenant the giants had, but they forfeited it when they misused it for pride and ungodliness. Similarly later on, when the Jews boast in a carnal manner of God, the Law, the worship, and the temple, they lose these gifts and perish. For Noah, however, God confirms this covenant, that he may firmly believe that Christ will be born from his descendants and that God, in His great wrath, will let a seedbed of the church remain. Accordingly, this covenant includes not only physical protection, about which Lyra and Burgensis are wrangling, but also eternal life.

Hence the meaning is: "I shall punish those who insolently despise the threats and promises. I shall deprive them in the first place of the protection and confidence that they derive from My covenant, that they may perish without any covenant and without mercy. But I shall convey this covenant to you, that you may be saved not only from the violence of the water but also from eternal death and damnation."

God expressly says: "With you." He does not mention the sons or the wives, whom He nevertheless also intended to save; He mentions Noah alone, by whom this promise was passed on to his son Shem. This, then, is the second promise of Christ, and it is taken away from all the other descendants of Adam and bestowed upon Noah alone.

[81] Lyra on Gen. 6:18, sec. s.

Later on this promise gradually became clearer; for it proceeded from the genus to the species, so to speak, and then from the species to the individual. From the entire race of Abraham it was passed on to David alone, from David to Nathan, and from Nathan to one virgin (who was like a dead stump or root of Jesse),[82] namely, Mary, in whom the promise or covenant reached its culmination and fulfillment.

The confirmation of this covenant was needed very much, for the unbelievable and incalculable wrath of God was near at hand.

But you will note also in this passage a special summons when God says: "And you shall come into the ark, you, your sons, etc." If he had not had this special summons, they would not have had the courage to enter the ark.

How terrible a situation it is that of the entire human race only eight persons are chosen to be saved and that even among these Ham, Noah's third son, is eventually rejected! By God's own mouth he is actually listed among the chosen and holy; yes, he is even protected and saved with them, and no distinction can be made between him and his father Noah. If he had not had the same beliefs and had not prayed, if he had not feared God, he would in no wise have been saved in the ark; and yet later on he is rejected.

At this point the sophists engage in a debate about an election made according to God's purpose,[83] but I have often warned that one must refrain from speculations about the uncovered Majesty. For just as they cannot possibly be true, so they are also useless for our salvation. Let us rather think about God in the manner in which He presents Himself in the Word and in the sacraments. Let us not assign occurrences of this kind to a secret election by which God has ordained everything with Himself from eternity. Such an election we cannot grasp with our mind, and we see that it is in conflict with the revealed will of God.

Someone may ask: What, then, shall we conclude from these occurrences? Nothing else than that they are presented to us to produce in us the fear of God, so that we do not assume that we cannot fall from grace after we have once received grace. Paul likewise issued the warning (1 Cor. 10:12): "Let anyone who thinks that he stands take heed lest he fall." Therefore these occurrences

---

[82] Here Luther follows the medieval tradition in applying Is. 11:1 to the Virgin Mary.

[83] Cf. p. 45, note 60.

should serve to keep us humble, so that we do not become proud about our gifts or slothfully come to a standstill with what we have received but rather press on to what lies ahead, as Paul says in Phil. 3:13, and not assume that we have fully obtained everything. Our enemy is vicious and very active, but we are weak and carry our great treasure in earthen vessels (2 Cor. 4:7). We must, therefore, not boast as though we were safe. We must come with our groanings to God, as people who are in immediate danger; for we observe that through their smugness such holy men have fallen from grace, even though they had received and possessed it for a long time.

This is a useful way to discuss such occurrences. But those who pay no attention to these things and pursue sublime matters involving an election according to God's purpose drive their souls to despair, toward which they already incline, and destroy them.

19. *And of every living thing of all flesh, you shall bring two of every sort into the ark, to keep them alive with you; they shall be male and female.*

20. *Of the birds according to their kinds, and of the animals according to their kinds, of every creeping thing of the ground according to its kind, two of every sort shall come in with you, to keep them alive.*

Here again an argument arises, the kind that comes when in historical accounts one takes up usage and incidental matters. The text seems to contradict itself; in this passage it speaks of two and two; but below, at the beginning of chapter seven, it speaks of seven and seven. Thereupon Lyra engages in a wrangle with a certain Andreas,[84] who believed that fourteen individuals were confined in the ark, because it is written: "But of the clean seven and seven." I favor Lyra's opinion; he declares that seven individuals of each variety were confined in the ark, three male and three female, and then also a seventh male, of which Noah could make use for his sacrifices.

Therefore the statement in this passage that two of each kind were brought into the ark compels us to apply the statement in the seventh chapter only to the unclean. For the number of the clean was larger, and seven of each sort were confined in the ark.

Here, however, we must discuss the difference in the designations:

[84] Lyra on Gen. 7:2-3, sec. d, contains this material.

every living thing, beasts, and cattle. They are indeed often confused; yet elsewhere Scripture employs them with a difference, as when it says: "Let the earth bring forth living thing" (Gen. 1:24), "Let the waters bring forth living thing" (Gen. 1:20). In these instances it is a general term for everything that lives on the earth and in the water. Varieties of this category are the animals named here, חַיָּה, רֶמֶשׂ, and בְּהֵמָה, although they are used indiscriminately at times.

Here Moses calls cattle בְּהֵמוֹת, although in the first chapter of Ezekiel (v. 5) the four animals are designated by the common name הַחַיּוֹת, a word that strictly denotes what we call either beasts or wild animals, not animals that eat hay or the other products of the earth, but carnivores, such as the lion, the bear, the wolf, and the fox.

בְּהֵמוֹת are beasts of burden or cattle that live on hay and herbage from the earth, such as sheep, oxen, deer, and goats.

רֶמֶשׂ denotes the creeping things, and the noun is derived from the verb רָמַשׂ, which means "to tread." If we compare ourselves with the birds, we, too, are רְמָשִׂים; for we creep and tread the earth with our feet, just like dogs and other beasts. But the term properly designates those animals that do not walk about with their faces lifted up. The animals that creep, such as those we call reptiles, have a special name and are called שְׁרָצִים, as is clear from Leviticus,[85] from the verb שָׁרַץ, which means "to move" and appears below in chapter seven (v. 21). The word עוֹף is familiar and denotes a bird.

This is the difference in these designations, although as I have stated, it is not observed elsewhere. But it must be applied only to the time after the Flood; otherwise it would follow that there were such savage beasts also in Paradise. But who has any doubt that before sin, inasmuch as man had the dominion over all the beasts of the earth, there was harmony not only among men but also between the dumb animals and men?

Although the first chapter proves clearly that those wild beasts were created with the rest, yet their natures were changed because of sin, so that now after the Fall those which would have been the most peaceful and harmless are wild and harmful. This is my opinion. Nevertheless, now that we have lost the state of living in innocence, it is easier to form an opinion about that life than to give an actual description of it.

But someone may say: If the natures of the animals were changed

---

[85] The reference is especially to Lev. 11.

in this manner because of sin, how could Noah control them, particularly the savage and huge ones? Surely the lion cannot be controlled, nor tigers, leopards, and whatever others are like them.

The answer given to this is that such wild animals entered the ark miraculously, and this seems likely to me too. If they had not been compelled to enter by the Lord's command (even though it was necessary for Noah to apply some effort), his skill, being that of a human being, would not have been adequate to control animals of such fierceness. Moreover, the text indicates both; for in the first place it states: "You shall bring them into the ark," and in the second place it adds: "Two of all will come to you." If this had not happened in a miraculous way, more than two or seven of each kind would have come running.

The fact that they come of their own accord in twos and sevens is a miracle and a sign that they had a premonition of the wrath of God and of the awful catastrophe that was about to take place. Dumb animals also have premonitions, as it were, and presentiments about impending misfortunes; often, as though moved by some feeling of compassion, they moan before a person who is in imminent danger. This is apparent in dogs and horses, which realize the dangers of their masters and indicate that they are affected by sensing these dangers; for dogs whine, and horses tremble and sweat freely. Indeed, in time of danger even wild beasts often take refuge with a human being.

Since this sensing occurs in other circumstances among dumb animals, what would be so remarkable if in this instance also they had been made conscious by God of the impending danger and had willingly joined Noah? The text indicates that they came willingly. History also bears witness, and experience confirms, that when a severe plague or a great disaster is imminent, wolves, which are very fierce animals, invade not only villages but also at times the very towns, take refuge with human beings, and humbly, as it were, seek their aid.

21. *Also take with you every sort of food that is eaten, and store it up; and it shall serve as food for you and for them.*

Because the Flood was to last an entire year, it was necessary to remind Noah about food, which had to be gathered from the herbage and from the fruits of the trees, in order to preserve human life as well as that of the other animals. But even though His wrath was great, inasmuch as everything the earth brought forth perished, the goodness of God still shone in so awful a disaster; for He is looking out for the human being and for the other animals, that they may be preserved and that through their preservation the species may be preserved. But just as the animals that were chosen to be preserved in the ark were of sound body and healthy, so through God's providence they also had food suited to their nature.

It is certain that man did not yet make use of meat as food, but only of the produce of the earth. But this was of far better quality before the Flood than it is now after that salty water has done such damage to the earth.

Thus in this passage we observe the providence of God, according to whose counsel the ungodly are punished but the good are preserved. This takes place in an amazing manner: while God punishes the ungodly, He nevertheless does not destroy nature in its entirety but graciously makes provision for future descendants.

Of course, it would have been easy for God to preserve Noah and the animals for an entire year even without food, as He preserved Moses, Elijah, and Christ for forty days without any food, yes, even as He made everything out of nothing, which is greater and more amazing. Nevertheless, as Augustine learnedly states, God governs the things He has created in such a way that He allows them to function with their distinctive activities;[86] that is (applying Augustine's statement to the instance before us), God makes use of definite means and tones down His miracles in such a manner that He makes use of the service of nature and of natural means.

And He demands from us too that we do not waste the products of nature (for that would be tempting God), but that we use with thanksgiving the means He has provided and offered. It would be a sin to expect food from heaven when one is hungry and not rather to provide it in some other manner or ask for it. Christ commands the apostles to eat what is set before them (Luke 10:7). Thus in this passage Noah receives the command to make use of the regular means of gathering food; he is not ordered to wait in the ark for some miraculous method of supplying food from heaven.

The entire monastic life amounts to nothing but tempting God. They cannot be continent, and yet they refrain from marriage. They also abstain from certain foods, although God has created these foods to be received with thanksgiving by believers, who know the truth

---

[86] One such passage is Augustine, *De Trinitate*, Book III, ch. 4.

that every creature of God is good and that nothing received with thanksgiving is to be rejected (1 Tim. 4:3-4). Thus the use of medicine is permitted, yes, even necessary; for it is the means created for the preservation of health. The study of the arts and languages should be pursued and, as Paul says (1 Tim. 4:4-5): "Nothing is to be rejected if it is received with thanksgiving or consecrated by prayer."

God could have saved Noah in the midst of the water, the way men tell fiction about St. Clement that he had a cell in the midst of the sea,[87] yes, even the way Israel was saved in the midst of the Red Sea and Jonah in the belly of the whale. But He did not want to do this. He wanted Noah to make use of the means provided by wood or trees, in order that human effort might have this race course, as it were, on which to train itself.

When the supply of these means or creatures is either lacking or depleted, then you must either suffer or wait for help from the Lord, as did the Jews, whom no further effort could sustain when they were standing at the sea and were surrounded by the enemy in their rear. In these circumstances they were obliged either to hope for a miraculous deliverance or to endure certain death.

22. *Noah did this; he did all that God commanded him.*

This expression is quite common in Scripture, but this is the first passage in which obedience toward God is praised in these words. Later on, however, it is repeated more frequently: "Moses or the people did according to all that the Lord had commanded them, etc."

Noah is praised as an example for us because he did not have a dead faith, which is actually no faith at all, but a living and active faith. He is obedient when God gives him a command; and because he believes God both when He gives a promise and when He utters a threat, he painstakingly carries out God's direction in regard to the ark, the gathering of the animals, and the food.

The particular praise of Noah's faith is that he stays on the royal road; he adds nothing, changes nothing, and takes nothing away from God's directive but abides completely by the command he hears.

The most common and at the same time the most pernicious plague

[87] This legend is taken from the apocryphal Greek acts of the martyrdom of Clement, relating his death under the emperor Trajan.

in the church is this: either a change is made in what God has commanded, or something is superimposed upon what God has commanded. Because there is only one royal road on which we must stay, those people sin who deviate too much to the left by not carrying out or by neglecting what God has commanded. Those also sin who deviate too much to the right by doing more than God has commanded, as Saul did when he spared the Amalekites (1 Sam. 15:9); indeed, they sin more flagrantly than those who deviate to the left. For in addition there is the pretense of godliness; the former, who deviate to the left, cannot excuse their error, while the latter even maintain that they have done something extraordinarily meritorious.

This error is very common; for God has the habit of commanding ordinary, unimportant, laughable, and at times even offensive things. Reason, however, takes delight in what is magnificent; either it is filled with disgust at those common things, or it undertakes them with resentment. Thus the tasks of a householder have filled the monks with disgust, and they have assigned to themselves other tasks, which are more magnificent in appearance. Today the masses (because they hear that in the Gospel the ordinary duties are preached) despise the Gospel as a common doctrine with nothing that is exceptional. What seems so important about teaching that servants should obey their masters and children their parents? These facts the learned papists not only disregard but even deride as things that are known to all and have already been taught previously by others. But they look for unusual things that are impressive for either their reputed wisdom or their seemingly great difficulty. Such is the madness of human wisdom.

The general rule is that one must consider, not who is saying something but what someone is saying; for the blunders of teachers are often manifest. But when we are dealing with God's commands and true obedience, this statement must be inverted. In this instance one must consider, not what is being said or commanded but who is speaking. If, in the instance of the divine commands, you should consider what is being said and not who is saying it, you would easily stumble. The example of Eve shows this. When she is not thinking of Him who gives the command, but looks only at the command, she considers eating the fruit to be of little consequence. But what great ruination that created for the entire human race!

He who considers the One who gives the commands will surely regard as most important even those things that seem most trivial.

To govern a state, to be a spouse, to rear children — these things the papists regard as something unimportant. And yet experience shows that they are most important attainments, which human wisdom cannot achieve at all; and we see that at times even the most spiritual men have failed shamefully. If, then, we consider Him who gives the command, it will readily become clear that even though God's commands appear ordinary and trivial, they are nevertheless of the highest order and cannot be carried out or fulfilled by any human being except with divine help.

The papists, who look only at the outward mask, as a cow looks at a barn door, can minimize the tasks of government and household, and fancy that they perform other and more perfect tasks. But because they are adulterers without shame, because they are blasphemers against God, because they profane what is holy and shamefully squander the church's possessions, they surely give living testimony, as it were, against themselves that they are altogether incapable of carrying out those small, trivial, ordinary, and common commands that have to do with the household and the state.

What kind of holiness is it, then, of which they boast so much? Obviously that they refrain from meat on certain days, that they bind themselves by certain vows, and that they select certain tasks. But please tell me who has commanded you to do these things? Nobody. Hence they do not care about what God has enjoined and commanded, but impose other things, about which God has given no command.

Therefore we must diligently adhere to this rule: We should consider, not what is commanded, but who gives the command. He who does not do this will often take offense at either the triviality or the senselessness, if I may express myself in this manner, of the task. But we must give God praise for wisdom and goodness, and maintain that whatever He Himself commands is commanded with the utmost wisdom and goodness, even though reason judges otherwise.

The papists disparage this wisdom of God when they disregard as trivial the tasks commanded by God and try to undertake something better or more difficult. By such tasks God is not appeased, but rather irritated, as the example of Saul shows (1 Sam. 9:15 ff.). Under the assumption that God was stupid, cowardly, and cruel when He commanded the destruction of the Amalekites and all their possessions, Saul adopted a more moderate plan and set aside the cattle for use at the sacrifices. What else did this mean than that he regarded himself as wise, but God as stupid?

In this passage Moses fittingly praises Noah's obedience when he states that Noah did all that the Lord commanded him. This is giving glory to God for His wisdom and goodness. He did not argue about the task, as Adam, Eve, and Saul did to their great misfortune. He complied with the majesty of Him who gave the command; this was sufficient for him, even though he was commanded to do things that were preposterous, impossible, and inconvenient. He passes by all these offenses as if with closed eyes and relies on this one fact, that it was God who had given the command. And so this is a familiar text so far as its sound is concerned, but in practice and performance it is familiar to few and very difficult.

CHAPTER SEVEN

1. *Then the Lord said to Noah: Go into the ark, you and all your household.*

Now that the extraordinary structure of the ark was completed, the Lord commanded Noah to enter it; for the time of the Flood, about which the Lord had given advance warning one hundred and twenty years before, was now at hand. The purpose of all this was that Noah should realize that he was the object of God's care; and not this alone but, as Peter (2 Peter 1:19) expresses it, also that he might have a rich and abundant Word by which his faith would be supported and strengthened in such great trouble. Since he had foretold the Flood for more than a hundred years, the world undoubtedly made him the object of various kinds of attacks.

Then, as I have repeatedly said, there was that unbelievable wrath; and the human mind — especially in the first and original world, in which there were better men than there are now — could not comprehend that by the Flood God would destroy the entire human race, all but eight souls. Therefore Noah, a holy, righteous, gentle, and compassionate man, had many a conflict with his heart; and only with the greatest disquiet did he hear the voice of the Lord as He threatened all flesh with sure destruction. For this reason it was necessary to comfort him with an eloquent word and to strengthen the faith of the distressed and troubled man, lest he doubt.

The command to enter the ark is the same as though the Lord were to say: "Have no doubts. It will surely happen, and the time to inflict punishment on the unbelieving world is already very close at hand. But do not be alarmed, and do not be afraid; for at times faith is very weak even in the saints. You will be an object of My care, you and your household." For us indeed this would have been impossible to believe, although we must conclude that it is possible for God to do anything.

In this passage Moses adheres to his way of speaking when he says: "The Lord said." I find it particularly pleasant to think that these words of God were not spoken from heaven but were said to Noah through a human agency. Although I do not deny that this could have been revealed by an angel or by the Holy Spirit Himself, nevertheless the ministry should be given the honor where it can be rightly maintained that God spoke through human beings. Thus we have shown above that many things which Moses says were spoken by God were spoken by Adam.[1] The Word of God is truly the Word of God even when it is uttered by a human being.

Since Methuselah, Noah's grandfather, died during the very year of the Flood,[2] it would not be improper to assume that this was the last statement of Methuselah to his nephew and, as it were, his testament — for Lamech, Noah's father, had died five years before the Flood — in which he bade his grandson farewell and added: "My son, just as you have obeyed the Lord so far, have waited in faith for this wrath, and have experienced God's protection and His faithful defense against the ungodly, so in the future have no doubt that you will be the object of God's care. Now the end is near, not only mine, which is an end of grace, but also that of the entire human race, which is an end of wrath. The Flood about which you have warned the world for so long, but in vain, will begin seven days from now." Thus, in my opinion, these words were spoken by Methuselah himself; but they are attributed to God because the Spirit of God spoke through him.

I like to apply this to the glory of the ministry where it can rightly be done, as in this passage.[3] Because it is sure that Methuselah died in the very year of the Flood, it can be assumed without any risk that this was his last address to his grandson, Noah, who heard his words and received them as the words of God.

The Jews also have their own special idea about these seven days, namely, that these seven days were added to the hundred and twenty years out of respect for Methuselah, in order that his descendants might mourn him.[4] This idea is harmless; for his descendants, especially the godly among them, certainly did not fail to do their duty.

But the former opinion, which involves the ministry of the Word, is not only likely; it is profitable as well. It is sure that God does

[1] Cf. *Luther's Works*, 1, p. 262.

[2] A reflection of Luther's work on his chronology, *Computation of the Years of the World*, first published in 1541; cf. W, LIII, 22—184.

[3] Cf. *Luther the Expositor*, pp. 103—106.

[4] Lyra on Gen. 7:4, sec. e.

not make a practice of speaking in a miraculous way and by means of special revelations, particularly where there is a lawful ministry that He has established in order to speak with men through it, to teach them, instruct them, comfort them, rouse them, etc.

In the first place, He has entrusted His Word to parents, as Moses often declares: "Tell your children these things." In the second place, He has given it to the teachers in the church, as Abraham says in Luke 16:29: "They have Moses and the prophets; let them hear them." Where there is a ministry, we should not wait for either an inward or an outward revelation. Otherwise all the orders of society would be confused. Let the clergyman teach in the church, let the civil officer govern the state, and let parents rule the home or the household. These human ministries were established by God. Therefore we must make use of them and not look for other revelations.

Nevertheless, I do not deny that even after Methuselah's death Noah heard God speaking. God speaks with men in a twofold way: in the first place and ordinarily, through the public ministry, that is, through parents and the teachers of the church; in the second place, through inner revelation or through the Holy Spirit. This latter method, however, He is wont to employ only in special situations and very rarely. It is profitable to be aware of this, so that we may not emulate the fanatics, who disregard the Word and expect new revelations. It is this idea that gives rise to the misguided spirits who later on bring confusion to the world by their dreams, as the example of the Anabaptists proves.

For I have seen that you are righteous before Me in this generation.

This is in truth an awful picture of the ancient and original world, as Peter calls it (2 Peter 2:5); by this designation he appears to attribute something extraordinary to that age in comparison with people in our age. What more awful statement can be made than what we hear in this passage, that Noah alone was righteous before the Lord? A similar picture of the world occurs in Ps. 14:2-3, where it is stated that the Lord looked down from heaven to see whether there was anyone with understanding or seeking God. "But," He says, "all have turned aside; they have been found useless, and there was none who did good, not even one." [5]

Moreover, this verdict about the world is in agreement with Christ's

---

[5] Luther cites Ps. 14:1-2 according to the paraphrase in Rom. 3:10-12.

statement; for because the last times will be similar to the times of Noah, Christ correctly declares (Luke 18:8): "When the Son of Man comes, will He find faith?" It is dreadful to live in such an evil and ungodly world. Since we have the light of the Word, this present time, by the grace of God, is still a golden age. The sacraments are properly administered in our churches, and godly clergymen disseminate the Word in its purity. Although the government is weak, wickedness is not yet beyond hope.

Christ's prophecy reveals that there will be very distressing times when the Day of the Lord is at hand, and there will be no sound teachers anywhere while the church is being suppressed by the ungodly. The counsels of our adversaries are threatening to bring about this very situation. The pope and ungodly princes are intent with all their might on destroying the ministry of the Word, so that when all true pastors have been either suppressed or corrupted, everyone may believe what he pleases.

The situation requires fervent prayer and great concern, that a purer doctrine may be handed down to posterity. If at Noah's time there had been more godly teachers, a larger number of righteous people might also have been expected. Since the righteous have been reduced to such a small number that Noah alone is declared righteous, it is now sufficiently clear that the godly teachers either had been killed or had been turned to heresies and idolatry, so that there was left only Noah, the one "herald of righteousness," as Peter (2 Peter 2:5) calls him. When the government had been turned into tyranny and the household had been ruined by adultery and fornication, how could the punishment hold off any longer?

Such a danger is also in store for us, since, of course, the last times will be similar to the times of Noah. Truly, the popes and the bishops are working hard to suppress the Gospel and to destroy the right established churches. In this way the world is striving with great effort to achieve an age similar to the age of Noah, in which all men will go astray in the darkness of ungodliness once the light of the Word has been put out. When preaching has been done away with, faith, prayer, and the right use of the sacraments will not be able to exist.

Such, writes Moses in this text, was the character of the original world at the time of Noah, even though that was the youth of the world and its best part, when the finest minds flourished everywhere and, on account of length of life, had acquired very great ability because of much experience. What will be in store for us in this insane state of a world that is growing old? Therefore we must not put aside our concern for our descendants, but we must diligently pray for them.

Just as the ancient world was the most corrupt, so it was also subjected to horrible punishment: not only did the adults perish, who had provoked God by their evil deeds, but even that innocent age which has no knowledge whatever and cannot tell right from left. Without a doubt many had been deceived because of their artlessness. But here God's wrath makes no difference; it overwhelms and destroys the adults together with the infants, the cunning together with the artless.

This horrible punishment seems to have induced the apostle Peter, like someone in a frenzy, to utter words we cannot understand even today. This is what he says (1 Peter 3:18-20): "Christ was made alive in the spirit, in which He went and preached to the spirits in prison, who formerly did not obey, when God's patience waited in the days of Noah, during the building of the ark, in which a few, that is, eight persons, were saved through water."

It is surely an amazing verdict and almost a frenzied utterance that this awful spectacle appears to have wrung from the apostle. Peter declares by these very words that there was some unbelieving world to which the departed Christ preached after His death. If this is true, who would doubt that Christ brought Moses and the prophets with Him to those people bound in prison, in order to make a new and believing world out of an unbelieving one? Peter's words surely sound as though they conveyed this meaning, although I would not make any authoritative statement about them.[6]

Furthermore, there is no doubt that those whom he calls the "unbelieving world" are not the godless despisers of the Word and the tyrants; of these it is sure that they were condemned if they were destroyed in their sins. He appears to be applying the term "unbelieving world" to infants and others whose artlessness prevented them from being able to believe; they were carried away by the offenses of the world as by a swift stream and were engulfed, so that they perished together with it and only eight souls were saved.

---

[6] The most familiar discussion of the descent into hell to come from Luther is contained in his Torgau sermon of 1533 (W, XXXVII, 62 ff.). Because the question came into controversy after his death, the caution expressed here in his *Lectures on Genesis* may come from an editorial hand.

Thus Peter emphasizes the vastness of the horrible wrath. But he also praises the patience of God for not removing the saving Word from those who, at the time, counted on God's patience and therefore did not believe or could not be persuaded that God would subject the entire world at the same time to such shocking punishments.

We do not know how this was done; but this we know and believe: that God is wonderful in His works and is all-powerful. Therefore He who preached to the living when He was alive, also was able to preach to the dead when He was dead; for all things hear, feel, and touch Him, even though human comprehension does not grasp this. Yet it is no disgrace, even if we lack knowledge about some mysteries of the Holy Scriptures. The apostles had their own individual revelations, about which it is presumptuous and foolish to engage in extensive discussions.

One such revelation dealt with Christ's teaching the souls of those who perished at the time of the Flood; to this it is perhaps fitting to apply the section in the Creed that speaks of Christ's descent into hell. Another such revelation was what was revealed to Paul about Paradise, about the third heaven (2 Cor. 12:2-3), and some other things. It is no disgrace not to know anything about these, but it is arrogance to pretend to know. St. Augustine and other theologians have an assortment of ideas when they discuss such passages.[7] But who would not believe that the apostles had revelations that Augustine and others did not have? But let us return to Moses.

It is truly an awful picture of the world when God testifies that He saw that Noah alone was righteous before Him and mentions neither the little children nor others who were led astray through no fault of their own.

We must take note of the phrase "before Me"; for it means that Noah was righteous not only in regard to the Second Table but also in regard to the First Table, that is, he believed in God, hallowed, preached, and called upon the name of God, gave thanks to God, condemned ungodly teachings, etc. To be righteous before God means to believe in God and to fear Him, not, as they were accustomed to teach in the papacy, to read Masses, to free souls from purgatory, to become a monk, etc.

This phrase serves to condemn the ancient world, which, after

---

[7] Cf., for example, Augustine, *De Genesi ad litteram*, Book XII, ch. 34, *Patrologia, Series Latina*, XXXIV, 482—483.

it had disregarded the worship of God in the First Table, was also most perverse in complying with the Second Table. They derided Noah as a fool and condemned his teaching as heresy. Meanwhile they complacently continued to drink, eat, and celebrate their feasts. Thus Noah was not righteous before the world; he was a condemned sinner.

The Lord, or grandfather Methuselah, comforts him with this statement in order that he may ignore the blind and wicked opinions of the world and not worry about what the world is thinking or saying, but close his eyes and ears and be intent only on the Word and opinion of God, in the faith that he is righteous before God, that is, that he is approved by God and is acceptable to God.

Surely, great was the faith of Noah that he was able to believe these words of God. I would certainly not have believed them. I realize how serious a matter it is if the opinions of all men assail one solitary individual and condemn him. We are condemned not only by the opinions of the pope but also by those of the Sacramentarians, the Anabaptists, and a thousand others. But these things are child's play and a pastime in comparison with the troubles of righteous Noah, who, apart from his own children and his godly grandfather, did not find one human being in the entire world who approved either of his religious views or of his life. We, by the grace of God, have many churches that are in agreement with us, and our princes shun no danger in defense of our teaching and religion. Noah had no such protectors; he saw his opponents leading a life in leisure and enjoying themselves in perfect peace. If I had been he, I would surely have said: "Lord, if I am righteous and please Thee, but they are unrighteous and displease Thee, why dost Thou bless them in this manner with riches? Why dost Thou heap all kinds of favors upon them, while I, together with my people, am maltreated in various ways and have almost no support at all?" In short, I would despair under such great misfortunes unless the Lord gave me the same spirit that Noah had.

Noah is an illustrious and grand example of faith. He withstood the opinions of the world with heroic steadfastness and was able to believe that he was righteous, but that all the rest of the world was unrighteous.

Whenever I think of those saintly men, John Hus and Jerome of Prague, I reflect with the greatest admiration on their great courage; for these two men withstood the verdicts of the entire world — the pope, the emperor, the bishops, the princes, all the universities and schools throughout the empire.[8]

It is profitable to reflect on such examples often. Such conflicts are fomented by the prince of the world, who with his flaming darts (Eph. 6:16) is trying to create despair in our hearts; and we must be equipped not to yield to the rage of the enemy but to say with Noah: "I know that I am righteous before God, even though the entire world forsakes me and condemns me as a heretic and an unrighteous man." Thus the apostles forsook Christ and left Him standing alone; but He said (John 16:32): "I am not alone." False brethren likewise forsook Paul. These perils are not new or unusual. Therefore we must not despair in them but courageously hold fast to the sound doctrine, no matter how much the world condemns and curses it.

2. *Take with you seven pairs of all clean animals, the male and his mate; and a pair of the animals that are not clean, the male and his mate;*

3. *and seven pairs of the birds of the air also, male and female, to keep their kind alive upon the face of all the earth.*

It is obvious that God enjoys talking to Noah. It is not enough for Him to have given him orders once about what he should do, but He repeats the same orders in the same words. Reason considers this wordiness absurd, but to a heart battling desperation nothing that gives instruction about God's will can seem to be enough or too much. God sees this attitude of the heart in its trial. He repeats the same words in close succession in order that Noah, as a result of that conversation and wordiness, may realize that he is not only not forsaken even though the entire world may have forsaken him but has a friendly and kindly disposed God, who loves him so much that it seems He cannot converse enough with this pious man. This is the reason why the same statements are repeated in this passage. I have stated above[9] in what manner God conversed with Noah: not from heaven but through a human being.

So far as language is concerned, this passage shows that הַבְּהֵמָה denotes not only cattle, that is, the larger animals, but also the smaller ones, which are generally offered as sacrifices, such as sheep, goats, and the like. For Moses did not originate the custom of offering sac-

---

[8] Cf. p. 21, note 32.
[9] See pp. 81—82.

rifices; this custom always existed in the world and was handed down from hand to hand, as it were, by the fathers to their descendants, as is evident from the example of Abel, who offered the firstlings of his herd to the Lord.

As for the rest, I have stated previously, at the end of the sixth chapter,[10] how to harmonize the statements that in this passage God commands Noah to take seven pairs into the ark, but there only one pair. Consequently, there is no need for us to repeat this. Because Noah was saved in a miraculous manner, he thought that he ought to add a seventh individual to the three pairs of the clean animals, in order that after the Flood he might give thanks to God for his deliverance.

4. *For in seven days I will send rain upon the earth forty days and forty nights; and every living thing that I have made I will blot out from the face of the ground.*

Here you see how carefully God is trying to give Noah the greatest possible assurance about everything. In advance He sets a limit of seven days and states that after these it will rain for forty days and nights.

He is especially emphatic when He says: "I will send rain"; for this was not an ordinary rain, but "both the windows of the heaven and the fountains of the deep were opened" (v. 11), that is, a large quantity of rain came down from heaven, and a huge mass of water poured forth out of the earth itself. The volume of water had to be huge to tower fifteen cubits above the peaks of the highest mountains. This was no ordinary rain; it was a rain of the Lord's wrath, by which He intended to destroy every living thing on the earth. Because the earth was ruined, the Lord ruined it too; and because the ungodly contended against the First and the Second Table, God used heaven and earth to contend against them.

Therefore this account is sure evidence that even though God is long-suffering and patient, nevertheless He will finally punish the ungodly. Peter states (2 Peter 2:5): "If He did not spare the original world." How much less will He spare either the popes or the emperors who persecute His Word? How much less will He spare us when we desecrate His name, when we lead an unworthy life in our vocation or profession, and when we sin daily against our conscience? Let us,

---

[10] Cf. p. 73, note 84.

therefore, learn to fear the Lord and with humility to receive His Word and to obey it; otherwise punishment will also overtake us, as Peter threatens.

5. *And Noah did all that the Lord had commanded him.*

6. *Noah was six hundred years old when the flood of waters came upon the earth.*

7. *And Noah and his sons and his wife and his sons' wives with him went into the ark, to escape the waters of the Flood.*

8. *Of clean animals, and of animals that are not clean, and of birds, and of everything that creeps on the ground,*

9. *two and two, male and female, went into the ark with Noah, as God had commanded Noah.*

10. *And after seven days the waters of the Flood came upon the earth.*

These words are clear from what precedes. Noah's faith is given the praise he deserves for obeying the command of the Lord and entering the ark with unwavering faith, together with his sons and their wives. God could indeed have preserved him by countless other methods. He did not use this all but silly method because He knew of no other. Do you suppose that anything is impossible for Him who preserved Jonah in the midst of the sea and in the belly of the whale for three days? But in this way the faith and obedience of Noah are praised, for the manner of his preservation, which had been divinely revealed to him, did not offend him; he accepted it in simple faith.

11. *In the six hundredth year of Noah's life, in the second month, on the seventeenth day of the month, on that day all the fountains of the great deep burst forth, and windows of the heavens were opened.*

12. *And rain fell upon the earth forty days and forty nights.*

In this passage we see Moses using a great abundance of words and repeating the same things to the point of being tiresome. How often he mentions the animals! How often the entrance into the ark! How often the sons of Noah, who went in at the same time! In this instance the decision must be left to men who are spiritual-minded; they alone know and see that the Holy Spirit repeats nothing in vain.

Others, however, who are weaker in spirit, can imagine that since Moses was deeply moved by the vastness of the wrath when he wrote these words, he wanted to emphasize the same points several times. Troubled hearts are fond of repetitions. Thus in 2 Sam. 18:33 David repeats his lament over his son Absalom. Thus the repetition in the present instance reflects the depths of Moses' feeling and the very great trouble of his soul. This example of wrath so dominates the attention of his eyes and ears that it is impossible for him not to mention the same event several times and even in the same words.

Poets and historians proceed differently; they portray various emotions, are prolix in their exaggerated presentation of events, and heap up a large number of words. Moses employs few words; but he repeats them several times, so that the reader, thus reminded, may himself ponder the significance of the events and imagine the real feelings instead of merely reading about those of others.

But it seems that by this constant repetition Moses wanted to give us some idea not only of his own exceedingly perplexed heart but also of the heart of Noah himself, who was filled with the Holy Spirit, was burning with love, and was almost overcome by his emotion over the coming disaster. When he realized that he could do nothing about it, what else could he do but regret the disaster? He saw that sure destruction was imminent for the wisest, the most distinguished, and the most outstanding of men. Thus David mourns when he is unable to bring Absalom back to life, and Samuel mourns when Saul's affairs have become hopeless (1 Sam. 15:35).

Therefore this is not a purposeless tautology or repetition. The Holy Spirit is not wordy without purpose, as the ignorant and sated spirits think who read the Bible through once or twice and quickly toss it aside as though they knew it well and there were nothing more in it for them to learn. By this procedure Moses wanted to thrust a goad, as it were, into the minds of his readers, to keep them from thinking that his message dealt with some unimportant matter.

Nonetheless in these very repetitions Moses presents certain facts unlike anything found in the writings of all the Gentiles, such as when he writes that Noah entered the ark in the six hundredth year of his life, in the second month, and on the seventeenth day of the second month.

At this point there arises an argument about the beginning of the year.[11] About this there is a twofold opinion. The first is that the beginning of the year occurs at the conjunction of the sun and the moon nearest to the vernal equinox. This month is therefore called the first by Moses in Exodus (12:2). Now if the Flood came in the second month and on the seventeenth day, it occurred approximately at the end of April, that is, at the time when the year is most beautiful and the world becomes green again, when the birds sing and the cattle frolic, and the world presents a new face after the raw winter weather. Surely the terror was all the greater, since death and destruction of all things closed in when the beginning of joy and of a new life for all things was being expected. The words of Christ in Matt. 24:38 are in agreement with this thought. Here He compares the last times of the world to the times of Noah and predicts that there will be banquets, marriages, and other signs of joy.

The second opinion about the beginning of the year is that it begins with the new moon nearest to the autumnal equinox, when all the crops have already been gathered from the field. They fix the beginning of the year at this point because Moses calls that month the end of the year. This beginning of the year they call the beginning of the civil year. The former one, at the vernal equinox, they call the beginning of the sacred year. The reason is that the Mosaic ceremonies and feasts extend from that time up to the autumnal equinox.

Hence if Moses is speaking here of the secular year, the Flood occurred in September or October, an opinion which I see that Lyra holds too.[12] And it is indeed true that because of the wet signs fall and winter are better suited for rains. In the second place, because Moses writes below that a dove was sent out in the tenth month and brought back a flowering olive branch, this also seems to agree well with assigning the beginning of the Flood to October.

But I disagree with this idea of the Jews who fix two beginnings of the year. Why not make four beginnings, since there are four distinct seasons on the basis of the equinoxes and the solstices? Thus the beginnings of these seasons will also be properly marked. It is safer to adhere to the divine order. According to it, the first month is the month of April, or the new moon that is nearest to the vernal

---

[11] Lyra on Gen. 7:11, sec. h.

[12] See the reference cited in the preceding note.

equinox. When the Jews assume that because the autumnal equinox is called the going-out of the year, a beginning of the year also comes in fall, they do this out of ignorance. Moses calls it the going-out of the year for no other reason than that at that time the labors in the field were coming to an end and all the fruits had been gathered and brought home.

It is my opinion, therefore, that the Flood set in at springtime, when the hearts of all men were full of the expectation of a new year. Such is the death of the ungodly that when they have said (1 Thess. 5:3): "Peace and security," then they perish. What is recorded below about the green olive branch presents no problem. Some trees are continually green, such as boxwood, fir, pine, cedar, laurel, olive, palm, etc.

But what does it mean when Moses speaks about the bursting fountains of the great deep and about the open windows of heaven? Nothing of this kind appears in the writings of any of the Gentiles, even though they have investigated the secrets of nature with great diligence.[13] But you must distinguish among these things in order to realize that the deeps of the earth are one thing, the sluice gates or windows of heaven another, and the rain still another. Rain is not uncommon, but for the sluice gates and the deeps to be opened is clearly something unusual and unnatural.

Nearly all the interpreters are silent on this point. But we know from the Holy Scriptures that by His Word God established a dwelling place for man and the rest of the animals on the dry land above the water, contrary to nature. It is contrary to nature for the earth, after it has been placed in water, to rise above the surface. If you throw a clod of earth into water, it immediately sinks to the bottom. But the dry land stands out in the water. It does so through the power of the Word, by which limits are set for the sea, as Solomon declares in Prov. 8:27 and Job in 38:11. If the water were not contained within a barrier by the power of the Word, it would overflow and lay everything waste. Thus our life is miraculously protected and preserved every single moment through the Word. Individual floods, by which at times entire cities or regions are covered with water, prove that we would experience such afflictions daily if it were not for God's providence.[14]

---

[13] Probably Luther is referring to the *De caelo* of Aristotle, quoted earlier in this commentary; cf. *Luther's Works*, 1, p. 24, note 39.

[14] Cf. *Luther's Works*, 13, p. 353, note 4.

Just as there is water beneath us under the earth, so there is also water above us above heaven. If, in keeping with its nature, this water were to come down, it would instantly destroy everything. The clouds move along as though they were suspended; but when they come down low at times, how much terror they spread! What would happen if they all fell down, as they would in accordance with their nature if they did not remain suspended by the Word in their place above us?

Thus we are surrounded by water on all sides and have no protection beyond a ceiling or a protective covering, and that composed of the flimsiest material, namely, the air we breathe. This supports the clouds and holds in place the vast mass of water, not indeed by its own nature but by the command of God or the power of the Word.

When the prophets contemplate these facts, they marvel;[15] for both are contrary to nature: that so huge a mass floats in the air, and that it does not fall down. But we neither see nor marvel at these great facts, since we are blinded, as it were, by daily familiarity with them. That at any moment we are not deluged by water both from above and from below we owe to the Divine Majesty, which so wonderfully directs and preserves the creatures and for this reason also deserves our praise.

That is why Moses says in this passage in careful and plain words that the deeps burst forth. He wants to point out that they had been closed by the divine power and sealed as though by God's seal, as they still are, and that God did not open them with a key but broke them open by force, so that the ocean, as though boiling over, covered everything with water.

Furthermore, nobody should imagine the statement that God broke open the deeps to mean that God moved His hand. Scripture speaks in accordance with our comprehension, to describe for us God's permission. He no longer confined the water or restrained it with His Word but allowed it to rage freely and to stream forth in accordance with its nature. The ocean, therefore, rose to such an extent that it appeared to be boiling over.

Among the salt wells in our neighborhood there is a spring named for the Germans. Unless it is drained, it gushes forth with such a volume of water at certain times that the water wells up and overflows beyond measure. It is said that once upon a time the town of Halle

---

[15] Luther is thinking of passages like Job 26:7 ff.

was destroyed by a huge and violent overflow of this spring.[16] But if a single spring could do this, what shall we suppose happened when the ocean and all the seas gave off such a huge volume of water and poured it forth? The people were overwhelmed even before they became aware of their danger. Where could they flee when the water was pouring forth with such force on all sides?

But this was not all that happened. The windows of the heaven were opened too. By these very words Moses points out that they had been closed up to this time, just as they are closed today. Indeed, the world was of the opinion that to open them would be impossible, but its sins made it possible.

Furthermore, what Moses calls windows are nothing else than openings in the sky. Nowadays, when it rains, it seems as though the water were dripping from the pores of the rain clouds. But at the time of the Flood it was discharged, not through pores but with great force through windows, as when water kept in a vessel is poured out by a single effort or when water bags burst in two. Then, too, Moses employs this mode of expression because of the manner in which these phenomena appear to us to occur.

Accordingly, a mass of water poured over the earth from everywhere, both from the heaven and from the lowest parts of the earth, until finally the entire earth was covered with water and the fertile soil or the entire surface of the earth was ruined by the saltiness of the water. Nothing like this is found in other writings;[17] it is Holy Scripture alone which relates that these things happened to a world smug in its sins, and that even today God's kindness holds in check the water that is suspended in the clouds and, according to its nature, could not but stream down in a great mass, the way it did in the Flood.

13. *On the very same day Noah and his sons, Shem and Ham and Japheth, and Noah's wife and the three wives of his sons with them entered the ark,*

14. *they and every beast according to its kind, and all the cattle according to their kinds, and every creeping thing that creeps on the earth according to its kind, and every bird according to its kind, every bird of every sort.*

[16] The Weimar editors reproduce a gloss inserted by an unknown hand: *Deutscher Brun zw Halle.*

[17] Cf. p. 131, note 1.

15. *They went into the ark with Noah, two and two of all flesh in which there was the breath of life.*

16. *And they that entered, male and female of all flesh, went in as God had commanded him.*

Here Moses begins to be amazingly wordy, so that his wordiness grates on sensitive ears because he repeats the same things so often and apparently without point. It is not enough for him to have said in general "every bird," but he mentions three kinds of birds. Among these צִפּוֹר is generally explained to be the sparrow. But this passage shows clearly enough that it is a term for a class, which no doubt received its name from its song, "zi, zi." He also mentions three kinds of animals.

Then he is also very wordy in his description of the Flood itself. He states that the water gained the upper hand, that it increased, that it overflowed, and that it ruined the surface of the earth. Finally, when he relates the result of this overflowing, he employs the same profusion of words: "All flesh expired, died, was destroyed," etc.

But I have said before that, contrary to his custom, Moses repeats the same statements in order to compel the reader to pause, to take more careful note of such an important fact, and to ponder it. For this wrath by which God destroys not only mankind but everything that it has is beyond comprehension. Through this knowledge of the wrath of God Moses wants to arouse obdurate and callous sinners.

These words are not without purpose, as it seems to empty-headed and dull readers. They impel us to fear God and bring us face to face with what is going on, in order that after we have been disheartened by the thought of such great wrath, we may begin to fear God in earnest and cease to sin. Moses seems to have written these words with a profusion of tears. His eyes and mind are so completely fixed on that terrible display of wrath that he cannot help repeating the same things several times. Surely, he is doing this in order to thrust the spurs of the fear of God into the hearts of his godly readers.

It is useful, however, for us to pause in our thought as though we were face to face with the event. In what frame of mind do you suppose we would have been if we had been brought into the ark and had seen the waters rushing in from all sides with such force and the wretched mortals swimming in the water and wretchedly perishing without any help? We must keep in mind that Noah and his sons were also flesh and blood, that is, they were human beings who, as the man in the comedy says, regarded nothing human as indifferent to them.[18] They sat in the ark for forty days before it was lifted from the earth. During these days whatever human beings and animals lived on the earth were destroyed. This disaster they saw with their own eyes. Who would doubt that they were profoundly shocked by it?

Furthermore, the ark floats on the water for one hundred and fifty days, buffeted by waves and gusts on all sides. In these circumstances no harbor could be hoped for, nor any association with other human beings. As exiles cast out of the world, they are driven hither and thither by the waves and winds. Is it not a miracle that these eight human beings did not die of grief and fear? We are indeed devoid of feeling if we can read this account with dry eyes.

What loud cries there are, what grief, and what wailing when, from the shore, we observe a boat overturned and human beings perishing wretchedly! But in this instance not only one skiff but the entire world perished in the water, which was full not only of grown people but also of infants, not only of villainous and ungodly people but also of many respectable matrons and virgins, all of whom perished. We may assume that this disaster drew from Moses this abundance of words, by which we are encouraged to look rather closely at this outstanding event. Extraordinary indeed was the faith of Noah, who comforted himself and his people with the hope of the Promised Seed and considered this promise of greater weight than the destruction of all the rest of the world.

And the Lord shut him in.

17. *The flood continued forty days upon the earth; and the waters increased, and bore up the ark, and it rose high above the earth.*

18. *The waters prevailed and increased greatly upon the earth; and the ark floated on the face of the waters.*

19. *And the waters prevailed so mightily upon the earth that all the high mountains under the whole heaven were covered;*

20. *the waters prevailed above the mountains, covering them fifteen cubits deep.*

21. *And all flesh died that moved upon the earth, birds, cattle, beasts, all swarming creatures that swarm upon the earth, and every man;*

[18] Terence, *Heautontimorumenos*, I, 1. 25.

22. *everything on the dry land in whose nostrils was the breath of life died.*

23. *He blotted out every living thing that was upon the face of the ground, man and animals and creeping things and birds of the air; they were blotted out from the earth. Only Noah was left, and those that were with him in the ark.*

24. *And the waters prevailed upon the earth a hundred and fifty days.*

Forty days the ark stood in some plain, but during that time the waters increased to such an extent that they lifted up the ark, which then floated on the water for one hundred and fifty days. This was truly a long voyage and one that abounded in mourning and tears. Yet they sustained themselves by their faith, never doubting the kindness of God toward them. They had become aware of His concern for them when they built the ark, gathered provisions, prepared other necessary things for this event, and finally also when the Lord closed the ark as the Flood rose.

But here the question arises: Was God truthful when He subjected the earth to man to till it and have dominion over it? God did not create the earth that it should lie waste, but that it should be inhabited and yield its fruits for man. How does it agree with this intention of the Creator when He destroys the entire human race except for eight souls?

There is no doubt in my mind that this argument induced the Cainites as well as the ungodly descendants of the godly generation not to believe Noah when he foretold the Flood. For how does it agree that God says to Adam and Eve: "You shall rule the earth," but that in this passage He says to Noah: "The water will rule over all human beings and will destroy them all"? Therefore they considered Noah's preaching ungodly and heretical.

The books of the prophets likewise bear witness that the threats about the captivity by the Assyrians and Babylonians were not believed by the priests and kings. They knew the grand promises: "This is My resting place forever; here I will dwell, for I have desired it" (Ps. 132:14); and the one of Isaiah: "Here is My furnace and fire" (31:9). For this reason they regarded it as impossible that either the city or the temple should be destroyed by the Gentiles. And although the Jews are a wretched people and without a country, even today they cling stubbornly to the promise that they are the people of God and heirs of the promises given to Abraham and the fathers.[19]

The pope is likewise puffed up with the promises given to the church in Matt. 28:20: "I am with you unto the end of the world"; in John 14:18: "I shall not leave you orphans"; in Luke 22:32: "Peter, I have prayed for you that your faith may not fail"; and so forth. Even though he sees and feels the wrath of God, he is enmeshed and caught in these promises and, together with his followers, dreams that his seat and power will remain unshaken. The papists blatantly confront us with the name "church" and assure themselves of all the greatest successes, as though they could compel God to establish such a church as they themselves dream of and desire.

In this connection the question is properly raised: How does the Flood, by which the entire human race perished, harmonize with the intention of God when He created man, and particularly with His promise or His bestowal of dominion on man? The answer to this question also applies to that concerning the church: God remains truthful and preserves the church, rules, and guides it, but in a manner that the world neither sees nor understands. He leaves the Roman pope, together with his followers, under the delusion that he is the church; He permits him to feel smug and to enjoy his prestige and title. But God has actually expelled him from the church and cast him aside because he casts aside the Word and establishes idolatrous forms of worship.

Meanwhile God has chosen for Himself another church, which receives the Word and shuns idolatry, although it is so hard pressed by cross and dishonor that it is not considered a church but a heretical body and a school of the devil. Thus Paul says in Rom. 2:17 that the Jews do not fear God but glory in the Law and in God; actually they deny God, blaspheme and provoke Him. While the Jews, who boast that they are the people of God, are doing this, God procures a church for Himself from the Gentiles who sincerely glory in God and receive His Word.

Who will accuse God of a lie because He preserves the church in a manner different from the way men either desire or know? The promises about preserving Jerusalem and the temple were similar. These promises were not annulled when Jerusalem and the temple were destroyed by the Babylonians. At that time God established

[19] Cf. *Luther the Expositor*, pp. 92—95.

another Jerusalem and another temple in the Spirit and through the Word, when Jeremiah promised (29:10) that the people would return after seventy years and would rebuild the temple and the city. For the Jews the temple and the city were destroyed at that time, but not for God, who promised in His Word that they would be rebuilt.

The argument of the Jews, therefore, is sound: God will not forsake His city and temple. But His manner of doing this was different from the way the Jews had in mind. They assumed that the city would not be destroyed, because the promise declared (Ps. 132:14): "This is My resting place forever." God permitted its destruction in order to punish the sins of His people. Nevertheless, He cares for the church and protects it when the godly are returned by King Cyrus and build the temple anew.

In the same way man was given dominion over the world at the beginning of creation. In the Flood this is taken away, not forever but for a time; and even then it is not taken away entirely. Even though the greater part of the world perishes, man nevertheless remains lord of the creatures; that lordship is preserved for him, if not in so large a multitude as the world believed and wanted, nevertheless in a few individuals, that is, eight souls, something that the world did not consider.

God's promise, therefore, did not lie. God kept His promise, but He did not keep it in the manner in which the world wanted it kept. He destroyed the sinners; but He saved the righteous, even though they were few and were like seed that God increased later on in various ways.

This judgment of God the papists ought to keep in mind. It teaches that God does not allow a large number, power, or even His own promise to prevent Him from punishing sins in the impenitent. Otherwise God would have spared the ancient world and the descendants of the patriarchs, on whom He had bestowed dominion over the earth. Now He destroys them all and saves only eight souls.

Why, then, would it be strange for Him to deal with the papists in the same way? Even though they boast of their titles, prestige, large numbers, and power, God will cast them aside for treading His Word underfoot and persecuting it; and He will choose for Himself another church which submits humbly to His Word and accepts the benefits of Christ with open arms, a church which the church of the pope, in reliance on its own merit, arrogantly despises.

One must not trust in the things that are at hand and in one's possession, even though they were promised by a divine Word; but one must pay heed to the Word itself and rely on it alone. Men who do not do this but depart from the Word and rely on what is at hand — even if such men are numerous, great, and powerful — will nevertheless not go unpunished for this defection from the faith. The Flood, the captivity of the Jews, and their present wretched state demonstrate this; so does the story of the seven thousand men in the kingdom of Israel (1 Kings 19:18).

This is adequate evidence that size does not make the church. Nor dare one consider how holy its origin is, who its ancestors are, and what they have in their possession and have received from God. The Word alone must be considered, and the verdict must be reached on the basis of it. Those who truly embrace it are the ones who, like Mt. Zion, will never be moved (Ps. 78:68-69), even though they are very few in number and are utterly despised before the world. Thus through Noah and his children, although they were very few, God preserved for man the truth concerning the dominion that had been promised him, even though man did not have the sole of his foot on the earth.

Our opponents lay great stress on this argument because they disregard the Word and consider only number, appearance, and persons. The apostles foretold that Antichrist would be a respecter of persons who would lay stress on large numbers and on antiquity, hate the Word, distort God's promises, and kill those who cling to the Word.[20] We are not going to consider such people to be the church, are we?

The church is the daughter who is born from the Word; she is not the mother of the Word. He who gives up the Word and hastens to put his reliance on persons ceases to be the church and becomes completely blinded. Neither a large number nor power gives him any support, just as by contrast those who keep the Word, like Noah and his people, are the church, even though they are very few in number, even only eight souls. Today the papists are more numerous than we are, and their prestige is greater than ours. We are not only reviled, but we also suffer in various ways. This must be borne until the judgment comes by which God will reveal that we are His church, but that the papists are the church of Satan.

In this instance one must adhere to the rule which appears in

---

[20] Probably a reference to 2 Thess. 2:3-12.

1 Sam. 16:7, where the Lord says to Samuel: "Do not look on his appearance or on the height of his stature, because I have rejected him; for the Lord sees not as man sees; man looks on the outward appearance, but the Lord looks on the heart."

Accordingly, let us not be concerned about how great and powerful the pope is. He boasts that he is the church and stresses apostolic succession and his personal majesty. Let us look on the Word. If he embraces this, let us consider him to be the church; if he persecutes it, let us consider him to be the slave of Satan.

This is what Paul says in 1 Cor. 2:5, namely, that the spiritual man judges all things. If I were the only one in the entire world to adhere to the Word, I alone would be the church and would properly judge about the rest of the world that it is not the church. Even though they have riches or office, they have them without the Word and actually have nothing. On the other hand, we, who have the Word even though we have no riches, nevertheless have everything through the Word. Therefore let the pope, the cardinals, and the bishops either ally themselves with us or stop boasting that they are the church, which cannot exist without the Word, because it is brought into existence by the Word alone.

Much hatred is heaped upon us when it is said that we have fallen away from the ancient church. The papists, on the contrary, boast that they remained with the church and are willing to submit everything to the judgment of the church. But the accusation is false. If we want to confess the truth, we fell away from the Word by remaining in their church. But now we have returned to the Word and have ceased to be apostates from the Word.

Even though they take the title of church away from us by their judgment, still we keep the Word and through the Word all the advantages of the true church. He who has the Creator of all things must also have the creatures. Thus Noah remains lord of the world, even though the waters prevail and the earth perishes. He loses his possessions. Nevertheless, because he keeps the Word by which everything was created, it is correct to say that he keeps everything.

CHAPTER EIGHT

1. *But God remembered Noah and all the beasts and all the cattle that were with him in the ark.*

AFTER the end of that awful wrath and after the destruction of all flesh, together with the earth, comes the beginning of the fulfillment of the promise that the Lord gave to Noah and his sons, that they would be the seed of the human race. Undoubtedly they were looking forward very eagerly to this promise. No life is more difficult than one lived in faith, like the one Noah and his sons lived, whom we see utterly dependent on heaven. Because the earth was covered with water and they had no ground on which to set foot, there was only the Word of the promise to give them support as they drifted over that vast mass of water.

When the flesh is out of danger, it regards faith as something altogether insignificant, as the discussions of the papists show. It chooses showy and tedious works and tortures itself with these. But as for you, look at Noah, who was surrounded by water on all sides and was all but overwhelmed by it. It is not works that preserve him, but solely his reliance on the mercy of God, to which the Word of the promise kept calling him.

This difficult situation Moses describes by implication in the statement, "The Lord remembered." He points out that Noah had drifted on the waters for so long that God seemed to have completely forgotten him. Men who live in such a conflict of thoughts — when the rays of divine grace are withdrawn, and we find ourselves in darkness or in a state of being forgotten by God — discover that it is far more difficult to live by the Word alone or by faith than to be a hermit or a Carthusian monk.

It is not idle chatter when the Holy Spirit says that God remembered Noah. It indicates that from the day when Noah entered the ark nothing was said to him, nothing was revealed to him, and he saw no ray of grace shining; but he clung only to the promise he had received, although meanwhile the waters and the waves were raging as though God had surely forgotten him. His children, the cattle, and the other animals of every kind experienced the same peril throughout the entire hundred and fifty days in the ark. Even though the holy seed overcame these perils, through a rich measure of the Spirit, it did not overcome them without great affliction of the flesh, without tears and great fear, which I think the dumb animals experienced too.

The evil by which they were troubled was twofold. The universal Flood which engulfed the entire human race could not take its course without great grief on the part of the godly, especially since they saw themselves reduced to such a small number.

In the second place, it was a serious matter to be tossed about on the waters for almost half a year without any comfort from God. Moses' statement, "The Lord remembered Noah," must not be weakened as though it were a figure of speech meaning that God acted as if He had forgotten, when actually God cannot forget His saints. A grammarian [1] does not understand what it means to live in such a manner as to feel that God has forgotten you. The most perfect saints are those who understand these matters and who in faith can bear with a God who is, so to speak, forgetful. For this reason the psalms and the entire Bible are full of such laments in which men call upon God to arise, to open His eyes, to hear, and to awake.

The more zealous monks have at times experienced this temptation; they called it the suspension of grace.[2] It may be felt also in light temptations. The fire of lust in young people is altogether unbearable if it is not moderated through the Word of God and the Holy Spirit. Similarly, intolerance and vindictiveness in adulthood simply cannot be overcome if God does not remove them from the heart. In more severe trials how much greater is the tendency to fall into the gloom of despair or into the snares of predestinarianism when one feels the suspension of grace!

This expression should not be passed over as a mere matter of grammar, the way the rabbis suppose.[3] But one must take into consideration the state of mind and the indescribable groaning of the heart when, in the very feeling of despair, a spark of faith still remains

[1] Cf. p. 15, note 23.

[2] Luther employs the technical term from medieval mysticism and spirituality: *suspensio gratiae*.

[3] Perhaps the source of this is Lyra on Gen. 8:1, sec. a.

and overcomes the flesh. Just as Paul complains of the angel of Satan (2 Cor. 12:7), so we must assume that Noah, too, felt similar barbs in his heart and often reasoned with himself: "You don't suppose that God loves only you this much, do you? You don't suppose, do you, that in the end God will save you, even though there is no limit to the waters and it seems that those immense clouds can never be emptied?"

Furthermore, when these thoughts also rose in the feeble hearts of the women, what outcries, laments, and tears do you suppose resulted? Although Noah was almost overcome by sorrow and grief himself, he nevertheless was obliged, practically against his own heart, to encourage and comfort them.

It was no joke or laughing matter for them to live shut up in the ark for so long, to see the endless masses of rain, to be tossed about by the waves, and to drift. In these circumstances there was the feeling that God had forgotten them, as Moses indicates when he states that the Lord at last remembered Noah and his sons. Even though they overcame this feeling through faith, they did not overcome it without great annoyance to the flesh. Similarly, a young man who leads a chaste life indeed overcomes lust, yet certainly not without the greatest discomfort and effort. But in this instance the danger was greater, for all their circumstances compelled them to debate whether God was favorably inclined and wanted to remember them. Therefore although they overcame these hardships, they did not overcome them without awful affliction. There is nothing that the flesh, which is inherently weak, is less able to tolerate than a God who does not remember us but has forgotten us. If by nature we are so constituted that we become puffed up and haughty when God remembers us, grants us success, and is favorable toward us, what is so remarkable about our becoming disheartened and despondent when God seems to have cast us aside and everything goes wrong?

Let us, then, remember that this story sets before us an example of faith, perseverance, and patience, in order that those who have the divine promise may not only learn to believe it but may also realize that they need perseverance. But perseverance does not come without a great struggle. In the New Testament Christ calls on us to persevere when He says (Matt. 24:13): "He who endures to the end will be saved."

This is the reason why for a time God seems to hide, so that He may appear to have forgotten us by suspending His grace, as they say in the schools. But just as in this temptation not only the spirit but also the flesh is troubled, so later on, when He again begins to remember us, there comes into the flesh a feeling of grace which was in the spirit alone at the time of the temptation and was very feeble at that.

Therefore the verb "He remembered" indicates that there was great sorrow among the human beings and the animals throughout the entire time of the Flood. Hence Noah and the others must have been exceedingly patient and courageous to endure the forgetfulness of God, which, without the Spirit, is altogether unbearable for the flesh, just as other temptations are, even though they may be light. Of course it is true that God always remembers those that are His, even when He seems to have forsaken them. Nevertheless, in this passage Moses indicates that God remembered His people also so far as their own perception was concerned, that is, by a sign and a clear display of what He had previously promised in the Word and in the Spirit. This is the main point of this entire chapter.

And God made a wind blow over the earth, and the waters subsided;

2. the fountains of the deep and the windows of the heavens were closed, the rain from the heavens was restrained,

3. and the waters receded from the earth continually. At the end of a hundred and fifty days the waters had abated.

Previously Moses stated that the Flood raged in three ways: the fountains of the deep burst forth, the windows of heaven were opened, and rain descended. When this came to an end on the one hundred and fiftieth day, a calm returned, and with it God's remembrance; and Noah, his sons, and their wives, together with the animals, were revived after their great and prolonged terrors. If a two-day storm drives sailors to despair, how much more difficult it was to endure being tossed about for half a year!

At this point the question is raised how the wind was brought over the earth, which till now was completely covered with water. It is nothing new for winds to dry up moisture, especially those from the east, which our people call *holewind* [4] but Vergil calls "burning" [5]

[4] Luther used *holewind* in his translation of Hos. 12:1.

[5] Luther is speaking of the *venti urentes* referred to in Latin literature.

because of the drought they bring upon the earth. Hosea, too, makes mention of this (13:15).

The answer is easy. The text says that a wind was brought over the earth, that is, over the surface of the water, until the dried-up waters again revealed the earth to the human beings. Thus in Exodus (14:21) it is stated that the Red Sea was dried up by a torrid wind. Even though the Lord could have achieved the same result without the wind, nevertheless He likes to make use of means that were created for a definite purpose.

Up to this time Noah lived in darkness and saw nothing else than the waters rushing and raging fearfully in a vast surge. Now the lovely light of the sun appears again, and the winds stop roaring at random from all directions. Only the east wind, which is capable of diminishing the waters, is blowing, and gradually it removes the standing waters. Besides this there are other means: the ocean no longer inundates the earth but again absorbs the waters it had discharged; and the floodgates of heaven are closed too.

These are the outward and palpable signs by which God comforts Noah and shows him that He has not completely forgotten him but remembers him. This is a useful and needed lesson, that when we are in dangers, we, too, may confidently look for the help of God, who will not forsake us if we persevere in faith and wait for His promise.

4. *And in the seventh month, on the seventeenth day of the month, the ark came to rest upon the mountains of Ararat.*

For forty days the waters increased, until the ark was lifted above the earth. Then it floated on the waters for one hundred and fifty days, driven by waves and winds during God's forgetfulness; finally the waters began to abate, and the ark came to rest.

At this point the Jews debate about the number of the months.[6] But why should we dwell too long on unessential matters, especially since the contributions of the rabbis are not particularly scholarly?

It is of greater importance for us to investigate what the mountains of Ararat are.[7] It is the common opinion of almost everyone that they are the mountains of Armenia near the highest mountains

[6] Lyra on Gen. 8:4, secs. f and g.

[7] From Lyra's comments Luther knew some of the principal theories about the location of Ararat.

of Asia Minor, the Caucasus and the Taurus. To me it seems more likely that this is a designation for the foremost mountain of all, the Imaus, which divides India.[8] Compared with this mountain the other high mountains are like warts. That the ark came to rest on the highest mountain is proved by the fact that the water continued to abate for almost three whole months, until the lower mountains were uncovered, such as the Lebanon, Taurus, and Caucasus, which are like feet or roots of the Imaus, just as the mountains of Greece are arms, as it were, of the Alps extending as far as our Hercynian forest.[9] The remarkable extent of the mountains is apparent to anyone who carefully examines them.

Josephus has some rather amazing statements about the mountains of Armenia. He records that remnants of the ark were found there in his time.[10] But I suppose that nobody will consider me a heretic if I doubt his reliability in some instances.

5. *And the waters continued to abate until the tenth month; in the tenth month, on the first day of the month, the tops of the mountains were seen.*

The text stated previously that by the seventh month the waters had diminished to such an extent that the ark came to rest on the mountains of Ararat. Thereafter, in the third month, the peaks of the smaller mountains began to be uncovered, so that from the mountains of Ararat, as from a watchtower, Noah saw the tops of the rest of the mountains, of the Taurus in Asia, of the Lebanon in Syria, and so forth. All these were signs of God's remembrance.

6. *At the end of forty days Noah opened the window of the ark which he had made,*

7. *and sent forth a raven; and it went to and fro until the waters were dried up from the earth.*

This is a historical account. The allegory we shall reserve for its place. Moreover, the carelessness of a translator has given rise to a question in connection with this passage. The Hebrew does not

---

[8] Ptolemy's map of the world contains a ridge of mountains identified as *Imaus m.;* presumably this is a reference to the Himalaya, for he identifies a *Scythia intra Imaum* and a *Scythia extra Imaum.*

[9] Present-day geology still speaks of the Hercynian Alps.

[10] Josephus, *Antiquities of the Jews,* Book I, ch. 3.

say that the raven did not return, as Jerome renders it.[11] There was, therefore, no need to invent a reason why he did not return; for it is alleged that he found everything full of dead bodies and that this delightful and abundant fare kept him from returning.[12]

Moses states the opposite, namely, that the raven which had been sent out returned, although it did not allow itself to be caught and shut up in the ark again, as the dove did. Moses reveals that Noah sent out the raven in order to learn through him whether the animals could now find a footing and have food. The raven did not carry out this mission carefully; but, as though he were glad to be set free from the prison of the ark, he flew to and fro as he rejoiced in the open sky and now paid no attention to Noah.

The Jews, like swine, reveal their impure minds everywhere. They invent the tale that the raven feared for his mate and suspected Noah's intention toward her.[13] Oh, what impure minds!

8. *Then he sent forth a dove from him, to see if the waters had subsided from the face of the ground;*

9. *but the dove found no place to set her foot, and she returned to him to the ark, for the waters were still on the face of the whole earth. So he put forth his hand and took her and brought her into the ark with him.*

After Noah has been disappointed in his hope by the raven, which impudently flies about but brings no indication about the state of the earth, he takes a dove; for he believes that she will perform this mission more successfully. The text almost forces us to accept the conclusion that the two birds were sent out together at the same time, in order that Noah might have two witnesses from which he could learn what he wanted to know. But the raven, which delights in the open sky, is unwilling to return into the ark, even though he keeps flying around it. The dove, however, which shuns dead bodies and unclean places, returns and permits herself to be seized. This story, as we shall hear,[14] will provide a striking allegory concerning the church.

[11] Jerome's translation is reflected in the Douay Version: "Which went forth and did not return, till the waters were dried up upon the earth."

[12] Cf. Lyra on Gen. 8:7.

[13] Lyra on Gen. 8:7, sec. p.

[14] Cf. pp. 161—164.

10. *He waited another seven days, and again he sent forth the dove out of the ark;*

11. *and the dove came back to him in the evening, and lo, in her mouth a freshly plucked olive leaf; so Noah knew that the waters had subsided from the earth.*

12. *Then he waited another seven days, and sent forth the dove; and she did not return to him any more.*

The dove is a faithful messenger. Therefore she is sent out a second time. Moses describes carefully how the waters gradually subsided, until finally the surface of the earth with the trees was free of the waters. When the dove fetches an olive leaf, we must not believe that the dove did this on her own impulse; but she was directed this way by God, who gradually wanted to indicate more clearly to Noah that He was remembering him and had not altogether forgotten him. For Noah and the rest, who were shut up in the ark as in a prison, this olive leaf was an extraordinary sign, in order that they might be encouraged by it and gain a sure hope of their coming release.

At this point the Jews violently debate where the dove found this olive leaf.[15] Some, in order to maintain the unique glory of their native country, make the silly assertion that it was taken from the Mount of Olives in the land of Israel, which God had spared, to keep it from perishing in the Flood like the rest of the earth.

The saner Jews properly refute these silly ideas by reasoning that if this were true, the olive leaf could not have been a sign from which Noah could conclude that the waters had subsided. Others come with the fiction that the dove was sent into Paradise and brought the olive branch from there. I have previously stated my opinion about Paradise several times,[16] and these silly ideas do not deserve a detailed rebuttal.

It is more profitable to point out that all this happened in a miraculous and supernatural way. The dove does not have a great impulse of herself to pluck a branch and bring it to the ark in order that through her Noah might reach a conclusion about the decrease of the waters. These things were done by divine direction. Other trees at that time also had leaves, especially those that are taller and emerged more quickly from the waters. The olive tree is low in

---

[15] See note 13 above.

[16] See p. 204, note 43.

comparison with the rest of the trees. Therefore it was suited to this purpose; through it Noah could become aware of the decrease of the waters, and by a practical process of reasoning could conclude that the wrath of God had now ceased and that the earth had returned to the condition in which it had been before the Flood. This he knew with greater certainty when the dove which was sent out the third time did not return; for she not only had food on the earth but could also build nests and walk on the ground.

13. *In the six hundred and first year, in the first month, the first day of the month, the waters were dried from off the earth; and Noah removed the covering of the ark, and looked, and behold, the face of the ground was dry.*

14. *In the second month, on the twenty-seventh day of the month, the earth was dry.*

Here we see that Noah was in the ark an entire year and ten days. In the second month, on the seventeenth day, he entered the ark, and when a whole year had passed, he left the ark in the same month, but on the twenty-seventh day. Hence poor Noah, with his children and the women, spent more than an entire half year in the ark, in deepest sorrow and in God's forgetfulness. After this, by means of various signs, God gradually shows him that He did not forget him, until finally, at the expiration of a year and ten days, he is established again as lord of the earth and the sea. On this day of the second month the earth was not only rid of the Flood but was also dry.

This is the account of the Flood and of how the waters decreased again. After this awful wrath there follows the boundless light of grace, as the sermon which God Himself addressed to Noah, and which now follows, will show.

15. *Then God said to Noah:*

16. *Go forth from the ark, you and your wife, and your sons and your sons' wives with you.*

17. *Bring forth with you every living thing that is with you of all flesh — birds and animals and every creeping thing that creeps on the earth — that they may breed abundantly on the earth, and be fruitful and multiply upon the earth.*

So far there has been only a factual account, or a description of a divine work. Although God's works are not mute but speak to us and, as it were, set before our eyes a view of God's will, God nevertheless comforts us far more effectively when to His works He adds the spoken Word,[17] which the eyes do not see but the ears hear, and which the heart understands as a result of the working of the Holy Spirit.

So far, by His work, God has shown that He has been appeased and, as it were, has been changed from an angry God to a merciful one, since He restrains the waters and dries up the earth. Now He continues to strengthen this comfort with His Word. He addresses Noah in a friendly manner and commands Him, together with the rest of the human beings and the animals, to leave the ark.

This is a passage which we repeatedly stress in our teaching,[18] and not without reason in order to establish that we are not permitted to institute or do anything, especially before God and in the worship of God, unless the Word instructs and commands us. Thus Noah entered the ark when he was commanded by God to enter, and thus he now leaves the ark when he is commanded by God to leave it. He does not follow superstitious ideas, such as those we observe among the Jews. When they have once been commanded to institute something that is temporary, they want to retain it forever as something necessary for salvation.

Noah could have thought thus: "Behold, at the command of the Lord I constructed the ark, and I was saved in it when all mankind was perishing. Therefore I shall remain in it, or I shall keep it as a temple or a place for the worship of God; for it has been hallowed by the Word of God and by the fact that saints, or the church, dwell in it." But the godly man does nothing of the kind, because the Word commanded him to leave. Therefore he complies; and now that the ark has served its purpose during the time of the Flood, he abandons it and is convinced that he and his children must live on the earth.

Likewise, let us institute nothing without the Word of God; but let us walk in a holy calling, that is, in one that has the Word and command of God. He who institutes anything without the command of God labors in vain.

Over against this one can put Noah's example, which follows a little later; without God's command he builds an altar, and on it he sacrifices to the Lord a burnt offering of clean animals. Now if Noah was permitted to do this, why should we, too, not be permitted to

[17] Cf. *Luther the Expositor*, pp. 48—70.
[18] Cf. *Luther's Works*, 23, pp. 347 ff., for one example.

choose certain forms of worship? And surely the papacy has arbitrarily heaped up innumerable works and forms of worship in the church. But one must keep in mind the axiomatic statement that whatever is not done out of faith is sin (Rom. 14:23). Faith, however, cannot be separated from the Word. Therefore whatever is done without the Word is sin.

Furthermore, the desire to do as the fathers did is manifestly dangerous. Just as individuals are different, so their duties are different; and in accordance with the diversity of their callings, God demands diverse works of them. For this reason the Letter to the Hebrews (11:2) relates the diverse acts of the fathers in a masterly manner to the one faith, in order to show that it is not the works of the fathers but their faith that should be imitated by each individual in his own calling.

Accordingly, the individual works of the holy fathers are by no means to be taken as a pattern for everyone to imitate, the way the monks imitate the fastings of Benedict, the garment of Francis, the shoes of Dominic, and so forth. This is the behavior of monkeys, who imitate actions without any understanding. Similarly, the monks imitate works but know nothing of faith.

Abraham is commanded to sacrifice his son. His descendants later on thought that they should follow this example with the utmost wickedness, and they filled the earth with innocent blood.[19] Thus his posterity worshiped the brazen serpent and sacrificed before it.[20] Both wanted to defend themselves with the example of their ancestors; but because they instituted these forms of worship without the Word, they were justly condemned.

Therefore let us remember not to institute anything without the command of God. Because duties are different, the works of individuals can not and need not be the same. How absurd it would be for me to shout that I must follow the example of the emperor and that I must dictate laws to others! How wicked it would be if I maintained that I must follow the example of the judge, and condemned someone to execution by the gallows or by the sword! Attention must, therefore, be directed, not to the works of an individual but to his faith. One faith is common to all the saints, although their works differ very much.

If Noah built an altar, beware of assuming that you are permitted

[19] Cf. Judges 11:29-40; 1 Kings 16:34; 2 Kings 16:3.
[20] Cf. *Luther's Works*, 22, pp. 346—347.

to do the same thing; but emulate the faith of Noah, who considered it proper to show his merciful Savior that he was aware of His kindnesses and was thankful for them. Emulate Abraham, not by sacrificing a son but by believing the promises of God and obeying His commands. With this in view, the Letter to the Hebrews (11:2) masterfully relates the examples or deeds of the fathers to faith and points out that it is this that we, too, must emulate.

But this objection can be answered also in this manner, that Noah did have a command to erect an altar and to bring sacrifices. God gave His approval to this custom of sacrificing when He commanded that the clean animals, which were suited for sacrifices, should be brought into the ark in larger number.[21] Nor was Noah permitted to withdraw from the priestly office, which, after it had been sanctioned in the primitive world, had passed on to him through the right of primogeniture. Adam, Seth, Enos, and others were priests.[22] From these the priestly office was handed on to Noah.

Noah, therefore, not only had the liberty to sacrifice as priest and prophet, but the obligation as well; and he did what he did by virtue of his calling. But because there is no calling without the Word, he built the altar and sacrificed in accordance with the Word and at God's command. Hence let a monk demonstrate the office and calling by virtue of which he may wear the cowl, call upon the Blessed Virgin, pray the rosary, and do similar things; and we shall praise his life. But because there is no such calling, because no word gives the direction, and because the office is lacking, both the life and all the works of all monks deserve to be condemned.

Lastly, leaving everything else out of consideration, there yet remains the argument *a posteriori*,[23] namely, that God approves Noah's action. Although reasoning *a posteriori* is not particularly reliable, it nevertheless has weight in the instance of such heroic and exceptional men. Even though they appear to be doing some things for which they have no command, nevertheless they are not cast aside by God but are approved by Him. Furthermore, they are convinced that they are not sinning, although this does not become apparent until the approval comes later on. There are many such instances, and we observe that God approved some actions of the heathen.[24]

[21] See p. 73, note 84.
[22] Cf. *Luther's Works*, 1, p. 247.
[23] The argument is *a posteriori*, that is, from effect to cause.
[24] Cf. *Luther's Works*, 13, pp. 199 ff.

Let this conviction remain unshaken: that everything must be done in accordance with God's command, in order that we may determine with assurance in our conscience that we are doing it because we have been commanded by God. Hence those who run in a calling that pleases God do not run in vain or beat the air, as those do who have no course on which they have been commanded to run. Therefore they cannot hope for a prize either (1 Cor. 9:24-26).

But I return to the text. Noah and his children, together with their wives, are commanded to leave the ark and to bring out on the earth the animals of every kind, that all His works may be hallowed and comprehended by the Word. About the animals in particular there is now added:

Be fruitful and multiply upon the earth.

18. *So Noah went forth, and his sons with him.*[25]

19. *And every beast, every creeping thing, and every bird, everything that moves upon the earth, went forth by families out of the ark.*

Because the Lord speaks in the ninth chapter about the procreation of Noah and his sons (9:1), I hold that here the Lord is speaking about the procreation of the dumb animals only. Lyra foolishly concludes from the manner of expression that at the time of the Flood sexual intercourse was forbidden and that now, beginning with the exit from the ark, it was again unrestricted or permitted because the Lord says: "Go out, you and your wife."[26] Such are the thoughts of monks, not of God, who concerns Himself, not with lust but with procreation; for procreation is a creature of God, but lust is the poison of Satan, which was instilled in human nature through sin.

Moses is rather wordy in this passage, in order to indicate and depict that their hearts were intoxicated with joy after they had been commanded to return from the prison of the ark to the earth, which was open on every side. Moreover, in this passage Moses follows a different arrangement in enumerating the kinds of animals; he divides them into families, in order to have you realize that God is concerned with procreation only. Without a doubt it was a most

[25] The latter part of verse 18 is missing from Luther's text, for no apparent reason.

[26] "This does not refer only to human beings but also to animals and birds." Lyra on Gen. 8:17, sec. d.

delightful sight that all the beasts, as they stood outside the ark, individually recognized the related animal and then repaired to the place to which they were accustomed: wolves, bears, and lions to the forests and woodlands; sheep, goats, and swine to the fields; dogs, chickens, and cats to human company.

20. *Then Noah built an altar to the Lord, and took of every clean animal and of every clean bird and offered burnt offerings on the altar.*

This is a clear text. It proves that Moses did not inaugurate sacrifices but collected them, like a rhapsodist, and then put into a system those that had been in use by the fathers and had been passed down from hand to hand.[27] Similarly, Moses was not the first to write the law of circumcision; this law was received from the fathers.

Previously, when he mentioned the sacrifice of Abel and Cain (Gen. 4:4-5), he gives that sacrifice a name, which was מִנְחָה, or offering; but in this passage there is the first mention of the burnt offering, which was burnt in its entirety. This, I say, is clear evidence that even before Moses there was a law about sacrifices. What Moses did was to bring into a system those rites which the fathers had observed.

21. *And the Lord smelled the pleasing odor.*

This means that the Lord approved of Noah's sacrifice, which he had offered in accordance with the example of the holy fathers and by virtue of his position as a priest.

But one must carefully note the difference in expression. Previously Moses stated that the Lord had regard for the offering. Here he states that the Lord smelled the delightful odor,[28] and after this Moses frequently makes use of such an expression. The heathen, too, copied it, as when Lucian ridicules Jove for being captivated by the odor of pieces of flesh.[29]

Actually the word does not mean "odor of pleasantness"; it means "odor of rest." For נִיחֹחַ, "rest," comes from the verb נוּחַ, which Moses used previously (Gen. 8:4), when he stated that the ark rested on

---

[27] Luther follows both Jewish and Christian writers in describing Moses as the codifier of patriarchal tradition.

[28] The phrase *odor suavissimus* occurs in passages like Ex. 29:18 and Lev. 1:13.

[29] Cf. Juvenal, *Satires*, Book V, l. 162.

the mountains of Ararat. Hence it is the odor of rest, because at that time God rested from wrath in that He gave up His wrath, was appeased, and, as we ordinarily say, was well pleased.

Here someone may interpose: "Why does he not say, 'God had regard for Noah and for his burnt offering,' instead of saying, 'The Lord smelled the odor of rest,' which indeed sounds offensive, as though He were not commending the person for his faith, but solely the work itself?" The answer generally given is to the effect that Scripture speaks of God in human fashion, for human beings are captivated by the pleasantness of an odor.

To me it seems that there is another reason for this expression, namely, that God was so close by that He perceived the odor. Moses wants to point out that this sacrifice was pleasing to God. Solomon says (Prov. 27:9): "A pleasant odor makes the heart glad." Physicians at times resuscitate lifeless people by means of pleasant odors, just as, on the contrary, a horrible stench is intensely offensive to our nature and often prostrates us.

Thus it may be said that God, who was offended by the horrible stench of ungodliness, is now recovering. He sees this one priest girding himself for sacrifice, in order to manifest some evidence of thankfulness and to indicate by a public act that he is not ungodly but has a God and fears Him; for it is with these matters that sacrifices are actually concerned.

Just as God thus far took pleasure in destroying the human race, so now He takes pleasure and rejoices in increasing it once more. It is for our sake, therefore, that Moses uses such an expression, in order that we may gain an understanding of God's grace and learn that He is a God who rejoices in doing good to us.

And the Lord said in His heart.

Moses is indicating that the Lord spoke these words, not in a perfunctory or superficial manner but from His innermost heart; for the meaning of the Hebrew is that God spoke *to* His heart.

I will never again curse the ground because of man.

God is speaking as though He repented of the punishment that has been inflicted on the earth because of man, just as He previously repented of the creation (Gen. 6:6), and as though He were finding fault with Himself for raging so greatly against man.

But this must not be understood as though a change of will could occur in God. These words are intended for our comfort; for He is accusing and blaming Himself, in order to encourage the little flock to rest assured that henceforth God wants to be favorably disposed toward them.

Their hearts were in great need of this comfort after they had been terrified by the greatness of God's wrath, which they had observed in its rage. Because it was impossible for their faith not to be shaken by the contemplation of such great wrath, God is, as it were, constrained to shape His acts and words in such a way that their hearts look for nothing but grace and mercy. It is for this reason that He now converses with them, is present at their sacrifices, indicates that He is delighted by them, finds fault with His counsel, and promises that He will never again do anything of this kind. In sum, He now begins to be a different God from the one He has been thus far. Not that God changes, but that He desires a change in the people, who are now swallowed up, as it were, in contemplation of His wrath.

People who have gone through spiritual trials know how necessary it is to support their heart with a sure and strong comfort that will finally bring them back to the hope of grace and help them to forget the wrath. Often a single day or a single month is insufficient for this purpose; but just as the alleviation of sickness requires a long time, so these wounds of the heart are not cured at once or by a single word. Since God is aware of this, He tries in various ways to bring back the frightened hearts to a sure hope of grace. He even finds fault with Himself by speaking to His heart, just as in Jer. 18:8, where He promises that He will repent of the evil He has in mind, provided that they, too, repent.

It must furthermore be noted that He states: "I will never again curse the ground." He is speaking of the universal destruction of the earth, not of partial ones, by which He destroys fields, cities, and kingdoms. Of these He makes use to warn others, as Mary says (Luke 1:52): "He puts down the mighty from their thrones."

For the imagination of man's heart is evil from his youth.

This is a highly important passage about original sin; those who disparage it surely go astray, like blind men in the sunlight, and take no notice of what they daily do and experience. Consider our infancy. In what a variety of ways sin revealed itself in our early age! What a heap of rods is needed until we are brought to order, as it were, and kept at our duty!

After this age comes adolescence. Then there is a greater feeling of rebellion. Besides, there is the unsubdued evil, the passion of lust and desire. If one takes a wife, there follows a loathing of one's own and a passion for strange women. When we are entrusted with the administration of the state, then especially there is a most abundant crop of vices: jealousy, excessive ambition, arrogance, hope of gain, avarice, anger, ill humor, etc.

Hence, as the Germans express it in a proverb, sins increase with the years: "There is no fool so stingy as an old fool."[30] Now all the vices of this kind are so crude and glaring that they can be recognized and observed. What shall we say of those that are within, namely, that unbelief, smugness, disregard of the Word, and ungodly thoughts thrive?

Nevertheless, there are some who are considered outstanding theologians and want to be so regarded, but who belittle original sin with specious arguments.[31] Surely, so many great vices cannot be disparaged. This is not a mild disease or shortcoming; it is the utmost lawlessness, the like of which all the rest of the creatures, the demons excepted, do not have.

Do those who belittle original sin have Scripture proofs on which they rely? Let us give consideration to Moses in this matter. As I pointed out previously, in the sixth chapter,[32] it is not lust, oppression, and other sins that he calls evil; but it is the imagination of the human heart, namely, industry, wisdom, and human reason, together with all their powers, of which reason makes use even in its best deeds. Even though we do not condemn civil and political activities, the human heart nevertheless taints these good works when it uses them for vainglory, gain, and oppression either against its neighbor or against God.

One cannot get around this passage with the claim that such people were the ones who perished in the Flood.[33] God uses a generic

---

[30] See *Luther's Works*, 21, p. 184, note 32.

[31] An attack on scholastic theologians; see p. 121, note 34.

[32] See pp. 13—14.

[33] Cf. Jerome, *Liber hebraicarum quaestionum in Genesim, Patrologia, Series Latina*, XXIII, 997—998, on Noah's righteousness in contrast with his contemporaries.

term and says that the heart of man is of that kind. But in those days there were no other people than those who had been saved in the ark, and yet He says that the imagination of the human heart is evil.

Hence not even the saints are excluded here. Later on this imagination betrays its nature in Ham, the third son. The other brothers were by nature no better. There is only this difference, that through their faith in the Seed the others continue to have the hope of the remission of sins and do not yield to the evil imagination of their heart but resist it through the Holy Spirit, who is given for the purpose of contending against this wickedness of nature and overcoming it. Because Ham yields to this nature, he is entirely evil and also perishes entirely. But because Shem and Japheth contend against it through the Spirit, although they, too, are evil, they are nevertheless not altogether evil; for they have the Holy Spirit, through whom they contend against what is evil, and for this reason they are saints.

Furthermore, it seems that God can be accused of inconsistency here. Previously, when He is about to punish man, He states as the reason for His counsel (Gen. 6:5): "Because the imagination of the heart of man is evil." Here, when He is about to promise grace to man, namely, that hereafter He does not want to indulge in such wrath, He gives the same reason. Hence these statements appear silly to an intelligent human being and in no wise compatible with divine wisdom.

I myself prefer to steer clear of lofty matters and to leave them to idle spirits. It is sufficient for me that these statements are made to suit our frame of mind, namely, that God is indicating that He is now appeased and is no longer angry. Parents, too, are in the habit of acting in the same way: after whipping their disobedient children as they deserve they finally win them over again, as it were, with caresses. This inconsistency not only does not deserve to be censured, but it ought to be praised. It benefits the children, lest, because they fear the rod, they also begin to hate their parents. This solution is sufficient for me, for it is conducive to faith. Others can contribute other explanations.

Careful note must be taken of this passage, since it clearly shows that the nature of man is corrupt. This knowledge of our corrupt nature is necessary above all else; without it the mercy and grace of God cannot be properly understood.

Accordingly, the sophists deserve our hate,[34] and we ought to indict the translator who gave rise to this error with his interpretation that the thinking of the human heart is not evil but is "inclined to evil." [35] This gives the sophists an opportunity to distort and get around the passages in which Paul declares that all are children of wrath (Eph. 2:3), that all commit sin (Rom. 5:12), and are under sin (Rom. 3:9). On the basis of this passage they argue as follows: "Moses does not say that our nature is evil, but that it is inclined to evil. This tendency or inclination is under the control of the free will, and it does not impel man to evil"; or, to use their own words, it does not put man under compulsion.[36]

Then they look for a reason for this opinion and declare that even after the Fall man has a good will and a sound reason, inasmuch as the natural endowments have remained unimpaired, not only in man but also in the devil.[37] Finally, they pervert Aristotle's axiom that reason is disposed toward what is best, and give it this meaning.[38]

Moreover, the seeds of these opinions are also to be found in the writings of the fathers. On the basis of Ps. 4:6, which speaks about the lifting of the light of the countenance of God over us, they differentiate between an upper part of reason, which speculates about God, and a lower one, which busies itself with outward and civil affairs.[39] Augustine, too, favors this distinction, as we stated previously when we discussed the fall of man.[40]

But if a trace of the knowledge of God had remained unimpaired

[34] By "sophists" Luther means the scholastics, whom he accuses of mitigating the gravity of original sin.

[35] The Latin version has *sensus et cogitatio humani cordis in malum prona ab adolescentia sua.*

[36] Luther makes use of the technical term from scholastic theology: *non necessitat.*

[37] Luther is discussing the Augustinian and scholastic distinction between *pura naturalia* and *donum superadditum.* When Adam was created, the added gift of grace was superimposed upon his natural endowments; his fall cost him the superadded gift, but he retained his natural endowments unimpaired. These were not enough to save him, since grace had to be restored for that; but they did make him good in his essence.

[38] Cf. p. 42, note 54.

[39] Not only Ps. 4:6 but Gen. 1:27 provided the exegetical support for this distinction; the parallelism of "image" and "similitude" in the latter passage was applied to the two parts of man.

[40] Cf. *Luther's Works,* 1, p. 184.

in man, we would be far different from what we are now. Therefore the sophists are immeasurably blind when they quibble about the clear statements of Paul in this manner. If they correctly appraised this passage as it stands in the Latin Bible and approach it with a godly mind, they would surely cease giving their support to such a wicked cause. He who says that the sensations and thoughts of the human heart are inclined toward evil from youth on is not making an insignificant statement, particularly since Moses declared previously, in chapter six (v. 5), that every thought of the heart is bent on evil at all times, that is, that it strives after evil and in its bent, impulse, and effort is under the influence of evil. For instance, when the adulterer is inflamed with desire, even though opportunity, place, person, and time are lacking, he is still plagued by lustful emotions and cannot concentrate on anything else in his thoughts. Such a nature, says Moses, is at all times directed toward evil. Hence, inasmuch as man is always bent on evil, the natural endowments are not unimpaired, are they?

If the sophists were as friendly toward the sacred teaching handed down through the apostolic and prophetic writings as they are to their own teachers, who maintain the free will and the merit of works, they surely would not have permitted something so slight as one little word to lead them from the truth. They would not maintain, contrary to Scripture, that the natural endowments are unimpaired and that man, according to his nature, is not under wrath and not under condemnation. Yet they themselves, too, seem to have been aware of this folly. Although they assumed that man's natural endowments remained unimpaired, they nevertheless declared that the grace which renders man acceptable is indispensable; that is, they taught that God is not satisfied with this natural goodness of man unless it is formed by love.[41]

But what need is there to argue at great length against the nonsense of these people, since we know from the true meaning of the Hebrew that the text does not state that the sensations and thoughts of the human heart are "inclined toward evil," but that the imagination of the human heart is evil from its youth?

As I have stated previously several times,[42] the "imagination"

[41] Scholastic theology identified saving grace (cf. note 37 above) as *gratia gratum faciens*, but it spoke also of *gratia (or fides) caritate formata*.

[42] See pp. 5—6.

denotes reason itself, together with the will and the intellect, even when it is engaged in thoughts about God and is occupied with the most honorable tasks, whether political or civil. For it is always opposed to God's Law; it lies in sin; it is under the wrath of God; and it cannot be freed of this evil by its own powers, as Christ says (John 8:36): "So if the Son makes you free, you will be free indeed."

Therefore if you want to give a true definition of man,[43] take your definition from this passage, namely, that he is a rational animal which has a heart that imagines. But what does it imagine? Moses answers: "Evil," namely, against God or God's Law, and against men. Holy Scripture ascribes to man a reason that is not idle but is always imagining something. But it calls this imagination evil, ungodly, and execrable. The philosophers, on the other hand, call it good, and the sophists call it "unimpaired natural endowments."

Hence one must take careful note of this text and stress it over against those quibblers, the sophists, because Moses declares that the imagination of the human heart is evil. For if it is evil, it clearly follows that the natural endowments are not unimpaired but corrupt. God did not create man evil; He created him perfect, rational, holy, with a knowledge of God, with sound reason, and with good will toward God.

Now inasmuch as there are clear proofs that man is evil and estranged from God, who is so foolish as to dare maintain that the natural endowments in man have remained unimpaired? This is the same as saying that the nature of man is still unimpaired and good, although we learn and experience by many examples that it is exceedingly depraved.

From this perverse opinion have originated many dangerous assertions, even some that are clearly false and ungodly, as, for instance, when they maintain: "When a man does that of which he is capable, God gives grace without fail." [44] With this trumpet signal, as it were, they have urged men on to prayers, fastings, bodily tortures, pilgrimages, and the like. Thus the world was convinced that if men did as much as they were able to do by nature, they were earning grace, if not by the merit of condignity, then by the merit of congruity.[45] The merit of congruity they have traced back to the idea

---

[43] Cf. *Luther's Works*, 12, pp. 310—311.

[44] Luther cites this principle often as an illustration of the scholastic doctrine of merit and grace.

[45] Cf. *Luther's Works*, 21, pp. 288—289.

that a work was not contrary to the Law of God but in accordance with the Law of God; for to an evil work punishment is due, not merit. The merit of condignity they ascribe not to the work itself but to the character of the work, if it was performed in a state of grace.

Of the same sort is the statement of Scotus [46] that as a result of his natural endowments man is able to love God above all things, for the basis of this statement is the claim that the natural endowments are unimpaired. He reasons thus: A man loves a girl, who is a creature. But he loves her so desperately that he risks himself and his life for her. A merchant loves riches, and indeed so passionately that he undergoes a thousand perils provided he can make some profit. Therefore if there is such love for creatures, who rank far beneath God, how much more will man love God, who is the highest good? Hence God can be loved on the basis of the natural endowments alone.

This is a fine conclusion, one worthy of a Franciscan monk! It shows that such a great theologian does not know what it means to love God. Our nature is so corrupt that it no longer knows God unless it is enlightened by the Word and the Spirit of God. How, then, can it love God without the Holy Spirit? It is true that there is no desire for anything that is unknown. Hence our nature cannot love God, whom it does not know; but it loves an idol and the dream of its heart. Furthermore, it is so completely bound up in its love for the creatures that even after it has learned to know God from the Word, it still disregards Him and despises His Word, as the examples of our own people show.

Foolish and blasphemous statements of this kind are a sure proof that scholastic theology has clearly degenerated into a kind of philosophy that has no true knowledge of God. But because it does not know the Word, it also does not know God and is in darkness. Aristotle and Cicero, who are the most eminent men in this class, teach many things about the virtues and bestow superb praise on them because of their civil purpose; for they see that they are beneficial both in public and in private life. Concerning God, however, they teach nothing. They do not teach that His will and command are to be considered in preference to either public or private advantage; for men who do not have the Word lack the

[46] Cf. p. 121, note 37.

knowledge of this will of God. Assuredly, the scholastic theologians have likewise been captivated by philosophical fancies and have failed to preserve the true knowledge either of God or of themselves. For this reason they have fallen into such fearful errors.

And indeed the fall is easy after one has departed from the Word, for the luster of civil virtues captivates the minds in a marvelous manner. Erasmus makes Socrates all but a perfect Christian, and Augustine bestows excessive praise on Marcus Attilius Regulus for keeping faith with the enemy.[47] Of all virtues truth is the most beautiful; and in his case the highest commendation is added because he combined this virtue with love toward his fatherland, which itself is an outstanding and most praiseworthy virtue.

But you may find many illustrious men who do not receive this praise for truth. Themistocles, for instance, surely did not receive it, even though he was a valiant man and useful to his fatherland. Accordingly, Augustine admires Attilius; for he observes a reason and will that is sound in the highest degree, that is, to the degree that one can expect it in human nature. What vice is there, or what evil, in this? Surely the work cannot be censured.

In the first place, Regulus lacks the knowledge of God. Although he does what is right, nevertheless consider whether a theologian could not criticize the final cause;[48] for with this zeal to help his fatherland there is combined a desire for glory. He scorns life in order thereby to gain immortal fame among later generations. If one considers the "phantom" of life and the outward mask, his was a most noble deed; but before God it is rank idolatry, for Regulus appropriates to himself the glory for this deed. And who has any doubt that other vices were connected with this eagerness for glory?

Hence Attilius is incapable of displaying this supreme virtue of truth and zeal for his fatherland without a mad and insane craving for evil, for it is evil that he wrests the glory from God and appropriates it to himself. Reason is unable to recognize this despoiling of the Godhead.

Therefore the virtues of the heathen must be distinguished from the virtues of Christians. It is true that the hearts of both are prompted by God. But among the heathen the zeal and ambition

[47] Augustine, *The City of God,* Book I, ch. 15.

[48] From the rest of the paragraph it is evident that Luther is using the word *finis* in the sense of "final cause."

for glory eventually corrupt these divine impulses in great men. Therefore if an orator should undertake to elaborate on the efficient cause but should disregard this final, depraved cause, who does not see that once the two chief causes, the formal and the final, are disregarded, this wretched shadow of virtue can be embellished by an eloquent man?[49]

But a dialectician will readily perceive the deception; for he is aware that the formal cause, that is, right reason, is lacking, inasmuch as there is no knowledge of God and no right will toward God. Moreover, he is aware that the final cause is corrupt; for the true goal, obedience toward God and love of one's neighbor, receives no consideration. What sort of virtue is it where nearly all the causes are missing except the natural one, which is only something passive, that is, a drive or impulse by which the heart is moved to keep faith with an enemy? Even the ungodly have these drives, as I have said. Therefore if they are followed in behalf of the fatherland, they become virtues; if against the fatherland, they become vices, as Aristotle learnedly argues.[50]

I am making these statements in order that students of the Sacred Scriptures may take note of this passage, which declares explicitly that nature is corrupt. For those semblances of virtues which occur among the heathen seem to prove the opposite, namely, that something has been left unimpaired in nature. Therefore these distinctions require careful judgment.

Moses adds "from his youth" because this evil lies hidden in early age and is dormant, as it were. The period of our infancy is spent in such a manner that reason and will seem dormant, and we are borne along by animal drives only, which pass away like a dream. We have hardly passed our fifth year when we look for idleness, play, wantonness, and pleasures, but shun discipline, shake off obedience, and hate all virtues, but especially the higher ones of truth and justice. Reason at that time awakes as from a deep sleep and becomes aware of some pleasures, but not yet the true ones, and of some evil things, but not yet the worst, by which it is possessed.

---

[49] Although the efficient cause is virtuous, its virtue is corrupted by the desire for glory; thus the formal cause and the final cause are wrong, and Luther is saying that these are decisive.

[50] See, for one example, Aristotle, *Politics*, Book III, ch. 5.

But when reason has matured, then, after the other vices have somehow become established, there are added lust and the hideous passion of the flesh, revelry, gambling, quarreling, fighting, murder, theft, and what not. Just as parents have need of the rod, so now the magistrate needs a prison and bonds to keep the evil nature under control.

Who is not aware of the vices of the more advanced years? It is then that greed, ambition, pride, treachery, envy, etc., come rushing and crowding in. Moreover, these vices are all the more harmful since this age is more adroit at covering them up and adorning them. Here the sword of the magistrate is not adequate; the fire of hell is needed to punish such great and numerous crimes. Hence it is correctly stated above, in the sixth chapter (v. 5): "The heart of man, or the imagination of his heart, is only evil every day, or at all times," and in this passage: "It is evil from its youth."

Even though the Latin translation employs a milder word,[51] he who says that the human heart is inclined toward evil states the case adequately. The comic poet similarly states: "It is man's nature to incline away from exertion toward sensuality." [52]

Those who want to misuse this word for the purpose of belittling original sin are convicted by the experience of all mankind, especially by that of the heathen or the ungodly. If spiritual human beings who have divine help from heaven can hardly stand firm against disgraceful acts and be controlled by discipline, what could a human being do without this help? If the divine aid contends and struggles against the captivity of the law of sin (Rom. 7:22), what folly it is to dream that the natural endowments are unimpaired without this divine help!

Reason per se, therefore, does not prescribe what is right; nor does the will per se desire what is right, as blind philosophy argues, which does not know the origin of these fearful impulses to sin in children, the young, and the aged. Hence it excuses them and calls them merely emotions or passions, but does not call them the wickedness of nature.

Furthermore, in the instance of great men, who hold these impulses in check and keep them under control, it calls them virtues. In the instance of others, who give free reign to their desires, it calls

[51] See p. 121, note 35.
[52] Terence, *Andria*, I, 1, 51.

them vices. This, however, amounts to virtual ignorance that human nature is evil. Holy Scripture agrees with experience and declares that the heart of man is evil from youth. Experience, too, teaches that even the saints remain steadfast only with difficulty and are often involved even in flagrant sins when they are overcome by the wickedness of nature.

The word נְעָרִים denotes the age when a man begins to make use of reason. This takes places at about the sixth year. Similarly, נְעָרִים is the term for youths and boys subject to the ministrations of parents and teachers, up to the age of manhood. But it is not without benefit for us individually to look back upon that age and reflect how willingly we obeyed the commands of our parents and teachers, how diligent we were to learn, and how uncomplaining whenever our parents took us to task for our mischievousness. To whom would it not have been much more agreeable to go for a walk, play games, and chat than to attend church when our parents commanded it?

Even though these inclinations can be corrected or restrained to some extent by discipline, they cannot be removed from the heart entirely, as their traces prove after we have grown up. The crude little verse is true: "In his old age the angelic child behaves like Satan."[53] God indeed incites some men to natural drives that are good; but this happens beyond nature, as when Cyrus is incited to restore the worship of God and to preserve the church (Ezra 1:2). These actions do not belong to human nature; for where God is with His Spirit, there is no longer the imagination of the human heart but the imagination of God. There God dwells through the Word and the Spirit of God. Of such things Moses is not speaking in this passage; he is speaking solely of men who lack the Holy Spirit. These are evil even when they are at their best.

Neither will I ever again destroy every living creature as I have done.

Moses is speaking of a universal smiting, such as was brought about by the Flood. But from this it does not follow that He will discontinue any particular smiting and will disregard the sins of all. The Last Day, too, will be an exception. Then not only every living thing will be smitten, but all creation will be annihilated by fire.

[53] Luther is referring to the German saying, *Junge Engel, alte Teufel.*

22. While the earth remains, seedtime and harvest, cold and heat, summer and winter, day and night, shall not cease.

On the basis of this passage the Jews divide the year into six parts; they assign two months to each part, as Lyra also remarks in connection with this passage.[54] But to me Moses seems simply to be speaking of a promise that a universal flood is no longer to be feared. For at the time of the Flood the disorder was such that there was no season for sowing and harvesting; and because of the great darkness resulting from the rains and the clouds day could not readily be distinguished from night. When dark clouds are floating in the sky, we see darkness being brought on for the earth. Yet how much greater it was when the water on the earth, set like a mirror beneath the clouds, reflected the darkness of the clouds into the faces and eyes of those who looked at it!

Hence the simple meaning is that in this passage God promises Noah that the earth will be restored; that it will be possible again to sow the fields; that the destruction which the Flood had brought about will come to an end; that the seasons will occur with customary regularity; and that in due order harvest will follow sowing, winter will follow summer, cold will follow heat.

Careful note must be taken of this passage over against the commonly held ideas about the signs that will precede the Last Day.[55] People imagine that at that time there will be who knows how many eclipses, and they fabricate the tale that no woman will give birth for an entire period of seven years, and so forth. But this text states that night, day, summer, and winter will not cease. These natural changes will, therefore, continue, and no eclipse will ever deprive the eyes of men of an entire day.

The statement of the text, "while the earth remains," is not without purpose; for it implies that at some time the days of the earth will come to an end and other days — of heaven — will follow. As long as the days of the earth endure, the earth will endure, and the changes of the seasons will endure. But when these days of the earth come to an end, everything will come to an end, and there will follow days of heaven, that is, eternal days, which will be Sabbath after Sabbath, when we shall not be engaged in physical

[54] Lyra on Gen. 8:22, sec. k.

[55] Here Luther is reflecting the notions characteristic of folk apocalyptic at the end of the Middle Ages.

labors for our subsistence; for we shall be like the angels of God (Mark 12:25). Our life will be to know God, to delight in the wisdom of God, and to enjoy the presence of God. We attain this life through faith in Christ. May the eternal Father, through the merit of His Son and our Deliverer, Jesus Christ, mercifully preserve us in it through the guidance and direction of the Holy Spirit. Amen. Amen.

CHAPTER NINE

1. *And God blessed Noah and his sons, and said to them: Be fruitful and multiply, and fill the earth.*

THESE words were a truly necessary comfort after the entire human race had perished by the Flood and only eight souls were saved. Noah realized that God is indeed favorably inclined toward him; for He is not satisfied with that first blessing with which He blessed the human race at the creation of the world, but He adds this new one in order that Noah may have no doubt whatever concerning the future increase of his progeny. This promise was all the more welcome because God had previously given the express promise that He would never again rage against the human race with so severe a punishment.

For one thing, this chapter confirms marriage; for through His Word and command God joins the male with the female, and that for the definite purpose of filling the earth with human beings. Because before the Flood God had been provoked to wrath by the sin of lust, it was necessary, on account of this awful expression of wrath, to show now that God does not hate or condemn the lawful union of a man and a woman but wants the human race to be propagated by it.

This was a sure proof for Noah that God actually loves man, is well disposed toward him, and has now put away all wrath. He wants human beings to be propagated through the union of a man and a woman. He could have brought them into being from stones, as in the poet's fable about Deucalion,[1] if He had not approved of this lawful union. This passage, therefore, deals with the honorableness of marriage, which is the source of both the family and the state, and the nursery of the church.

At this point it is objected that this promise was pointless, because

[1] The myth of Deucalion, Pyrrha, and the Deluge was probably known to Luther in the version of Ovid, *Metamorphoses*, Book I, ll. 244—415; cf. p. 95, note 17.

Noah had already reached an age that was no longer suited for procreation; and indeed Scripture makes no mention of his having begotten any children later on. My answer is that this promise was made, not to Noah alone but also to his sons, likewise to the entire human race, and that the hope for descendants has reference to grandfather Noah as well.

This passage, moreover, leads us to believe that children are a gift of God and come solely through the blessing of God, just as Ps. 127:3 shows. The heathen, who have not been instructed by the Word of God, believe that the propagation of the human race happens partly by nature, partly by accident, especially since those who are regarded as most suited for procreation often fail to have children. Therefore the heathen do not thank God for this gift, nor do they receive their children as the gift of God.

2. *The fear of you and dread of you shall be upon every beast of the earth, and upon every bird of the air, upon everything that creeps on the ground and all the fish of the sea; into your hand they are delivered.*

Here the dominion of man appears to be increased for the purpose of consoling him even more. Even though all the animals were put under the rule of man after the creatures had been called into being, we do not read that the beasts feared and shunned man to the same degree as Moses asserts in this passage. The reason is that until now the animals did not have to die in order to provide food for man, but man was a gentle master of the beasts rather than their slayer or consumer.

But here the animals are subjected to man as to a tyrant who has absolute power over life and death. Because a more oppressive form of bondage has now been imposed on them and a more extensive and oppressive dominion has been assigned to man, the animals are dominated by fear and dread of man. Thus we observe that even tame animals do not readily permit themselves to be handled. They feel the authority of man to be oppressive and naturally are influenced by their danger. This, I think was not the case before the Lord made this statement. Up to that time man had used animals solely for the tasks for which they were suited and for sacrifices, but not for food and nourishment.

By this increase of man's authority over that which the patriarchs had had, God gives a special indication that He is favorably inclined and friendly toward man.

This blessing, which gives this authority over the beasts to man, must not be taken lightly. It is an extraordinary gift, of which the heathen, who are without the Word, have no knowledge. And we enjoy the benefit of this gift most. When these words were addressed to Noah and this privilege was granted to him, there was no need for it. A small number of human beings occupied the entire earth; so there was a superabundance of the fruits of the earth, and it was unnecessary to add the flesh of the beasts. But today we could not live on the fruits of the earth alone if this great gift had not been added, which permits us to eat the flesh of beasts, birds, and fish.

These words, therefore, establish the butcher shop; attach hares, chickens, and geese to the spit; and fill the tables with all sorts of foods. Necessity also keeps men busy. Not only do they hunt forest animals, but at home they give particular care to tending and fattening cattle for food.

In this passage God sets Himself up as a butcher; for with His Word He slaughters and kills the animals that are suited for food, in order to make up, as it were, for the great sorrow that pious Noah experienced during the Flood. For this reason God thinks Noah ought to be provided for more sumptuously now.

We must not assume that these things happen by chance, as do the heathen, who are of the opinion that the custom of butchering animals always existed. These things are established, or rather permitted, by the Word of God. An animal could not have been slain without sin unless God by His Word had clearly given permission to do so. It is a great liberty that with impunity man may kill and eat animals of every edible kind. If only one kind of animal had been designated for this purpose, it would still be a great blessing. How much greater a blessing it must be considered that all animals fit for food are permitted!

The ungodly and the heathen are not aware of all this, and the philosophers have no knowledge of it either; for they assume that this custom has always existed. But we ought to lay emphasis on it in order to make our consciences relaxed and free about using the things created by God and permitted to us for use; for in this matter there is no law to forbid our eating them, and consequently there can be no sin in their use. Yet the villainous popes have wickedly imposed burdens on the church in this matter too.[2]

Accordingly, in this passage the dominion of man is increased, and the dumb animals are made subject to man for the purpose of serving him even to the extent of dying. They fear and shun man because of this regulation, which was new and hitherto had not been observed in the world. For Adam it would have been an abomination to kill a little bird for food; but now, because the Word is added, we realize that it is an extraordinary blessing that in this way God has provided the kitchen with all kinds of meat. Later on, when He shows man how to cultivate the vine, He will also concern Himself with stocking the cellar.

These are reliable and excellent proofs that God no longer hates man but is kindly disposed toward him. Accordingly, this historical account gives examples of both facts: just as God's wrath is unbearable when He has begun to be incensed, so His compassion is boundless and without measure after it begins to shine again. Therefore His compassion is more abundant because it is a part of God's nature, since wrath is truly God's alien work,[3] in which He engages contrary to His nature, because He is forced into it by the wickedness of man.

3. *Every moving thing that lives shall be food for you; and as I gave you the green plants, I give you everything.*

Here a question arises. Previously (Gen. 7:2) Moses pointed out the difference between the clean and the unclean animals, but here he speaks without any distinction and in general of all the animals. Did God grant man the use also of the unclean animals as food? His statement is general: "Everything that creeps upon the earth."

There are indeed some who think that at the time of Noah human beings made use of all animals without distinction, both the clean and the unclean, for food. But to me the opposite seems true. Because a difference was made earlier between the clean and the unclean and this is later carefully maintained in the Law, I believe that so far as food is concerned, man made use of only the clean animals, that is, of those that were offered at the sacrifices.

[2] A reference to the rules of fasting and of abstinence.

[3] From Is. 28:21 Luther derived the idea of the *opus alienum* of God: His proper work was to comfort, but His alien work was to terrify. Cf., for example, *Luther's Works*, 14, p. 335.

Hence the general statement must be understood with a stipulation: "Every moving thing that lives [namely, among the clean] shall be food for you." Our nature loathes serpents, wolves, ravens, mice, and dormice, although somewhere you may find some nations who relish the flesh even of these. The terror and fear of man is on all the animals of the earth because man is permitted to kill them, but this does not mean that man eats all the animals. It is likely that Noah made use of the clean only, which he knew were the only ones that could be sacrificed to the Lord.

But here something else turns up that troubles the mind even more. How can it be that the terror and fear of man is on all the animals when wolves, lions, bears, boars, and tigers devour human beings and for this reason are a terror to man, as is the entire class of the serpents, from which we all flee the moment we see them? What shall we say about this? The Word of the Lord is not untruthful, is it?

My answer is: Even though we flee from and dread such animals because we are warned by our danger, it is still true that the fear of man rests on them. Even the wildest animals become filled with fear and flee at the first sight of a human being; but if they are infuriated, they finally overwhelm him with their physical strength.

Why, then, you say, are they filled with fear when they are stronger? My answer is that they know that the human being is endowed with reason, which has the advantage over all the animals. Man's diligence tames even elephants, lions, and tigers. What man cannot do with his strength he accomplishes with his skill and the power of his reason. Otherwise how would it be possible for a ten-year-old boy to manage entire herds of cattle and to drive a horse, an animal of extraordinary spirit and strength, in whatever direction he wishes, now urging it on to a run, now forcing it to go at a slower pace? All this is achieved by human diligence, not by strength. Thus there are clear indications that the fear of man continues in the animals, although they harm people when they are infuriated. For this reason they are also feared by man.

Besides, I have no doubt that at the time of Noah and of the fathers close to him in time this terror in the animals was greater, since righteousness flourished and there was less sin. When saintliness of life declined and sin increased, this blessing also began to wane, and wild animals began to be a punishment for sin, as Moses threatens in Deuteronomy (32:24) that God will send the teeth of beasts against Israel. How frightful was the plague of the fiery serpents in the desert (Num. 21:6)! Bears tore to pieces the children who mocked the prophet (2 Kings 2:24). Why did the terror of man not remain in the beasts in this instance? Why did they rage against people? Was not sin the reason?

Hence, as we have stated previously, when new sins increase, new punishments also increase. Within our own time unusual kinds of diseases and disasters have become widespread, such as the English sweat, the locusts that laid waste the fields over wide areas throughout Poland and Silesia in the year 1542, and so forth.[4]

Thus the Lord has promised seasons of seedtime and of harvest, of heat and of cold; and yet this does not mean that He closes His eyes to our sins and that the seasons, both of seedtime and of harvest, are not occasionally unsettled by unseasonable weather. There was a vast drought in the year 1540, and during the following two years there was almost continuous rainfall.[5] Since the present age is the worst age, is it any wonder that the blessing is taken away from us and a curse takes its place, with the result that the animals, on which there would be a terror *of* us if we were good, are now a terror *to* us and harm us?

The land of the Sodomites was a sort of Paradise, but because of their sin it became a lake of pitch. People who have seen that region report that the most beautiful apples grow there; but when they are sliced, the inside is full of ashes, as it were, and emits a most disgusting odor.[6] The reason for this is that the Sodomites did not recognize the gifts of God when He blessed them but willfully misused those gifts. Furthermore, they blasphemed God; and, puffed up by their advantages, they persecuted His saints. As a result, the blessing was taken from them, and a curse was put on everything.

The true solution of this question is this: Although there are signs

---

[4] Luther is referring to the sweating sickness that spread through England several times in the sixteenth century, and from there to the Continent. The reference to the locusts of 1542 is evidently an editorial interpolation. Cf. Introduction.

[5] Since it is evident that Luther was lecturing on this ninth chapter earlier (cf. Introduction), these references must likewise be regarded as insertions by a later hand.

[6] On "the apple of Sodom," cf. J. Penrose Harland, "Sodom and Gomorrah II. The Destruction of the Cities of the Plain," *The Biblical Archaeologist*, VI (1943), 49—52.

of terror in the wild animals, it is nevertheless we who fear them and whom they harm.

I have no doubt that once upon a time the worst of men lived in this region of ours. For whence come the dryness of the earth and the barren sands? The names also indicate that at some time Jews inhabited this region.[7] Where wicked men dwell, there the land is gradually ruined because of the curse of God.

At Bruges in Flanders there was a very famous harbor; but ever since they held King Maximilian captive, the sea has receded, and there has ceased to be a harbor.[8] About Venice they report the same thing today.[9] Nor is this a great wonder after the defense of idolatry and the persecution of the Gospel were added to the countless sins that are characteristic of powerful states.

4. *Only you shall not eat flesh with its life, that is, its blood.*

The things we have heard so far have been matters pertaining to the household; now the Lord adds a commandment that concerns the state. Because it was no more a sin to kill an ox or a sheep for food than it is a sin to pick a flower or a herb growing in a field, there was a danger that men would abuse this liberty, which the Lord had granted them over against the animals, and would proceed to shed the blood of other human beings as well. Therefore He now gives a new law about not shedding human blood, and He also restricts their liberty to eat flesh. He does not want them to eat any meat unless it has first been cleansed of its blood.

In the Hebrew the text is extremely obscure, and it is for this reason that the opinions of the interpreters differ. It is superfluous to relate all of them here. I steadfastly follow this rule: the words ought to serve the subject matter and not, conversely, the subject matter the words.[10] Therefore I do not care for the opinions of those

---

[7] In his treatise *On the Abuse of the Mass* (1521) Luther had spoken about the Hebrew origin of many place names in Germany (even of Wittenberg!) as proof that God had let His Word arise even in this out-of-the-way place (W, VIII, 562). But Luther makes it clear that he is joking when he suggests this.

[8] The Flemish city of Bruges had lost its access to the sea by about 1490, when the silting-up of the Zwyn was complete.

[9] The decline of Venice at the end of the fifteenth century had been brought on by diverse factors — the new trade routes, the wars with the Turk, the alliance of pope and emperor against the city (1508—10).

[10] See p. 15, note 23.

who interpret the words in accordance with their own notions and want them to serve ideas that they themselves bring to the text.

In the first place let us, therefore, take a look at the language. נֶפֶשׁ properly denotes an animated body or a living animal, such as the ox, the sheep, man, etc. It does not denote the body alone, but the living body, as when Christ says (John 10:15): "I lay down My soul for My sheep." Here "soul" means nothing else than physical life.

But בָּשָׂר denotes flesh, which is part of a denser element and yet is given breath and has a pulse, not from the body but from the soul. The flesh or the body per se and without a soul is no different from a block of wood or a stone; but when it is provided with breath by the soul, then the fluids and everything else in the animal are set in motion.

Now in this passage the Lord forbids the eating of a body that still has in it a functioning, active, and living soul, the way a hawk devours chicks and a wolf sheep that have not been killed first but are alive. This cruel procedure the Lord forbids in this passage, and He restricts the permission to kill. It may not be carried out in the inhuman fashion whereby living bodies or parts of living bodies are consumed; but a lawful manner of killing is to be followed, such as took place at the altar and at the sacrifices, where the animal was killed without any cruelty and ultimately was offered to God after its blood had been carefully washed off.

This I believe to be the simple and true meaning, which also some Jewish teachers espouse, namely, that we must not eat pieces of raw flesh and limbs that are still quivering, as was the practice of the Laestrygones or of the Cyclopes.[11]

5. *For your lifeblood I will surely require a reckoning; of every beast I will require it and of man; of every man's brother I will require the life of man.*

In this passage the Hebrew text is even more obscure than in the preceding one. Lyra, following an opinion of the rabbis, assumes four kinds of murder here; for he divides this statement into two parts and explains each in a twofold manner.[12]

The first part he applies to those who commit suicide. If this

[11] Lyra on Gen. 9:4, sec. e.
[12] Lyra on Gen. 9:5, secs. g and h.

opinion is correct, there is an assertion of immortality in this passage; for how could God punish him who is nothing, since he is already dead? Hence the punishment of sins after this life is meant in this passage. But it seems to me that grammar is opposed to this meaning. Even though I do not presume to have a perfect knowledge of the Hebrew language,[13] I am nevertheless fully convinced that the words do not convey this meaning.

He makes the practice of casting human beings before wild beasts, as used to be done in former times in the theaters, a second kind of murder. Truly, an uncivilized spectacle and one that violates every humane feeling!

The third variety involves hiring a murderer.

The fourth is when relatives are slain, etc.

This division would not be altogether unattractive if it could be supported on the basis of the text. But it is a Jewish invention, resulting from their hatred of the Roman laws.

The meaning is simpler if one understands this passage as a prohibition of murder in general, in accordance with the Fifth Commandment, which says (Ex. 20:13): "You shall not kill." God wants not even an animal killed except in a scrupulous manner, that is, either for sacrifice or for human consumption. Much less does He want a human being killed except by divine authority, just as logically follows.

In the first place, therefore, wanton and irreverent killing or slaughter is forbidden. For it is a matter of good order not to kill animals without a purpose and not to consume their raw flesh. Thereafter God forbids the human being to kill another human being in any manner whatever. For if God will require the blood from an animal that kills a human being, with how much greater severity He will require it from the hand of a human being! Therefore this passage has reference to the Fifth Commandment, that no one should shed the blood of a human being.

6. *Whosoever sheds the blood of man, by man shall his blood be shed.*

In this passage we must find fault with the carelessness of the translator, who has omitted the altogether necessary phrase בָּאָדָם, "by man."[14] For this indicates the difference between the time before

---

[13] See p. 34, note 43.

[14] The Latin translation has merely "*Quicunque effuderit humanum sanguinem, fundetur sanguis illius.*"

the Flood and that after the Flood. Cain had killed his brother Abel, but at that time God held human blood in such high esteem that He threatened sevenfold punishment for anyone who would kill Cain (Gen. 4:15). He did not want the murderer killed even through a public trial. Therefore even though Adam severely punished his son's sin with excommunication,[15] he did not dare impose the death penalty upon him.

In this passage, however, the Lord establishes a new law and wants murderers to be killed by men. This was something that had not been customary in the world until now, for God had reserved all judgment for Himself. It was for this reason that He Himself finally exacted punishment from the wicked world by means of the Flood when He saw that the world was daily becoming more and more corrupt. Here, however, God shares His power with man and grants him power over life and death among men, provided that the person is guilty of shedding blood. Whoever does not have the right to kill human beings and yet kills a human being, him God makes liable not only to His own judgment but also to the human sword. Therefore if such a person is killed, even though he is killed by the human sword, he is nevertheless correctly said to have been killed by God. If it were not for this command of God, it would be just as unlawful to kill a murderer now as it was before the Flood.

Here we have the source from which stem all civil law and the law of nations. If God grants to man power over life and death, surely He also grants power over what is less, such as property, the home, wife, children, servants, and fields. All these God wants to be subject to the power of certain human beings, in order that they may punish the guilty.

In this connection the following difference must be maintained between the authority of God and that of human beings: even if the world should be unable to bring a charge against us and we should be guiltless before the world, God still has the power to kill us. For sin, with which we were born, makes us all guilty before God. But human beings have the power to kill only when we are guilty before the world and when the crime has been established. For this reason courts have been established and a definite method of procedure has been prescribed. Thus a crime may be investigated and proved before the death sentence is imposed.

[15] Cf. *Luther's Works*, 1, pp. 291 ff.

Therefore we must take careful note of this passage, in which God establishes government, to render judgment not only about matters involving life but also about matters less important than life. Thus a government should punish the disobedience of children, theft, adultery, and perjury. In short, it should punish all sins forbidden in the Second Table. For He who allows judgment in matters involving life also permits judgment in less important matters.

This text is outstanding and worthy of note; for here God establishes government and gives it the sword, to hold wantonness in check, lest violence and other sins proceed without limit. If God had not conferred this divine power on men, what sort of life do you suppose we would be living? Because He foresaw that there would always be a great abundance of evil men, He established this outward remedy, which the world had not had thus far, in order that wantonness might not increase beyond measure. With this hedge, these walls, God has given protection for our life and possessions.

Hence this, too, is a proof of the supreme love of God toward man, no less than is His promise that the Flood would no longer rage and His permission to use meat for sustenance.

For God made man in His own image.

This is the outstanding reason why He does not want a human being killed on the strength of individual discretion: man is the noblest creature, not created like the rest of the animals but according to God's image. Even though man has lost this image through sin, as we stated above,[16] his condition is nevertheless such that it can be restored through the Word and the Holy Spirit. God wants us to show respect for this image in one another; He does not want us to shed blood in a tyrannical manner.

But the life of one who does not want to show respect for the image of God in man but wants to yield to his anger and grief — his worst advisers, as someone has said [17] — this life God turns over to the government, in order that his blood, too, may be shed.

Thus this passage establishes civil government in the world, something that did not exist before the Flood, as the examples of Cain and Lamech show. They were not put to death, even though the

---

[16] Cf. *Luther's Works,* 1, pp. 62—65.

[17] Apparently a paraphrase of the Latin proverb, *Ira atque cupido* [Luther has *dolor*] *pessimi consultores.*

holy fathers were the arbiters or judges of public deeds. But in the passage before us those who have the sword are commanded to use it against those who have shed blood.

This passage, therefore, solves the problem that engaged the attention of Plato and all the sages.[18] They come to the conclusion that it is impossible to carry on government without injustice. Their reason for this is that among themselves human beings are of the same rank and station. Why does the emperor rule the world? Why do others obey him, when he is a human being just like the others, no better, no braver, and no more permanent? He is subject to all human circumstances, just as others are. Hence it seems to be despotism when he usurps the rule over men, even though he is like other men. For if he is like other men, it is the height of wrong and injustice for him not to want to be like others but to place himself at the head of others through despotism.

This is how reason argues. It is incapable of coming up with a counterargument. But we who have the Word are aware that the counterargument must be the command of God, who regulates and establishes affairs in this manner. Hence it is our duty to obey the divine regulation and to submit to it. Otherwise, in addition to the rest of our sins, we shall become guilty of disobeying God's will, which is, as we can see, so beneficial to this life of ours.

Accordingly, this passage gives permission to slaughter animals for religious and private purposes but utterly forbids the killing of human beings, because man was created according to the image of God. Those who do not obey this will He turns over to the government to be put to death.

7. *And you, be fruitful and multiply, bring forth abundantly on the earth and multiply in it.*

After God has permitted the killing of cattle, not only for sacrifices but also for food, and has forbidden homicide, there now follows the reason why He detests homicide so intensely: He wants the human race to multiply on the earth; but homicides lay waste the earth and bring on desolation, just as we observe in war. God did not create the earth without a purpose; He wanted it to be inhabited, as Isaiah says (45:18). For this reason He also makes it fruitful by means of rain and sunshine. Hence He hates those who remove

[18] See *Luther's Works*, 13, pp. 152 ff.

from the earth those who inhabit it. For His will is life, not death (Ps. 30:5).

These and similar statements of the prophets are derived from promises like this one, where God commands mankind to increase. For He is clearly shown to be more inclined toward making alive and showing kindness than toward wrath and killing. Else why would He forbid murder so sternly? Why would plagues be so infrequent? Within a decade hardly one plague or pestilence occurs; but every day human beings are born, animals increase, and fruits are produced without limit.

All this bears witness that God does not love death, but life, just as in the beginning He also created man, not that he should die but that he should live; "but through the devil's envy death entered the world" (Wisd. of Sol. 2:24). Yet even after sin the remnants of the blessing are preserved in such a manner that God's will toward us cannot be unclear, namely, that He loves life more than death. Moreover, it is beneficial to give much thought to these issues; for in this manner we shall truly derive joy from the Lord, as Solomon says (Prov. 18:22).

8. *Then God said to Noah and to his sons with him:*

9. *Behold, I establish My covenant with you and your descendants after you,*

10. *and with every living creature that is with you, the birds, the cattle, and every beast of the earth with you, as many as came out of the ark.*

11. *I establish My covenant with you, that never again shall all flesh be cut off by the waters of a flood, and never again shall there be a flood to destroy the earth.*

On several previous occasions we have stated the reason for such an abundance of words.[19] The Holy Spirit is prolix, but not without purpose. Therefore those who consider in what great trepidation, fear, sorrow, and danger Noah and his people have been will conclude that there was the utmost need for God to repeat and impress the same facts rather frequently.

Moreover, because the covenant of which this passage is speaking

[19] See p. 115.

involves not only mankind but every living soul, it must be understood, not of the promise of the Seed but of this physical life, which even the dumb animals enjoy in common with us: this God does not intend to destroy in the future by a flood.

12. *And God said: This is the sign of the covenant which I make between Me and you and every living creature that is with you, for all future generations:*

13. *I set My bow in the cloud, and it shall be a sign of the covenant between Me and the earth.*

14. *When I bring clouds over the earth and the bow is seen in the clouds,*

15. *I will remember My covenant which is between Me and you and every living creature of all flesh; and the waters shall never again become a flood to destroy all flesh.*

16. *When the bow is in the clouds, I will look upon it and remember the everlasting covenant between God and every living creature of all flesh that is upon the earth.*

Careful note must be taken of the phrase "for all future generations," for it includes not only the human beings of that time and the animals of that time but all their offspring until the end of the world.

Moreover, this passage also teaches us how God is wont always to link His promise with a sign, just as previously, in the third chapter, we called attention to the garments of skins with which He clothed the naked human beings as a sign that He wanted to protect, defend, and preserve them.[20]

The allegory proposed by some is not inappropriate, namely, that just as the skin of a dead sheep warms the body, so Christ, after He has died, warms us with His Spirit and on the Last Day will raise and revive us. Others suggest that the skins were added as a sign of mortality;[21] but of this there was hardly any need, since our entire life reminds us of our mortality. There was need for them

---

[20] This is discussed in *Luther's Works*, 1, pp. 221—222.

[21] For a collection of patristic citations on this cf. Gerhart B. Ladner, *The Idea of Reform. Its Impact on Christian Thought and Action in the Age of the Fathers* (Cambridge, Mass., 1959), p. 176, note 27.

to have a sign of life, from which they could learn God's blessing and good will. For this is the particular nature of signs, that they dispense comfort, not terror. To this end also the sign of the bow was established and added to the promise.

Just as God previously says to Himself that He repents of so horrible a punishment and promises that He will never again use such punishment, because the imagination of the human heart is evil from its youth (Gen. 8:21) — if, therefore He wanted to punish evil, there would be need daily of a new flood — so in this passage, by a word spoken to mankind either by an angel or, as is possible, by the mouth of Noah, He promises that in the future no flood will come over the earth.

When the same matter is repeated so many times, this is an indication of God's extraordinary affection for mankind. He is trying to persuade them not to fear such a punishment in the future but to hope for blessing and for the utmost forbearance.

Noah and his people were in great need of such comfort. A man who has been humbled by God is unable to forget his hurt and pain, for affliction makes a far deeper impression than an act of kindness. We observe the same reaction in children. Even though a caressing mother tries to calm them with rattles and other allurements after they have been chastened with the rod, the grief still persists in their heart to such a degree that they have to sigh frequently and sob bitterly. How much more difficult it is for a conscience that has experienced God's wrath and the terrors of death to let comfort come in! These experiences remain so firmly entrenched later on that a heart becomes fearful and terrified even in the face of kindnesses and comforting words.

It is for this reason that God shows Himself benevolent in such a variety of ways and takes such extraordinary delight in pouring forth compassion, like a mother who is caressing and petting her child in order that it may finally begin to forget its tears and smile at its mother.

This comfort is expressed in many eloquent words and emphasized in various ways, to meet the need of these wretched people who had been watching the immeasurable wrath of God rage for an entire year. Therefore they could not be talked out of their fear and terror by a word or two; a great abundance of words was needed to drive back their tears and to soften their grief. Even though they were saints, they were still flesh, just as we are.

We, too, need this comfort today, in order that despite a great variety of stormy weather we may have no doubt that the sluice gates of the heavens and the fountains of the deep have been closed by the Word of God. The rainbow makes its appearance even now, to be a sure sign that a universal flood will not occur in the future. Hence this promise demands also from us that we believe that God has compassion on the human race and will not rage against us in the future by means of a universal flood.

There is further discussion at this point whether there are natural causes in the rainbow that convey this meaning. And the discussion of the philosophers is familiar, especially that of Aristotle in his *Meteorologica*, about the color of the rainbow, about the nature of the cloud in which it originates, and about its curvature.[22] Rather appropriately, they include a comparison with mirrors, in which an image is reflected in the same way the rays of the sun are reflected, and produce a rainbow when they fall upon a moist and concave cloud. In such matters reason sees what is most likely to be the case, even though it is incapable of determining the truth in every instance; for this is the prerogative, not of the creature but of the Creator. Yet I for my part have never given less credence to any book than to the *Meteorologica*, because it is based on the principle that all things have their origin in natural causes.[23]

Even though people maintain that the rainbow presages a storm of three days' duration — something I readily grant [24] — nevertheless, it certainly signifies that no further flood will occur. It does not have this significance as the result of some natural reason, but solely as the result of the Word of God, because God so determines and establishes through His Word. Similarly, circumcision was the sign that the people was the people of God. Circumcision did not have this meaning per se, however, but solely through the Word that was attached to it. Likewise, the garments of skins signified life and preservation, not because they were able by their nature to offer these things, but because God had given His promise that they would. In the same way, because of the Word of God, not because of some natural cause, the bow in the clouds has the meaning that no further flood will occur.

[22] Aristotle, *Meteorologica*, Book III, ch. 4.
[23] Cf. also *Luther's Works*, 1, pp. 3—4.
[24] Apparently a popular belief.

I do not despise human thoughts and surmises about these things; but because the proofs are not substantial, I do not place too much confidence in them. Furthermore, the surmises of Aristotle about a moist and concave cloud are not reliable, because such clouds can exist even when no rainbow develops. Indeed, from either a denser or a more tenuous medium there can develop a rainbow that either is larger or forms a greater arc. Here in Wittenberg I personally observed a rainbow round like a circle and closed on all sides, not cut off on the surface of the earth, the way it ordinarily appears.[25] Why, then, do rainbows develop sometimes in one way, sometimes in another? A philosopher, I am sure, will figure out something, for he will regard it as a disgrace not to be able to give reasons for everything. But he certainly will never persuade me to believe that he is speaking the truth.

There is one reliable and sure explanation, namely, that all these phenomena,[26] as they are called, are works of God or of the demons. I myself have no doubt that leaping goats, flying dragons, spears, and the like are the workings of evil spirits, who carry on this way in the air either to frighten human beings or to deceive them. The heathen thought that the flames that appeared on their ships were Castor and Pollux, and sometimes a moon appears above the ears of horses.[27] It is certain that all these phenomena are antics of the demons in the air, although Aristotle is of the opinion that they are air that has been set on fire, just as he also argues that a comet is vapor that has been set on fire.[28]

To me it seems to be far safer and surer for us to explain these matters on the basis of a general law,[29] namely, that when God wills it, a comet glows as a sign of terror, just as when He wills it, the rainbow in the heaven flashes back His sign of grace. For who would be able to comprehend all the reasons why the rainbow appears in so beautiful a combination of colors and so perfectly semicircular in shape? The arrangement of the clouds surely does not produce this so accurately. Hence this bow stands there by divine pleasure, because of the will and promise of God, to give

[25] See also Luther's *House Postil* (1544), W, LII, 17.

[26] Luther's word is *impressiones*.

[27] Castor and Pollux, the Dioscuri, were said to be responsible for the electrical phenomenon now known as corposant or St. Elmo's fire.

[28] Aristotle, *Meteorologica*, Book I, chs. 6—7.

[29] Luther uses the phrase *a priore* to mean "as a general law."

assurance to both man and beast that no flood will ever take place at any future time.

This sign should remind us to give thanks to God. For as often as the rainbow appears, it preaches to the entire world with a loud voice about the wrath which once moved God to destroy the whole world. It also gives comfort, that we may have the conviction that God is kindly inclined toward us again and will never again make use of so horrible a punishment. Thus it teaches the fear of God and faith at the same time, the greatest virtues. Philosophy has no knowledge of these and carries on a discussion solely about the material and the formal cause; it does not know the final cause of this beautiful creature. But theology points it out.[30]

Here another discussion arises: whether the bow was in existence even before the Flood. And much effort is expended on the matter. Since it is written above that God created the heaven and the earth in six days and then rested from all His work, they reach the conclusion that the rainbow was in existence from the beginning; otherwise it would follow that God created something new outside those six days. But what happened at the time of Noah was that God took the rainbow, which He had created in the beginning, and by means of a new Word appointed it as a special sign; it had indeed existed previously, but it had meant nothing. In support of this opinion they make use also of Solomon's statement (Eccl. 1:9) that there is nothing new under the sun. Consequently, they maintain that after the six days no creature was created anew.

I am of the opposite opinion, namely, that the rainbow was never in existence before and was created now. Similarly, the garments of skins with which God clothed the first human beings certainly were not created in those six days, but after the fall of the first human beings; therefore they were a new creature. The statement that God rested is not to be understood to mean that He created nothing thereafter.[31] For Christ says (John 5:17): "My Father is working still, and I work."

As for Solomon's statement that there is nothing new under the sun, it has troubled the theologians in various ways.[32] Nevertheless, who does not see that it is speaking, not of the works of God but

[30] Cf. p. 126, note 49.

[31] See *Luther's Works*, 1, pp. 74—79, for Luther's discussion of this problem.

[32] Cf. Augustine, *De Genesi ad litteram*, Book IV, chs. 11—12, *Patrologia, Series Latina*, XXXIV, 303—306.

of original sin, namely, that the same reason that was in Adam after the fall and the same debates about morals, vices, virtues, the nourishment of the body, and the management of human affairs still go on among human beings? It is just as the comic poet declared in another statement: "Nothing has been said that has not been said before." [33] Truly, in human works and endeavors there is nothing new; for there are the same words, thoughts, endeavors, passions, griefs, loves, and failings that have always been. Hence it is silly to apply this statement to the works of God and His creatures.

I hold that the rainbow was a new creature, not seen by the world until now, in order that the world might be reminded of the past wrath, of which the rainbow shows traces, and might also be assured of the mercy of God. It is like a book or a picture that shows both the bygone wrath and the present grace.

There is also a discussion about the colors, which some consider to be four: fiery, yellow, green, and watery or blue. But I myself think there are only two, a fiery one and a watery one. Moreover, the fiery one is uppermost, except when the rainbow is reflected; for then, just as in a mirror, the uppermost parts are changed to the lowest. When the fiery and the watery color come together or are mixed, the result is a yellow color.

The nature of the colors was so decreed by God with the definite purpose not only that the watery color might be a reminder of the bygone wrath, but also that the fiery one might depict the future judgment for us. The inner surface, which has the color of water, is finite; but the outside, which has the color of fire, is infinite. Thus the first world perished by the Flood, but the wrath had limits. For some remnants were saved; and afterwards another world came into being, yet one that was finite. But when God destroys the world with fire, this physical life will not be restored; but the wicked will bear the eternal judgment of death in fire, while the godly will be raised into a new and everlasting life — not a physical one, even though it is in bodies, but a spiritual one.

Let us, therefore, be reminded by this sign to fear God and to trust Him, in order that, just as we have escaped the punishment of the Flood, we may also be able to escape the punishment by fire. This knowledge is more profitable than those philosophical discussions about the material cause.

[33] Terence, *Eunuchus*, 41.

CONCERNING ALLEGORIES

At last we have finished the story of the Flood, which was related by Moses at considerable length as an awful example of the vast and almost boundless wrath of God, which no words can adequately express. It remains for us to say something about the allegorical meaning, although I have often asserted that I take no great delight in allegories.[34] Nevertheless, I was so enchanted by them in my youth that under the influence of the examples of Origen and Jerome, whom I admired as the greatest theologians, I thought that everything had to be turned into allegories. Augustine, too, makes frequent use of allegories.

But while I was following their examples, I finally realized that to my own great harm I had followed an empty shadow and had left unconsidered the heart and core of the Scriptures. Later on, therefore, I began to have a dislike for allegories. They do indeed give pleasure, particularly when they have some delightful allusions. Therefore I usually compare them to pretty pictures. But to the same extent that the natural color of bodies surpasses the picture — even though, as the poet puts it, the pictures are adorned with the colors of an Apelles, which closely approximate nature [35] — the historical narrative itself surpasses the allegory.

In our own age the unlearned mob of the Anabaptists, no less than the monks, are in the clutches of an excessive zeal for allegories.[36] Because of this they have a great affection also for the more obscure books, such as the Revelation of John and the worthless fabrication going by the name of Ezra, which appears in translation in the last two books.[37] There one is free to fabricate anything whatever. We recall that Münzer, that rebellious spirit, turned everything into allegories.[38] But truly, he who either fabricates allegories without discrimination or follows such as are fabricated by others

---

[34] Cf. *Luther's Works,* 9, pp. 24 ff.

[35] Statius, *Silvae,* V, 1, 5.

[36] Luther seems to mean not so much that Anabaptist exegesis allegorized the literal texts of the Scriptures as that it had a predilection for the figurative, especially the apocalyptic texts. This was not true, of course, of all the Anabaptist groups.

[37] Luther is referring to 4 Esdras.

[38] Apparently the "allegory" mentioned here is Münzer's interpretation of "This Is My Body."

is not only deceived but also most seriously harmed, as these examples show.

Hence allegories either must be avoided entirely or must be attempted with the utmost discrimination and brought into harmony with the rule in use by the apostles, of which I shall say something a little later. Let us not fall into these abominable and ruinous absurdities because of the example not only of the theologians but also of the canonists, or rather the "asinists" — something to which the decretals and decrees of His Most Execrable Lordship, the pope, bear witness.

Yet these remarks must not be understood to mean that we condemn all allegories indiscriminately, for we observe that both Christ and the apostles occasionally employed them. But they are such as are conformable to the faith, in accordance with the rule of Paul, who enjoins in Rom. 12:6 that prophecy or doctrine should be conformable to the faith.

When we condemn allegories, we are speaking of those that are fabricated by one's own intellect and ingenuity, without the authority of Scripture. The others, which are made to agree with the analogy of the faith, not only embellish doctrine but also give comfort to consciences.

Thus Peter turns this very story of the Flood into a beautiful allegory when he says in 1 Peter 3:21-22: "Baptism, which corresponds to this, now saves us, not as a removal of dirt from the body, but as an appeal to God for a clear conscience, through the resurrection of Christ from the dead," who is at the right hand of God, swallowing up death in order that we may be made heirs of eternal life, and "who has gone into heaven, with angels, authorities, and powers subject to Him." This is truly a theological allegory, that is, one in agreement with the faith and full of comfort.

Of the same nature is Christ's allegory in John 3:14 about the serpent that was raised up in the desert and those who looked up at it and were healed from its bite. Likewise Paul's (1 Cor. 10:4): "Our fathers all drank from the supernatural rock."

These allegories are such that they not only agree nicely with the subject matter but also instruct hearts about faith and are profitable to the conscience.

Consider, on the other hand, the majority of the allegories of Jerome, Origen, and Augustine. These men do not concern themselves with the faith when they devise allegories; they look for philosophical ideas, which are profitable neither for morals nor for the faith, not to mention that they are even rather silly and absurd.

We have previously heard Augustine's allegory about the creation of the man and the woman. He applies it to the upper and the lower part of the human being, that is, to reason and the emotions.[39] But, I ask you, what is the value of this fabrication?

The pope deserves praise for piety and learning in the matter of allegories when he thunders thus from his exalted position: "God made two large luminaries, the sun and the moon. The sun is the papal office, from which the imperial majesty derives its light, just as the moon does from the sun."[40] Oh, such audacious insolence and such villainous desire for power!

Similarly, in this historical account they compare the ark to their own church, in which the pope is with his cardinals, bishops, and prelates.[41] The laity, however, is swimming in the sea; that is, it is involved in secular affairs and would not be saved unless those helmsmen of the ark, or the church, held out to the swimmers either planks or ropes to draw them into the ark. The monks everywhere have used such a picture to depict the church.

Origen has better sense than the popes, for he usually devotes his allegories to matters of morality. Nevertheless, he should have observed Paul's rule, who enjoins that the analogy of the faith must be preserved in prophecy; for this edifies and is truly applicable to the church. Concerning morals the philosophers of the heathen, too, are capable of giving instruction, although they are completely without a knowledge of faith.

In his letter to the Corinthians (1 Cor. 10:2) Paul declares that the Israelites were baptized under Moses in the cloud and in the sea. If in this passage you look merely at conduct and words, then Pharaoh, too, was baptized, but in such a way that he perished with his men, while Israel passed through safe and unharmed. Similarly,

[39] Cf. *Luther's Works*, 1, p. 184.

[40] "Just as God, founder of the universe, has constituted two large luminaries in the firmament of heaven, a major one to dominate the day and a minor one to dominate the night, so He has established in the firmament of the universal church, which is signified by the name of heaven, two great dignities . . ., the pontifical authority and the royal power." Innocent III, *Sicut universitatis Conditor* (November 3, 1198).

[41] Cf. p. 68.

Noah and his sons are preserved in the baptism of the Flood, while the entire remaining world outside the ark perishes because of this baptism of the Flood.

These are fitting and learned statements, for Baptism and death are interchangeable terms in the Scripture. Therefore Paul says in Rom. 6:3: "As many of us as have been baptized, have been baptized into the death of Christ." Likewise, Christ says in Luke 12:50: "I have a Baptism to be baptized with, and how I am constrained until it is accomplished!" And to His disciples He said (Mark 10:39): "You will be baptized with the Baptism with which I am baptized." [42]

In accordance with this meaning, the Red Sea is truly a baptism, that is, death and the wrath of God, as is manifest in the case of Pharaoh. Nevertheless, Israel, which is baptized with such a baptism, passes through unharmed. Similarly, the Flood is truly death and the wrath of God; nevertheless, the believers are saved in the midst of the Flood. Thus death engulfs and swallows up the entire human race; for without distinction the wrath of God goes over the good and the evil, over the godly and the ungodly. The Flood that Noah experienced was not different from the one that the world experienced. The Red Sea, which both Pharaoh and Israel entered, was not different. Later on, however, the difference becomes apparent in this: those who believe are preserved in the very death to which they are subjected together with the ungodly, but the ungodly perish. Noah, accordingly, is preserved because he has the ark, that is, God's promise and Word, in which he is living; but the ungodly, who do not believe the Word, are left to their fate.

This difference the Holy Spirit wanted to point out in order that the godly might be instructed by this example to believe and hope for salvation through the mercy of God, even in the midst of death. For they have Baptism joined with the promise of life, just as Noah had the ark. Hence even though the death of the wise man and of the fool is the same (Eccl. 2:16) — for Peter and Paul die no differently from the way Nero and other ungodly men die later on — they nevertheless believe that in death they will be preserved for eternal life. Nor is this an idle hope; for they have Christ to receive their spirits. On the Last Day He will revive also the bodies of believers for eternal life.

This allegory is of great value and serves to comfort our hearts,

[42] The original has "Matt. 20."

for it points out how differently things will turn out in the end. If you heed the eyes of the flesh, Solomon's statement is true (Eccl. 2:16) that the wise man and the fool die alike and that the righteous man dies as though he were not beloved of God. But here the eyes of the spirit must be applied and the difference noted: Israel enters the Red Sea and is saved, but when Pharaoh follows on the heels of Israel, he is submerged by the waters and perishes. Therefore the death by which the godly and the ungodly perish is the same; indeed, the death of the godly is almost always ignominious, while that of the ungodly is grand and magnificent. But in the eyes of God the death of sinners is the worst, while the death of the saints is precious (Ps. 116:15); for it has been sanctified by Christ, through whom it becomes the beginning of eternal life.

Just as the Deluge and the Red Sea are helpers, as it were, to deliver Noah and Israel from death and to preserve their life, so our own death, if we abide in the faith, is clearly the opportunity for life. When the Children of Israel were in extreme peril, the sea suddenly opened and stood to the right and to the left like an iron wall, so that Israel passed through without danger. Why did this happen? Manifestly in order that in this manner death might serve life. For this is the divine power by which the assaults of Satan are overcome, as was the case in Paradise. There, too, he was endeavoring to kill the entire human race with his poison. But what happens? Through what was truly a "happy guilt," as the church sings,[43] it was brought about that the Son of God came down into our flesh and delivered us from such great evils.

Accordingly, this allegory teaches, comforts, and encourages us in an excellent manner. As a result, we fear neither death nor sin but disdain all dangers while we give thanks to God for calling us and dealing with us in such a way. Death itself, by which the entire world perishes, is compelled to serve life, just as the Flood, in which the rest of the world perished, was the occasion to preserve Noah; and the Red Sea, by which Pharaoh was destroyed, served the welfare of the Children of Israel.

This must be applied also to other trials. We must learn to disdain dangers and to have hope even when no hope appears to be left, so that when death or any other danger befalls us, we may

---

[43] The expression *felix culpa* does not come, as the Weimar editors suggest, from Lazarus Spengler but from the hymn *Exultet* in the liturgy for Holy Saturday; this hymn may have been written by Ambrose.

encourage ourselves and say: "Behold, here is your Red Sea, your Flood, your baptism, and your death. Here your life — as a philosopher used to say about those who were going to sea [44] — is barely a handbreadth away from death. But do not be afraid. This danger is like a handful of water, whereas through the Word you have a flood of grace. Therefore death will not destroy you but will be a thrust and aid toward life." Far from being able to destroy the Christian, death is the most immediate escape from death. For the death of the body immediately precedes the liberation of the spirit as well as the resurrection of the flesh. Similarly, in the Flood it is neither the earth nor the trees nor the mountains that carry Noah; it is the Flood itself, even though it kills the rest of the human race.

Therefore the prophets have reason for their frequent praise of the wonderful deeds of God, such as the passage through the Red Sea, the exodus from Egypt, and the like. For there the sea, which by nature cannot do otherwise than overwhelm and destroy man, is compelled to stand still and protect him, lest he be covered by its waves. Hence that which by its nature is nothing but wrath becomes grace for those who believe; that which is nothing but death becomes life. Thus whatever misfortunes there are, of which this life surely has countless numbers and by which our bodies and goods are beset — all this will be turned into salvation and joy if you are in the ark, that is, if you believe and lay hold of the promises made in Christ; for death, which carries you away, must be turned into life, and hell, which engulfs you, into a way to heaven.

It is for this reason that in 1 Peter 3:21 Peter declares that we, too, are saved through water in Baptism, which is symbolized by the Flood, because pouring water over us or immersing us is death. And yet from that death or immersion there arises life because of the ark in which we are preserved, that is, because of the Word of promise to which we hold fast. The canonical Scriptures put forward this allegory, and it is something not only trustworthy but also worthwhile in every way. We should consider it carefully, for it provides glorious comfort even in extreme perils.

To this allegory the fathers added another, one derived from the geometrical shape and proportion of the ark.[45] From the crown of

[44] Perhaps a reference to Juvenal, *Satires*, XII, 1. 58: "four or seven inches from death."

[45] See p. 68 ff.

the head to the sole of the foot the human body is six times longer than it is wide. Now the ark was fifty cubits wide; but its height was six times greater, namely, 300 cubits. Hence they declare that the ark signifies the man Christ, to whom all promises apply. Therefore those who believe in Him are saved; and in the Flood, that is, in death itself, they remain alive.

This thought is not unscholarly. Nor is it unattractive. I am most pleased that it is conformable to the faith. Therefore even if there were an error in the application, the basis nevertheless is sure and solid. There is no doubt that the Holy Spirit used various ways to depict the promises that were to be realized through Christ and the wonderful way in which the human race was to be saved through faith in Christ. If one devises allegories in this manner, therefore, they are nevertheless not ungodly or offensive, even though they may be somewhat inappropriate.

Thus if someone should state that Christ is the sun and the church the moon, illuminated by the grace of Christ, he might be in error; nevertheless, his error is such that it rests, not on an incorrect basis but on a solid one. But when the pope declares that the sun is the papal office and the moon is the emperor, then not only is the application silly and foolish, but even the basis is evil and wicked. Such allegories are thought out and devised, not by the Holy Spirit but by the devil, the spirit of lies.

In order to comfort and strengthen our hearts, allegories must be directed toward the promises and toward the teaching of the faith, as the example of Peter teaches us. Because he sees that Noah is delivered in the midst of death and that the ark is the means of life, the ark is properly made to signify Christ. For it takes a divine power to save in the midst of death and to carry across to life. Thus in Ps. 68:20 Scripture calls God the One who delivers from death and makes death an occasion or even an aid to life.

As a result of this, there arose those common expressions in the Holy Scriptures in which afflictions and perils are compared to an intoxicating cup. Surely, a striking understatement.[46] Thus in Ps. 110:7 the passion of Christ is called a draught from a brook, as though one were to call it a medicinal potion or syrup, which, though bitter, heals by its bitterness and makes alive through its killing action.

These disparaging terms have the effect of comforting us, that we

[46] Luther is referring to the figure of speech known as *tapinosis*, "understatement."

may learn to disdain death and other perils, and to endure them with a more ready heart.

Satan, too, has his cup; but it is a sweet one and one that intoxicates to the extent of bringing on vomiting. Those who have been seduced by its sweetness and drain it lose their life and die an eternal death. Such was the cup that the Babylonian drained, as the prophet says (Jer. 25:15). Let us, therefore, receive the salutary cup with thanks, just as Paul says that the believers glory in tribulations (Rom. 5:3).

Now that we have presented this picture of the ark and the meaning of the Flood on the basis of the canonical Scriptures, something must also be said about the remaining portions of the historical account: about the raven which did not return; and about the doves, the first of which returned when she did not find a place where she could set her foot, the second returned and brought back an olive branch, and the third did not return, because the earth had now been cleared of water.

In our discussion of the historical account we stated that these events took place for the comfort of Noah and his sons, to give them the assurance that the wrath of God had come to an end and that He was now reconciled. It was not through her own effort that the dove brought back the olive branch; this was a divine power and miracle, just as the serpent in Paradise did not speak by its own effort but through the influence of the devil, by whom it was possessed. Just as in that instance the serpent spoke under the influence of Satan and seduced mankind into sin, so in this instance the dove did not bring back the olive branch through her own effort and instinct but under God's influence, in order that Noah might derive sure comfort from this most delightful sight. For the fruit of the olive tree is not the food of a dove, which likes wheat, barley, or peas.

It is certain, therefore that this miraculous action had some particular meaning, especially since the prophets also frequently mention doves in their prophecies about the kingdom of Christ, such as Ps. 68:13 and Is. 60:8. In the Song of Songs, Solomon also seems to take special delight in the name of the dove.[47] Therefore the picture that this allegory presents should not be regarded with complete indifference; it should be treated with fitting skill.

The allegory that the scholars fabricated about the raven is

---

[47] Song of Solomon 1:14; 2:10, etc.

familiar.⁴⁸ They were of the opinion that because ravens are fond of carrion, they represent carnal people like the Epicureans, who delight and indulge in carnal pleasures. The thought is indeed good, but it is not fully satisfactory; for this allegory is merely moral and philosophical, the sort that Erasmus has been accustomed to fabricate, somewhat after the pattern of Origen.

We for our part should look for a theological allegory. Those moralists fail to note, in the first place, that Scripture praises the raven for not leaving the ark of its own accord; it is sent out by Noah as his messenger, to investigate whether the waters have ceased and the wrath of God has come to an end. But the raven does not return, nor is it the bearer of a favorable omen. It remains outside the ark; and although it goes and comes, it does not let itself be caught by Noah but remains outside the ark.

All this agrees most beautifully with the ministry of the Law. The black color characteristic of the raven is a symbol of sadness, and the sound of its voice is unpleasant. All the teachers of the Law who teach a righteousness of works are of the same kind: they are ministers of death and of sin. Thus Paul calls the ministry of the Law the ministry of death: "The Law kills" (2 Cor. 3:6); "the Law brings wrath" (Rom. 4:15); "the Law causes sin to increase" (Rom. 5:20).

And yet Moses is sent by God with this doctrine, just as Noah sends out the raven. God wants people to be instructed about morals and a holy life, and He wants His wrath and sure punishments announced to the transgressors of the Law. Nevertheless, such teachers are nothing else than ravens; they fly back and forth around the ark and bring no sure pronouncement of a reconciled God.

It is characteristic of the Law that its teaching cannot make fearful consciences sure, strengthen and comfort them. Rather it frightens them, because it does nothing else than teach what God demands from us, what He wants us to do. Moreover, it bears witness against us through our conscience, because not only have we not done the will of God revealed in the Law, but we have even done the opposite.

Hence it is correctly stated about the teachers of the Law in Ps. 5:9: "There is nothing sure in their mouth." (Our translation has: "In their mouth is no truth.")⁴⁹ For when they present their doctrine

⁴⁸ Cf. p. 109, note 13.

⁴⁹ That is, the Vulgate: *non est in ore eorum veritas*.

in their most perfect manner, they say: "If you do this and if you do that, you will be saved." Therefore when the scribe gives a superb formulation of the teaching of the Law, Christ answers him ironically (Luke 10:28): "Do this, and you will live." He shows him that the teaching is holy and good, but that since we are imperfect, the guilt lies on us, who neither keep nor can keep it.

We, therefore, declare correctly that by the works of the Law — not those dealing with ceremonies but those chief ones dealing with the love of God and one's neighbor — we are not justified. The reason is that we cannot perform them.

What is more, we have the right to censure the effrontery of our opponents, who shout that when we deny the righteousness of works, we are forbidding good works and condemning the Law of God.[50] We would be doing this if we did not acknowledge that the raven had been sent out from the ark by Noah. We do assert that the raven was sent out from the ark; but this we deny, either that there was no raven or that it was a dove. Yet all the shouts, calumnies, and abuses of our adversaries aim to force us into the lie of making a dove out of the raven.

Yes indeed, examine their books, and give careful consideration to their doctrine. Is it not merely a doctrine of works? They say: "This is fine, this is honorable, this you must do. That is detestable and disgraceful. Therefore shun it." When they teach this, they consider themselves true theologians and teachers. But how about showing [51] that there is anyone who either has done or will do all those things, especially if you carefully set before him not only the Second Table, as they do, but also the First?

Therefore he who stands on the teaching of the Law is actually nothing but a hearer (James 1:22), who learns nothing else than to know what he ought to do. For those who want to learn nothing else, it would be enough to provide Cato's poem or Aesop, whom I consider the better teacher of morals.[52] Nevertheless, it is profitable to put both into the hands of young people. Let the older ones learn Cicero, to whom, to my surprise, some prefer Aristotle as a teacher of morals. This is, in a sense, a course in rational conduct.

[50] This was the constant criticism of Luther's doctrine of justification.

[51] The Latin phrase is *Da demonstrandi!*

[52] Cf. *Luther's Works*, 13, p. 200, note 55, on Aesop; "Cato" refers to the author of the *Disticha*, which Luther often quoted, e. g., ibid., p. 82.

So far as moral precepts are concerned, one cannot find fault with the industry and earnestness of the heathen. Nevertheless, they are all inferior to Moses, who gives instruction not only in morals but also in the worship of God. Yet it is true that he who stops with Moses has nothing but the raven flying back and forth outside the ark; of the dove and of the olive branch he has nothing.

Hence this is a picture, not only of the Law given by God but of all human reason and wisdom, of all laws and of all philosophy. They merely state what one must do, but they do not supply the ability to do it. Therefore Christ's statement in Luke 17:10 is true: "When you have done all that is commanded, say: 'We are unworthy servants.'"

The raven is indeed sent out: God wants the Law to be taught, and He Himself reveals it; nay, He even writes it upon the hearts of all human beings, as Paul demonstrates in Rom. 2:15. From this natural knowledge have originated all the books of the more sensible philosophers, such as Aesop, Aristotle, Plato, Xenophon, Cicero, and Cato.[53] It is a good idea to set these books before uneducated and unruly individuals, that their wicked impulses may in some measure be counteracted through this training.

But really, if you inquire about peace of conscience and a sure hope of eternal life, they are like the raven, which flies back and forth around the ark and finds no peace outside, but does not seek it inside the ark either. It is as Paul says about the Jews (Rom. 9:31): "By following the righteousness of the Law Israel did not attain righteousness." The reason is that the Law is like the raven: it is the ministry of death and sin, or it makes hypocrites.

Now let anyone who wants to do so enlarge on this allegory and investigate the peculiar features of this bird. It is an impure animal, black and gloomy in color, with a hard beak and an unpleasant and doleful voice. It scents carrion from any distance, and for this reason men shudder at its voice as though it were a sure sign of an impending funeral. It feeds on carrion and likes places that are horrible because they are used for public executions.

Even though we do not apply all these features individually to the Law, yet who is not aware that they fit the papists, priests, and monks very well? These men were not only richly fed as a result of the consciences that were murdered through their false doctrine;

[53] Cf. *Luther's Works*, 1, p. 4, note 5.

but they also drew on carrion for their support by making use of vigils, anniversaries, holy water at graves, and even of purgatory to provide money. In fact, their concern for the dead brought them greater gain than their concern for the living.

They are truly ravens, for they live on carrion and screech dolefully while they sit on it. These characteristics fit the papists and the ravens well; but truly the entire ministry of the papacy, even at its best, does nothing but mangle and murder consciences. It does not lead to true righteousness; it merely produces hypocrites, just as the Law does too.

In Ezek. 13:19 there appears among the other sins of the false prophets also this one, that for a handful of barley and a piece of bread they put to death souls that are not dying and keep alive souls that are not living.

This is characteristic of the ravens, or the teachers of the Law. They declare righteous those who live according to the precept of the Law, but these are actually souls that are not alive. On the other hand, they condemn those who violate the traditions. The Pharisees similarly condemned the disciples for plucking ears of grain, not washing, and not fasting. This is the doleful and deadly voice of which the ravens should remind us as they sit on the carrion.

When the Greeks wanted to invoke evil, they used the expression: "To the ravens with you!" [54] The Germans do likewise when they tell someone to become the food of ravens: "I hope the ravens devour you!" [55] If we give this curse a place in the allegory, it surely is a very serious one. What can be more ruinous than to have teachers who, when they do their best teaching, do nothing but commit murder? They involve consciences in difficulties from which it is impossible to be disentangled.

Someone may say that this allegory about the raven has been improperly applied to the ministry. Nevertheless, it is true, and it agrees with the basic principle.[56] Besides, it is not only suited for teaching; it is also very profitable.

What Moses relates about the dove is really a delightful likeness of the Gospel, especially if you carefully trace the characteristics of the dove, which are ten in number: (1) it is devoid of malice; (2) it

[54] Aristophanes, *Wasps*, ll. 852, 982.
[55] The German is *das dich die Raben fressen!*
[56] See p. 156.

does no harm with its mouth; (3) it inflicts no damage with its claw; (4) it picks up clean grain; (5) it feeds other young birds; (6) instead of singing, it moans; (7) it stays near water; (8) it flies in flocks; (9) it nests in a safe place; (10) it flies swiftly. These ten characteristics have been summed up in the following six lines:

> Felle columba caret, rostro non laedit, et ungues
> Possidet innocuos, granaque pura legit.
> Estque frequens ad aquas, pennaque per aëra fertur
> Praepete, pro cantu lugubre voce gemit.
> Educat alterius pullos, volitatque gregatim,
> Et studet in tutis nidificare locis.[57]

The New Testament relates that the Holy Spirit appeared in the form of a dove. Therefore we rightly apply the allegory to the ministry of grace.

Moses relates that the dove did not fly to and fro about the ark, like the raven; but she was sent out, and when she did not find a place to light, she returned to the ark and was caught by Noah.

This dove is a figure of the holy prophets, who were indeed sent to teach the people; but the Flood, that is, the era of the Law, had not yet come to an end. Thus although David, Elijah, and Isaiah did not live to see the era of grace or of the New Testament, they were nevertheless sent to be messengers of the end of the Flood, even though it had not yet ended. After they had performed their mission, they returned to the ark, that is, they were justified and saved without the Law through faith in the Blessed Seed, in whom they believed and for whom they were waiting.

After this dove another is sent out; it finds the earth dry and not only the mountains but also the trees free of water. This one alights on an olive tree and brings to Noah a branch she plucked.

Scripture suggests this allegory also, since in several passages it compares olive oil to grace or mercy or the forgiveness of sins.[58] This the dove brings in its mouth, to represent the outward ministry or the spoken Word. For the Holy Spirit does not — as the enthusiasts and the Anabaptists, truly fanatical teachers, dream — give His instruction through new revelations outside the ministry of the Word. God wanted the branch of a green olive tree brought to Noah by mouth, to make us realize that in the New Testament, when the

---

[57] Cf. Aristotle, *Historia animalium*, Book IX, ch. 7, on some of these characteristics.

[58] Cf. *Luther's Works*, 12, pp. 175—176.

Flood or the era of wrath comes to an end, God wants to reveal His mercy to the world through the spoken Word.

The messengers of this Word are doves, that is, devout men and without malice, full of the Holy Spirit. Isaiah (60:8) likewise compares the ministers of the Gospel, or of grace, to doves that are flying to familiar windows. Even though Christ commands His disciples in Matt. 10:16 to imitate doves in their simplicity, that is, to be sincere and without venom, He nevertheless urges them to be wise as serpents; that is, they should be on their guard against insincere and treacherous people, and they should be cautious, the way a serpent in a fight is said to protect its head with extraordinary skill.

That the olive tree is green, this agrees with the Word of the Gospel, which endures forever and is never without fruit. The psalm (1:3) also compares people who apply themselves to the Word to a tree whose leaves do not fall. We heard nothing like this when we spoke about the raven flying to and fro near the ark. Hence this dove, the second one to be sent out, is a type of the New Testament, where forgiveness of sin and grace are plainly promised through the sacrifice of Christ. That is why in the New Testament the Holy Spirit wanted to appear in the form of a dove.

The third dove did not return. When the promise of the Gospel, announced to the world through the mouth of a dove, has been fulfilled, there is nothing left to do, and no new doctrine is expected. All we still expect is the revelation of the things we have believed. Hence this also serves to give us a sure testimony that this doctrine will endure until the end of the world.

The text also expressly mentions the time. It states that after Noah had sent out a dove for the first time, he waited seven days. These seven days are the time of the Law, which had to precede the time of the New Testament.

Similarly, it is said of the second dove that it returned to the ark toward evening and was carrying an olive branch. The last age of the world is set aside for the Gospel. Nor should any other kind of doctrine be expected. For this reason Christ compares the Gospel to a supper (Matt. 22:2; Luke 14:16).

The doctrine of the Gospel has been in the world ever since our first parents fell, and by various signs God confirmed this promise to the fathers. The earlier times knew nothing of the rainbow, circumcision, and other things that were ordained later on. But all ages had the knowledge of the Blessed Seed. Since this has been revealed, there is nothing left except the revelation of what we believe and our flight with the third dove into another life, never to return to this wretched and distressful life.

These are my thoughts about this allegory. I wanted to present them briefly. Allegories do not deserve as much time as do the historical accounts and the articles of faith.

Origen, Jerome, Augustine, and Bernard allegorize a great deal. The trouble is that since they spend too much time on allegories, they call hearts away and make them flee from the historical account and from faith, whereas allegories should be so treated and designed that faith, to which the historical accounts point in every instance, may be aroused, increased, enlightened, and strengthened. As for those who do not pay attention to the historical accounts, it is no wonder that they look for the shade of allegories as pleasant bypaths on which to ramble.

We see that in the papacy the music of the chants is very pleasing, although the words are commonly not only inappropriate but even wicked and contrary to Scripture. Thus with their foolish allegories the scholars have often corrupted the good sense of a historical account, the sense that was profitable for faith.

I have often stated what kind of theology there was when I began to engage in this sort of study. It was continually stated that the letter kills (2 Cor. 3:6).[59] Therefore I disliked Lyra above all other exegetes, because he tried to ascertain the literal meaning with such care. But now, just because of this commendable quality, I prefer him to almost all other interpreters of Scripture.[60]

I urge you with all possible earnestness to be careful to pay attention to the historical accounts. But wherever you want to make use of allegories, do this: follow closely the analogy of the faith, that is, adapt them to Christ, the church, faith, and the ministry of the Word. In this way it will come to pass that even though the allegories may not be altogether fitting, they nevertheless do not depart from the faith. Let this foundation stand firm, but let the stubble perish (1 Cor. 3:12-15). But let us return to the story.

[59] For this application of 2 Cor. 3:6 cf. Augustine, *On Christian Doctrine*, Book III, ch. 5.

[60] Some scholars (see Introduction) suggest that this praise for Lyra may be the work of Luther's editors.

20. *Noah was the first tiller of the soil. He planted a vineyard;*
21. *and he drank of the wine, and became drunk, and lay uncovered in his tent.*
22. *And Ham, the father of Canaan, saw the nakedness of his father, and told his two brothers outside.*

The account of the Flood itself reveals adequately what kind of man Noah was during the Flood. Moreover, what sort of man he was before the Flood, Moses reveals in a few words when he says that he was just and perfect. Nothing else is recorded about this great man, except that his remarkable and almost unbelievable continence is faintly indicated and praised when it is stated that he did did not begin to beget children until he was five hundred years old. This itself shows that at that time the nature of man was far stronger and better, and that the Holy Spirit was more active and more abundant in the holy men of the original world than He is today in us, who are, as it were, the dregs and end of the world.

It is surely high praise for Noah when Moses mentions that he was just and perfect before God, that is, that he was full of faith and the Holy Spirit, endowed with chastity and with all good works, and pure in his worship and religion, although he had endured many temptations from the devil, from the world, and from himself. Yet he successfully overcame all these temptations. Such a man was Noah before the Flood.

Even though Moses has little to say about Noah after the Flood, anyone will realize that since he lived for approximately three hundred and fifty years after the time of the Flood, such a great man could not have been inactive but was busy with the government of the church, which he alone established and ruled.

In the first place, Noah filled the office of bishop; and because he had been plagued by various temptations, it was his foremost concern to oppose the devil and comfort the tempted, to restore the erring, to give confidence to the wavering, to encourage the despairing, to shut out the impenitent from his church, and to receive back the penitent with fatherly joy. These are almost the same duties that must be performed by a bishop through the ministry of the Word.

In the second place, Noah had his civil tasks, because he established the state and formulated laws, without which human lust cannot be kept under control. In addition to this, there was the management of his own home or care for the household.

Although reason tells us that after the Deluge Noah was occupied with so many varied tasks, Moses makes mention of none of these. To Moses it seemed necessary to record only this one item: how he began to plant a vineyard, became drunk, and lay naked in his tent.

This is indeed a silly and altogether unprofitable little story if you compare it with the rest of Noah's outstanding achievements through the course of so many years. If other events were recorded, they could edify people and help them arrange their lives properly. Moreover, this story also seems to give a cause for offense and to defend people who get drunk and then sin because of their drunkenness.

But the intention of the Holy Spirit is familiar from our teaching. He wanted the godly, who know their weakness and for this reason are disheartened, to take comfort in the offense that comes from the account of the lapses among the holiest and most perfect patriarchs. In such instances we should find sure proof of our own weakness and therefore bow down in humble confession, not only to ask for forgiveness but also to hope for it. This is the true theological reason why the Holy Spirit makes mention of the extraordinary lapse of this great man, although He disregards other important matters.

Lyra excuses Noah on the grounds that he did not know the effect of wine and that he was deceived by drinking a little too much.[61] Regardless of whether wine had been in existence previously or was first produced through the skill of Noah as the result of a divine impulse, it is my opinion that Noah was not unfamiliar with the nature of this juice and, together with his family, often made use of wine before this both for the benefit of his own body and also in sacrifices or libations. But occasionally, when he wanted to use wine for refreshment, I believe he drank too much.

This I simply cannot excuse. Anyone who wanted to excuse it could find weightier reasons than Lyra could, for example, that a man of advanced age, tired out by a large number of daily tasks and cares, was overcome by wine, to which he had already become accustomed. For wine more readily overcomes those who are either worn out by labors or weak because of old age. On the other hand, robust and carefree men are able to consume a very large amount of wine without any special impairment of their reason.

Those who excuse the patriarch this way dispense of their own

[61] Cf. Lyra on Gen. 9:21, sec. x.

accord with the comfort that the Holy Spirit considered necessary for the churches, namely, that even the greatest saints sometimes fall.

Even though this fall seems very insignificant, it is still the cause of great offense. It is an offense not only to Ham but also to the rest of the brothers, perhaps also to their wives. We are not to assume that Ham was a seven-year-old child; for he was born when Noah was five hundred years old. Thus he was at least a hundred years old and had one or two children himself.

So Ham did not laugh at his father because of some childish thoughtlessness, as children do when they stand around a drunken peasant in the street and make sport of him. He was actually offended by his father's fall, because he regarded himself as more righteous, holier, and more pious than his father. We have here more than a mere appearance of offense; the very situation is an offense, because son Ham is so offended by his father's drunkenness that he passes judgment on his father and takes delight in his sin.

If we want to discuss Ham's sin correctly, we must take original sin into consideration, that is, we must keep in mind the depravity of the heart. The son would never have laughed at his father, who was overcome by wine, if he had not first put out of his heart that reverence and esteem which, by God's command, children should have for their parents.

Therefore just as the majority of the world regarded Noah as a fool before the Flood, condemned him as a heretic, and looked down upon him as a madman, so his son here laughs at him as a fool and condemns him as a sinner.

Furthermore, since Noah alone ruled the church, the state, and his household with unremitting attention and effort, who has any doubt that he did many things that offended the proud and arrogant mind of his son? But up to this time the son concealed this malevolence of his heart. Now it comes to light on the occasion of his father's manifest sin.

The source of this sin must be taken into consideration; only then does the hideousness of the action become really apparent. Nobody becomes an adulterer, and no one commits murder unless he has first cast the fear of God out of his heart. Thus a pupil does not rebel against his teacher unless he has first lost all due respect for his teacher.

Similarly, Ps. 14:2 declares that the Lord looked down from heaven to see whether there was anyone who either understood or sought

God. But when He sees that there is no one, He adds that they did not do what is good, that they were unprofitable, that they sinned with their tongue, that they sinned with their hand, that they feared where there was nothing to fear, etc.

Thus Ham appeared wise and holy to himself, and in his own judgment he regarded many things that his father had done as evil or foolish. This points to a heart that despises not only its parent but also the commands of God. Therefore nothing is left for the wicked son except to wait for an opportunity he could use as evidence to bring his father's foolishness to public attention. Hence he does not laugh at his drunken father like a child, nor does he summon his brothers as though for some laughable sight. He wants this to be conclusive evidence that God has forsaken his father and has accepted Ham. He gleefully broadcasts this sin among other people; for, as I have said before, he is not a seven-year-old child; he is a hundred-year-old man.

This perverseness is characteristic of original sin; it makes men arrogant, proud, and wise beyond measure, although as Paul admonishes in Rom. 12:3: "One ought to think with sober judgment, each according to the measure of faith which God has assigned him." But original sin does not let Ham stay within these bounds. Therefore he arrogantly goes beyond his right to pronounce judgment upon his father.

We observe the same thing in Absalom. Before he foments the rebellion against his father David, he passes unfavorable judgment on David's rule. This displeasure in his father's rule is later followed by unconcealed contempt and open violence, designed to overthrow his father. When Ham's heart was full of this poison, which, like a spider, he drew from his father as from a beautiful rose, there resulted this kind of fruit.

These examples give us warning and instruction concerning the conflict that has been going on from the beginning of the world between the church and Satan with his members, the hypocrites or false brethren. Ham's deed must be traced back, not to some childish playfulness but to the bitter hatred of Satan, who inflames his members against the true church, especially against those who are in the ministry, and makes them constantly watchful, so that they may be on the lookout for anything that can be turned into slander.

Thus we see that the papists today do nothing but watch our entire way of life, in an endeavor to slander us. If we make a human mistake — and indeed we are weak and have our failings — then they plunge into our dirt like hungry swine and make it an object of delight, while they expose our weakness after the pattern of the cursed Ham and bring it to everybody's attention. They truly hunger and thirst for our offenses. Even though, by the grace of God, they cannot reproach us with adultery, murder, or other crimes, except with such as they invent — these brazen men shrink from no lie — yet they pick up other matters and exaggerate them before the public.

The example of David is well known. He had been surrounded on all sides by his enemies, who were intently watching for any chance he might give them. They envied him for the kingship to which he had been called by God. Hence when that awful fall of his occurred, they were elated.

All this serves for our instruction. Because at times God permits even righteous and holy men to stumble and fall either into actual offenses or into such as seem so, we must be on our guard lest we immediately pass judgment, as Ham did. He had despised his father long since, but only now does he do so openly. Moreover, he maintains that his father is feeble-minded from senility and has evidently been forsaken by the Holy Spirit, because he, on whom lay the rule of the church, the state, and the home, has not refrained from drunkenness. But, O wretched Ham, how happy you are that now at last you have found what you were seeking, namely, poison in a lovely rose!

God should be praised and blessed forever for dealing with His saints in a truly wonderful manner. For while He permits them to be weak and to stumble, while He lets them abound with actions that result in displeasure and offense, and the world judges and condemns them, He forgives them these weaknesses and has compassion on them. On the other hand, He leaves to Satan and utterly rejects those who are angels in their own eyes.

The first value of this account is that the godly have the comfort they need in their weaknesses, because they see that at times even the saintliest men fell disgracefully as the result of a similar weakness.

In the second place, the account is also an example of the terrible judgment of God. Prompted by Ham's peril, we should not at once pass judgment if we see a person who holds an official position in the state or the church or the home — such as our parents — make a mistake and fall. For who knows why God is doing this? Even though such lapses should not be excused, we see that they are profitable to comfort the godly; for they show that God is able to put up with the mistakes and faults of His people. When we are assailed by sins, therefore, we, too, may hope for God's mercy and not despair.

But this medicine for the godly is poison for the ungodly. They are not looking for instruction and comfort from God. Therefore they do not deserve to see the glory of God in His saints. They see nothing except what offends and ensnares them so that they fall, and in the end they themselves perish.

Let us, therefore, cultivate respect for our elders. Do not be offended if they act rashly. Remember that they are human, and keep in mind that God, who wants the ungodly to be offended and provoked, has amazing ways with His saints. Thus Moses threatens the Jews in Deut. 32:21: "I will provoke you with a foolish nation." Because they were unwilling to listen to the prophets during the entire time of the kingdom, God brought about a great offense: He cast aside the people that was wise and religious, had the promises, and was descended from the fathers; and He chose the dirt and dregs of the world, a foolish nation, one that was not a nation, that is, one without godliness, without religion, without worship, and without divine wisdom or the Word. This offense drove the Jews mad.

The same thing will happen to our papists; they will be stricken by some irreparable offense. Ham had given up his devotion toward God and his father when he came to believe that he could rule the church better. Secretly he either laughed at or condemned his father. Now he makes such an exhibition of himself that he displays also before others his wicked and disrespectful attitude toward his father.

The other two brothers, Shem and Japheth, do not share Ham's wickedness; they continue in their respect for God and their father. They see the offense, that their father is drunk and that he lies there naked without any shame, just like a child. They realize that this is not proper for a ruler of the church and of the state.

But Shem and Japheth do not let this destroy the respect they owe their parent. They overcome this offense; they cover and extenuate this weakness as they approach their father with eyes turned away and cover him with a garment. They would not have had this outward and truly admirable respect for their father if they had not been rightly disposed toward God in their heart and had not been convinced that their father had been appointed priest and king by divine power.

We have before us the horrible example of Ham, who, though he was preserved with the few during the Flood, forgets all piety. Still it is profitable to consider carefully how this fall happened to him. The outward sins we commit with the body must first take form in the heart. That is, before one sins by an act, the heart departs from the Word and the fear of God; it does not know and seek God, as the psalm states (14:2). After the heart gets to the point that it pays no attention to the Word and despises the ministers and prophets of God, there follow ambition and pride; those whom we see standing in the way of our desires we overwhelm with hatred and defamation, until finally our abusive language even brings on murder.

Hence let those who are to rule either churches or states strive with all zeal to remain humble, and let them ask God in their daily prayers to enable them to do so. Accounts of this kind should move us to such concern. We see what occasioned Ham's horrible fall.

Hence when we see saints fall, let us not be offended. Much less let us gloat over the weakness of other people, or rejoice, as though we were stronger, wiser, and holier. Rather let us bear with and cover, and even extenuate and excuse, such mistakes as much as we can, bearing in mind that what the other person has experienced today we may perhaps experience tomorrow. We are all one mass, and we are all born of one flesh. Therefore let us learn St. Paul's rule that "he who stands should take heed lest he fall" (1 Cor. 10:12).

This is the way Ham's brothers looked upon their drunken parent. They thought: "Behold, our father has fallen. But God deals in a wonderful way with His saints. Sometimes He lets them fall for our comfort, lest we despair when we are overcome by a similar weakness."

Let us, too, emulate the wisdom of these men. The sins of other people do not give us the power to judge them. "They stand and fall for their own lord" (Rom. 14:4). Furthermore, if the downfall of others displeases us — since many actions surely neither should nor can be excused — let us be on our guard all the more diligently, lest something of the same sort happen to us; but let us not judge proudly and presumptuously. For this is the vicious character of original sin, that it wants to be wise beyond measure and seeks to acquire praise for righteousness as the result of other people's failings.

We are indeed weak sinners, and we readily confess that since we are human our behavior is not always free of offense. But although we have this fault in common with our opponents, we diligently do our duty by planting the Word of God, teaching the churches, correcting defects, exhorting to what is right, comforting the weak, and whatever else is called for by the ministry that God has committed to us.

On the other hand, our adversaries, who strive for nothing but hypocrisy and the appearance of holiness, add most serious sins to the weakness that they have in common with us; for they do not devote themselves to their calling but are busy with their concern for prestige and wealth. They neglect their churches and let them go to a miserable ruin; they condemn sound doctrine and teach idolatry. In short, abroad they are wise, at home extremely unwise. This evil is very destructive in the church.

This is the first part of the only historical account that Moses wanted to record, although righteous Noah was certainly endowed with many outstanding qualities and accomplished very much both in the church and in the state. For it takes much effort to found states and to establish churches. Besides, these two aspects of life, to say nothing of the management of the household, are fraught with many perils. For Satan, who is a liar and a murderer (John 8:44), bitterly hates both church and civil government.

But all these real achievements Moses passes by and does not touch on them with a single word. This one fact he records: how Noah became drunk and was ridiculed by his younger son, as an outstanding example from which the godly may learn to trust in God's mercy. On the other hand, the proud, the would-be religious, the sanctimonious, and the wiseacres should learn to fear God and refrain from rashly judging others. For God is wonderful in His dealings with His saints, as King Manasseh says, and terrible "against the ungodly and sinners" (Pr. of Man. 5). This the example of Ham shows; this was not the first time he went astray, but he nourished this hatred against his father for a long time and later on filled the world with idolatry.

23. *Then Shem and Japheth took a garment, laid it upon both their shoulders, and walked backward and covered the nakedness of their father; their faces were turned away, and they did not see their father's nakedness.*

24. *When Noah awoke from his wine and knew what his youngest son had done to him,*

25. *he said: Cursed be Canaan; a slave of slaves shall he be to his brothers.*

In this passage Moses records a truly outstanding and noteworthy example of respect toward a father. It would not have been sinful if the sons had approached and covered their father without turning their faces away. What sin would there be if someone came upon a naked human being by chance and saw what he did not want to see? But this is not what the two sons do. When they hear from their proud and laughing brother what happened to their father, the two place a garment on their shoulders, enter the tent backwards — how amazing! — lay down the garment with their faces turned away, and so cover their father.

Who does not see here a heart that has a concern for the will and the Word of God, and a respect for a father's majesty, which God wants held in honor and not despised or ridiculed by children?

Therefore God indicates that He regards this deference as a most welcome sacrifice and as the highest form of worship and obedience. On the other hand, He hates Ham with the utmost hatred; for he could have looked at what he saw, provided he came upon the sight by chance, if only he had covered it, if only he had kept silence and had not revealed that he took pleasure in his father's sin. But this despiser of God, of His Word, and of divinely instituted order not only does not cover his father with a garment but even makes sport of him and so leaves him naked.

Hence in his description of what the two brothers did Moses points out the extraordinary malice of Ham, namely, that he had a satanic and bitter hatred against his father. Who of us would not at least cover with his own garment an unfamiliar and strange human being who has been overcome by wine and is naked on the road, in order to avoid disgrace? How much more this should have been done for a father! But Ham not only fails to render this service to his father, who was at that time the supreme sovereign of the world — something that human reason teaches us to do for strangers — but he even reveals Noah's plight with pleasure, derides his drunken father, and reveals their father's sin to his brothers as though it were good news.

Moses, therefore, holds up Ham as a horrible example that should be carefully impressed in the church, in order that young people may learn to respect their elders, the magistrates, and their parents. This account is not recorded for Noah's sake or for Ham's sake; it is recorded for the sake of their descendants and of every one of us. Ham, the despiser of God and of his parent, is depicted in the most hideous colors.

Moreover, the penalty for such great wickedness is pointed out with special care. For Noah, a foolish, feeble-minded, and ridiculous old man in the eyes of his son, now comes forward in prophetic majesty and announces to his sons a divine revelation about future events. Thus it is true what Paul says: "Strength is made perfect in weakness" (2 Cor. 12:9). The assurance with which Noah makes his pronouncement here is proof that it is full of the Holy Spirit, even though his son derided and despised him as though he had been altogether forsaken by the Holy Spirit.

At this point I am passing over the discussion on which I touched above — the discussion concerning the order of the sons of Noah, who was the first-born and who the youngest.[62] More profitable and more deserving of notice is this: the Holy Spirit is moved to such great wrath against the disobedient and contemptuous son that he even refuses to call him by his own name but designates him as Canaan, after his son. Some maintain that because God was willing to save Ham in the ark with the others as though he were one who was blessed, Noah wanted to curse his son Canaan, not him. Nevertheless, the curse upon the son recoils upon the father, who deserved it. Hence the name Ham disappears at this point because the Holy Spirit hates it, and this is indeed an ominous hatred. Thus the psalm also states: "I hate them with perfect hatred" (139:22). When the Holy Spirit begins to hate and to be angry, eternal death follows.

Even though son Ham sinned against his father in many ways, yet this sin was the most striking. In it the fruit of the first sin and the malice of Satan revealed themselves as the drunken father lay there naked. When through this sin the rest of his sins have been made full and complete, the Holy Spirit condemns him and, to deter others, also threatens him with everlasting servitude.

26. *He also said: Blessed be the Lord God of Shem; and let Canaan be His slave.*

These are two great and important prophecies, and they must be given careful consideration. They concern even our own age, although the Jews have signally misapplied them. They observe that Ham is cursed three times, and this they interpret to the glory of their own nation, promising themselves a physical rule or empire.

But the reason why the curse is repeated so many times is a different one, namely, that God is unable to forget such great disrespect toward parents and does not permit it to go unpunished. He wants

[62] Cf. *Luther's Works*, 1, pp. 357—358.

parents and magistrates treated with respect, and honor shown to older people, because He commands in Lev. 19:32 that one should rise before a hoary head. And about the ministers of the church He says: "He who rejects you rejects Me" (Luke 10:16).

Disobedience toward parents is, therefore, a clear indication of an impending curse and disaster; likewise also contempt for the office of the ministry and the government. When people in the ancient world began to deride the patriarchs and to despise their authority, the Flood followed. When among the people of Judah a child began to be insolent against an old person, as Is. 3:5 shows, Jerusalem fell, and Judah collapsed. This deterioration of morals is the surest indication of impending ruin. We have reason to be fearful for Germany too, where the infraction of law and order is so widespread.

But in this connection note must be taken of the rule that both experience and the Holy Scriptures teach: because God delays the punishment with which He is threatening, He is laughed at and is charged with lying.

This rule we must attach to all prophecies as a seal. Ham hears himself cursed; but because he does not feel the curse immediately, he smugly despises it and laughs at it.

Similarly, the ancient world laughed at Noah when he made predictions about the Flood. If it had believed that such great punishments were impending, you do not think, do you, that it would have continued to be so smug and would not have improved its life and repented?

Thus if Ham had considered true what he heard from his father, he would have sought refuge in mercy and would have begged for forgiveness of the crime of which he was guilty. But he does neither. He leaves his father haughtily and goes to Babylon; there, together with his descendants, he engages in building a city and a tower, and establishes himself as lord of all Asia.

What is the reason for this smugness? This no doubt, that divine prophecies are trustworthy only to faith; they are not perceptible to the senses or subject to tests, regardless of whether they are promises or threats. Therefore to the flesh the opposite always appears to be true.

Ham is cursed by his father, but he takes possession of the largest part of the world and establishes extensive kingdoms. On the other hand, Shem and Japheth are blessed; but if you compare them with Ham, they and their descendants are actually beggars.

How, then, can this prophecy be true? My answer is: this prophecy and all others, whether they are promises or threats, are beyond the grasp of reason and understandable solely by faith. For God delays both the punishments and the rewards. Hence perseverance is needed. "For he who endures unto the end will be saved," as Christ says in Matt. 24:13.

The whole life of the godly is one of faith and hope. If one were to take reason or the achievements and the examples of the world into account, they all stand for the opposite. Ham is cursed, and yet he alone becomes a lord; Shem and Japheth are blessed, but they alone bear the curses and are afflicted in various ways. Hence because God delays with His promises as well as with His threats, one must wait in faith. "Even though," as Habakkuk says, "it should be slow, it will nevertheless surely come and not tarry" (2:3).

The Holy Spirit's great wrath is exhibited in this passage when it states about Ham: "He shall be a slave of slaves," that is, the lowest and most abject slave. If you consult history, however, you will see that he rules in Canaan, but that Abraham, Isaac, Jacob, and other descendants who had the blessing live like servants among the Canaanites. Furthermore, since the Egyptians are the descendants of Ham, with what pitiful servitude Israel is oppressed in that country!

How, then, is it true that Ham is cursed and Shem is blessed? Evidently in this way, that the fulfillment of the divine promise and threat had to be awaited. The delay occurs in order that the ungodly may fill their cup and God cannot be accused of not giving an opportunity for repentance. While the godly are oppressed by the ungodly and actually serve those who are their servants, they go through trials and training for the purpose of increasing their faith and love toward God. They are to be disciplined through many vexations and tribulations; and only after they have been disciplined, may they at last attain the promise. For when the time was fulfilled, it was impossible for Ham's descendants to be powerful enough to avoid yielding to the descendants of Shem. Then was fulfilled the curse that Ham and all his descendants had regarded with arrogant contempt and unbelief for so long.

Our situation today is no different. We have the true doctrine and the true worship. We can boast that we are the true church and that we have the promises of spiritual blessings in Christ. Because the pope's church condemns our doctrine, we know that it is not the church of Christ but the church of Satan and truly, like Ham, " a slave of slaves." Yet the actual situation is that the pope is the ruler and we are the slaves and the offscouring, as Paul calls us (1 Cor. 4:13).

What shall we wretched and oppressed people do? In the meantime we comfort our hearts with our spiritual sovereignty, that is, with our knowledge that we have forgiveness of sins and a God who has been reconciled through Christ, until on the Last Day the liberation of the body comes also. Yet we experience some small part of the liberation of the body even in this life; for because tyrants stubbornly oppose the Gospel, they are utterly exterminated from the earth.

Thus the Roman Empire perished after all the other realms of the world had fallen, but the Word of the Lord and the church abide forever. Similarly, Christ is gradually weakening the power of the pope. But until he is completely removed and becomes a slave of slaves with ungodly Ham, there is need for faith and patient waiting. Meanwhile Ham is excluded from the kingdom of God and for a time has possession of the kingdom of the world. Thus the pope is excluded from the church of God and holds the kingdom of the world for a time, in such a manner, however, that finally he will not endure.

The procedure of divine justice is this, that the godly should have a kingdom, but in faith, and should be satisfied with the spiritual blessing that they have a reconciled God and a sure hope of the kingdom of heaven. Meanwhile they should leave the possession of the kingdoms of the world to the ungodly until God scatters them even physically, but appoints us heirs of all things through Christ.

Furthermore, this prophecy reveals that Noah was enlightened by the Holy Spirit in an extraordinary degree, because he saw, in the first place, that his descendants would abide forever, and, in the second place, that the family of Ham, even though it would rule for a time, would finally perish, and, in particular, would be deprived of the spiritual blessing.

But this must be understood just as I stated previously about the descendants of Cain.[63] I do not think that all were condemned without exception. But those who were converted to the faith were not saved as the result of a definite promise made to them; they were saved as the result of what I would call "irregular grace."[64] Thus the Gibeonites and others were saved when the people of Israel occu-

[63] Cf. *Luther's Works*, 1, pp. 301—302.

[64] The phrase is *vaga gratia;* cf. also *Luther's Works*, 1, p. 301, note 58.

pied the land of Canaan. Similarly, Job, Naaman the Syrian, the Ninevites, the widow of Zarephath, and others from among the heathen were saved, not as the result of a promise but as the result of irregular grace.

Why, however, does he not say: "Blessed be Shem" but: "Blessed be the Lord God of Shem"? My answer is that this is done because of the excellence of the blessing. For here Noah is speaking, not of a material blessing but of the future blessing through the Promised Seed. He sees that this blessing is so great that it cannot be expressed in words. For this reason he turns to thanksgiving. Zacharias seems to have patterned after this very passage in Luke 1:68, when, by the same reasoning, he says: "Blessed be the Lord God of Israel."

Thus Noah directs his blessing toward God Himself, after the fashion of a thanksgiving. "God, who is the God of Shem," says he, "is blessed," as though he wanted to say: "There is no need for me to extend my blessing over Shem, because he has already been blessed with a spiritual blessing. He is already a child of God; and from him the church will be expanded, just as it was expanded from Seth before the Flood." It is extraordinarily meaningful that he links God with his son Shem in this manner and, as it were, betroths them.

Great must have been the enlightenment in the heart of Noah, who thus distinguishes between his sons: Ham with his descendants he repudiates; but Shem he places among the line of the saints and the church, because on him would rest the spiritual blessing that was given in Paradise concerning the Seed (Gen. 3:15). It is for this reason that the holy man blesses God and thanks Him.

27. *God will speak gently with Japheth, and he will dwell in the tents of Shem; but Canaan will be their slave.*

This prophecy is amazing because of the remarkable aptness of the words. Noah does not bless Shem; he blesses the God of Shem. Thus he gives thanks to God for having cherished Shem and for having endowed him with the spiritual blessing, the blessing concerning the Seed of the woman. But when he gets to Japheth, he does not use the same expression he used concerning Shem. His obvious purpose was to point to the mystery of which Paul speaks in Rom. 11:11 and Christ in John 4:22, that salvation is from the Jews. Yet the Gentiles, too, share in this salvation. For although Shem alone is the true root and stock, nevertheless the Gentiles are grafted into this stock like a foreign scion, and they become partakers of the fertility and the sap that are in the chosen tree.

This light Noah sees through the Holy Spirit, and vaguely but precisely he foretells that the kingdom of Christ must be extended into the world from the stock of Shem, not from that of Japheth.

The Jews prate that Japheth signifies the neighboring nations round about Jerusalem which were admitted to the temple and its worship.[65] But Noah does not concern himself at all with the temple at Jerusalem or with the tabernacle of Moses; he is dealing with more important matters. He is dealing with the three patriarchs who were to replenish the earth. Moreover, he states about Japheth that while he was not of the stock of the people of God, which has the promise concerning Christ, he is nevertheless to be called by the Gospel into the fellowship of that people which has God and the promises.

Hence the church of Gentiles and Jews is depicted here. Ham is a castaway and is not given access to the spiritual blessing of the Seed except insofar as this takes place through irregular grace. But Japheth, even though he does not, like Shem, have the promise of the Seed, is nevertheless given the hope that he will be embodied into the fellowship of the church. Thus we Gentiles, who are the children of Japheth, do not indeed have the promise given to us; and yet we are included in the promise that was given to the Jews, for we have been foreordained to the communion of the saints of the people of God. All this has been recorded, not for the sake of Shem and Japheth but for the sake of their descendants.

We see here the reason why the Jews are so puffed up and boastful. They see that their father Shem alone has the promise of the eternal blessing that is through Christ. But then they err by supposing that the promise is received as the result of natural descent and not as the result of faith. Paul treats this passage masterfully in Romans (9:6) when he says that the children of Abraham are not those who are descended from Abraham according to the flesh but those who believe as Abraham believed (Gal. 3:7).

In this passage Moses expresses the same idea dimly when he expressly declares: "Blessed be the Lord God of Shem"; for this means that the blessing is nowhere except where the God of Shem is. Therefore not even a Jew will share in this promise unless he has the God of Shem, that is, unless he believes. Nor will Japheth share in the

---

[65] Lyra on Gen. 9:27, sec. e.

promise unless he dwells in the tents of Shem, that is, unless he is his partner in the same faith.

This is an outstanding promise. It remains in force until the end of the world. But just as we said that it applies only to those who have the God of Shem, or to those who believe, so the curse, too, applies only to those who continue in the ungodliness of Ham. For since Noah is not speaking these words as a human being or on his own authority and reason, but through the Spirit of God, he is speaking not merely of a temporal curse but of a spiritual and eternal one. Moreover, the curse must be understood as applying not only before the world but before God.

We made a similar statement previously about the curse of Cain.[66] If you look at the events, Cain had a greater physical blessing than Seth. God wants the church to be in such a condition in this world that the curse of the ungodly appears to be transferred to it, and that, in contrast, the ungodly should appear to be blessed. Therefore Cain built the city of Enoch while Seth was dwelling in tents.

Similarly, Ham built the city and the tower of Babel, and also ruled over a wide area, while, on the contrary, Shem and Japheth were in want, living wretchedly in tents. Thus the outcome proves that the promises and the curses of God are to be understood, not in a carnal sense concerning the present life but in a spiritual sense. Although the godly are oppressed in the world, still they are most certainly the heirs and sons of God. The ungodly, on the other hand, even though they flourish for a time, are nevertheless finally cut off and wither, as the psalms often declare.[67]

The deed as well as the lot of Ham and of Cain are almost alike. Cain kills his brother. This deed is proof enough that there was no respect for his parent in his heart. He is excommunicated by his father, secedes from the church that had the true God and the true worship, builds the city of Enoch, and devotes himself completely to civil concerns. Ham likewise sins against his father by his disrespect. When he later hears the verdict of the curse, by which he is excluded from the promise of the Seed and from the church, he smugly withdraws from God and from the church; for he is cursed, not in his own person but only in his son, and he goes to Babylon and there builds a royal city.

[66] *Luther's Works*, 1, pp. 310 ff.
[67] Luther is thinking of passages like Ps. 94:3.

These are very fine examples. The church needs them. The Turk and the pope today permit us to glory in the heavenly and enduring blessing that we have the doctrine of the Gospel and are the church. They know our verdict about them, namely, that we regard and condemn both the pope and the Turk as the very Antichrist.[68] Yet with what smugness they disregard this verdict, since they feel secure because of the riches and the power that they have, and because of our weakness and small number! We observe exactly the same attitude in the cursed and excommunicated Cain and Ham.

These experiences teach us that we must not look for a city or a secure place in this earthly life; but in the diversity of our mishaps and of our lot, which this life brings with it, we must look to the hope of eternal life that has been promised to us through Christ. This is, after all, the harbor toward which we, like anxious and attentive sailors, should steer with all our strength in the great violence of the storms.

What if the Turk should subject the entire world to his rule, something that will never happen? For according to Daniel (10:13), Michael will bring aid to the holy people, the church. What if the pope should acquire the wealth of the entire world, something he has been striving to attain with the utmost zeal for many centuries? Will they, perhaps, escape death for this reason or provide an enduring place for themselves in this life? Then why are we offended by their worldly blessings or even by our own misfortune and perils, since they have been banished from the fellowship of the saints, while we shall enjoy eternal blessings through the Son of God?

If, then, because of their brief and small good fortune in this life, Cain and Ham, as the ancestors, and the pope and Turk, as their descendants, can disregard the verdict of the true church, why do we, who are in sure possession of eternal blessings, not disregard their power and verdicts in turn? His father's curse makes no impression on Ham; he is displeased with him, and despises him as a feebleminded old man. Ham goes away and provides himself with the power of the world. This he values more highly than if he had been blessed by his father along with Shem.

This passage serves to give us strength when we go through the same experience today. The popes and the bishops hold us in utmost

---

[68] Sometimes Luther said that the pope was the head of Antichrist and the Turk his body; he frequently linked the two, as in his hymn, *Erhalt uns, Herr* (W, XXXV, 467).

contempt. What, say they, could these beggarly heretics do? They are puffed up by their wealth and power. But as for ourselves, let us calmly bear this insolence of the ungodly, just as Noah bore it at that time in the case of his son, and let us comfort ourselves with hope and faith in the eternal blessings, which we know they lack.

I stated previously that the Holy Spirit was so perturbed by Ham's sin that He could not even endure to mention him by name in the curse.[69] And it is true, as the punishment also indicates, that Ham committed a serious sin. But the following reason is not inappropriate either, as I stated above: after Noah had seen that Ham was called by the voice of God, was received into the ark, and was also saved with the others, he wanted to spare him whom God had spared in the Flood. Therefore he transfers the curse, which Ham had deserved by his sin, to his son Canaan, whom Ham undoubtedly wanted to remain with him.

The Jews hand down another reason, namely, that son Canaan first saw that his grandfather Noah was lying there naked and reported this to his father, who himself also saw it; and so Canaan was the instigator of this sin for his father.[70] But let the reader judge what this is worth.

In connection with this passage a linguistic question should be raised; for the philologists debate why all interpreters render it "May God enlarge Japheth," although the Hebrew manner of speech does not tolerate this translation. Yet by general agreement not only the Hebrew but also the Aramaic translators accept the word יַפְתְּ in the sense of "to make wide." Sometimes such linguistic discussions are of great value and bring out the real meaning of a statement.[71]

Some derive Japheth from the verb יָפָה, which means "to be beautiful," as in Ps. 45:3: יָפְיָפִיתָ מִבְּנֵי אָדָם, "You were the fairest of the children of men." But these translators can readily be shown to be wrong, for its true derivation is from פָּתָה, which means "to persuade," "to deceive with kindly words." Thus Moses uses it in Ex. 22:15: וְכִי־יְפַתֶּה אִישׁ בְּתוּלָה, that is, if anyone deceives a girl with gentle words, he shall give her a dowry. Also in Jer. 20:7: פִּתִּיתַנִי יְהוָה וָאֶפָּת, "You have deceived me, Lord, and I was deceived." Likewise Prov. 1:10: אִם־יְפַתּוּךָ, "If sinners entice you." There is no need

---

[69] See p. 174.
[70] Lyra on Gen. 9:22, sec. y.
[71] See p. 15, note 23.

of additional examples, for this word is encountered all along; and I have no doubt that the Greek πείθω is derived from it, for it has altogether the same meaning.

But to get back to the question. Why do all have the translation "May the Lord make Japheth wide," although the verb is not פָּתַח, which means "to make wide" or "to open," but פָּתָה? I have no doubt that the translators were prompted by an incongruity. Since this is a promise, it appeared difficult to maintain that Noah is saying: "May the Lord deceive Japheth"; for this seems to have the sound of a curse, not of a blessing. They therefore adopted a milder expression, although it is not in agreement with usage; and since the difference between פָּתַח and פָּתָה is small, they took the one for the other because the situation seemed to require it, inasmuch as this is a promise.

But there is no need of twisting the text in this fashion and doing violence to the rules of language, especially since the verb פָּתָה conveys a very suitable meaning. It is a neutral verb, like "persuade" in our language, and can be understood in a good or in an evil sense. Therefore it involves no reproach for God if one applies this word to Him. A clear example of this is Hos. 2:14, where the Lord speaks thus: "Behold, I מְפַתֶּיהָ, shall persuade or with kindly words entice her and bring her into the wilderness and speak tenderly to her. I shall allure her, I shall speak sweetly with her; and thus I shall deceive her, as it were, so that she gives Me her approval, so that the church allies itself with Me."

Thus in this passage too it is correctly understood in the sense of "allure," "to persuade," "to influence with friendly and kindly words." Let God allure, persuade, and move Japheth by means of persuasive words, so that Japheth himself, in harmony with his name, becomes the persuaded one, the lovingly invited one, and also the deceived one.

But you will say: What can be the meaning of this statement? Or why should Japheth be deceived or persuaded, and by God at that? My answer is: In this prophecy Noah seizes upon the opportunity provided by the names. He thanks God that He has so placed Shem that he stands like a solid root from which Christ should be born; for the verb שׂוּם denotes "to put," "to place," or "to establish."

Concerning Japheth he prays that he may be a true Japheth. Because he was the oldest, to whom the right of primogeniture ordinarily belonged, Noah asks that the Lord may lovingly persuade him, in the first place, not to begrudge his brother the honor and not to be too impatient because this prerogative was taken from him and transferred to his brother. In the second place, because this pertains solely to the person of Japheth, Noah includes all his descendants and prays that although the promise was given to Shem alone, God would nevertheless not exclude the descendants of Japheth from it but would speak to them lovingly through the Gospel, in order that they, too, might be a יָפְתְּ and be persuaded by the voice of the Gospel. This is a divine persuasion. It is the work of the Holy Spirit, not of the flesh or of the world or of Satan; it is a holy and life-giving work.

Paul employs this expression when he says in Gal. 1:10: "For am I now persuading God or men?" And in Gal. 3:1: "Who has bewitched you τῇ ἀληθείᾳ μὴ πείθεσθαι, that you do not believe the truth or that you do not permit yourselves to be persuaded of the things that are true?"

Thus Japheth denotes one whom we call "artless" in the proverb,[72] one who readily believes, who readily permits himself to be persuaded of something, is not contentious, not obstinate, but takes his reason captive for the Lord and believes His Word, remains a learner, and does not want to teach God what to say and do.

This passage presents the very charming prayer that God would persuade Japheth, that is, that He would speak kindly with him, so that although He does not speak to him because of the promise, as with Shem, He would nevertheless speak with him because of His grace and divine goodness.

This prayer of Noah deals with the promulgation of the Gospel throughout the entire world. Shem is like the stock, for from his descendants or line Christ was born. For it is the church of the Jews, who had patriarchs, prophets, and kings. Yet here God reveals to Noah that even the poor Gentiles are to dwell in the tents of Shem, that is, that they are to share in the benefits that the Son of God brought into this world, namely, the forgiveness of sins, the Holy Spirit, and life eternal. He clearly prophesies that Japheth, too, in harmony with his name, will hear the friendly message of the Gospel; although he does not have the name that Shem has, who "was placed" that he should be the stock from which Christ would be born, he may still have the persuasion, that is, the Gospel.

It was Paul through whom this prophecy was fulfilled. Almost single-handedly he instructed the family of Japheth in the doctrine of the Gospel, as he states in Rom. 15:19: "From Jerusalem and as

[72] Perhaps Luther is thinking of the proverbial saying, *O sancta simplicitas!* ascribed to John Hus.

far round as Illyricum I have fully preached the Gospel of Christ." For nearly all Asia, with the exception of its eastern peoples, together with Europe, belongs to the descendants of Japheth. The Gentiles did not receive from God, as did the Jews, kingdom and priesthood, or the Law, or the promise; as a result of God's mercy they received only the friendly voice of the Gospel, the persuasion to which the very name Japheth points.

The translators, whom God permitted to err in this manner, did not see this true meaning; and yet them did not miss the actual sense by much.[73] For the verb הִרְחִיב, which means "to make wide," denotes "to comfort" in a Hebrew idiom, just as, conversely in Latin "narrowness"[74] denotes griefs, perils, and disaster. Thus in Ps. 4:1 there appears בַּצָּר הִרְחַבְתָּ, "Thou hast given me room in distress"; but the only true room or comfort is the Word of the Gospel.

Thus the two ideas agree if one interprets them properly. But the first idea, involving persuasion, is the true and actual one. Moreover, it provides the outstanding insight that even though the promise was not given to us Gentiles, we are nevertheless called to the Gospel through divine Providence. The promise belongs to Shem alone, but Japheth has the persuasion and, as Paul says: "Like a wild olive tree is grafted into the olive tree and becomes a sharer in the natural fatness or sap of the olive tree" (Rom. 11:17). In Holy Scripture the earlier statements are in agreement with the most recent; and what God promised at the time of Noah, that He now carries out by actual events.

Ham means one who is hot and glowing. I believe that this name was given to him by his father because of the great hope he had formed about his youngest son, as though in comparison with him the other two were cold. Eve similarly exulted greatly when Cain is born, for she believed that he would remedy whatever mishap had occurred (Gen. 4:1). But he is the first to harm the human race in a new way, for he kills his brother.

Thus in His unfathomable counsel God changes even the plans of His holy men. At Ham's birth his father foretold that he would be inflamed more than his brothers with outstanding zeal to promote the church. After he has grown up, he is indeed growing and hot, but in a different direction. He is incensed against his father and

[73] The Vulgate has *Dilatet Deus Japheth.*
[74] Cf. *Luther's Works,* 13, p. 7, note 6; the Latin word is *angustiae.*

against God, as his deed reveals. Thus he bears an ominous name, although his father did not understand it this way when he gave it to him.

This is Noah's prophecy about his sons, who have filled the world. The fact that by the mercy of God the Word of the Gospel has begun to shine for Germany is due to this prophecy about Japheth, and so what Noah foretold at that time is being fulfilled today. Even though we are not of the seed of Abraham, we nevertheless live in the tents of Shem, and we have the benefits of the fulfilled promises concerning Christ.

28. *After the Flood Noah lived three hundred and fifty years.*

29. *All the days of Noah were nine hundred and fifty years; and he died.*

The historical account reveals that Noah died in the fifty-eighth year after Abraham's birth. Therefore Abraham, having availed himself of such an excellent and outstanding teacher for up to fifty years, was able to make considerable progress in religion. There is no doubt that Noah, full of the Holy Spirit, cherished this grandson with extraordinary fondness and love as the only heir of the promises given to Shem.

Nevertheless, the descendants of Ham were flourishing at that time, and they spread idolatry in the eastern regions. This idolatry Abraham observed, yet not without offense. But he was saved by Noah; Abraham was almost the only one to admire Noah as a remnant of the ancient world. The rest, who had forgotten the wrath that had raged during the Flood, even laughed at the godly old man, but especially the descendants of Ham, who were puffed up by their wealth and power. They scoffed at their father Noah and, crazed by their success, ridiculed his curse about their servitude as the dream of a feeble-minded old man.

CHAPTER TEN

1. *These are the generations of the sons of Noah, Shem, Ham, and Japheth; sons were born to them after the Flood.*

EVEN though this tenth chapter is seemingly barren and appears to serve no purpose, and though we, born after so many changes of kingdoms and peoples, have nothing to say about the individuals who are mentioned here, we should nevertheless not pass it over in silence.

In the first place in this chapter Moses divides the world after the Flood into three parts, corresponding to the three sons of Noah. Although our literature also divides the world into three parts — Asia, Europe, and Africa — Moses deviates from this division; for he includes in Europe also that part which we designate as Asia, together with the North, which extends as far as the Mediterranean Sea where it touches Palestine. That northern part, together with Europe, he assigns to the sons of Japheth, who, being more numerous, occupy a more extensive area.

The second part of the world he makes the one we call Africa, which also includes the Ethiopians and extends as far as the Strait of Gibraltar.

The third part he assigns to Shem, namely, Judea, but not it alone; for he adds Persia and other peoples, both eastern and southern.

THE GENERATION OF JAPHETH

2. *The sons of Japheth: Gomer, Magog, Madai, Javan, Tubal, Meshech, and Tiras.*

Japheth left seven sons. The names of all the others recur in Holy Scripture; only the name of Tiras perished and is not found anywhere else in Scripture.

Gomer is the first son, and Jerome thinks that he is the father of the Galatians.[1] But to me that group appears too small to fit this patriarch; besides, it is certain that the Galatians are Germans, for it

---

[1] Jerome, *Liber hebraicarum quaestionum in Genesim, Patrologia, Series Latina,* XXIII, 999.

is maintained that even today they use the German language, that is, the idiom of the Saxons.[2]

From Ezekiel (38:6) it is certain that they are northern peoples. I am of the opinion that they are those nations which dwell near the Cimmerian Bosporus, for the close relationship of the names is an important piece of evidence.[3] Although the peoples who today inhabit those places are immigrants and not autochthonous, that is, indigenous, this is still no reason to be in doubt about the place. The interchange of the letters *g* and *s* or *c* is common, as the pronunciation of the Italians and of the Belgians proves. I think that Gomer with his descendants inhabited the Cimmerian Bosporus, Maeotis,[4] and the neighboring region toward the north.

Who Magog is I regard as certain. Ezekiel mentions Gog and Magog (38:2). The meaning of גוֹג is "roof." Therefore Gog is considered to be the Scythians, who do not live in houses, as we do, but only in huts or tents.

Similarly, the Turks, too, boast that they do not build magnificent structures, as do we, who adorn our cities with magnificent buildings and erect castles as though we were going to live forever. The Turks laugh at this ambitious endeavor of ours, and they regard it as a part of saintliness not to dwell in stately houses. Hence they lay waste vineyards and demolish stately buildings.[5] The northern peoples whom we call Tartars follow a similar way of life; for they also dwell in huts, or, as the Hebrews say, are מָגוֹג, like the Scythians and other nations.

The Madai are familiar. As their name proves, there is no doubt that they are the Medes. More certain evidence is derived from sacred history, which calls Darius a Mede. Moreover, secular history also declares him to have been a Mede.[6]

Javan is undoubtedly Janus, from which the place Janiculum received its name.[7] Even though it seems to some that the Ionians

[2] It is not clear just where Luther got this startling notion.

[3] This is still the interpretation of many scholars on the location of Gomer.

[4] *Palus Maeotis* was the ancient name for the Sea of Azov; it appears, for example, on the map of Ptolemy (cf. p. 107, note 7).

[5] Cf. p. 181, note 68.

[6] Luther is thinking of the Book of Ezra and probably of Herodotus.

[7] The Janiculum is on the west bank of the Tiber; by his reference to Greek Luther may mean the Etruscans, but more probably he means the area known as *Magna Graecia*.

were named for him, it is certain that Italy, too, used the Greek language once upon a time. For this reason the maritime areas were called Magna Graecia, and historical accounts say that Pythagoras taught there.[8] Hence there is nothing to prevent us from maintaining that Javan and his descendants occupied Asia Minor and all the coast of the Mediterranean Sea from the Gulf of Cilicia to the farthest parts of Spain. The text expressly states later on that the islands of the sea were divided by his sons, for the Mediterranean Sea has many islands. What the situation was in Italy prior to the time of Troy is unknown, and so I believe that those areas underwent many changes.

Jerome believes that Tubal are the Spaniards,[9] but to me he seems to suit the Tartars. Mention is also made of him in Ezekiel 38:2-3.

Jerome thinks that Meshech are the Cappadocians;[10] but from the psalm (120:5) it appears that it is Greater Armenia, where the Georgians and the Caspians are located. The psalm says that the writer is dwelling with the inhabitants of Kedar and Meshech. Moreover, about Kedar it is sure that it is Arabia Petraea,[11] which later on had Moabites, Edomites, and Ammonites as inhabitants. On the northern side of these is Meshech. On the strength of the name, I for my part would readily maintain that they are the Muscovites; and it may be that they migrated from Armenia to the areas they now occupy, just as peoples have often migrated to other areas and occupied them after driving out the inhabitants.

It is unknown who is meant by Tiras, for Scripture nowhere mentions this name again. Jerome believes that they are the Thracians,[12] and this name does resemble Tiras to some extent.

These are the descendants of our father Japheth. The poets also have knowledge of him and call him Japetus.[13] From him all the Northern people have their origin: the Medes, the Scythians, the Tartars, the Cimmerians, the Poles, the Vandals, the Danes, the Germans,

[8] Pythagoras worked in Croton, one of the Achaean towns of Italy.

[9] Jerome, *Liber hebraicarum quaestionum in Genesim, Patrologia, Series Latina,* XXIII, 999—1000.

[10] Cf. Lyra on Gen. 10:2, secs. g and h.

[11] See *Luther's Works,* 1, p. 101, note 31.

[12] Lyra on Gen. 10:2, sec. i.

[13] "His [Japetus'] name yields no plausible Greek etymology, and it is far from unlikely that it is to be connected with that of Japhet son of Noah." H. J. Rose in *The Oxford Classical Dictionary* (Oxford, 1949), p. 418.

the Greeks, the Italians, the French, and the Spaniards. The languages, which have undergone so many changes, prove that the inhabitants often change.

3. *The sons of Gomer: Ashkenaz, Riphath, and Togarmah.*

By common consent the Jews maintain that Ashkenaz represents the Germans.[14] Although this cannot be proved from the Holy Scriptures, we gladly agree, since we have nothing else to suggest. Jeremiah mentions him in chapter 51:27, although our translation does not have the proper name but renders it by an appellative.[15] Eusebius maintains that they are the Goths,[16] but it is established that these were the Germans.

Hence we Germans throughout our entire line are descended from the first-born of Japheth. Although this is no glory before God, it does indicate that there would be some kingdom of this Ashkenaz, since he is the first-born. In the second place, it is also faintly intimated that he would come to a knowledge of the Gospel; for both are the prerogatives of primogeniture. The clear meaning is this: God had merciful regard for this nation and wanted to honor it in an outstanding manner, and history bears witness that the German nation was always considered highly praiseworthy.

Of Riphath, just as of Tiras, there is no further occurrence in the Holy Scriptures. Nor is there anything in the writings of the Gentiles, except that they make mention of the Rhipaeans and of mountains of the same name among which, according to fable, the griffins gather gold.[17] But nobody has any doubt that the stories about the mountains are fiction.

We maintain only that these, too, were northern peoples, but that they were destroyed or subjugated by the Tartars; for God is wont to punish the sins of kingdoms in this manner. Thus He states in Amos (9:8): "Behold, the eyes of the Lord God are upon the sinful kingdom, and I will destroy it from the surface of the ground"; and in Dan. 2:21: "He removes kingdoms and establishes them." Hence the names of the kingdoms do indeed persist, but the inhabitants

---

[14] Cf. Lyra on Gen. 10:2, sec. c.

[15] The Vulgate of Jer. 51:27 has *Annunciate contra illam regibus Ararat, Menni, et Ascenez.*

[16] Cf. Jerome, *Liber hebraicarum quaestionum in Genesim, Patrologia, Series Latina,* XXIII, 1000.

[17] Cf. Aristotle, *Meteorologica,* Book I, ch. 13.

are destroyed and perish on account of their sins. Thus the Turks engulfed Greece, and the Goths Spain; yet the ancient names persist. This is the course of events in the world, and these facts are recorded to the honor of Holy Scripture.

Who Togarmah is nobody knows. Ezek. 27:14 mentions him and lists him among the northern peoples. To me he appears to belong to the Tartars. Some guess that they are the Phrygians and try to find some relationship to the name in Tigranes;[18] but what these ideas are worth I leave to the reader.

4. *The sons of Javan: Elishah, Tarshish, Kittim, and Dodanim.*

5. *By these were divided the islands of the Gentiles in their areas, each one according to their language and families in their nations.*

Jerome thinks that Elishah are the Aeolians,[19] but I am of the opinion that it was a wider dominion. Ezekiel mentions him in chapter 27:7.

Tarshish, it is maintained, is Cilicia, in which is the city of Tarsus, the native land of Paul; I have nothing against this.

Kittim is renowned in Holy Scripture and is generally understood to be Italy. But in my judgment it is actually Greece, together with the neighboring shores of Italy and France. Bileam mentions it in Num. 24:24: "Ships shall come from Kittim"; likewise Zechariah,[20] when he predicts that the destruction of Tyre and of Ashdod will be brought about by Alexander.

Moreover, Macedonia got its name from Kittim; for if the letter *m*, which the Hebrews use as a prefix, is combined with כִּתִּים, there results מַכְתִּים, which we call Macedonia.[21] But one may ask why Greece got its name from Macedonia when this is such an unimportant part of Greece. My answer is that this unimportant part produced the ruler of the entire world.[22] Hence it deserves to be celebrated as the chief part of Greece, since it is the chief part of the entire world.

Dodanim, I believe, has perished. For if Dodona, famed for its

[18] See the passage in Jerome referred to in note 16 above.

[19] Jerome, loc. cit.

[20] The original has "Zechariah," but Luther is evidently thinking of Is. 23:1.

[21] Macedonia traced its name as well as its origin to the eponymous hero Macedon.

[22] This is, of course, a reference to Alexander.

temple of Jupiter,[23] received its name from him, he remains as a single small branch of his entire empire, just as Rome today is ever so small a part of the extensive monarchy it used to be.

Accordingly, these sons of Javan were very great kings and, without a doubt, were properly instructed in religion by their grandfather Japheth. They were also very holy men, especially up to the time when the Jewish people was distinguished from the rest of the nations by a definite Law.

Now when the text declares that the islands of the sea were divided by these people, it means that they were skilled in navigating, which they undoubtedly learned from the example of the ark. But since God gave permanence to their rule, I believe that they retained the true forms of worship that they had received from their fathers and that were in use in the church. God overturns the kingdoms of the ungodly and the idolaters; He does not found them. I do not know whether what Pliny says is true, that some islands emerged from the sea;[24] to me it appears more likely that they were found and inhabited by men who were skilled in navigating, as Moses indicates in this passage.

These are the descendants of Japheth, among whom, without a doubt, were holy fathers who ruled their descendants properly in both a spiritual and a physical way, and erected altars wherever they happened to live. Because no law had yet been given about worship in a certain place, they were free to sacrifice everywhere, just as we today are free to pray everywhere.

Gradually, however, the descendants degenerated into idolatry and began to worship the sun, the stars, etc. This very idolatry undoubtedly took its origin from the true worship, just as superstition always has its origin in true godliness. Godly parents taught their children to pray at sunrise and to give thanks for the beautiful light by which all things are not only illuminated but preserved; but their descendants turned this practice into idolatry. Similarly, the Chaldeans later on worshiped fire; the Turks practiced circumcision; and we ourselves, departing from the teaching of the apostles, have fallen into the abominable idolatry introduced into the church by the papal gang for its own profit. Stupid imitation by the ungodly has always followed upon the faith of the godly, and this has been the source and origin of all misfortune in the church.

[23] Homer, *Iliad*, Book XVI, ll. 233—235; *Odyssey*, Book XIV, ll. 327—328.
[24] Pliny, *Natural History*, Book IV, ch. 23.

Our ancestors were great and extraordinary men, among whom Ashkenaz was an outstanding hero renowned for his godliness and quick to act. In addition to the other eminent endowments that Germany possesses, it now enjoys the clear light of the Word, which is the greatest gift. Blessed are those who make faithful use of it!

Moses records particularly that the languages and families of these men were dispersed to definite places, and he indicates that in this manner empires were established. This was done no doubt by their own father Noah, who ordered one to sail to Asia, another to Greece, and still another to Italy, and there to establish states and churches. The obedient sons and grandsons experienced the blessing of the Lord. Hence these events are put before us as examples of their extraordinary obedience to their father Noah and of their extraordinary diligence in the establishment of churches and kingdoms, as well as of the true harmony that flourished in the churches and states until the infamous Ham troubled the world, as we shall hear in the next section.

Because historical records of these events have perished, it would be profitable to know the etymologies of the names. I believe that the holy fathers, being full of the Holy Spirit and foreseeing future events in the church as well as in the state, followed a definite procedure in assigning these names. On several previous occasions we have pointed out similar examples where names revealed the nature either of the times or of the events.[25] But since the historical accounts have perished, we would have to guess at the reason underlying the etymologies, even if we were able to trace the etymologies themselves.

גָּמַר means one who finishes, or it means an end or a completion. It seems, therefore, that some extraordinary misfortune had occurred to make them believe that the church was finished. But we speculate in vain about matters that are unknown. Therefore we leave this concern to those who have the time for it.

THE GENERATION OF HAM

6. *The sons of Ham: Cush, Egypt, Put, and Canaan.*

It is surely strange that the descendants of the ungodly Ham should be enumerated before those of the blessed Shem. Perhaps this is done in accordance with Christ's statement in the Gospel that

[25] Cf. *Luther's Works*, 1, p. 327.

in the kingdom of God the last become the first (Matt. 19:30). Just as Ham is placed in the middle here, between Japheth and Shem, so we see that the ungodly are sown in the midst of the church and get the best and most prominent place.

In addition, the descendants of Ham are not satisfied with their lot. They encroach upon the generation of Shem and Japheth; for they took possession not only of some eastern and northern parts but also of some southern ones. Cush are the Ethiopians, as we call them today; they occupy not only the interior lands of the South but also its coasts. There is no doubt that מִצְרַיִם is Egypt.

About Put there is nothing certain. I, therefore, assume that he, too, quickly perished on account of sin. Commentaries state that these are the Libyans or Africans, that is, Africa, where it touches the Mediterranean: Numidia, Mauritania, and Cyrenaica. They further declare that in Numidia there is a river by the name of Put.[26]

Canaan is the most famous of all, because he occupied the kingdom that was given to the Children of Israel later on. Consider, however, what the lot of the true church in this world is. Ham is cursed by his father Noah, while Shem and Japheth are blessed. But do not the historical events indicate the opposite? Canaan, Ham's son, has possession of the best and most excellent part of the earth; for I believe that Paradise was in the land of Canaan,[27] and that it alone is the place where God wanted the church and His people to be eventually. While Ham and his descendants are in possession of this delightful area of the world, the church is afflicted and poor. Nevertheless, the good fortune of the ungodly is not everlasting; for in the end Canaan is woefully laid waste, but God's people triumph.

The name Canaan is prophetic; it means merchant, and its centers of commerce have always been most renowned in the world. Thus Tyre and Sidon, in which the merchants resided, gave their name to this entire kingdom. Nor are there any other centers of commerce of greater renown in the Holy Scriptures. Pagan accounts, too, reveal that these cities were most renowned throughout the whole world.[28] For Carthage was their colony, and Ezekiel calls Tyre the "might of the sea" or its mistress (26:17).

[26] Lyra on Gen. 10:6, sec. p.

[27] See p. 204, note 43.

[28] Tyre and Sidon achieved commercial and political prominence in the Roman empire.

Thus with the exception of Arabia and the Persian and Indian gulfs Ham was master of the entire southern area, the most excellent part of the world. What, then, has become of the curse? It has been deferred but not removed, in order that the ungodly might fill their measure and begin to feel all the more smug. The church, on the other hand, is subjected to afflictions, in order to enable it to hold fast even more firmly to the eternal benefits and the true blessing.

7. *The sons of Cush: Seba, Havilah, Sabtah, Raamah, and Sabteca.*

These five sons of the Ethiopian took possession of Arabia Felix, the Persian Gulf, and the Indian Gulf, where Havilah is located (Gen. 2:11). Some say that even today Seba is a famous city of the Ethiopians.[29]

The sons of Raamah: Sheba and Dedan.

Rama or Raamah is the father of Arabia Felix. His son Sheba had possession of the richest region of the South, which is more highly extolled in the historical accounts than any other part of the earth. In short, Shem and Japheth get the barren sands and the swampy and desolate areas; but Ham takes possession of what remains of Paradise, where nothing but spices, gold, and gems are found.

But this happens by the definite counsel of God, who freely grants the ungodly an abundance of everything, even as they strive for it greedily and apply themselves to this endeavor. God does not permit their efforts to be in vain. Meanwhile the sons of God hunger, thirst, freeze, and die by hanging or fire. Why does this happen? Undoubtedly to make us understand that riches of another kind are promised to us in the Word and have been won for us by the Son of God. The ungodly are not concerned with these; they are interested in material things, which come to them in abundance, since they strive so vigorously to get them.

Thus God heaped unbelievable power upon the Roman Empire. Today the Turks are extending their territory with astounding success. This counsel of God is an offense to His weak children. It vexes them when they see the prosperity of the ungodly, who laugh at God and men, while they themselves are in sorrow and are all but overwhelmed by their misfortunes. But this has been the way of God

[29] Luther apparently means Addis Ababa.

since the beginning of the world, as the examples of the first patriarchs bear witness. The murderer Cain is the first to build a city (Gen. 4:17), and Ham acquires the best part of the earth.

Then what is so unusual if today, too, the Turk and the popes are successful? Throughout all ages this has been a universal experience, that the ungodly flourish "like the grass of the earth" (Ps. 92:7). The godly, on the other hand, are stricken daily, in the fine phrase of Ps. 73:14. Yet while they are flourishing in this manner, they are actually being set on a slippery place to be hurled headlong to their destruction.

It was not easy for Lazarus in his great distress to see the rich man with his great abundance of everything (Luke 16:21). But does not the same rich man present a sorry spectacle in hell after his death? Let us, therefore, not be offended by the good fortune of the ungodly; but let us open our spiritual eyes and keep in mind that such people are enjoying transitory and deceptive advantages in this world. We, however, who are afflicted and who live in the fear of God, have the hope of an eternal kingdom, when the ungodly will be subjected to eternal punishment.

NIMROD

8. *Cush became the father of Nimrod; he was the first on earth to be a mighty man.*

9. *He was a mighty hunter before the Lord; therefore it is said: Like Nimrod a mighty hunter before the Lord.*

Nimrod is not listed among the rest of the sons of Cush, perhaps because he was the child of a harlot. Moses presents a careful account of him and extols him above all the other descendants of Noah. He related that Cain's son Enoch was the first before the Flood to strive for sovereignty and to build a city, which he wanted called by his own name. I believe that it was located at the place where Babel stood after the Flood; for, as the historical accounts of the heathen testify,[30] the plain of that region was very beautiful. Similarly, Nimrod was the first after the Flood to strive for the sovereignty of the world. Not satisfied with its southern part, he extended his grasp toward the east, in the direction of the lands of Shem. Moses presents a rather careful account of him so that he might be in full view in a conspicuous place, to inspire fear in the ungodly and to give comfort to the godly.

[30] Cf. *Luther's Works*, 1, pp. 314 ff.

The name is indicative of the events. He is called Nimrod from מָרַד, which means "to fall away" and "to rebel," either because he went to war with his brothers, and especially with the families of the godly, in order to extend his territory, or because at that time this nation began to turn away from the sons of Shem and their religion, and sought to gain for itself the sole sovereignty over all the sons of Noah.

Therefore Moses adds: "he was the first on earth to be a mighty man," not by divine command or by the will of the fathers Shem and Arpachshad but through tyranny. We must not suppose that he achieved this without murder and bloodshed. Thus he was the first Turk or pope on earth after the Flood. His hand was against all the churches as well as all the states, while he used tyranny to gain for himself a sovereignty that did not belong to him but to Shem, who also had the priesthood. A son of the devil must be like his father, for Satan is a murderer (John 8:44).

Furthermore, to be a mighty man on earth is not in itself evil; for he was free to rule in his own area, and without a doubt he possessed the best part of the earth. Not satisfied with his own territory, however, he encroaches on his neighbors.

And, what is worse, he wants to be a mighty hunter, not only on earth but also before the Lord. That is, he not only wanted to be mighty in government, but he also wanted to rule in religion; he invades it and exercises tyranny over it, just as the pope does today. He who has this tyranny does not hunt hares, deer, or boars, as the hunters do; but he lies in wait for the righteous, the holy, the prophets, and the priests of God. He hunts, traps, and kills those who are dear to God, who have faith, and in whom God Himself dwells through His Spirit.

Can there be any doubt that the holy fathers always had their gatherings and meetings, where they instructed the youth, where they preached, prayed, prophesied, and praised God? The church cannot exist without the constant use of the Word, and the church always had its sacraments, or tokens of grace, and its ceremonies. Thus Abel and Cain had been accustomed by their father to sacrifice, which at that time was the proper form for the worship of God; and they continued to offer sacrifices. In the same manner Shem had meetings, sermons, forms of worship, sacrifices, and other ceremonies, which continued in existence up to the time of Abraham.

On these religious practices, which Shem was carrying out at God's command, this hunter makes inroads. Not satisfied with his tyranny in the state, he also wants to be lord in the church. He sets up new forms of worship, and he oppresses those who stand before God. Moses clearly distinguishes how a thing appears before God from how it appears before men. What is good and righteous before God the world always regards as evil and unrighteous.

In his own eyes and before the entire world Nimrod was considered to be a mighty hunter before God, that is, he was regarded as the high priest, as the head of the church, and altogether as what the pope would like to be today. For the eyes of the flesh are incapable of passing the judgment that the papacy is evil. Those who have the Holy Spirit and adhere to the Word can pass this judgment. But just as this judgment of ours is intolerable to the pope, who wants to be the head of the church, so Nimrod seized this title by force of arms, because he wanted to be a mighty hunter before God, that is, a lord in the church.

Thus Scripture depicts a tyrant who makes inroads not only on other kingdoms but also on religion. He does so under the most noble pretense. As a result, no one notices that he is doing this in order to be a mighty hunter before God or in order to strive for authority in the church, as the pope did when he called himself "the servant of servants." [31]

Nimrod, too, concealed his plans this way. He wanted to be regarded as godly and benign, as one who is of service to the state and is needed by the church; otherwise he would not have received such great acclamation from the masses. But he is truly a Nimrod, an apostate and a tyrant, an abuser and pillager of the human race, and finally a persecutor and slayer of holy men and true priests. They attempted to promote human welfare by taking that grand title from him. The godly, who adhere to the Word, neither can nor should disregard the plans and endeavors of the ungodly. But when they act accordingly, they are threatened with the sword and war, and the church suffers under unjust tyranny.

That Nimrod is called "a hunter" must not be understood of the usual sort of hunting. Some princes devote themselves to hunting with such senseless passion that they prefer it to grave affairs of state and would rather be regarded as bold hunters than as wise

[31] Luther is referring to the papal title *servus servorum Dei*, first used by Gregory I (d. 604).

rulers.³² But Moses points out that Nimrod hunted and pursued human beings, not wild beasts, and especially those who ruled the church by teaching.

Hence this title should be added to the titles of ungodly princes and should be inscribed on their coats of arms. Thus Moses declares that a saying had its origin from Nimrod, as though he wanted to say: "Later on this was the common title of all tyrants and princes." Following his example, they not only invaded states and kingdoms in order to increase their prestige and power, but they even usurped authority over the church. Thus at our time the Bishop of Mainz, besides plundering his bishopric, also troubles the churches by keeping out sound doctrine and forcing men to accept ungodly and idolatrous forms of worship.³³

Moses calls Nimrod "a valiant hunter," one whom no one can resist. Along with their apostasy and treachery, the tyrants have power; armed with this, they easily achieve whatever they wish. I have no doubt that by this picture Moses wanted to present the story of all tyrants who would rage against the state and the church in later times; for he calls Nimrod a mighty persecutor of the saints of God, an enemy of the Word and of the church. What follows deals with the description of the kingdom Nimrod acquired for himself.

10. *The beginning of his kingdom was Babel, Erech, Accad, and Calneh in the land of Shinar.*

Look how this worst of all scoundrels first encroaches on the people of God and the line from which Christ was to be born; for to it, as we stated above, Judea, with the eastern regions, fell after the Flood. It is known that the land of Shinar is the name of the plain on which Babel was later built, and this was the beginning of Nimrod's kingdom.

This passage is usually explained in the following way: that one and the same city Babylon was divided into four parts, and that their names were Babel, Erech, Accad, and Calneh. Pliny declares that it was so big that it had forty-six political subdivisions and communes.³⁴ Aristotle relates that Babylon was not a city but a province surrounded by a wall.³⁵ It is not remarkable that so large a city was

³² Cf. *Luther's Works*, 9, p. 194, note 2.
³³ A reference to Albert, Bishop of Mainz (1490—1545).
³⁴ Pliny, *Natural History*, Book VI, ch. 26.
³⁵ Aristotle, *Politics*, Book III, ch. 3.

divided into four main parts. Rome was similarly divided into patricians — or the Senate — knights, plebeians, and farmers; and Hebron is called קִרְיַת אַרְבַּע because it was a tetrapolis.

This is the explanation some give for the passage before us. I do not follow this opinion, because I notice that the prophets extol Calneh; later on this was called Seleucia, and to it Seleucus transferred the commercial center in order to weaken and reduce Babylon. But it would be ridiculous to fancy that Seleucia was a part of Babylon, which was far away from it. Therefore even though I am unable to identify Erech and Accad, I do not share the opinion that Babylon was a tetrapolis.

For us it is enough to know that Babylon was built by Nimrod, perhaps at the same place where Cain had built the city of Enoch (Gen. 4:17); likewise, that the Babylonian kingdom had its beginning through Nimrod, and that gradually it became vaster, so that Daniel counts it as the first monarchy.[36] Just as kingdoms have their fate, by which they die, so sacred history reveals that the royal power was transferred later on to Nineveh and the Assyrians, although from there it returned to the Babylonians.

But here the question is raised whether Babel was built before the famous tower that the sons of Ham erected in the land of Shinar. Even though I have nothing certain to say on this, I am of the opinion that Nimrod built that structure in order to make an everlasting name for himself in the world and among his descendants. When he saw that this building project was brought to naught and was interrupted by God through the confusion of tongues, then he began to build the city of Babel. Besides, the designation בָּבֶל induces me to adopt this opinion; for what took place proves that the name was given to the city as a result of the event.

Now we have the first king and ruler of the world, who, although he is an enemy of the church and of God, seizes power over the entire East.

11. *From that land went forth Asshur, and built Nineveh, and Rehoboth-Ir, Calah,*

12. *and Resen between Nineveh and Calah; that is the great city.*

In the course of time, after the Babylonian kingdom was established, Asshur went out from there and also built himself a city,

---

[36] Cf. *Luther's Works*, 9, p. 204, note 4.

Nineveh, which the secular accounts also mention; and to it was transferred the rule of the entire East. But on what occasion and in what circumstances Babylon was destroyed is nowhere recorded.

They relate that Nineveh, too, was a tetrapolis; and the story of Jonah (Jonah 3:3) points out that it was a very extensive city, the like of which Europe does not have today. But if it was a tetrapolis, Nineveh was the center and best part of the city, in which the royal palace was located. רְחֹבֹת was the quarter of the businessmen; עִיר, that of the supreme council; and Calah, that of the farmers. Somewhat remote from these areas was Resen, in which the truck gardeners lived. Actually we have nothing certain about this; we are making guesses about things that are very ancient.

There is a discussion also about Asshur, whether he is the one listed in the genealogy of Shem (v. 22) or really someone else.[37] Although I am unable to give any assurance of certainty, I personally — if I may make a guess — would assume that Asshur, Shem's son, went out from the land of Babylon, just as Abram later on departed from the land of the Chaldeans, was called Abraham by God, and did not leave his native country of his own accord.

It was the wickedness and the violence of the ungodly generation of Ham that forced Asshur to depart. He was unable to put up with the ungodly forms of worship and the idolatry of Ham's descendants. He yielded before their madness and joined our ancestors, the descendants of Japheth, to be somewhat closer to them; and he built Nineveh. For this reason the Lord was fond of Nineveh, as appears from Ezekiel and Jonah, and bestowed on it the honor of becoming a monarchy. Ezekiel (31:9), therefore, compares it to a beautiful tree with wide-spreading branches.

Finally Jonah was sent to these remnants of Shem; and after Nineveh was converted, it repented, acknowledged the Lord, and was saved. It is not without reason that Jonah calls it a great city of God (Jonah 3:3). That he should call it a city of God because it was great, as the Jews fancy,[38] is altogether ridiculous. Whatever God does is great, even if it concerns only one human being. Nineveh is called a city of God because it had the true religion and was preserved by God on account of the good man Asshur, who, being intolerant of idolatry, abandoned ancient Babylon and migrated

[37] Lyra on Gen. 10:11-12, sec. e.
[38] Cf. p. 342, note 31.

toward the northern regions, toward the Japhethites, and there gathered a little church.

I like this surmise in preference to others about this Asshur, who left Babylon because he wanted to get away from the offense of idolatry and because he was concerned about leaving a church for his saintly descendants. Since the accounts tell nothing about this, we can only speculate.

Here also, as previously in the instance of Babylon (Gen. 10:10), the text states that Nineveh was built together with three other cities, Rehoboth, Ir, and Calah.[39] Therefore I am now inclined to the idea that a tetrapolis was not one place surrounded by a single wall but four cities in different places, although they were ruled by one prince.

Silesia has six-city districts, which, although they differ in names and location, nevertheless individually bear the name "hexapolis" and acknowledge the same ruler.[40] Thus Calneh, which is Seleucia, may be Babylon comprising four cities. In our time the Swiss have many powerful cities, but there is one council for all, similar to that of the amphictyonies among the Greeks;[41] and perhaps the four-city districts in the Babylonian and Assyrian kingdom were of this kind.

The Assyrian kingdom is given great praise in the Scriptures, not only on account of its civil administration but on account of its religion and because it believed the preaching of the one man Jonah, who had been sent to them. It had not only a king and monarch but also other classes, namely, princes, priests, etc. If they had been like our princes, cardinals, and bishops, they not only would have kept Jonah out but would even have killed him. And the godly descendants of Shem, even though they had deteriorated, nevertheless received the Word and returned to the former way; and the Lord received them in mercy.

Later on they deteriorated again, for it generally happens that angels become devils and the church becomes heretical. Therefore Assyria was destroyed, as Is. 37:21 ff. threatens, perhaps at the time of Esarhaddon, the son of Sennarcherib; at that time his sons were at enmity with one another after the slaying of their father, and

[39] Does this indicate that some time had elapsed since the comment on p. 201?

[40] The six cities to which Luther is referring are Bautzen, Görlitz, Lauban, Löbau, Camenz, and Zittau. As the Weimar editors point out, they did not belong to Silesia at this time, but to the Bohemian crown.

[41] The Greek amphictyonies were relatively autonomous leagues dedicated to the maintenance of temples.

the monarchy was transferred to Babylon. This was not that ancient Babylon built by Nimrod and later destroyed; it was the new Babylon, whose first monarch, Nebuchadnezzar, laid waste the kingdom of Judah.

13. *Egypt became the father of Ludim, Anamim, Lehabim, Naphtuhim,*

14. *Pathrusim, and Casluhim (whence came the Philistines), and Caphtorim.*

These, too, are mostly mere names and, so to speak, corpses either of regions or of peoples. The Ludim are thought to be the Lydians, and the Lehabim the Libyans. The Pathrusim are considered to be the people whom Is. 11:11 calls "Pathros," and today they are perhaps the ones who inhabit Africa; in the opinion of others they are the Numidians and Mauritanians, for Isaiah connects them with the Egyptians.

The Jews propound the ludicrous idea that the Pathrusim and the Casluhim exchanged their wives and that, as a result of that adultery, there "came out," that is, there were born, the Philistines and the Caphtorim.[42] This is a silly invention. For the verb "to go out" must be understood as referring not to procreation but to a migration, namely, that the Philistines and the Caphtorim were unwilling to dwell together with the Pathrusim and the Casluhim. The Jews invent this tale for the purpose of extolling their own glory, although it is contrary to grammatical usage; for "to go out" does not mean to be born as a result of adultery.

We now have the three sides of the world: the North, the West, and the South. There remains the East.

15. *Canaan became the father of Sidon his first-born, and Heth,*

16. *and the Jebusites, the Amorites, the Girgashites,*

17. *the Hivites, the Arkites, the Sinites,*

18. *the Arvadites, the Zemarites, and the Hamathites. Afterward the families of the Canaanites spread abroad.*

19. *And the territory of the Canaanites extended from Sidon, in the direction of Gerar, as far as Gaza, and in the direction of Sodom, Gomorrah, Admah, and Zeboiim, as far as Lasha.*

[42] Lyra on Gen. 10:13-14, sec. g.

20. *These are the sons of Ham, by their families, their languages, their lands, and their nations.*

Sidon is known. Moses saw the Hittites, the Jebusites, the Amorites, the Girgashites, and perhaps others too; but they were later exterminated, partly by the people of God and partly by other nations which took possession of those regions. The Zemarite is known, as is Hamath, which is Antioch.

At this point turn your eyes and minds to the previous statements. Canaan was cursed by his grandfather Noah; yet here he not only has the advantage because of the large number of his children, but he also occupies the most excellent part of the entire world. For the peoples whom Moses enumerates here left the area that their father Ham had occupied. Ham had received only the southern region as his share, while the godly Shem had received this region as his possession, together with the East. But the lot of the ungodly in this life is always better than that of the godly. And so the descendants of the ungodly Ham, even though they were cursed, drove the descendants of blessed Shem out of their own territory and took possession of Palestine, Syria, and the adjoining areas, as far as Babylon.

This proves that man was not created for this life; for since the ungodly fare so well in this life, there remains another life, in which they will be afflicted. On the other hand the godly will experience an eternal compensation in the other life for the afflictions that they bear here.

I have no doubt that the land of Canaan was the most delightful part of the entire world. Therefore I readily agree with those who believe that Paradise was situated in that area before the Flood. Nor does anyone sin if he believes that the very place where through His death Christ restored life to the world was the location of the tree that brought ruin upon man when he was deceived by the serpent.[43]

Yet the bliss of the Canaanites did not continue forever, for they paid the penalty for their ungodliness when they were cast out and exterminated by the people of God. In the end the people of God must prevail, although some remnants of the ungodly have remained. Thus in our own flesh, even when we are justified, there remain the

[43] Luther discusses this earlier in the *Lectures on Genesis;* cf. *Luther's Works,* 1, p. 310.

remnants of sin, obviously in order that we may not become remiss but may practice our godliness.

The boundary from Sidon as far as Gaza includes the shore of the Mediterranean Sea, embellished by the wealthiest and most beautiful cities. Sidon is situated toward the north, Gaza toward the south. Not far from Sidon was Tyre, the most famous commercial center of all Asia. East of it are Ptolemais, Caesarea, Apollonia, Joppa, Azotus, etc. Sodom was the boundary toward the east. Lasha is believed to be the place the Romans called Caesarea Philippi, in the tribe of Dan.

THE GENERATION OF SHEM

21. *To Shem also, the father of all the children of Eber, the elder brother of Japheth, children were born.*

22. *The sons of Shem: Elam, Asshur, Arpachshad, Lud, and Aram.*

Here some raise the question why Shem is called the father of all the sons of Eber, although the latter is not a son of Shem but the grandson of Arpachshad, who is the third son of Shem. The Jews generally argue in favor of the opinion that this is done because from this Eber the people of God got the name "Hebrews." [44] Yet they would prefer to derive this designation from Abraham. But to me the former opinion appears to be more correct. This Eber was the father of Peleg, at whose time, as Moses relates later on, the languages began to be divided, when Nimrod and the descendants of Ham were building the Tower of Babel.

It has been stated previously that Asshur departed from the land of Shinar because he was unwilling to acquiesce in the idolatrous forms of worship introduced by Nimrod. Therefore when he could not live safely among the idolaters, he turned toward the north, where the descendants of godly Japheth were living.

Hence in order that there may be a distinction among the sons of Shem, Moses calls Shem the father of all the sons of Eber, to make it clear that Christ would be born from the descendants of Eber. This is such a great privilege that Moses did not want the others regarded as the sons of Shem in preference to this Eber, the father of Christ, although they, too, excel in prestige.

Elam are the Persians, who were famous not only because they had that excellent sovereign Cyrus as their monarch, but because

[44] See p. 371, note 12.

they had a knowledge of God and of the true religion, which was revealed to them by Daniel.

Perhaps the Greeks have reproduced the name Arpachshad in the name Arbaces,[45] in the passage stating that he was the one who defeated Sardanapalus.

Asshur are the Assyrians.

Some believe that Lud are the Lydians; but previously, among the descendants of Canaan, the Ludim were called the Lydians.

Aram is Syria. But it is known from history that there were two Arams, the one in Mesopotamia and the other in Phoenicia. Armenia is supposed to have got its name from Aram.

23. *The sons of Aram: Uz, Hul, Gether, and Mash.*

These are unknown to us, except Uz, from whose land Job came (Job 1:1).

24. *Arpachshad became the father of Shelah; and Shelah became the father of Eber.*

25. *To Eber were born two sons: the name of the one was Peleg, for in his days the earth was divided, and his brother's name was Joktan.*

Eber is the fourth from Shem; and he is extolled as second only to Shem, because he also is among the ancestors of Christ. At his time it happened that Nimrod came from the southern region, invaded the East, and drove out from there the godly descendants. Therefore the good patriarchs changed their habitations, just as we stated previously about Asshur.

26. *Joktan became the father of Almodad, Sheleph, Hazarmaveth, Jerah,*

27. *Hadoram, Uzal, Diklah,*

28. *Obal, Abimael, Sheba,*

29. *Ophir, Havilah, and Jobab; all these were the sons of Joktan.*

30. *The territory in which they lived extended from Mesha in the direction of Sephar to the hill country of the East.*

31. *These are the sons of Shem, by their families, their languages, their lands, and their nations.*

[45] Arbaces was the name of the first king of Media.

32. *These are the families of the sons of Noah, according to their genealogies, in their nations; and from these the nations spread abroad on the earth after the Flood.*

All these are peoples of India, unknown to us, because India is least known to us of all the parts of the entire earth;[46] otherwise perhaps the similarity of the names might give some clarification, although these, too, are being changed by the seafarers in the present age.[47]

Mt. Sephar is perhaps Ararat or the Imaus.[48] Whenever I read these names, I think of the wretched state of the human race. Even though we have the most excellent gift of reason, we are nevertheless so overwhelmed by misfortunes that we are ignorant not only of our own origin and the lineal descent of our ancestors but even of God Himself, our Creator. Look into the historical accounts of all nations. If it were not for Moses alone, what would you know about the origin of man?

Aristotle was a very sharp-witted man. I like to compare him with Cicero. Nevertheless, I regard Aristotle as superior for the achievements of his genius, because Cicero's researches were hampered in no small measure by state affairs. But when Aristotle gives thought to the origin of mankind, his very reason constrains him to maintain that there is neither a first nor a last human being.[49] I hold that Plato did not discuss this problem seriously but wanted to poke fun at the philosophers of his time.[50] Therefore I do not use his evidence at this point.

But if one should follow the opinion of Aristotle, who gave serious thought to these matters, what absurd conclusion will follow![51] In the first place, it will follow with inevitable consequence that the soul is mortal; for philosophy not only does not recognize anything that is potentially infinite but simply maintains that more than one infinite is an impossibility, just as are a vacuum and the reciprocal

[46] Cf. *Luther's Works*, 1, pp. 100—101.

[47] On Luther's awareness of the voyages of discovery in his day see also *Luther's Works*, 1, p. 207, note 52.

[48] See p. 108, note 8.

[49] Cf. *Luther's Works*, 1, p. 3.

[50] Perhaps a reference to Plato, *Timaeus*, 69 ff.

[51] In both language and content what follows here seems closer to Melanchthon than to Luther; see Introduction.

penetration of contained bodies. It recognizes the actually infinite, as when we observe human beings passing away and others coming into being during a long succession of years, which Aristotle considers as being potentially infinite.[52] This is the wisdom our reason supplies, with the result that we know nothing about our origin if the Word is lacking.

But even as I rate Aristotle above Cicero in native ability, so I have to realize that Cicero discussed these very matters with far greater discernment.[53] He keeps clear of this topic of the infinite as of a dangerous crag and takes up the subject of religion; that is, he shifts the discussion to a consideration of the creature, about which it is possible for reason to make certain judgments. He observes the harmony of the motions of the celestial bodies; he observes the unvarying changes of the seasons and of the fixed forms of the products of this earth; and he observes that man was created both to have an understanding of these things and to derive benefit from them.

Therefore he is disposed to assert both that God is the eternal Mind by whose providence all these things are controlled in this way, and that the soul of man is immortal. And yet, even though he makes these assertions, he seems to be overturned by some currents in his thought. As a result this very opinion, to which he held so firmly at times, appears to slip out of his hands. For the discussion of the infinite is a very emotional one; and when we observe that our nature is burdened by such a variety of mishaps, our reason drops the subject of religion.

Of this wretched state, that is, of our awful blindness, we are reminded by the passage before us, which gives us instruction about things that are unknown to the whole world. What do we have about the very best part of the second world besides words, not to mention the first one, which antedated the Flood? The Greeks wanted to have the account of their activities preserved, the Romans likewise; but how insignificant this is in comparison with the earlier times, concerning which Moses has drawn up a list of names in this passage, not of deeds!

Hence one must consider this chapter of Genesis a mirror in which to discern what we human beings are, namely, creatures so

[52] Cf. Aristotle, *Metaphysics*, Book II, ch. 2.
[53] Cf. Cicero, *De natura deorum*, Book I, ch. 13.

marred by sin that we have no knowledge of our own origin, not even of God Himself, our Creator, unless the Word of God reveals these sparks of divine light to us from afar. Then what is more futile than boasting of one's wisdom, riches, power, and other things that pass away completely?

Therefore we have reason to regard the Holy Bible highly and to consider it a most precious treasure. This very chapter, even though it is considered full of dead words, has in it the thread that is drawn from the first world to the middle and to the end of all things. From Adam the promise concerning Christ is passed on to Seth; from Seth to Noah; from Noah to Shem; and from Shem to this Eber, from whom the Hebrew nation received its name as the heir for whom the promise about the Christ was intended in preference to all other peoples of the whole world. This knowledge the Holy Scriptures reveal to us. Those who are without them live in error, uncertainty, and boundless ungodliness; for they have no knowledge about who they are and whence they came.

CHAPTER ELEVEN

THIS chapter, too, deals with the extraordinary example of the holy patriarch Noah and of his family, especially those who were godly. It is intended to show us how much faith and godliness there was in these holy men despite the incredible wickedness, envy, and tyranny that were widespread and dominant among the children of men.

For some time after the Flood the entire earth was in a blessed state; for all people had one language, no small bond for maintaining harmony and a particular asset for maintaining the teaching of religion. The fresh memory of the immeasurable wrath of God in the Flood kept their hearts in the fear of God and in reverence for their ancestors.

Noah's son Ham is the first to disturb this blessed state. As though he had forgotten the great wrath, he first despises the authority of his father and makes a mockery of him whom he ought to have respected, as we have previously heard. Then he leaves his father and his godly brothers and sets up a new kingdom for himself on the earth. Finally his oldest son presents him with a grandson, Nimrod, who, after setting up his power through tyranny, afflicts the godly descendants of Noah in various ways, establishes a kingdom for himself, and assumes sole sovereignty over it.

Similarly, when two sons had been born to Adam, two kinds of people took their origin from them. Cain left his father, established a special church without God's command, and held the true church in contempt. The same thing happens here among the sons of Noah. From Ham, as from an ungodly and wicked source, the false and lying church takes its origin. In the present chapter Moses unfolds this story about the beginnings of the pestilence that rages against the church.

This chapter does not indicate clearly wherein the sin of the builders of the Tower of Babel consisted. Consequently, opinions vary both about the structure or tower itself and about the sin of its builders. The more daring a man is in answering each of these two questions, the more outspokenly he expresses himself. And the common people, too, did not refrain from inventing stories.[1] Thus they say that the height of the tower was nine miles, but that when the languages were confused, a third of it was destroyed by the force of wind and weather and the rest sank into the earth, so that now only one third of it is still in existence. Moreover, they claim that it was so high that from it one could hear the voices of the angels singing in heaven.

But we disregard these foolish tales. It is worthier of our inquiry to give thought to the sin of the builders, something that cannot be clearly understood from the text.

Lyra is of the opinion that the descendants of Ham undertook this construction with the idea of having a safe place of refuge if the Lord should again want to destroy the world by a flood.[2] I do not agree. In the first place, Ham also heard the plain promise that the earth would never again perish by a flood. In the second place, Ham knew that the Flood had risen fifteen cubits above the highest mountains of the entire world. Therefore I believe that they were not stupid enough to think that they could erect a pile so high that it would protect them from a flood.

I believe their motive is expressed in the words: "Come, let us build *ourselves*[3] a city and a tower." These words are evidence of smug hearts, which put their trust in the things of this world without trusting God and despise the church because it lacks all power and pomp.

Hence what Lyra says about a safe place against the violence of a raging flood I consider to be an allegorical tale. The fathers used it to depict men whose extreme contempt for God makes them think that in their own power there is some protection against God's wrath. Indeed, you may invent any story you please about a heart that is smug and does not fear God, and it would still be impossible to depict ungodliness adequately.

I have no doubt that this very account gave rise to the story about the giants who formed the plan to expel Jupiter from heaven and heaped mountains upon mountains, just as the story of Deucalion

---

[1] The story of Babel had a place in medieval folklore and legend, from which these items are taken.

[2] Lyra on Gen. 11:4, sec. h.

[3] In the original this is in capital letters.

originated from the account of the Flood.⁴ These accounts became known among the Gentiles through the sermons of the patriarchs. Therefore I think that here the sin was nothing else than extraordinary smugness and pride linked with contempt for God. The ungodly are wont to behave in such a way. When they are puffed up by success, they suppose that they are sitting on God's lap; and in their great self-reliance they have the audacity to do anything they please.

Similarly, Ham's sin was a sin not only against the church but against the government as well; for he laughed at his holy father and despised his religion and doctrine. After he had separated from his father, as we heard previously, he established both a new government and a new religion. His grandson Nimrod likewise sinned against both the government and the church. He did not cultivate the true religion; and he practiced unjust tyranny on his cousins, whom he expelled from their paternal lands. There is no doubt that these people who, as Moses says, migrated toward the east were Nimrod and other descendants of Ham; for Moses gives a clear indication to this effect at the beginning of this chapter. These sins brought on their own punishment, which Moses will describe a little later.

Therefore these words, which Moses has set down so simply — that they urged one another to build a tower and a city — must be interpreted in a harsh manner, as though Moses were saying: "Was this not colossal pride and great contempt for God, that without asking God for advice they dared undertake so massive a project on their own responsibility?" They drive out the godly descendants of Shem from their habitations and are intent on subjugating the entire world, but especially on suppressing the church. Therefore this sin is a horrible apostasy from the church, from the Word, and from the very angels of God to the devil; it involves sins not only against the First Table but also against the Second.

Hence the emphasis lies on their saying: "Let us build *ourselves* ⁵ a city and a tower," not for God, not for the church of God, but to suppress the church; and on the words: "Let us make a name for *ourselves*." These men who are gripped by such an intense desire to exalt their own name are surely not concerned that the name of

⁴ Cf. p. 131, note 1.
⁵ The original has capitals in both these places.

God may be hallowed; and without a doubt they looked with profound contempt upon the humble cabins of the holy fathers and of their brothers, since they were building in such grand style.

Nor is it without purpose when they declare that the top of the tower should reach to heaven. These words must not be applied to the height alone; they also denote that this was to be a place of worship. The implication was that God was dwelling very close to this tower. This is Satan's way. He adorns himself with the title of God and wants to have superstition regarded as religion.

The church in our age has no deadlier enemies than the Turk and the pope. But both make a display of the name of God, and they suppose that there is nothing they cannot get by means of this title. Meanwhile we hear ourselves called heretics, the seed of Satan, apostates, and rebels.

This is the way things have always gone, even in those earliest times before and after the Flood. In this passage the descendants of Ham are portrayed as people who despised the lowliness and godliness of the church and built Babylon, not only for political purposes but also for the sake of a religious impression, namely, that the place might be regarded as very close to heaven and as a habitation most pleasing to God.

Therefore the saying is true that every apostate is the persecutor of his own kind.[6] Because Ham and his descendants separated from the church, he made it his business later on to oppress the church and to elevate himself and his own people. Satan likewise persecutes God and the church with a fierce hatred now that he has separated from God and the angels, who are the heavenly church. In order to be able to do this with some success, he transforms himself into an angel of light (2 Cor. 11:14) and arrogates divinity to himself. Thus here in the midst of Babylon he makes himself a kind of god and sets up a church for himself in order to suppress the true church.

Now it is up to the godly to act in like manner. After they have separated from the church of Satan and have deserted it, they should also begin to hate it. Thus, by the grace of God, we are holy apostates; for we have defected from the Antichrist and the church of Satan

---

[6] Edward Gibbon has paraphrased this epigram in his comment on Julian the Apostate: "He affected to pity the unhappy Christians, who were mistaken in the most important object of their lives; but his pity was degraded by contempt, his contempt was embittered by hatred." *The Decline and Fall of the Roman Empire*, ch. XXIII.

and have allied ourselves with the Son and the true church. It befits us to stand with this and to assail the false church.

In this passage Moses points out the sin of apostasy, namely, that the descendants of Ham, Nimrod, and others separated from God and the Word, from the fathers and the church, not only so far as their outward association was concerned but so far as religion and worship were concerned. They lived in accordance with their own devices and desires.

It was no sin in itself to erect a tower and to build a city, for the saints did the same; and Asshur, whom I believe to have been altogether a saint, built Nineveh because he could no longer live with the ungodly (Gen. 10:11). This, however, is their sin: they attach their own name to this structure; having despised Noah and the true church, they are intent on sovereignty; they maintain that they are the people who are very close to God, to whom God listens, and to whom He grants success; and they conclude that Noah, in turn, has been abandoned and cast aside by God.

Thus this account portrays the ungodliness, the schemes, the ambition, and the plots of all ungodly men, especially of the hypocrites who alone appear to themselves to be holy and very close to God and who want to rule the earth. If you want to call this sin by another name, it is truly blasphemy of the name of God and a violation of the Sabbath; it is rank idolatry, by which the glory of the living God is changed into a calf, that is, into an idol of the heart. These sins beget others, namely, hatred of the true church, persecution, tyranny, murder, robbery, and even fornication and adultery. For the false church is always the persecutor of the true church, not only spiritually, by means of false doctrine and ungodly forms of worship, but also physically, by means of the sword and tyranny.

Moses states that upon this sin there followed a punishment, namely, the division of languages. This may appear to have been a light punishment, but surely it is a terrible one if you take into consideration the extreme hardships that resulted from this division of languages. For one thing, identity of language is a very strong bond in human association and harmony among men. In this instance, too, the statement of the proverb is true: "Birds of a feather flock together." A German likes to converse and associate with a person of his own nationality. But where the languages differ, there not only no commerce develops, but hatred arises in the heart against that nation whose language you do not understand. Thus a Frenchman hates and despises the Germans; the Italians hate and despise all nations except themselves.

Thus it is clear that as a result of this division of languages hearts were disunited, customs changed, and dispositions and endeavors altered. Consequently, you can truthfully call it the seedbed of all evils, since it has caused political as well as economic [7] confusion.

Although these are very serious inconveniences, they are nothing in comparison with the confusion that this division of languages has brought to the churches and the endless occasions it has provided for idolatry and superstition. Who does not realize that the function of the ministry was almost entirely disrupted by this change of languages? Eber, who undoubtedly retained the first and true language, was unable thereafter to instruct others whose language he did not know and who could not understand him.

Therefore it is a great blessing and an outstanding miracle of the New Testament that by means of various languages the Holy Spirit on the day of Pentecost brought men of all nations into the one body of the one Head, Christ (Acts 2). Christ joins and unites all into one faith through the Gospel, even though the different languages remain; and He tears down the wall (Eph. 2:14), not only by reconciling us to God through His death and speaking to us in a new language but also by bringing about outward harmony, so that different flocks are brought together under one Shepherd and are gathered into one fold (John 10:16). This is Christ's blessing; and since it is common to all, differences in outward life cause no offense.

Let us, therefore, give Him the credit that through the Holy Spirit He has removed this most severe punishment, which was the beginning and seedbed of all evils and discords, and has brought us a holy harmony, even though the different languages remain. For where Christ the Mediator is not acknowledged, there is a disagreement of hearts like that of the languages, and there is horrible blindness. Hence when we survey the histories of all nations and times, we see that various wars broke out and a great variety of customs, religions, and ideas arose because of the diversity of languages. This evil Christ wanted to remedy by means of a new miracle.

I myself do not understand an Italian, nor does an Italian understand me; and so there exists a natural opportunity for anger and enmity between us. But if we both understand Christ, we mutually

---

[7] The term *oeconomia* usually means "household" in Luther, but in this passage it seems to have acquired its later and broader signification.

embrace and heartily kiss each other as fellow members. But where Christ is not present, there the punishment of Babylon still prevails, the division of languages, which brings on a sure division of hearts and gives rise to confusion, not only in the administration of the home and government but also in religion and the church.

This punishment, which is so horrible, warns us to be on our guard lest we fall away from the Word or prefer ourselves above others as though we were better and holier. Because Ham's descendants did this, a horrible punishment followed, which, in my estimation, brought greater harm to the human race than did the Flood itself. The latter harmed only the human beings of one time, but the former lasts until the end of the world. Although Christ brought us some help through His Spirit, yet how small is the part that receives the Word and believes it! The remaining multitude is as divided in its opinions as it is in its languages and renders welcome service to Satan, the instigator of wars and of discord.

In the third place, after we have discoursed on the sins and on the punishment of the builders, it is not without profit to calculate the time, namely, how many years there were between the Flood and the birth of Peleg, at whose time the Tower of Babel was built and the division of languages occurred. This amounts to about a hundred years after the Flood, and Noah was already seven hundred years old. Ham and his grandsons, who had promptly forgotten the horrible wrath of God, despised Noah together with his entire church and the descendants of the holy fathers while he was still living, ruling, and preaching about the great wrath of God. Must we not suppose that it grieved pious Noah and his people that descendants of his were engaging in such enterprises while their father looked on and warned them to no avail? Thus this saint is ridiculed a second time as a feeble-minded old man.[8]

Consequently, our temptations, crosses, and vexations are nothing in comparison with the temptations, crosses, and vexations of the fathers. Even though we, too, observe monstrous evils in the world, we do not observe them for long and for this reason are more fortunate; for we leave such a wicked generation more quickly. Noah observed his degraded grandsons for three hundred and fifty years, and how much misery do you suppose he experienced during this time? In respect to this share of misfortune Noah is surpassed by

[8] Cf. p. 87.

his godly son Shem, who lived for five hundred years after the Flood. Oh, what martyrs! All the generations of men should thoughtfully consider them and learn patience from their example.

St. Peter declares about righteous Lot that his soul was distressed when he beheld the ungodly actions of the Sodomites (2 Peter 2:7). Simeon states about Mary that a sword would pierce through her soul (Luke 2:35). The saints cannot behold the wickedness of the world without intense grief. But these crosses of later generations are nothing in comparison with those of the holy fathers, who were compelled to behold the great perversity of the world for five hundred years and more. Therefore let us, too, patiently bear these sad sights and the darts of Satan (Eph. 6:16), which he drives into our hearts; for we should not expect our situation to be better than that of the holy fathers, although, as I have said, it is better in this respect that we have a shorter span of life.

These thoughts I wanted to express briefly as an introduction to this chapter. Now we shall look at the text.

1. *Now the whole earth had one language and few words.*

2. *And as men migrated in the east, they found a plain in the land of Shinar and settled there.*

We discussed the word מִקֶּדֶם previously, in the second chapter.[9] It is my conviction that east is the term for that region which is closest toward the east in relation to the land of Canaan. Thus in the Books of Kings the Arabs are called sons of the east (1 Kings 4:30).

Shinar is a place name familiar from the tenth chapter (10:10). In ancient times this name was given to the region that later began to be called Babel or Babylon.

3. *And they said to one another: Come, let us make bricks, and burn them thoroughly. And they had brick for stone, and bitumen for mortar.*

This is clear evidence that the city of Babel and the tower were constructed of bricks or baked stone, just as Rome was built of bricks. I further conclude that at that time this was a new method of construction, unknown to previous generations, which were unfamiliar with the process of baking bricks and did not make use of bitumen to join the bricks.

[9] *Luther's Works*, 1, p. 88.

4. *Then they said: Come, let us build ourselves a city, and a tower with its top in the heavens, and let us make a name for ourselves, lest we be scattered abroad upon the face of the whole earth.*

What is the meaning of this? Who put these words into their mouth, to cause them to foretell their future dispersion over the entire world? They are not prophesying like Caiaphas (John 11:49-51), are they, and saying something of which they have no knowledge? It is a common occurrence, as Solomon bears witness somewhere (Prov. 10:24), that the ungodly foretell evil for themselves, and that what they dread happens to them. Similarly, Ezekiel declares (11:8-9): "You have feared the sword; and I will bring the sword upon you, says the Lord God. And I will bring you forth out of the midst of the land." On the other hand, the hope of the godly is not futile; but what they hope and believe is sure to take place and not to fail them. Nevertheless, the foreknowledge in the instance before us is not a prophecy like that of Caiaphas; it has a different cause.

In such passages I myself generally follow this rule: just as the statements and actions of the godly cannot be understood except from their spirit and temper, so I also maintain that the words and deeds of the ungodly cannot be understood unless we comprehend the disposition and temper of the spirit that urges them on, namely, Satan's; and that disposition and temper is always opposed both to God and to the church. On the other hand, both the utterances and the actions of the godly aim at the glory of God and the welfare of the church. He who pursues this goal cannot be deceived by any of the pretense and hypocrisy toward which Satan always directs his efforts by word and deed. He who hears things that are not in agreement with the Word of God gives a correct description if he declares that they have come from Satan. He is right too if he maintains that they were spoken in order to deceive and kill.

I have followed this rule when passing judgment on the dogmas of the pope. Because I saw that they were not in agreement with the Word of God, I continued to maintain that his dogmas are from the devil, designed to deceive and to kill. Nor have I allowed myself to be swayed from this conviction by any of the outward show with which the outrageous impostor has deceived the entire world. Therefore since this is a reliable rule for judging and evaluating the words and deeds of God and of Satan, of the godly and of the ungodly, we shall do well to follow it also in the present instance.

The descendants of Ham, namely, Nimrod and the others, had invaded the region that had fallen to Shem, the heir of the promise concerning Christ. Because they were inclined toward despotism, they had a desire not only to drive out the descendants of Shem but also to establish a new government and a new church. Even though there is no written record of what they attempted against the true church, against Noah himself, the ruler of the church, and against his pious posterity, it can nevertheless be surmised by analogy if we carefully consider the actions of our opponents at the present time. For Satan, who incites the ungodly against the true church, is always the same.

Therefore when Noah and the other godly men saw themselves hard pressed and new forms of worship being introduced, they became prophets through a logical deduction, although they also had positive knowledge of the nature of the punishment, since the Holy Spirit was giving them warning. They reasoned in this manner: "Adam did not go unpunished for having sinned in Paradise, and the punishment of his sin adheres to us all up to the present time. Cain was likewise punished for killing his brother and for his wicked notion about God, until at last God destroyed the entire world through the Flood. Surely, these men will not go unpunished, either, for making an attempt at tyranny and for disturbing and corrupting religion. But God has promised that in the future He will not resort to a flood." Hence they maintained under the guidance of the Holy Spirit that a punishment was to follow: just as these men were joining efforts to suppress the true church, so the true church would be preserved, and they themselves would be scattered over the entire world.

Because this prophecy tended to give strength and comfort to the church of the godly, it was spread abroad by Noah himself, not in secret or in only one place but publicly and with great courage. Therefore it could not remain unknown to the generation of the ungodly, which, though it smugly disregarded these voices of the Holy Spirit, still could not disregard them altogether. This is what happens to the ungodly: though they know that they are sinning and that punishment for sin is imminent, they smugly overcome their fear when their wickedness gains the upper hand.

Thus in the passage before us the words reveal a conscience that is troubled and yet smugly keeps on disregarding the punishment. Such a conscience is attributed to Medea by Ovid when she says:

"I see and applaud the better things, but I follow the worse." [10] And we ourselves once heard Carlstadt say at this very place, when he was conferring a doctor's degree, that he knew that it was a sin to create doctors of theology, but that he was doing it nevertheless.[11] It is no trivial sin to harden oneself against conscience and to glory in a sin willingly and knowingly.

So far as the present passage is concerned, we now understand the disposition of the ungodly and of Satan. As a result, we shall readily pass judgment on their words. It is not enough for the ungodly descendants of Ham to have sinned in driving the godly out of their habitations, but they also laugh at the punishment and make a joke of the threats that they hear from their parent Noah. Similarly, our papists laugh gently when we threaten them with the advent of Christ; for they think that if the case is postponed until then, they will fare well.

The ungodly in this passage act just like that. From their father Noah they hear that they will be punished by being scattered. "What?" say they, "Are we to be scattered? Well, then let us be scattered! But first we shall build a city and a tower as a memorial to our achievements." They do not fully believe that their dispersion will take place, nor are they altogether sure that it will not take place; and to show their contempt for the godly church they make ready for the new structure. These are, therefore, extremely arrogant words of Satan and his children against God.

We observe that the papists are doing the very same thing. It is impossible for the tyranny of the popes to continue any longer, for Rome is so tainted with every kind of wickedness that it cannot be any worse unless it becomes hell itself. In addition to this, there is the horrible craze for idols, and they incite kings and princes to give their support to ungodliness and to the suppression of the truth. Since no one can live in such great sins without fear of punishment, of which we also are prophets, they nevertheless grow horns [12] and, as the prophet puts it (Is. 48:4), assume a forehead of brass and pretend to be without fear. It is for this reason also that they do not curtail their ungodliness but boldly practice and increase it.

Thus the nature of ungodliness is always the same: it derides God

[10] Ovid, *Metamorphoses*, Book VII, l. 20.

[11] Carlstadt had based this condemnation of academic degrees on Matt. 23:10.

[12] The German expression *horn gewinnen* is a colloquial metaphor for *mutig werden*, "to grow brave."

both while it is full of hope and while it is full of fear. We see that these two emotions are mixed in the ungodly, just as they are mixed in the godly, who have the true faith. But even though the godly fear more than they hope, yet their hope and faith ultimately prevail. In the ungodly, on the other hand, even though they also fear, insincerity and wickedness prevail, drive away fear, and make them smug. As a result, they lunge forward without regard for their own peril. But finally what they fear comes to pass, and hope fails them. Thus we see that the ungodly descendants of Ham were wretchedly scattered, but Noah and his people were spared.

Therefore this entire account must be applied for the comfort of the church. Even though the church is troubled by the ungodly in sundry ways, nevertheless it ultimately triumphs, while the ungodly perish and are prophets of their own disasters, as Caiaphas was with his "lest perchance the Romans come and take away our nation" (John 11:48). And in Hosea it is stated: "I will chastise them as they have heard in their congregation" (7:12).

5. *And the Lord came down to see the city and the tower, which the sons of men had built.*

Now there takes place what the ungodly were fearing and yet smugly disregarding, since, as we have stated, their wickedness prevailed. Therefore this is a text with theological significance, for it reveals the frame of mind of the godly as well as of the ungodly. We observe the course of events to be this: while the sinner is engaged in sinning and is engrossed by it, he does not see God, does not speak of Him, and is not aware of Him; for the sinner assumes that God does not see and is not aware of what he is doing.

While Adam is bringing the fruit to his mouth, he gives no heed to the Word. Therefore if you were to look into his conscience, you would observe that he is no more concerned about God and His Word than if God were something dead and nonexistent. Thus Ps. 10:11 describes the thoughts of the ungodly remarkably well when it states: "He thinks in his heart, 'God has forgotten, He has hidden His face, He will never see it.'" While Cain falls upon his brother and kills him, he is likewise thinking that God is asleep and does not notice what he is doing. But this happens because God is long-suffering and does not immediately punish the deeds that deserved punishment.

Thus the godly also get the impression that God is asleep and has His eyes closed while they are crying and sighing for deliverance.

God puts off their deliverance, and for this reason the following expressions are frequent in the psalms: "How long wilt Thou forget, O Lord?" (13:1); "Why sleepest Thou? Arise, awake" (44:23); "Lift up Thy hand" (10:12). And those statements in which God asserts that He sees the works of men, that nothing is hidden from His eyes, that He is a God who detests iniquity, and so forth, are intended for the comfort of the church.

Therefore Scripture speaks here of the attitude of God by which He does not pay attention to the sins of the ungodly and the prayers of the godly. This attitude we make our own when we suppose that God is actually asleep during the time when He either does not immediately punish sins or does not immediately hear our prayers.

Thus in this passage God is said to come down as though He had not been present previously, for while the contempt of the ungodly was intense and Noah's prophecy was ridiculed, they thought that God was absent and had no knowledge of what the sons of Ham are attempting. But after the sin has been committed, God "comes down"; that is, then at last it is realized that He is at hand and is angry. Thus Gen. 22:12 says: "Now I know that you fear God," as though previously God had had no knowledge of Abraham.

The papists likewise believe that God is dead, that He does not see, that He does not hear, and that He is not present. Hence they are smug in their rage against the church and their various acts of oppression against it; for they say, as we read in Ps. 73:11: "How can God know? Is there knowledge in the Most High?"

As we stated previously, in the third chapter,[13] it is the nature of sin to lie still and be quiet for a time while the day is hot, that is, while lust and sin reign and man, overwhelmed and engrossed by Satan, pays no attention to the Word of God but disregards it, as if God were sleeping or simply did not exist.

But toward evening, after the heat of the day, the Lord begins to walk about in Paradise; and His voice is heard, no longer a pleasing and delightful voice, as it was before sin, but a terrifying one, which Adam is unable to bear. Therefore he hides among the trees and wants neither to hear nor to see God, but he cannot remain hidden.

The poets fancied that souls were terrified by the bark of Cerberus; but real terror arises when the voice of the wrathful God is heard, that is, when it is felt by the conscience. Then God, who previously

---

[13] Cf. *Luther's Works,* 1, pp. 163—172.

was nowhere, is everywhere. Then He who earlier appeared to be asleep hears and sees everything; and His wrath burns, rages, and kills like fire.

These are expressions of Holy Scripture to which one must become accustomed. God "comes down," not really or essentially — for He is everywhere — but He ceases to take no notice, He ceases to be long-suffering, and begins to reveal, punish, and convict sin. Therefore the smug people who used to think that He was far away now see that He is present, and they begin to tremble.

All this is intended to frighten us, that we may learn to beware of sin. For God will not ignore it forever; but just as by His arrival He finally frightened and killed Adam, Cain, and the entire world in the Flood, so at some time He will destroy us also if we do not forestall Him through repentance.

For the godly, however, the descent of the Lord is most delightful and most welcome; and for this reason they earnestly request it in fervent and unceasing prayers. But the flesh often makes them have doubts; for the pope, the Turk, and other enemies of the church appear to have established their power to such an extent that no force seems able to overthrow them. Yet someday God will descend and scatter them both. Over against our weakness and the smugness of the ungodly, Scripture bears witness that finally God descends, punishes, and opens His eyes, ears, and mouth. This the godly believe, but with a feeble faith, while the ungodly smugly disregard it.

Hence let us be warned by the example before us and learn this: the longer God puts up with idolatry and other sins, and the longer He pays no attention to them, the more intolerable will His wrath reveal itself to be later on. Therefore we ought to consider it a great kindness if He does not permit our sins to go unpunished for a long time. Ps. 30:5 exhorts the church to give thanks because the wrath of the Lord is "for a moment" and because He loves life. It says: "Weeping may tarry for the night, but joy comes with the morning"; and Ps. 89:30, 32: "If his children forsake My Law and do not walk according to My ordinances, I will punish their transgression with the rod and their iniquity with scourges." This is a wrath of grace, when the punishment comes quickly and calls us back from sin.

But when God pays no attention to sin and seems to connive at it, then there follows an unbearable wrath that has no end. Such was the wrath of the Flood and the wrath that Moses mentions in this passage. God permits the descendants of Ham to be prosperous and permits them to continue in sin as long as they are building the tower and the city, but then there follows a disaster that is all the greater.

Let us recognize, therefore, that a horrible judgment, such as no one has experienced since the beginning of the world, is in store for the pope and the Turk, who have been prospering for so long. God has never disregarded the ungodliness and the extreme blasphemies of anyone else for so long. Therefore their punishment will surpass the punishment of the Flood, of the dispersion, and of the Sodomites, for the wrath against them will be everlasting.

Moses says not only that God is descending, but that He is descending in order to see. We have stated how this is to be understood. Thus far God has conducted Himself as though He did not see, and the ungodly were also sure that God was not taking notice of their activities.

He shows a striking contempt for these tyrants and proud builders when He calls them sons of Adam or sons of men. He does this with the same intention as above (Gen. 6:2, 3), namely, to make a difference between the true and the false church, between the sons of God and the sons of men. For He calls those who are without the Word the sons of men; they are lost and abandoned hypocrites. "What are these men trying to do?" says God. "They are building a city and a tower against My church, surely a laughable undertaking, since they are sons of men."

This also serves to comfort the true church, that God not only sees the enterprises, machinations, and counsels of the ungodly who oppose the church but also laughs at them, as the second psalm (2:4) says: "He who sits in the heavens laughs; the Lord has them in derision." But it is a scornful laughter; for fury, wrath, and dispersion follow upon this laughter. "He will speak at some time in His wrath," says David, "and terrify them in His fury" (Ps. 2:5).

Therefore it should not frighten us if we see the pope, like Nimrod, building a citadel for the purpose of suppressing the church, while he incites the Turk and the world against us. The Lord is certainly laughing at these futile plans and will confound him also.

Thus the Holy Spirit comforts the true church, which is being troubled by the church of Satan, lest it believe that God is paying no attention to it. He says: "The Lord sees what the ungodly are doing. And now He is getting ready to descend, that those who laugh smugly at all threats and mistakenly suppose that their power cannot be broken may become aware that their plans are not hidden from God."

Yet God does not make use of battering-rams to break down walls, nor does He use other engines of war; He merely confuses their languages. This is truly an astounding method of conquering cities and of demolishing walls, but it is the surest and easiest of all. Similarly, Christ asserts in the Gospel (Luke 11:17): "Every kingdom divided against itself is laid waste." If the languages had not been confused, the unity of hearts would have continued. But now Babylon falls, Nineveh falls, Jerusalem falls, Rome falls — in short, all kingdoms fall as a result of the confusion of languages, which gives rise to a disunity of hearts.

6. *And the Lord said: Behold, they are one people, and they have all one language; and this is only the beginning of what they will do; and nothing that they propose to do will now be impossible for them.*

The verb זָמַם is familiar, for it means to reach some decision as a result of some proposal and to consider whether it is good or evil. Such is its meaning in the passage before us: "They have decided to do this; they have made up their minds; and they will not allow themselves to be turned away from what they have undertaken." This is a sort of complaint from God, who is amazed and grieved at the great arrogance of men, because to their own great harm, they smugly despised the authority of Noah and of godly Shem.

Yet this is written for our comfort (Rom. 15:4); for our faith is feeble, and even for one who is ever so patient the cross is heavy. Therefore when we see the plans of the ungodly and so many violent offenses, we get thoughts such as these: that the church is about to go to ruin and that ungodliness is about to take over everything. Against these thoughts of despair the passage before us is effective; as though the Holy Spirit were saying: "Do not observe only what men have in mind; for they are reckless, stubborn, proud, and smug. But leave the earth for a while, ascend into heaven with your thoughts, and see what God is doing and how He is disposed. Surely He is not idle, nor is He sleeping; but He looks upon this human smugness with grief, and these matters distress Him as much as they distress you. Therefore have no doubt; someday He will come and will confound these זְמָמִים." This is the name the Hebrews give to stubborn people who have set their hearts on carrying out some deed. Hence these words of God denote the sobs and sighs of the godly when they are frightened and unnerved by the stubborn disposition of the ungodly, who have made up their minds that even against the will of the gods they want to carry out what they have undertaken.

Thus we see that the holy fathers were troubled and tempted by their weakness in faith when they saw so many offenses from the ungodly men who were blaspheming God and His Word. Otherwise they would not have been so fearful or sighed so much that for their comfort God was constrained to reveal His own grief, which stemmed from the arrogance of the ungodly. Now follows the punishment.

7. *Come, let Us go down, and there confuse their language, that they may not understand one another's speech.*

8. *So the Lord scattered them abroad from there over the face of all the earth, and they left off building the city.*

9. *Therefore its name was called Babel, because there the Lord confused the language of all the earth; and from there the Lord scattered them abroad over the face of all the earth.*

This is a description of the awful punishment from which wars, murders, and evils of every kind throughout the entire world have resulted. One should not think that this punishment has come to an end. It continues until now, and especially the church is conscious of this severe affliction. How often has it happened that churches were at variance with one another because of one little, inconsequential ceremony! Pope Victor excommunicated all the churches of the East because they differed from the Western churches in their celebration of Easter.[14] The Eastern churches adhered to the same day that the Jews observe until now, but those in the West preferred to make use of their Christian liberty.

There are similar occurrences in government, for truly there is no more harmful plague for kingdoms and state affairs than division. If we Germans had been united in heart and effort, what could the Turk have achieved against us, or what could he achieve now? But now that we are divided among ourselves on account of petty titles,[15]

[14] Pope Victor I (d. 198) excommunicated Polycrates, Bishop of Ephesus, and other Eastern bishops for observing the fourteenth day of Nisan as the Christian Easter.

[15] Cf. Luther's comments in his exposition of Ps. 101, *Luther's Works*, 13, pp. 146 ff.

he is gradually sapping the strength of Germany and taking possession of one area after another.

Thus we also are punished by the confusion of languages, and ever since Babel was built all kingdoms have felt this plague. What Sallust says is true: Small undertakings grow through harmony, but great ones go to ruin through disharmony.[16] And the Greeks have rather cleverly invented the story of Eris,[17] which may have had its origin in this very account; for the sacred stories became known to the Gentiles through oral accounts. "Babylonian evil" would, therefore, deserve the status of a proverb to express the idea that discord is the most ruinous plague in human affairs; for it utterly subverts religion, laws, good habits, and whatever good this life has. Of this we have examples before our eyes in the church, in the government, and in the household.

Previously, in the first chapter,[18] we explained Moses' use of the plural number in this passage when the one God is speaking. We said that this is sure evidence of the most holy Trinity, of our belief that the Father, who begets; the Son, who is begotten; and the Holy Spirit, who proceeds from the Father and the Son, are one God. We are not going to spend any time on the trivial objections of the Jews, who prattle that God was speaking with the angels.[19] For we were not created in the likeness of the angels; but they, together with us, are the likeness of God. We maintain, as the words reveal, that there is a plurality in God characterized by an undivided essence and an inseparable unity. The angels are unable to confuse languages; this is the work of the Creator Himself. As He gave uniformity of speech, so He alone is able to change and abolish it; a creature cannot do this. The angels are able to adopt human speech, as very many examples of Scripture prove; but they can neither create nor change it in man.

Let us, therefore, abide by the true meaning that the Father is God, the Son is God, and the Holy Spirit is God; that is, that in this passage the one Godhead Itself is speaking to Itself and saying: "Let Us descend." Hence that descent is the work of God alone. The angels have no part in it. Through it He frightens and crushes the ungodly after they have fallen into sin.

[16] Sallust, *Bellum Iugurthinum*, 10, 6; cf. *Luther's Works*, 9, 221.
[17] Cf. Homer, *Iliad*, Book IV, ll. 440—441.
[18] *Luther's Works*, 1, pp. 57—59.
[19] Cf. Lyra on Gen. 11:7, sec. o.

Thus Moses reveals the plurality of Persons in God, but he did not explain its number and nature; for this was being reserved for the glory of the New Testament, which expressly designates the Persons, namely, that there is in God a Person who begets, a Person who is begotten, and a Person who is, so to speak, "breathed," who proceeds from the Father and the Son. In the Old Testament, therefore, this article about the Trinity was included in the general faith [20] in which the holy fathers died and were saved. Let us, therefore, not permit ourselves to be deprived of such evidences by the ungodly and blinded Jews. Words that are so clear and that are used in their strict sense should not be distorted and twisted into an absurd meaning.

THE LINEAGE OF THE ANCESTORS OF CHRIST FROM THE FLOOD UP TO ABRAM

10. *These are the descendants of Shem. When Shem was a hundred years old, he became the father of Arpachshad two years after the Flood.*

This latter part of the eleventh chapter seems to be of little importance, because it contains nothing except the generations of the fathers. In reality, however, there is need of this account, especially as an example for our time. For we hear that after the division of languages not only governments and the affairs of the home but also the church was thrown into disorder in various ways. And so, lest we suppose that Satan had been allowed to remove the sunlight of the Word utterly from the world and to suppress the church, the generation of the holy fathers is set before us, to show us that by the mercy of God the remnants were preserved and the church was not completely wiped out.

After Seth the remnants of the church were Methuselah and Noah, together with their households. After the Flood, when the ungodly descendants of Ham had suddenly increased and were filling everything with offenses, Noah, together with his son Shem and his grandsons, governed the church. This shows that the article of our creed is true when we believe one, holy, catholic church in all ages, from the beginning of the world until the end of the world. God has always preserved for Himself a people that would cling to the

---

[20] Perhaps Luther is distinguishing here between this *fides generalis* and the *fides specialis* or personal faith by which an individual is saved. Cf. p. 27.

Word and would be the guardian of religion and of sound doctrine in the world, lest everything degenerate into ungodliness and there be no knowledge of God among men.

This list of the fathers teaches us the basic doctrine that God has never altogether abandoned His church, even though on some occasions it was larger and on others smaller, just as also on some occasions its teaching was purer and on others less clear. Let us sustain ourselves with this hope against the great wickedness of the world and of the opponents of the Word. Christ also gives us the comfort (Matt. 24:22) that the days of the last time will be shortened for the sake of the godly, namely, that the church will be preserved and Antichrist will not encompass everything with error and falsehood.

These grandsons of Shem were heirs of the promise concerning Christ, and God wanted them preserved and defended, in order that there might be people among whom the church or the Word might be found. For these cannot be separated: where the Word is, there the church is, there the Spirit is, there Christ is, and everything. Who cares how much the pope shouts his vile objections or denies that there can be a church where he himself is not the head!

The fathers had a physical succession, just as later on in the Law there was a physical succession to the priesthood. But in the New Testament there is no such physical succession. Christ did not beget sons according to the flesh. Therefore the church is not confined to a place or to persons but is only where the Word is. Where the Word is not, even though the titles and the office are there, the church is not, because God is not there either.

Similar examples out of later ages bear witness to the extraordinary counsel and the inexpressible mercy of God, who, even in His fury and wrath, does not cast away the human race without preserving what Isaiah calls "the remnant" of the church (1:8-9; 10:20). Thus at the time of the Babylonian captivity Jeremiah, Daniel, and others were preserved. These men He cherished and supported with the promises of the Word, that they also might pass the church on to their descendants.

Thus at the time of the Romans, when the iniquities of the ungodly synagog were full, remnants were preserved like a seedbed. Through them the Gentiles, too, came to a knowledge of Christ. Thus the church has always been divinely preserved in the world through Him who crushed the head of the serpent (Gen. 3:15).

After this comfort, which the list before us gives, it is a pleasant task to draw an inference on the basis of chronology [21] as to the outward appearance of the church and to see who its rulers and their contemporaries were.

Noah lived for three hundred and fifty years after the Flood. But who can imagine how he exerted himself in reproving the ungodly followers of Nimrod, or how much he prayed to keep the godly with him and away from entanglements with the ungodly? Not a single day passed on which the good old man did not battle against offenses and against the heresies that were arising. Therefore I stated previously that these fathers occupy the highest rank among the martyrs [22] because they underwent such great conflicts with the ungodly for so long.

Noah saw his grandsons up to the tenth generation, for he died when Abraham was fifty-eight years old. Shem outlived Abraham by thirty-five years. Therefore he lived for one hundred and ten years together with Isaac and for fifty years together with Jacob and Esau. What a beautiful church this was! To be ruled by so many fathers living for so long at the same time! God wanted these lights of the church to shine among a host of offenses, lest everything degenerate into idolatry.

But godly Noah excelled them all. He had seen the former world for such a long time; and he hoped that his offspring would abide by the Word and in the fear of God, since they had been warned by the awful example of the Flood. But the good father is mistaken. For scarcely after a hundred years had passed since the Flood, Nimrod attacked the godly generation, drove it from its abodes, and established a new church and new forms of worship. In this he was following the example of his father Ham, who made a mockery of his father when he was drunk, not so much from wine as from worry.

Thus the outward appearance and the lot of the church are the same from the beginning of the world until our time. We also endeavor to oppose and remedy offenses; but these examples remind us that, as Christ says (Matt. 18:7): "Offenses must come," and Paul (1 Cor. 11:19): "There must be heresies among you."

Let us, therefore, prepare ourselves to be patient, and let us learn to endure the rage and the blows of Satan as he tries to tear the church of Christ to pieces and establish his own church. We are no

[21] Cf. p. 82, note 2.
[22] See pp. 216—217.

better than the fathers. Even with much sweat and effort they barely succeeded in preserving the Word and in snatching some from the jaws of Satan. Even Abraham was almost swallowed up by the church of Nimrod; but he was called back by the voice of the Lord, who admonished him to separate from the ungodly race and to seek a new abode. I believe that this was done by Shem himself. Since he was the ruler of the church and had the promise concerning Christ, he was held in high esteem by his grandsons; for his ministry was in truth a ministry of God, and what he ordered, his grandsons received as the voice of God.

Thus when it is written that Rebecca consulted the Lord (Gen. 25:22), I think that she consulted Shem himself, whom the Lord wanted to be at the head of the church.[23] For Shem died when Jacob and Esau were fifty years old; and when men who are full of the Holy Spirit speak, it is God who is speaking. At about this time the kingdom of Egypt had its beginning, for the account states that Abraham went down to Egypt.

Hence it is the main point of this chapter to have us realize where the church was at that time, by which fathers it was governed, and finally which fathers were contemporaries.

In the second place, this chapter points out that after men were permitted to eat meat, they became weaker, and that they began to beget children as well as to die at an earlier age. Having originally brought on our death by eating the fruit, we hasten our death by the variety of our food and by our gluttony. If we used plain foods, without foreign spices, which stimulate the appetite, we would undoubtedly enjoy a longer life.

When I was a boy, very many people, even some who were rather wealthy, used to drink water and to use foods that were very simple and easily prepared. Some barely began to drink wine when they were thirty years old. Nowadays people become accustomed to wines almost in childhood, and either foreign or distilled wines at that. They use them when the stomach is empty. Is it any wonder, then, that they cut their span of life in half, and that very few live to be fifty years old?[24] Just as the eating of the fruit brought on death, so through gluttony and the variety of our foods we lose what we have left of life.

[23] Cf. *Luther the Expositor*, pp. 103—105.

[24] See *Luther's Works*, 13, p. 122, note 71, on the expectation of life and the mortality rate in the Germany of Luther's day.

11. And Shem lived after the birth of Arpachshad five hundred years, and had other sons and daughters.

Perhaps it will appear strange to the reader that Moses did not add the sentence "And he died" to this list, as he did to the previous one. The reason is simple. Previously Moses used this sentence to clarify and emphasize the example of the resurrection and of the future life, which God exhibited to the first world in the person of Enoch. Moses wanted to make this statement repeatedly to be sure that even a careless reader, when he read "and he died" about all the others, would pause at Enoch, of whom alone it is not stated that "he died," but that "the Lord took him." Thus the reader is to reflect on to what place the Lord took Enoch, where Enoch is, and what he is doing. This reflection leads even the reader who is thinking of something else to a sure hope of immortality and of the life that is lived, not before the world but [25] before God.

Here another question arises: "How is it that Arpachshad is begotten two years after the Flood, although he is Shem's third son, as Moses asserts in the previous chapter (Gen. 10:22)? For Shem's first son was Elam, and from him the Persians are descended. To him belonged the kingdom of Babylon, but he was driven out by Nimrod. Asshur is listed as the second son. In order to get away from the cursed idolatry of Nimrod, he emigrated to Assyria and built Nineveh. After these comes Arpachshad. Moses states that he was born two years after the Flood, and yet he plainly declares that he was born when Shem was one hundred years old. Shem, however, was one hundred years old at the time of the Flood."

Some give one answer, others another.[26] In the first place, no great harm would result even if there were no information available about these matters. In the second place, in order that we may give at least some answer, it is not at all inappropriate if one applies to the beginning of the Flood the expression "two years after the Flood" which Moses uses here. Then the meaning would be that Arpachshad was born two years after the Flood had begun. The Flood, however, lasted one year and ten days.

But it is objected: "If this is true, how is it that Elam and Asshur were born before Arpachshad, for then three births occurred in one

---

[25] Although the Weimar text has *seu*, the reading should certainly be *sed*, as it is in all the other editions.

[26] Lyra on Gen. 11:10-11, sec. s.

year?" I answer that even this does not cause any difficulty if we assume that there were twins at the first birth. As I stated above, our faith is not endangered if we should lack knowledge about these matters. This much is sure: Scripture does not lie. Therefore answers that are given in support of the trustworthiness of Scripture serve a purpose, even though they may not be altogether reliable.

12. *When Arpachshad had lived thirty-five years, he became the father of Shelah;*

13. *and Arpachshad lived after the birth of Shelah four hundred and three years, and had other sons and daughters.*

You observe that these fathers hasten to beget children after the great disaster of the human race; otherwise they would have refrained for a longer time out of grief, just as Adam and Eve did after their son Abel had been killed by his brother.[27]

14. *When Shelah had lived thirty years, he became the father of Eber;*

15. *and Shelah lived after the birth of Eber four hundred and three years, and had other sons and daughters.*

16. *When Eber had lived thirty-four years, he became the father of Peleg;*

17. *and Eber lived after the birth of Peleg four hundred and thirty years, and had other sons and daughters.*

18. *When Peleg had lived thirty years, he became the father of Reu;*

19. *and Peleg lived after the birth of Reu two hundred and nine years, and had other sons and daughters.*

20. *When Reu had lived thirty-two years, he became the father of Serug;*

21. *and Reu lived after the birth of Serug two hundred and seven years, and had other sons and daughters.*

22. *When Serug had lived thirty years, he became the father of Nahor;*

23. *and Serug lived after the birth of Nahor two hundred years, and had other sons and daughters.*

[27] *Luther's Works*, 1, p. 339.

24. *When Nahor had lived twenty-nine years, he became the father of Terah;*

25. *and Nahor lived after the birth of Terah a hundred and nineteen years, and had other sons and daughters.*

26. *When Terah had lived seventy years, he became the father of Abram, Nahor, and Haran.*

Here we finally come to Eber, whom Moses mentioned previously (Gen. 10:21) when he called Shem "the father of all the children of Eber." We have already stated the reason for this,[28] namely, that it was done primarily out of deference to Christ and also because at his time that awful confusion of languages occurred. Therefore Shem, who had an extraordinary affection for his people, put him in charge of the church and appointed him as a kind of pontiff, that the line of descent of the church and of Christ might be known. It is clear that this Eber was an outstanding man, who loyally and steadfastly persevered in the faith and promise of the earlier fathers when Nimrod disturbed the church of God.

Because of this devotion it was appropriate that the church took its name from him, with the approval of the holy father Shem, and that those who adhered to the doctrine and faith of the holy father Eber were called Hebrews. This designation of the church persisted up to the time of Christ.

Let us, therefore, reject the fiction of Rabbi Solomon, who maintains that the Hebrews received their name from having crossed the Euphrates. Burgensis, who likes argument for its own sake, follows him. Lyra has a more correct opinion.[29] But even he does not point out the reason for the name very clearly, namely, that the sons of Eber adhered to sound doctrine and true religion, which was anxiously guarded by Eber, lest it be corrupted by Nimrod and the other apostates. From this church came Abraham, who lived with this man Eber throughout his life. Therefore he, too, is called a Hebrew, because he lived in the promise and faith of Eber; for Eber died sixty-four years after Abraham.

You now have the history of the first world, which has been faithfully presented by Moses as proof of the uninterrupted transmission of the promise concerning Christ. Therefore if you call

[28] See p. 371, note 12.
[29] Lyra on Gen. 11:28, sec. a and *Additio*.

this a history of the first church, you are not mistaken; for the Holy Spirit does not concern Himself with the ungodly. They are removed from the memory of men and are buried in hell. But we observe that the true church is the object of God's concern, and that the Holy Spirit carefully describes its propagation from the beginning of the world.

The church has always held this book in the highest esteem, and with good reason; for if we did not have it, we would have no knowledge about the situation of the church for two thousand years. But now we, who follow the patriarchs after such a long interval, have cause to marvel at those holy rulers of the first church, Adam, Seth, Noah, and Shem; and we appraise their conflicts on the basis of our own trials, which the brevity of our life makes bearable. After standing in the battle line for many centuries, those men overcame the furious assaults of Satan and of the world through faith in the promise of the woman's Seed; and finally, when they were called away from this station, they left their descendants well equipped and following in the footsteps of their ancestors. Therefore even though the church was never at peace, it nevertheless weathered the fiercest tempests of its trials.

In these eleven chapters Moses has preserved the memory of this great blessing. From it we, who have sound doctrine and pure religion, may gain the sure hope that also in our era the ungodly will fall, but that the church will be victorious and triumph.

DR. MARTIN LUTHER TO THE GODLY READER [30]

I hope that this work of mine will be of some benefit to the godly, and that it will please them. Yet who will not grant us indulgence if we, who have been born in the world's old age and indeed almost in its dotage, have not always grasped the lofty thoughts of those great men who ruled the first world and passed on religious teaching and true worship to the time of Abraham, who was a ruler of the third millennium? His story we shall also discuss, with the help of God. To God, the Father of our Lord Jesus Christ, together with the Holy Spirit, be glory and praise for this and all His other blessings forever and ever. Amen.[31]

[30] See Introduction, p. x.

[31] Here there appears the following colophon: *IMPRESSUM VUITTEM-BERGAE per Petrum Seitz Anno 1.5.44.*

At this point we shall begin the third book. The first contains the account of the first world up to the Flood; the second describes the events that took place after the Flood up to the time of Abraham. It is indeed a brief account if you consider what kind of history the world usually admires. But it surpasses all other accounts, however grand, in this respect: it reveals both that God spoke with a holy man and that the promise concerning the future Christ was given to the patriarch Shem with the proviso that Japheth, too, should become a partaker of the promise. In those times this promise shone before them like a sun. The godly saw the day of Christ from afar; and in that hope they overcame whatever hardships the thankless world and Satan, the malevolent enemy, put in their way.

Now follows the third book, in which not only a new generation but also a new promise appears. For why not call that generation "new" to which a new Word is sent from heaven? Thus it is an outstanding distinction that God bestows on Abraham when He speaks with him and gives him the promise concerning the Seed who was to bless all nations.

Secular histories have nothing like this. Whatever is extraordinary in them has to do entirely with the glory and privilege given to man when he is commanded to have dominion over the fish of the sea, the birds of the heaven, etc. (Gen. 1:28); that is, secular histories present nothing but what mankind has achieved by dint of reason and effort. But the Word of God is a greater gift, just as the Spirit, by whom the hearts of the godly are ruled, is a greater gift than reason. The former are earthly, but the latter are heavenly and divine; and for this reason they deserve our highest praise and admiration.

It is true that at the time of Abraham many patriarchs were still alive; for Abraham was fifty-eight years old when Noah died, while Shem survived Abraham by thirty-one years, and some of his ancestors were alive after him. Nevertheless, it is correct for us to say that with Abraham a new world and a new church began; for with Abraham God begins once more to separate His church from all nations, and He adds a very clear promise concerning Christ, who was to bless all nations.

Therefore it is also proper that we begin a new book at this point, where a new light comes from heaven. This light reveals that Christ will be born from the descendants of Abraham; and it makes the very sweet announcement concerning His ministry that He will bring a blessing for the world, that is, that He will atone for the sins of the world and thus reconcile us to God and give us eternal life. Added to this is the designation of the place where Christ is to be born. Because the land of Canaan is promised to the descendants of Abraham and Christ was to be born of the descendants of Abraham, it is sure that Christ will be born in the land of Canaan and from the Jews. This light the church did not have before Abraham. Therefore there now arises almost a new church, because a new Word is beginning to shed its light.

THE LATTER PART OF CHAPTER ELEVEN

27. *Now these are the descendants of Terah. Terah was the father of Abram, Nahor, and Haran; and Haran was the father of Lot.*

28. *Haran died before his father Terah in the land of his birth, in Ur of the Chaldeans.*

This passage belongs to the most obscure of the entire Old Testament. Therefore it has given rise to a variety of questions, which the attentive reader will find here and there among both old and more recent writers.[32] Even if I do not arrive at its true meaning, however, it seems to me that I shall be doing the right thing to defend myself with a statement of Paul, who, when he encountered the same difficulties, stated (1 Tim. 1:4) that one should keep away from genealogies, which give rise to endless questions. Moreover, there is this other failing, that ambitious minds think they can acquire a great reputation if they express themselves freely on difficult passages and then tenaciously defend their opinion. This is a malady of our nature against which expounders of the Sacred Scriptures must be on their guard.

There are many obscure passages and, as they are sometimes called, "crosses of the philologians"[33] in secular writers too. Ingenious people may try their skill on these without peril. In the Sacred Scriptures, however, nothing should be defended tenaciously except what is definite; about dark and doubtful matters other people must be allowed their own judgment.

In connection with this passage the first question is: "Since Abram is mentioned in the first place here, was he the first-born or not?"

[32] Cf. Lyra on Gen. 11:27, sec. t.
[33] Cf. p. 15, note 23.

Lyra and Rabbi Solomon line up hostile armies against each other on this issue.³⁴ Lyra denies that Abram was the first-born and submits this mathematical reason: Sarah, he says, was the daughter of Haran, but Abraham was only ten years older than his wife. For he says below (Gen. 17:17): "Shall a child be born to a man who is a hundred years old? Shall Sarah, who is ninety years old, bear a child?" Hence it is impossible that Abraham was older than his brother Haran, whose daughter is only ten years younger than Abraham. This is a mathematical reason and a sound one; for if Abraham was only ten years older than his brother's daughter and is represented as older than his brother, it follows that his brother Haran was at the most eight years old when he begot Sarah. This is clearly ridiculous.

Someone will say: "Then why is Abraham put in the first place?" Augustine answers that one must take notice, not of the order of birth but of the mark of future prestige, in which Abraham surpassed his brothers.³⁵ As the head and ruler of the generation that followed, he had to be placed first. This is Lyra's opinion, and it actually cannot be refuted if Sarah was the natural daughter of Haran. But it is also possible that Haran married her mother, a widow, and that the daughter was brought along by the mother, or that she was adopted by Haran himself. In either case she would be properly called Haran's daughter, but not by blood. If Sarah was the daughter of Haran in one of these ways, Lyra's evidence is not conclusive.

Rabbi Solomon ignores this calculation and maintains that Abram was literally the first-born. Even though he does this out of the usual desire to honor the father of the Jews with this distinction, I also tend to incline toward that opinion, with the result that I consider Abram to have been the first-born.

The second question is far more difficult, and yet neither Lyra nor other writers take note of it, namely, that in the instance of Abraham himself we are sixty years short. The computation which the text gives is simple. Terah is seventy years old when he begets Abram, but Abram leaves Haran in the seventy-fifth year of his life, in the course of which Terah died. If you add up these years, you will have one hundred and forty-five years. But when the account mentions the years of Terah, it plainly states that he died when he

---

³⁴ Lyra on Gen. 11:27, sec. t.
³⁵ See Lyra as referred to in the preceding note.

had lived two hundred and five years. Hence the question is how these years can be accounted for.

It is senseless to imitate the foolhardy geniuses who immediately shout that an obvious error has been committed whenever such a difficulty arises and who unabashedly dare emend books that are not their own.[36] As yet I have no real answer for this question, even though I have carefully computed the years of the world.[37] Therefore with due and humble admission of my lack of knowledge (for it is the Holy Spirit alone who knows and understands all things) I offer the conjecture that in the case of Abraham God wanted these sixty years to be lost because of a definite plan, that no one might venture to foretell anything definite about the end of the world on the basis of an accurate calculation of the years of the world. He does indeed give signs of the Last Day, and He wants them to be prominent and to be observed. But He does not want this day to be known, no, not even the year, so that in expectation of this most momentous day the godly might continually display their faith and fear of God. I have nothing further to say about this question.

I wanted to call attention to these facts concerning the first two questions in order that no one might get the impression that we either have no knowledge of such matters or have not read about them. If we are in error when we maintain that Abraham was the first-born, the error is one that does not impair faith or condemn us. Nor am I striving for fame as a result of these discussions; for I know that God distributes His gifts the way He does, not for us to lord it over others through them or to scorn the opinions of others but to serve those who have need of our labors in this area.

When the text states about Haran that he died עַל־פְּנֵי תֶּרַח, in the presence of his father, in the land in which he was born, this is easy to understand. This is intended to point out that Haran died before Abraham and his father Terah left Chaldea. I am purposely not taking into account the Jewish prattle, which Lyra repeats: that Haran perished when he was cast into a fire, but that Abraham was preserved in the fire because he had a stronger faith.[38] Joshua is a more trustworthy witness, and he expressly states (24:2): "On

---

[36] This refers not only to the emendation of Scripture but to tampering with any books.

[37] Cf. p. 82, note 2.

[38] Lyra on Gen. 11:28, sec. a.

the other side of the river [that is, in Mesopotamia], your fathers originally dwelt, Terah, the father of Abraham, and Nahor, and they served other gods." This is a different pronouncement from that which the lying Jews make up for Abraham. They praise his faith solely for the sake of temporal distinction, so that they themselves might have a greater claim to fame because of such a father. But if they want to praise Abraham as Scripture praises him, they must admit that he was an ungodly idolater; for such is the testimony Joshua gives.

Therefore this is an awful indication that the faction or heresy of Nimrod in Babylon grew to such an extent that it infected even the descendants of the saints with its poison. Godly Shem adhered to the true worship and did not depart from the sound doctrine. But how much he must have been despised by the followers of Nimrod, when even Terah, Nahor, and Abram separate from him and ally themselves with the church of Satan!

Having been warned by this example, we ought to put aside smugness and walk in the fear of God; for we observe that not only the collateral branches among the patriarchs fell into error and idolatry but even the very root of the church, Terah and Abraham. This is also an outstanding example of God's mercy, that God does not cast aside these idolaters but calls them back from error and restores them through His Word. The pope makes sheer angels of his saints, indeed even blocks and logs of wood not subject to human failings.[39] But the Scriptures reveal that even the greatest heroes of the church were human beings, that is, that they often fell, often sinned, and nevertheless were received back into grace by a merciful God. So these examples are useful both to instill the fear of God into hearts and to sustain faith or trust in mercy.

29. *And Abram and Nahor took wives; the name of Abram's wife was Sarai, and the name of Nahor's wife, Milcah, the daughter of Haran, the father of Milcah and Iscah.*

30. *Now Sarai was barren; she had no child.*

Nearly all the commentators are of the opinion that Iscah is the one who is called Sarai above and who was taken in marriage by Abraham. But it seems to me that the reason why Moses expressly

[39] Cf. Luther's *Lectures on the Minor Prophets* (1524—26), W, XIII, 242; *Luther the Expositor,* pp. 75—77.

calls Haran the father of Milcah and Iscah in this passage is to indicate that Sarai was not the natural daughter of Haran but was either his stepdaughter or his adopted daughter. But I will not keep anyone from following what he considers nearest to the truth, for it does not imperil our faith.

The reason why Scripture says concerning Sarai that she was barren is to make us realize that also at that time procreation was a wonderful blessing, since the Scriptures mention it as a singular misfortune of Sarai that she was barren. The marriage of Abraham is the only one that is barren, while all the ungodly have large families and numerous descendants — with this misfortune, this hell,[40] Almighty God punishes, or rather tests, this holy man. But it was not only that God wanted to test Abraham in this manner; for it makes the miracle greater and bears witness to God's mercy, power, and truth when the barren and even feeble Sarah gives birth to a son from whom so large a people and so many descendants have sprung. Moreover, we properly note in this passage that the Holy Spirit differentiates between the malady of human nature, corrupted by sin, and its work, namely, procreation. He does not take away the gift because of that nature; but even in the corrupt nature, which, like a monster, is carried away by its lust and rabid desire, He praises the gift of procreation as an outstanding blessing. If this were not the case, He would not have mentioned the barrenness of Sarah, who was married to Abraham.

31. *Terah took Abram his son and Lot the son of Haran, his grandson, and Sarai his daughter-in-law, his son Abram's wife, and they went forth together from Ur of the Chaldeans to go into the land of Canaan; but when they came to Haran, they settled there.*

32. *The days of Terah were two hundred and five years; and Terah died in Haran.*

This is the second knot, but it is a little less complicated than the first. The difficulty arises from the statement of Stephen in Luke's Acts of the Apostles 7:2-3: "The God of glory appeared to our father Abraham when he was in Mesopotamia, before he lived in Haran, and said to him, 'Depart from your land and from your kindred, and go into the land which I will show you.'" Here, however, Moses says that Abraham migrated to Haran at his father's

---

[40] The phrase is obscure: *in isto peccati infernalis inferno.*

request; and in the next chapter (12:1) he says that Abraham was called away from Haran by the voice of God after his father had died in the land of Haran. But if one is willing to be wise with humility and not to overindulge his reason, he will easily reconcile Moses and Stephen.[41] We shall state our own idea below, in chapter twelve.[42] At this point it will be sufficient to recall that Terah was deceived by the Nimrodic faction, departed from the faith with his household, and became an idolater. Yet when he was rebuked by the holy patriarch Shem, he decided that he had to give up the Nimrodic fellowship.

A third question must be treated here, a linguistic one, about Ur of the Chaldeans, whether it is the name of a place or of a Chaldean idol. The word אוּר denotes light or fire. From it comes the name of the אוּרִים in Ex. 28:30, which were in Aaron's breastplate and from which the Lord gave His answers. Even though the nature of this object cannot be definitely stated, it is sure nevertheless that it gets its name from light or brilliance. I am of the opinion that Ur is the name of a place, which, however, as is frequently the case, got this designation from an idolatrous cult that especially flourished there. We in Germany have similar place names, but given for other reasons: Lichtenfels, Lichtenstein, and Lichtenberg. It seems, moreover, that this cult originated when God gave the fathers an indication of His favor by light or fire sent down from heaven, which consumed the sacrifices that were being offered. This was a sign that God was pleased with this form of worship, as the story of Elijah reveals (1 Kings 18:38). And in the Law (Lev. 6:12) the Lord commanded to maintain continually the sacred fire from which the sacrifices should be burned. The heathen imitated this form of worship, as the historical accounts show. I think that in just this way the Nimrodic faction imitated the pure religion and consecrated its own special fire, to make the worship of the fathers look contemptible, as though they had nothing unusual and outstanding. From this fire the name was given later on to the place, so that the city in which that form of worship flourished most was called אוּר, where the people gathered in large numbers, just as

---

[41] In their discussion of this apparent contradiction Luther and Melanchthon had disagreed. Luther said: "Luke manifestly contradicts this text." Melanchthon replied: "This is a casual error." W, *Deutsche Bibel*, III, 179. This suggests the possibility that the text as given here has been revised by an editorial hand.

[42] See pp. 277—278.

they did at Jerusalem among the Jews and in our times in Rome. And according to Joshua, Terah, Nahor, and Abraham adhered to this idolatry and approved of it (Joshua 24:2).

The examples of all times teach that the Word of truth and the true forms of worship are despised by the common people. Hence when new teachers arise, they present itching ears to them; and truly, as Moses says (Deut. 29:19): "The drunkard seizes the thirsting." Perverse teachers are most ready to teach, and the common people are most eager to listen. In this manner the Word and the true forms of worship become lost. The Anabaptists proclaim the new doctrine that children should not be baptized, because they cannot have faith, since they are without reason and do not understand the Word. The common people had heard nothing of this kind from us, and so they received that idea with great applause. The Sacramentarians, Zwingli, Oecolampadius, and their like contend that when Christ says: "This is My body," He does not mean that with the bread or under the bread He is giving His body, but that only bread is received and wine is drunk, and that the body of Christ is not received and His blood is not drunk. These teachers the ignorant common people admire and follow. But we, who do not allow ourselves to be diverted from the words of Christ, are regarded as not one whit sounder or better than the papists. Such is the custom of the world: it despises the Word and admires what is new. This is what made that אוּר, of which Moses is speaking here, famous and extolled above the remaining cities of Chaldea, on account of the new worship there.

The word כַּשְׂדִּים means Chaldeans. However, I am of the opinion that on account of the new worship אוּר was called אוּר חֲסִידִים, as though one were to call it the city of saints. Similarly, people have called Rome the chief church and the head of all the rest of the churches. But Moses changes the name to its opposite, as if to say: "You are not חֲסִידִים but כַּשְׂדִּים, not saints but Chaldeans." The prophets take delight in such plays on words. Micah (1:11) similarly calls צָאֲנָן שַׁאֲנָן, and Hosea (10:5) calls בֵּית־אֵל בֵּית־אָוֶן.

Traces of this idolatry remained for a long time among the Persians, as the historical accounts of the heathen prove. For the Persian king demanded that the sacred fire, which the historical accounts designate by the corrupt Hebrew word *Orimasda*,[43] be

[43] The name is Avestan in origin.

carried before him in solemn procession on a horse without a rider. Similarly, the pope lets the body of Christ, as he calls it, be carried before him on a horse without a rider, but on one that is highly ornamented. He is deceiving himself and others, however; for it is not the body of Christ but plain bread. Christ did not want His body to be present when the bread is carried about in parade, but when it is taken and eaten in church in accordance with His institution. The pope misuses the public procession in order to give support to his error concerning the one kind.[44]

Thus ungodliness and superstition always remain the same. Even though the practices and signs, or the outward form of worship, may change, the tendencies and endeavors remain the same. Today the pope does not make use of fire for adoration; he has other ungodly endeavors and practices. These are different in appearance, but they have the same objective. Thus אוּר of the Chaldeans remains until the end the way it was almost from the beginning of the world. For people abandon the Word, persecute the faith, and meanwhile busy themselves with new endeavors, which they imagine to be the only true form of worship.

The Jews think that אוּר is not the name of a place, but that it was the fire into which those who condemned the Nimrodic idolatry were cast, just as they relate a tale about Abraham and Haran.[45] But I do not follow their opinion. I believe that it is the name of a place at which men gathered from everywhere as though for most sacred worship. Similarly later on Jerusalem, Bethel, and Shechem were famous places of worship, where God revealed Himself to the fathers through various acts.

[44] Cf. *Luther's Works*, 22, pp. 265—266.
[45] See p. 239, note 38.

CHAPTER TWELVE

1. *Now the Lord said to Abram: Go from your country and your kindred and your father's house to the land that I will show you.*

THIS is the third age [1] (as it is called), in which Holy Scripture begins the description of the church from a new stem. Thus far the line of descent was traced from Adam, through many patriarchs, down to Noah, and from there down to Abraham. During this time the church suffered great damage, for ungodliness had increased to such an extent that even the descendants of the saints were carried away into error. Therefore it was necessary for Moses to point out how in this great peril God accomplished the rebirth of the church, lest it collapse entirely and true religion be utterly blotted out.

This account deserves our attention as an extraordinary example of mercy. It should encourage and persuade us that God will preserve the church also in our own time, when everything is threatening religion with destruction. Despite the great importance of their content the preceding accounts are very brief. In these which follow, however, the Holy Spirit will speak at greater length and will discuss everything in greater detail. Accordingly, up to this point the church looks like a brook that is flowing along peacefully; but now it receives accessions and rushes along with the roar of a real river until, through the marvelous blessing of God, the holy nation expands into a vast ocean and fills the world with its name. It is highly gratifying and comforting to observe these beginnings and increases of the church. Moreover, we see that the prophets, too, were delighted by these thoughts, for Isaiah refers more than once to this marvelous guidance and increase of the church.[2]

Above, when Moses was describing Noah (Gen. 6:9), he called him a righteous and perfect man in his generation. No such title is bestowed on Abraham in this passage. No doubt this is because, as Joshua bears witness, Abraham, with his father and brothers, was

[1] On the first and second age cf. p. 236.
[2] Luther is thinking of passages like Is. 60:3 ff.

an idolater and was righteous, not before God but before Nimrod, whose worship he was imitating (Joshua 24:2). Moses, therefore, says nothing about Abraham's person and has no praise for anything in him. For idolatry must be reproved, not praised. But he does praise God's mercy and extol Him because He did not allow this idolater to remain in idolatry any longer but called him out of the church of the ungodly to another place.

This call is grand and praiseworthy, and Isaiah extols it in chapter 41:2: "Who stirred up one from the east?" Who called him that he should teach righteousness wherever he went? (For the Hebrew way of saying this is contained in the word רַגְלוֹ.) And the Letter to the Hebrews states (11:8-9): "By faith Abraham obeyed when he was called to go out to a place which he was to receive as an inheritance; and he went out, not knowing where he was to go. By faith he sojourned in the Land of Promise, as in a foreign land." Moses intimates the very same thing in this passage by saying that he was called by God to go out.

This blessing of deliverance from idolatry has its source, not in his own merits or powers but solely in a God who pities and calls him. Similarly, Moses reminds his people that they were chosen by the Lord, not because they had deserved this but because the Lord had loved them and was keeping the oath that had been given to their fathers.[3] In this passage we see that the beginnings are in agreement with the end. For what is Abraham except a man who hears God when He calls him, that is, a merely passive person [4] and merely the material on which divine mercy acts?

Therefore this passage is important as proof for the doctrine of grace over against the worth of merits and works, which reason extols so highly. For if you should ask what Abraham was before he was called by a merciful God, Joshua (24:12) answers that he was an idolater, that is, that he deserved death and eternal damnation. But in this wretched state God does not cast him away; He calls him and through the call makes everything out of him who is nothing. I readily believe that Abraham was a very honorable man if one considers his civil virtues, and a very good man so far as nature makes this possible, one who did not yield to lust, greed, and other vile

---

[3] It is not clear which specific passage in the Pentateuch Luther has in mind; perhaps, as the Weimar editors suggest, it is Deut. 29:13.

[4] Cf. *Luther's Works*, 13, p. 137, note 90.

desires but practiced moderation to overcome or control the blind impulses of his corrupt nature.

To be sure, the Babylonian religion of Nimrod was most pretentious. They worshiped God under the title of light, which is the best figure or representation of the Divine Majesty; the Holy Scriptures themselves call God "Light."[5] Added to this worship, which had a fine outward appearance, were an excellent life and morals. Therefore even the descendants of the saints embraced this religion. Superstition is a pernicious empress, who rules in the world in every age; and the world eagerly accepts her reign. But in this dazzling and magnificent religion Abraham is Satan's captive slave, who worships God, not in the manner in which God Himself wanted to be worshiped but as he sees Him worshiped by those whose number, prestige, and power surpassed the holy remnants of the godly fathers.

Thus, as I said above, Abraham is merely the material that the Divine Majesty seizes through the Word and forms into a new human being and into a patriarch. And so this rule is universally true, that of himself man is nothing, is capable of nothing, and has nothing except sin, death, and damnation; but through His mercy Almighty God brings it about that he is something and is freed from sin, death, and damnation through Christ, the Blessed Seed.

I surmise that at that very time the patriarch Shem was in the land of Canaan, not alone, to be sure, but with his church. He was living in Salem, as is recorded below (Gen. 14:18), and he is called a priest of the Most High. Therefore he was not alone, but he had with him some whom he would teach, perhaps his sons Elam, Asshur, Shelah, Eber, etc.; all these were fleeing the church of Satan in Babylon and followed the holy patriarch. And yet the Lord seemingly disregards all these; God elects as patriarch an idolater, who is estranged from God and a prisoner of Satan, one who had not been abandoned among the Nimrodites but remained among them without cause and voluntarily.

Why does He do this? Why does He not rather take one of those who were in the company of the holy patriarch Shem and kept the true worship? Doubtless in order that God may commend and emphasize His mercy, which is in truth, as Paul calls it in Eph. 3:8, "His unsearchable riches." Thus in later generations, as Paul relates about himself in the same passage, He calls Paul to the apostolate of

[5] Probably a reference to 1 John 1:5.

the heathen, a very wicked man, a murderer, a blasphemer, one who is inflamed with hatred for Christ and for His church. God could have called one of the seventy-two [6] or some other excellent man; but He does not do this, obviously in order to reveal to us His superabundant mercy.

Moreover, these words are written, not in order that the ungodly may be confirmed in their ungodliness and sin all the more wantonly, but in order that the fainthearted and fearsome, who are tempted to despair because of their sins, may find comfort and, encouraged by such examples, may learn to place their hope in such a merciful God. For God's wrath and sin are intense, and the conscience cannot bear His wrath unless it is buoyed up by the Word of God. We need examples like these to show that the mercy of God is boundless, so that we may hope for pardon and call upon God.

It is a great and inexpressible gift that Abraham is physically the father of the Son of God. But what is the beginning of this honor? That Abraham is an idolater and a very great sinner, who worships a God he does not know! The Son of God wants this ancestor in His line of descent to be exalted, just as other ancestors of Christ are noted for their great sins.

Why should this be the case? In the first place, in order to show that He is the Savior of sinners. In the second place, to inform us of His limitless kindness, lest we be overwhelmed by our sins and plunged into despair. In the third place, to block the road to haughtiness and pride. For when Abraham has been called in this way, he cannot say: "I have deserved this; this is my work." Even though he was guiltless before men so far as the Second Table is concerned, yet he was an idolater. He would have deserved eternal death had it not been for the call by which he was delivered from idolatry and finally granted the forgiveness of sins through faith. Therefore the statement stands (Rom. 9:16): "It depends not upon man's will or exertion but upon God's mercy."

The Jews are extravagant in their praise of Abraham.[7] They claim that in Ur of the Chaldeans he was cast into the fire because he had condemned the wickedness of the idolaters, and that he was saved by faith. They suppose that in this way they bring great honor to their race; but they are shameful liars, for their own leader

---

[6] Apparently Luther is referring to the Sanhedrin.
[7] Lyra on Gen. 11:28, sec. a.

and ruler Joshua manifestly refutes them (Joshua 24:2). The monks are in the habit of doing the same thing. Their sermons are nothing but prodigious praises of Francis, Dominic, and Augustine; and one who is able to expand and adorn these praises is regarded as the best preacher. But God is the last in line, and at the end He is also given a little praise because He endowed those great saints with such gifts.

But this is philosophical, rationalistic, and truly Turkish preaching; it maintains that we obtain salvation and righteousness through our works. Let us, therefore, follow the example of Moses when we wish to preach about the saints. Let us not forget Ur of the Chaldeans, and that Abraham was an idolater when he lived there. That is, let us teach that even the greatest saints were human beings who could fall into sins and often fell horribly; but when they were saved and later on were endowed with various gifts, this is entirely the result of God's mercy, who calls us by His Word and does not cast us aside.

In this respect all the saints are like Abraham; even if they are good and holy in appearance, they are nevertheless subject to death and damnation as long as they have no divine call and no Word. But when they have been called and enlightened through the Word, they believe, they give thanks to God, they lead a godly life, and they please God — yet in such a way that even then they need the forgiveness of sins. Therefore even when they live in the saintliest way, they still remain humble and do not become proud.

But here the question arises: How was Abraham called, and did he hear this voice from God Himself? I am convinced that he was not called directly by God without the ministry, as it is related below (Gen. 18:2) that God visited him, conversed with him, and was even the guest of Abraham; but I believe that this command was brought to him either by the patriarch Shem personally or by some others who had been sent by Shem.[8]

What grieved pious Shem was not only this, that Terah and his children were perishing in that fire of the Chaldeans, that is, in Nimrodic idolatry, but that through divine revelation, or as a result of divine inspiration, he saw that Abraham would be the only one of his descendants from whose loins the Deliverer of the human race was to come. Moved by this revelation, he did not permit him to tarry any longer among the idolaters, especially since father Noah had now died. For Abraham was commanded to leave Ur about sixteen years after Noah's death.

[8] See p. 231, note 23.

Some saintly men called him out because the Holy Spirit inspired them to do so. Therefore it is stated that the Lord called him out. Whatever men speak at the prompting of the Spirit of God, that God Himself speaks, as Christ says (Luke 10:16): "He who hears you, hears Me."

Furthermore, the expression לֶךְ־לְךָ, which our text renders "go out," is very emphatic in the Hebrew. Literally rendered it denotes: "Go for yourself out of your land." Its meaning, however, is that the entire religion in which Abram had lived until now was ungodly and abominable. It is as though Shem wanted to say: "If you remain in that place, you will not be saved. Therefore if you desire to be saved, abandon that land, abandon your kindred, abandon the house of your father. Go away as far as possible from those idolaters, among whom there is no faith, no fear of God, but only superstition and blind delusion, which results from a lack of the knowledge of God." If there had been no ungodly worship in Babylon, God would not have commanded Abraham to migrate elsewhere. Therefore this very expression implies the First Table. Abraham gives ear to it and begins to fear God; that is, he believes this threat and follows the holy advice. For this reason there follows such a grand promise later on.

But just as godly Shem preached to Abraham, so David also preaches to his people in Ps. 45:10, when he says: "Hear, O daughter, consider and incline your ear; forget your people and your father's house." This is an earnest admonition that the Jews should not make light of the Word of the Gospel but should subordinate the Law and everything else to this doctrine and forget their fathers altogether. "If you do this," says David, "the king will desire your beauty (Ps. 45:11); that is, He will lovingly embrace you through His grace and will adorn you with His Holy Spirit, righteousness, and other gifts." Hence this is the glorious blessing of the Word, or of the ministry, that it points out or reveals sin, which reason by itself not only cannot know, but which it regards as the height of righteousness and a worship most acceptable to God. For idolatry is recognized only through the Word of God.

If the Jews really desire to praise their father, let them begin their praises right here at this passage. Until now he lived in idolatry, had no true knowledge of God, and lacked both faith and the fear of God, even though in appearance he was not a bad man. But now, when the Word reveals the true worship of God and condemns idolatry, he does not behave like our papists, who, when they have been admonished, go their way with a hardened heart and against their conscience insist on ungodly forms of worship. Instead, he submits to the Word when he is commanded to leave Babylon, where he had set up his household, and obeys immediately. He does not argue with himself as the ungodly are accustomed to do: "What if we should be better men than those who are calling me away from here? We, too, are the grandsons of the patriarch Shem. For all that, there will be some holy men also in this land. Why, then, should I alone migrate from here?"

He has no such thoughts; but when he hears the religion condemned to which his father's house and his entire kindred had adhered until now, he forsakes it and willingly follows God at His call, without giving any consideration to the advantages he already had and was about to acquire. This is surely remarkable obedience; we should praise and admire it. That the head of a household leaves his home, his fields, his dear fatherland, and his dear relatives, and goes into exile, uncertain where he would be able to settle — this is surely no insignificant example of obedience, and few will imitate it.

But it is something far greater and more difficult that he allows himself to be convinced that the religion in which he was reared by his parents was ungodly and contrary to the will of God. It is our experience too that it is by far the most difficult of all tasks to win those who were brought up in the papistic religion, even though it is manifestly ungodly and blasphemous. Yes, even we ourselves, who renounced the doctrine of the pope long ago, still have to struggle often and hard to overcome this wretchedness, which has been doubled by habit; for we are born as hypocrites, and afterwards we are confirmed in our hypocrisy by ungodly teachers.

Therefore we are right to praise Abraham, who, after the admonition of holy Shem, gave up both what nature had provided and what had been established through the authority of the fathers and habit. Even though this was not accomplished without great conflict in his conscience, nevertheless faith and the Word finally achieved the victory. Therefore the fathers of the monks, Augustine, Francis, and Dominic, are nothing at all in comparison with this man.

But let us not overlook Sarah either, who so promptly imitates her husband's godliness and herself leaves her native country and dear relatives as well as a household that was surely well established — all to follow an uncertain hope. There is no doubt, moreover, that her relatives urged her to give up her husband, especially when they learned of his intention to go away. But the godly wife bravely disregarded the flatteries, entreaties, and threats, and followed her husband. The household servants, too, were far better and more obedient than they are nowadays, and they were unwilling to desert the head of the household.

The monks consider it a matter of great praise that they forsake everything, although they find more in the monasteries than they left in the home of their parents. But whom will one compare to this monk Abraham, who forsakes his native country, relatives, paternal estate, home, and everything, and simply follows God when He calls him into exile? Among others, of course, he has godly Sarah as his companion in this monastic state. She does not realize that she will have to spend the first night in some inn when she could be living in luxury and comfort at home.

It is not merely because of her wifely affection that she follows her husband. She was aided by the Holy Spirit, who moved her womanly heart so that she also, disregarding everything else, followed God when He called, since she also desired to be saved and not be condemned with the idolaters. Peter, therefore, properly praises this obedience in 1 Peter 3:6 and wants wives to imitate this extraordinary virtue of Sarah. "You are," he says, "her children if you do right and let nothing terrify you."

Hence the true praises of the holy patriarch are these: he permits himself to be reproved, acknowledges that he is an idolater and an ungodly man, and is terrified by the threatened wrath of God. In the second place, he sets out without knowing where he is going. He gives up a sure habitation and goes in pursuit of an uncertain one. In faith it was indeed a certain one, yet in appearance it was uncertain; yes, so far as possession and enjoyment are concerned, it was no habitation at all, as the account shows. David bestows grand praise on this and presents it as a notable example in Ps. 39:12. "I am," he says, "Thy passing guest, a sojourner, like all my fathers."

Someone may say: "What? Was not David a king and lord of the land that was promised to the seed of Abraham? And even though Abraham himself was an exile, he was nevertheless in easy circumstances and had very great wealth." These claims are indeed true, and yet they were exiles because they had these possessions as though they did not have them, as the Letter to the Hebrews bears witness: "Dealing with the world as though they had no dealings with it."[9]

Thus they live in the world at all times. They do indeed concern themselves with the affairs of the home and of the state, govern commonwealths and rear families, till fields, carry on commerce or manual occupations; and yet they are aware that they are exiles and strangers, like their fathers. They make use of the world as an inn from which they must emigrate in a short time, and they do not attach their heart to the affairs of this life. They tend to worldly matters with their left hand, while they raise their right hand upward to the eternal homeland. Moreover, if some disturbance ever occurs either in the state or in the household, they are perturbed very little, if at all. No matter how they may be treated in this inn, it is satisfactory to them; for they know that eternal mansions have been prepared by the Son of God.

Scripture, therefore, has good reason to praise the faith of these holy people, Abraham, Sarah, and Lot, and to present them as a notable example for us to contemplate throughout our life. And yet this is only the beginning of faith and the first call. Because the second call is even more important and grander, we shall have to bestow greater praise on Abraham's faith. At present only food and physical shelter are at stake. This difficulty Abraham overcomes with courage and confidence, and they follow God when He calls them into an exile whose outcome they do not see.

Then what about the idle and indolent pride of the monks, who declare that they have forsaken everything? Let Jerome, Augustine, and Gregory remain silent. They are nothing in comparison with our sojourner and exile, who follows the divine commands and clings with great faith to this one word, that the Lord will show him another land in which he is to have a better habitation.

2. *And I will make of you a great nation.*

This is a most outstanding passage and one of the most important in all Holy Scripture. For this reason it should not be dealt with lightly or read through casually; it should be examined repeatedly and carefully unfolded and explained. Just as we correctly assign the censure of the idolatry in which Abraham lived to the doctrine of the Law, by which sins are reproved, so one may properly call

---

[9] Actually this is a quotation from 1 Cor. 7:31.

this great comfort or promise the Gospel. But what the Lord promises briefly here is explained at greater length in the following chapters.

First of all, you should consider that what the Lord promises Abraham here is altogether impossible, unbelievable, and untrue if you follow reason, because it cannot be seen. If the Lord has something like this in mind for Abraham, why does He not let him remain in his land and with his kindred, where Abraham undoubtedly had some influence or reputation? Is the way to success easier among strange people, where one does not even have a place to set one's foot, than at home, where one's fields, friends, neighbors, and relatives are, where one's household has been well established?

Therefore the power of the Holy Spirit was great and extraordinary in Abraham, because he was able to apprehend with his heart these impossible, unbelievable, and incomprehensible things, as though they were real and already present. Such must have been the case, especially since he was already approaching old age. For he was seventy-five years old, but Sarah was ten years younger and barren at that.

How, I ask you, do these facts agree with this promise: "I will make of you a large nation"? This means that his descendants would be a great and numerous people. But where are the descendants to come from, since Abraham's marriage is childless? These huge masses of unbelief and these high mountains, which could suppress his faith completely, the holy patriarch overcomes and crosses by faith. He simply clings to this one thought: "Behold, God is promising this. He will not deceive you, even though you do not see the way, the manner, or even the time of the fulfillment of this promise."

The Lord calls Abraham's descendants a great nation, not only because of temporal or physical greatness but also because of spiritual greatness, which would, nevertheless, belong to its physical life. For this people must be distinguished from all the kingdoms and peoples of the entire world, however great and powerful. God gives kingdoms also to the Gentiles and fixes their bounds, as Daniel declares (2:21). But He gives these things by His hidden counsel, without the knowledge even of those to whom He is giving them. They suppose that being born or becoming a king is something that happens by chance; they do not realize that these events are directed and controlled by God.

Therefore the word "luck" is such a common word among the

heathen, even though they do not know what luck is.[10] But this people had this prerogative above all the other peoples and kingdoms of the world: God had revealed Himself in His Word, manifested Himself by many and sundry miracles and signs, and declared Himself to be the God of this people.

The exploits of the Jewish people do not seem to equal the triumphs of the heathen. The other kingdoms — the Babylonian, the Persian, the Greek, and the Roman — are considered to be far greater in power and in wealth. Nevertheless, if you take into consideration the ruler of this people — namely, God, who, as appears in the prophet (Is. 31:9), had His home in Jerusalem and was, as it were, a fellow citizen — the victories and triumphs of all the other kingdoms and peoples will seem paltry. Then only those exploits will be judged worthy of the admiration and praise of all men which are shown to be the work of this Master of the house, who is the eternal God, the Creator and Preserver of all things. Even though He rules the remaining kingdoms too, He does this in a hidden manner, without the knowledge of the very people who experience these blessings.

But among this people He reveals Himself; and among this people He wants to be known, praised, and worshiped. He chooses a tabernacle and commands that a temple be built, in order to have a definite dwelling place among this people. To them He reveals Himself through the Word, signs, wonders, rites, ceremonies, etc., that they may know that He is present everywhere and may all but feel Him with their hands. This prerogative Moses includes in these words.

The heathen indeed rank higher in power and wealth, and their exploits strike the eyes and arouse admiration. But these are nothing in comparison with this privilege, which Moses praises in a most exalted manner in Deut. 4:7, that this people has a God who draws near. That is, He dwells in its midst, reveals Himself in the Word, in the worship, and in the holy prophets, who were filled with the Holy Spirit and gave this people instruction concerning the will of God.

These are true and substantial blessings, which the world indeed does not comprehend, because it completely lacks them. Therefore Moses' reason for calling his people a great nation was different from the reason Cicero and Demosthenes had to make the same statement about their nations. Yet his people was also great in a physical sense if you consider its origin, namely, solitary Abraham, from whom

[10] Luther uses the word *fortuna*.

sprang a people so numerous that it is compared to the sand of the sea and the stars of the heaven (Gen. 22:17). The Lord is not yet speaking of the spiritual blessing and the eternal life also promised to this people. These are material blessings, which this people enjoyed in this life, both to prevent others from despising it because of its size and to assure that it would have God dwelling in its midst, speaking, ruling, and defending it. These are superb gifts, which cannot be adequately praised, that God in this manner enclosed Himself, as it were, in this people so that He not only dwelt in its midst but also wanted to be born as a human being from its line. But this belongs to the spiritual and eternal gifts about which we shall speak a little later.

Abraham saw none of these things. In fact, he had abundant reason not to believe them if he had wanted to follow his flesh; for his marriage was childless. Although Isaac was born to him later on and he himself saw his grandson Jacob up to about his fifteenth year, who does not realize that these are very feeble beginnings in comparison with that great promise? Thus the faith of this holy man was outstanding, because he believed these things as though he were already seeing them before his eyes and had no doubts about the promises that were given to him.

With this great faith let us compare our own lack of faith. We know that Christ will come on the Last Day and will destroy all His enemies: the Turk, the Jews, the pope, the cardinals, the bishops, and whatever ungodly men there are, who either persecute the Word or proudly despise and disregard it. We also know that meanwhile Christ will be with His church and will preserve sound doctrine and the true forms of worship.

But if we firmly believed what we know, do you think that it would be possible for any misfortune to perturb us? Or do you think that in our hearts there would arise the smugness we feel in ourselves, as though we were sure that the day of the Lord is a thousand years away?

If, then, we believe at all, our faith is surely weak. We are truly people of little faith and can in no wise compare ourselves to holy Abraham, who receives these invisible things with a firm faith, as though he were already holding them in his hands and touching them. He hears the Lord: "I will make of you a great nation"; and yet he is aware that he is like a dry trunk, for he has a barren wife. And at last, when she is impregnated by her husband and bears a son as a result of God's promise and contrary to nature, he realizes that the promise depends on that only son, who would be exposed to countless hazards, considering the uncertainty of this life. He sees that from Isaac too there is born a single heir of the promise, Jacob. Thus far there is nothing here to bear out the promise that he would have a very numerous posterity. Yet his faith stands firm and unshaken. This is the first part of the promise.

The ungodly Jews consider גּוֹיִם a contemptuous term; for this is the name they give to those who differ from them in worship, just as we term "ungodly" those who are outside the church. Yet they do not realize that in this promise to their own father the true church is given this name. For in this passage all the descendants of Abraham are called by this name: "I will make of you לְגוֹי גָּדוֹל, a great nation."

And I will bless you.

In Scripture the verb "to bless" denotes increase or growth. Therefore this part of the promise means that Abraham should believe not only that he will have a numerous posterity, but also that it will constantly grow and be increased more and more.

Therefore the first gift is that Abraham will be "a great nation," that is, that his descendants will have a kingdom, power, wealth, laws, ceremonies, a church, etc. For this is what is properly called a nation.

But the second gift is that this nation will endure, as Ps. 89:30-33 explains uncommonly well: "If his children forsake My Law and do not walk according to My ordinances, if they violate My statutes and do not keep My commandments, then I will punish their transgressions with the rod and their iniquity with scourges; but I will not remove from him My steadfast love, or be false to My faithfulness."

Truly, that people was often afflicted. The tribe of Benjamin was almost entirely slain. The kingdom of Israel was utterly destroyed. The tribe of Judah, too, was weakened in various ways by the Babylonian kings and then by the Syrians and the Egyptians. And yet that people was preserved by God until the promise concerning Christ would be fulfilled. Then began the real blessing and the real increase, because in place of the few unbelieving Jews the fullness of the Gentiles came in, and the seed of Abraham truly became like the sand of the sea and the stars of the heavens (Gen. 22:17). Therefore it endures to this day and will endure until the end of the world.

No other kingdom of the world enjoyed such a blessing. For how short the time is during which the four monarchies endured![11] But the seed of Abraham will endure forever. If anyone wants to observe the beginnings of this blessing, let him read in order the historical accounts of Moses, Joshua, Judges, Kings, etc., and he will realize that this nation was truly great and blessed.

And make your name great.

That is, you will be extolled far and wide, even among the heathen, as Moses explains in Deut. 4:6-7: "That will be your wisdom and your understanding in the sight of the peoples, who, when they hear all these statutes, will say, 'Surely this great nation is a wise and understanding people.' For what great nation is there that has a god so near to it as the Lord our God is to us?"

But the Jewish people was renowned not only because of the promises, its worship, and the utterances of God entrusted to it, but also because of its heroic men. For out of all heathendom whom shall we pit against David, Hezekiah, Daniel, Joseph, Samson, Gideon, Joshua, and their like, or the prophets or the kings and leaders?

Therefore the heathen regarded this people with admiration and called it blessed. The Syrian Naaman even took with him to Syria some soil of Jerusalem (2 Kings 5:17). Nebuchadnezzar, Darius, and Cyrus commend this people's worship and God to their own peoples and openly condemn whatever other gods and forms of worship there were.[12] Shall we not say that all this is of great significance?

"But," someone will say, "Abraham did not see these events but died long before." This is indeed true, but he still believed and sincerely rejoiced, while if he had lived, Satan would have disturbed this joy; for he disfigures the church and government with so many offenses. But now he derives perfect joy from what he knows as a certainty, that whatever true wisdom the other nations have, they would receive from his descendants. Thus he has a right to glory in the great name that not he himself but the Lord made.

So that you will be a blessing.

Here is presented the amazing promise that this people will not only be increased among itself and be blessed materially and spir-

---

[11] See *Luther's Works*, 9, p. 204, note 4, on the four monarchies of the Book of Daniel.

[12] Cf. 2 Kings 5:17; Dan. 4:31 ff.; Dan. 6:26; Ezra 1:2.

itually, but that the blessing will also overflow to the neighboring nations and peoples. This happened to the Pharaoh in Egypt.

Thus Job, the king of Nineveh, the kings of Babylon, Nebuchadnezzar and Evilmerodach, the Persian kings Darius and Cyrus, and countless others of whom no account is extant — all became partakers of the blessing bestowed on Abraham. Even though Abraham was no longer alive when these things were fulfilled, he nevertheless saw them in the spirit and believed.

3. *I will bless those who bless you, and him who curses you I will curse.*

The church never runs out of enemies and opponents. For Satan hates it, and for this reason he plots against it in various ways and stirs up perils of every kind. When the descendants of Abraham, as the true church, would experience this, the Lord here threatens that the enemies of the church would be punished; for He Himself would inflict punishment upon them. Thus the Pharaoh of Egypt perished, and this very threat drowned him in the Red Sea (Ex. 14:28). This same threat brought about the death of the heathen kings Sihon, Og, etc., and destroyed their kingdoms (Deut. 2:33; 3:3). In fact, the kingdoms of the entire world were destroyed because they harmed the church: the Babylonian, the Assyrian, the Greek, the Roman, etc.

On the other hand, it promises a blessing to those who befriend the church. Thus God built houses for the midwives in Egypt because they did not hate this people (Ex. 1:20). Thus the harlot Rahab, with her household, is preserved through this promise (Joshua 6:25). The interested reader [13] may gather more examples of the various ways in which the Lord blessed those who showed kindness either to the church or to its leading members, the teachers and prophets. Thus the woman of Zarephath (1 Kings 17:8-24), the Ethiopian in Jeremiah (38:7-13), and others were blessed.

And in you all the families of the earth will be blessed.

So far the Lord has promised material blessings. For even though these are properly called spiritual blessings — that the Lord dwelt among this people, and that He revealed Himself through signs, miracles, and His Word in the holy prophets — these were nevertheless blessings that belonged to this earthly life.

[13] Cf. Introduction, p. x.

But now there follows that promise which should be written in golden letters and should be extolled in the languages of all people, for it offers eternal treasures. For it cannot be understood in a material sense, namely, that it would be confined to this people only, as the previous blessings were. But if, as the words clearly indicate, this promise is to be extended to all nations, or families of the earth, who else, shall we say, has dispensed this blessing among all nations except the Son of God, our Lord Jesus Christ?

Therefore the simple, true, and incontrovertible meaning is this: "Listen, Abraham, I have given you and your descendants grand promises; but this is not yet enough. I shall distinguish you also with a blessing that will overflow to all the families of the earth." Abraham understood this promise well. For he reasoned thus: "If all the families of the earth are to be blessed through me, then of necessity this blessing must not depend on my person. For I shall not live till then. Furthermore, I am not blessed through myself, but through the mercy of God the blessing has come to me too. Therefore all nations will not be blessed because of my person or through my power. But from my posterity will be born One who is blessed in His own person and who will bring a blessing so long and wide that it will reach all the families of the earth. He must necessarily be God and not a human being, although He will be a human being and will take on our flesh so that He is truly my seed."

No doubt Christ referred to these thoughts of the holy patriarch when He said (John 8:56): "Your father Abraham rejoiced that he was to see My day; he saw it and was glad." The statement of the text, "all the families of the earth," is not to be understood of extent only, of the families of one time, but of duration, as long as the world will stand. It is altogether in accord with the statement of Christ (Mark 16:15-16): "Go, preach the Gospel to the whole creation. He who believes and is baptized will be saved; but he who does not believe will be condemned." This blessing has now endured for one thousand five hundred years, and it will endure until the end of the world, since the gates of hell (Matt. 16:18), tyrants, and ungodly men will oppose it and rage against it in vain.

But above all it must be noted that the text does not say that all the nations will flow together to the Jews and will become Jews; but it declares that the blessing this people is to possess will be transferred from this people to the heathen, that is, to those who are not circumcised and who know nothing of Moses and of his statutes.

Therefore it is proper for us to contrast the blessing in this passage with the curse under which all human beings are because of sin. The curse has been taken away by Christ, and a blessing will be bestowed on all who receive Him and believe in His name. The remarkable blessing is this, that after being freed from sin, from death, and from the tyranny of the devil, we are in the company of the angels of God and have become partakers of eternal life.

Out of this promise flowed all the sermons of the prophets concerning Christ and His kingdom, about the forgiveness of sins, about the gift of the Holy Spirit, about the preservation and the government of the church, about the punishments of the unbelievers, etc. They saw that these conclusions were definitely implied: If the Seed of Abraham does this, He must necessarily be a true human being by nature; on the other hand, if He blesses others, even all the families of the earth, He must necessarily be something greater than the seed of Abraham, because the seed of Abraham itself stands in need of this blessing on account of its sin.

In these few simple words the Holy Spirit has thus encompassed the mystery of the incarnation of the Son of God. The holy patriarchs and prophets explained this more fully later on in their sermons, namely, that through the Son of God the entire world would be made free, hell and death would be destroyed, the Law would be abrogated, sins would be forgiven, and eternal salvation and life would be given freely to those who believe in Him. This is the day of Christ about which He discourses in John (8:56), the day which Abraham did not see with his bodily eyes but did see in the spirit, and was glad. To the flesh these things were invisible, impossible, and for this reason incredible.

This passage is profitable not only for instruction and encouragement but also for refuting the perfidious Jews. Because God promises Abraham the material blessing that his descendants will be a great nation, let them declare about themselves whether they are a blessed and great nation today! But if their very situation compels them to declare that they are both an afflicted and a small band, what else can be concluded from this passage except that God is a liar in His promises or that they themselves are in error and are not the true seed of Abraham? But to maintain the former is wicked; therefore the latter necessarily follows. For what the blessing consists of is familiar.

Furthermore, a people is called a nation when it has a government, a body politic, laws, and liberty. But what of this do the Jews have today? They are a people scattered here and there, oppressed in various ways, and all but held in captivity wherever they live. They fancy that they have great power and prestige and wealth in some Babel, of which I know nothing, and among the Turks.[14] And it is true that the Turks favor them because of their traitorous activities. For whatever secret plans the Jews are able to fish out from all the courts of Christian princes, they immediately betray to the Turk. Great is not only the folly but also the ungodliness of some princes, that they have Jews as such close friends.[15] But if you consider the actual situation, the Jews are prey for the Turks themselves, as I know for sure from those who lived not only at Constantinople but in Damascus itself, where the number of the Jews is very great.[16]

Therefore let the miserable Jews confess that they are not the true seed of Abraham, that is, that they are in error and are under God's wrath because they oppose the true religion; or we ourselves shall drive them to the blasphemy of maintaining that God is a liar. For what middle ground can there be?

The statement we have made about the blessing and about the great nation, however, we also make about the great name that God promises to make for Abraham. What sort of name have the Jews today? Are they not the reproach of all human beings? Nothing is more despised than the Jews, as the discourses of the prophets threaten that they will be a reproach and laughingstock for all nations.[17] Where, then, is their great name? Must they not declare by their own witness that they have lost it? And yet the seed of Abraham must have a great name, for God does not lie.

But consider this too: whether those who bless the Jews and intimately associate with them are blessed. There are obvious examples, not only of private individuals but also of great princes, who can bear witness concerning this blessing that they experience because of their intimacy with Jews, namely, that they are being ruined with respect to fortune, body, and soul.

But perhaps the Jews will object that the psalm (109:11) says:

[14] As "people of the Book," Jews were entitled to religious toleration, according to the provisions of the Koran.

[15] Cf. Luther's letter to Anton Lauterbach, February 9, 1544, on princes who had taken Jews into their confidence.

[16] Cf. *Luther's Works*, 9, p. 215, note 8.

[17] Luther is thinking of passages like Is. 57:4.

"May the creditor seize all that he has; may strangers plunder the fruits of his toil!" They will say that the Jews do not experience this from Christians, but the Christians from the Jews; for it is well known how much harm they cause the state with their excessive interest.

My answer is this: In the first place, reason itself teaches that interest or usury is contrary to nature and for this reason is actually a sin.[18] Therefore Christians have the rule (Luke 6:35): "Lend, expecting nothing in return." Those who are disciples of Christ observe this rule and beware of interest as of a real sin. Moreover, experience also shows that riches gained in this manner are cursed by the Lord and do not last. Therefore if the Jews consider interest or usury a blessing, let them enjoy it. For it is certain that it is a sin; and a sure penalty is attached to this sin, as Scripture teaches again and again, and as the Jews themselves prove by their own example.

Consider whether they are not being drained of their possessions. While they are scraping together their wealth by pennies, they pay a large number of tolls, levies, and real estate taxes. And yet they are being treated considerately by Christian governments in comparison with what they suffer from the Turks. These would not even spare their bodies and life if they did not recall the great advantages of the treason for which the Jews are very well trained by their hate of the Christians.

However this may be, let them boast of their wealth for all I care; let them glory that they do not pay interest but collect it. What a small matter this is in comparison with what they are compelled to admit that they have lost! They were driven out of the land that God had given them and had blessed; they lost the kingdom; they lost their worship; they live in deepest darkness and have no understanding of the sacred prophecies. In short, they have no hope for salvation except to invent some idea about God's mercy and goodness. If all this does not compel those unhappy people to confess that they are thrice wretched, let them be happy with this blessing, that they lend money to others at interest and do not borrow money.

But how much better it is to seek alms from street to street than to use this sinful means to gain riches, out of which others, in turn, cheat them later! And to this supposedly extraordinary blessing, of which they boast so much, there are attached many great liabilities.

[18] Luther wrote several treatises on usury, including his *Address to the Clergy to Preach Against Usury* (1540), W, LI, 331—424.

Nowhere do they have a continuing abode; they are hated and despised by all men; they live most wretchedly in dirt and filth; they are not permitted to engage in the more honorable occupations — and who could enumerate all the hardships of the enemies of Christ?

Hence this is a most powerful argument to support our religion and faith and to refute the deceitful Jews, namely, that they have lost everything promised here to Abraham, and especially what is promised last, that the blessing will spread from the seed of Abraham to all the families of the earth.

They are hard pressed by this reasoning. Therefore they prate that this statement was fulfilled in Solomon, the son of David, and that he was blessed by the nations, that is, was renowned and was praised by everybody.[19] But what has it to do with the text if he was blessed or praised by others? What the words mean is this, that this seed will bring a blessing to all nations. Now what did Solomon bring to the nations?

Therefore this text clearly compels us to confess that the Messiah or Christ has long since come and was revealed, and that He brought a spiritual and eternal blessing with Him into the world. When the unbelieving Jews rejected this and would not have it, it was brought to the heathen. But the wretched Jews were deprived of both their material and their spiritual blessing, as experience demonstrates. They have now been living for almost one thousand five hundred years under great hardships and in uninterrupted captivity, and they have nothing of the promises of which the Lord is speaking here. If God is truthful in His promises, then they must be liars; and through their unbelief they have forfeited these promises and are no longer the seed of Abraham to which these promises were given.

The error under which all Jews labor today is well known: they are waiting for a Messiah to beat down all the heathen and restore to them an earthly kingdom over all nations, just as under Ahasuerus (Esther 8:10). For then the power and the prestige of the Jews was great.

The passage before us clearly gives the lie to this vain hope. It does not state that the heathen will be oppressed by the seed of Abraham or will be reduced to servitude, but that they will be "blessed," that is, that they will be given aid against death and sin. But for all I care, let the gloss of the Jews stand that "to bless" has

---

[19] Lyra on Gen. 12:3, sec. j.

this meaning; for then it will become apparent that they have the greatest blessing, that is, that they are most severely oppressed by the heathen. To call this a blessing is the devil's language.

Because God is good, He uses "blessing" to mean deliverance from the curse and wrath of God, and He promises that this will occur through the seed of Abraham, not only for the descendants of Abraham but for all the families of the earth. This blessing the Son of God, Jesus Christ, brought us. He was born from the seed of Abraham by the Virgin Mary. But because the unbelieving synagog did not want this blessing, it was withdrawn; and it lost not only this eternal blessing but also those earlier material ones. Therefore it is manifest to all that this is a nation that is cursed and subjected to God's wrath.

Hence this passage is profitable for us in various ways, and therefore it deserves to be noted by students of the Holy Scriptures. Not only does it emphatically refute the stubborn Jews and portray the person of Abraham, whom all godly people ought to contemplate in order that they may learn to believe from his example; but, together with Abraham, it also describes the progress and the good fortune of this entire people, indeed of the entire church to the end of the world. Whatever will be achieved in the church until the end of the world and whatever has been achieved in it until now, has been achieved and will be achieved by virtue of this promise, which endures and is in force to this day.

If you desire to reduce to a few words the history of the church from the time of Abraham until today, carefully consider these four verses. You will see the blessing, and you will also see some who curse; but these, in turn, God has cursed so that they utterly perished, while the eternal blessing of the church has remained unshaken. Hence this passage is in agreement with the first sermon about the Seed who crushes the head of the serpent (Gen. 3:15). The church does not lack enemies; it is troubled, and it sighs; and yet it overcomes through the Seed and finally triumphs forever over all its enemies.

But just as the Lord gave a warning above about the bite of the serpent, so here He warns that the seed of Abraham will encounter some who will curse it. But if we are hurt by the world and the devil, the damage is slight, since we have the angels, yes, even God Himself to bless us and annihilate our adversaries. But such an explanation of this passage must be looked for in the prophets. This is the source from which they drew both their consolations and their threats. Hence the divine wisdom is truly admirable, that such important matters and the history of all ages, so far as it concerns the church, have been reduced to a few words in this passage.

Now there follows an example or corollary, as they call it in the schools,[20] of this promise, namely, how Abraham obeyed God when He called him.

4. *So Abram went, as the Lord had told him.*

Promise and faith belong together naturally and inseparably.[21] For what is the use of making any promise if there is no one to believe it? On the other hand, what would be the advantage of faith if there should be no promise? Hence promise and faith are related terms; and the natural sequence demands that after Moses has described the promise, he also give information about Abraham, who believed, that is, appropriated, the promise.

Satan also has his promises, and very fine ones at that. Therefore keen judgment is needed to distinguish properly between the promises of God and those of Satan, that is, between the true and the false. Satan's promise is pleasurable and is readily received; it makes men smug and neglectful of themselves and of God's judgment, just as we see that the Turks, the Jews, and the false brethren among us are of a very smug disposition and maintain that nothing matters less than to fear the wrath and judgment of God.

But when God makes a promise of some kind, faith wrestles much and long; for reason, or flesh and blood, regards God's promise as altogether impossible. Therefore faith must wrestle with doubt and against reason.

This the sophists do not realize. Consequently, when they hear us teaching about faith, they suppose that it is a quarrel about a rather insignificant matter. They are not aware that faith is a change and renewal of the entire nature, so that the ears, the eyes, and the very heart hear, see, and feel something altogether different from what everyone else perceives.

For faith is a vigorous and powerful thing; it is not idle speculation, nor does it float on the heart like a goose on the water. But just as

[20] Cf. Boethius, *The Consolation of Philosophy*, Book III, ch. 10.

[21] Cf. The Apology of the Augsburg Confession, Art. IV, par. 324, *The Book of Concord* (Philadelphia, 1959), p. 157.

water that has been heated, even though it remains water, is no longer cold but is hot and an altogether different water, so faith, the work of the Holy Spirit, fashions a different mind and different attitudes, and makes an altogether new human being.

Therefore faith is an active, difficult, and powerful thing. If we want to consider what it really is, it is something that is done to us rather than something that we do;[22] for it changes the heart and mind. And while reason is wont to concern itself with the things that are present, faith apprehends the things that are not present and, contrary to reason, regards them as being present. This is why faith does not belong to all men, as does the sense of hearing; for few believe. The remaining masses prefer to concern themselves with the things that are present, which they can touch and feel, rather than with the Word.

This, then, is the mark of the true and divine promises, that they are in conflict with reason, and that reason does not want to accept them. Because those of the devil, on the other hand, are in agreement with human reason, they are accepted by reason readily and without hesitation.

Mohammed promises those who keep his law a temporal kingdom in this life and after this life physical pleasures, and this the heart readily accepts and firmly believes. Unlike Abraham, therefore, Mohammed stays at home, and he is unwilling to go out from home and from the kindred of his father. He is fond of the things that are present, and in them he finds his comfort. But Abraham simply clings to the divine Word and disregards the dangers he will encounter, for he believes that God will be his protector.

Similarly, the pope proposes the merits and intercessions of the saints and praises the efficacy of works, which is really an attractive fiction. These are things that are welcome to reason, which is vain and for this reason is delighted by the lie, that is, by flattery and the glory of its virtues; it enjoys hearing that by its own works it is able to earn salvation, fulfill the Law, and obtain righteousness. But this is not killing reason, but giving it life. Therefore the flesh readily accepts this doctrine and believes these promises without hesitation. But when it hears what Abraham heard — "Go out from your country, from your kindred, and from your father's house to an unknown place; I shall be your God" — it immediately draws back. The flesh

[22] Luther's phrase is *magis passio quam actio*.

considers it stupid to give up the things that are present and to strive after the things that are not present; it fears the dangers and flees, and it looks for security.

In short, the promises of Satan, even though they are lies, are welcome to the flesh because they give pleasure at the beginning. The divine and true promises immediately point out the cross, but after the cross they promise a blessing. Reason is offended by both: the invisible and far distant things it regards as worthless; but for the cross it has an aversion, and flees from it as from an incessant evil that never comes to an end. And this is why, though God gives abundant promises, only a few believe, namely, those whose hearts the Spirit moves, so that, like Abraham, they disregard all dangers and cares, and simply cling to the voice of God when He calls them.

Hence in this passage Moses is setting before us an outstanding example of faith, and in a few words he completes the legend or the account of the most holy patriarch when he says: "Abraham went, as the Lord had told him."

From what place did he depart? From Ur of the Chaldeans, where he had a sure home, fields, an established household, kindred, relatives, and friends. Leaving all these behind without delay, he looks for an uncertain abode. For the Lord had not yet showed him the land he was to have. He had this one hope, that the Lord had promised a blessing; but when, where, and how He would bless him, of this Abraham was not yet aware.

Thus these are brief words. Outwardly they appear to teach nothing. For reason does not perceive true good works and true obedience, nor does it consider them pleasing to God. On the contrary, it is captivated by counterfeit performances and empty outward appearances.

Therefore the books of the monks are full of praises for their fathers, whom they praise for forsaking the world and following Christ. But if you compare Francis, Dominic, and Bernard with this obedience of Abraham and judge such important matters with spiritual eyes, you will see that the whole crowd of the monks is like children who are deceived by the outward appearance and who save the gilded shells of nuts as gold and admire them. For what do the saints have apart from their own outward appearance? In fact, their entire way of life, of which they make so much, is nothing but empty pretense if you compare it with our own monk, who forsakes everything in true faith.

It is recorded about the apples near the lake of asphalt where Sodom was sunk beneath the waters by God that in outward appearance they are most beautiful; but if one opens them, they are full of ashes and a vile odor.[23] Similarly, the hypocritical obedience of the monks is combined with contempt for God and for true religion. Nevertheless, the world admires it and praises it. But these excellent works and acts of worship that are most welcome to God, namely, the outstanding faith and obedience of Abraham, it regards as something unimportant, insignificant, and contemptible. The world is not in the habit of doing anything else, nor does it know how.

I admit indeed that Francis, Dominic, Bernard, and the others who are said to have founded the orders of the monks, were not without their gifts; and I prefer Bernard to all the others, for he had the best knowledge of religion, as his writings show.[24] But these are gifts that belong to an individual and must be praised in a manner that does not disparage the glory of Christ and the mercy of God. But what happened? The men who came after them employed those gifts to establish sects and almost to blot out the name of Christ. For the stupid and wretched people placed their trust, not in their Christianity and their Baptism but in their dedication, whether to Francis or to Dominic. This was considered the most direct road to heaven.

We have reason to find fault with monasticism and to remove those offenses that have been placed beside the way of truth and of faith; for we set forth Christ, who both atoned for our sins with His death and made us worthy of the Holy Spirit. This is the true way of righteousness; it does not rely on our merits and works but on the Son of God and on the pure and free mercy offered in the Word.

The monks regard themselves as blessed because they enter a monastery. But we refuse even to maintain that Abraham was justified because he forsook everything when he went out from Ur of the Chaldeans. He had already been justified when he believed the promise of God that was revealed through the holy patriarchs. If he had not been righteous, he would never have gone out and would never have obeyed God when He called. Therefore he heard the Word and believed the Word; and later on, after he had been

[23] Cf. p. 136, note 6.
[24] Cf. *Luther's Works*, 14, p. 38, note 42.

justified thereby, he also became a righteous doer of works by wandering about and following Christ, who had called him.

For this is the true order, that outward obedience follows upon inward obedience. But the monks turn this around. In the first place, they have no word that they follow; but actually they live in what Anselm calls a manufactured religion,[25] which was established without the Word by the will of man. In the second place, they maintain that this outward change will bring about a change in the heart and in the entire human being; this makes hypocrisy unavoidable. For they dream of righteousness while their hearts are impure.

Who does not see how badly this agrees with the example of Abraham? He forsakes his home, fields, and kindred, and wanders about without knowing where he is going. But the monks leave their families with the knowledge that they will find an abundance of everything in the monasteries, while at home with their parents they barely have black bread. What do those swine, who are looking for nothing but fattening food, lack in their diet, and a most luxurious one at that? Yet they boast loudly that they have forsaken everything and have followed Christ.

Abraham was not entertained like that among the heathen, who, as the account shows, caused him trouble in various ways. If you compare Benedict, Francis, and the other fathers of the monks with him, you will realize that they are utter filth in comparison with the precious jewels of our own monk. These comparisons are indeed odious; nevertheless not only men but also God has need of them, now that monastic life has come to be so misused that ungodly men even put it on a par with Baptism.[26]

At this point there arises an opportunity to discuss obedience, which is extolled to such an extent in the monasteries that no monk has been too unlearned not to leave some writing about it.[27] And in his decretals the pope puts greater stress on obedience to his laws than on anything else. As a result, the statement of Samuel (1 Sam. 15:22-23) has been heard from every pulpit: "To obey is better than

[25] Cf. also *Luther's Works*, 13, p. 90.

[26] A monastic adaptation of the idea current in the ancient church that martyrdom, as a "baptism of blood," was the equivalent of Baptism. Tertullian, *On Baptism*, ch. 16.

[27] Luther is referring to treatises on the threefold monastic vow of poverty, chastity, and obedience.

sacrifice. Rebellion is as the sin of divination."[28] To this true statement they appended the inference: "Hence no kind of life is better than that of the monks." Surely a fine conclusion, which, as used to be said in the schools, has the force of the argument from the staff to the corner![29] Thus it is clear that the entire papacy had no knowledge of what obedience is.

True obedience is not to do what you yourself choose or what you impose upon yourself, but what the Lord has commanded you through His Word. This definition is drawn from this very passage of Moses when he states about Abraham (Gen. 12:4): "So Abraham went, as the Lord had told him." Here you have obedience defined after the manner of the dialecticians,[30] as something that requires the Word of God. Therefore when God is not speaking but is keeping silence, there can be no obedience.

Moreover, it is not enough that God speaks; but it is necessary that He speaks *to you*. Thus the Word of God came to Abraham that he should sacrifice his son. It was, therefore, true and praiseworthy obedience that Abraham wanted to carry out this command; for it was directed to him. But the fact that the descendants of Abraham wanted to imitate this same action was not obedience, even though the work was the same. For they had not been commanded to do this, as Abraham had been commanded. Similarly, the young man in the Gospel is told to sell everything and to follow Christ (Mark 10:21), and it would have been a most admirable work of obedience if he had obeyed. The monks boast that they are doing the same thing, and they regard this as a true praise of obedience; but it is not obedience, because Christ did not give them this command.

Careful note should be taken of this description: "Abraham went, as the Lord had told him." The Lord, it says, has spoken, and He has told Abraham that he should go out. Therefore this going out was a most sacred work, an obedience that was most pleasing to God.

One must note, however, that the Lord also speaks to us through human beings. When parents give orders to their children, the tasks may seem insignificant and unimportant in their outward appearance;

[28] Cf. Luther's *Notes on Ecclesiastes* (1532), W, XX, 86—89.

[29] The phrase is *a baculo ad angulum*.

[30] By a definition formulated *dialectice* Luther appears to mean a definition in the precise sense; cf. Aristotle, *Topics*, Book I, ch. 5.

yet when the children obey, they are obeying not so much men as God. For God has commanded that parents should be obeyed. This divine Word is the true diadem that is customarily depicted on the heads of the gods, and it brings about obedience.

You students are living here with the approval of your parents, and it is their will that you should be both industrious in learning and obedient to your teachers. When you try to satisfy this desire of your parents as much as you can, you are offering a most pleasing sacrifice to God; for "to obey is better than sacrifice" (1 Sam. 15:22).

Thus when the government, by virtue of its office, calls citizens into military service in order to maintain peace and to ward off harm, obedience is shown to God. For the Lord tells us (Rom. 13:1): "Let every person be subject to the governing authorities." But someone will say: "Obedience is dangerous, for I may be killed!" My answer is: "Whether you kill or are killed is immaterial, for you are going as the Lord has told you. It is, therefore, a holy and godly deed even to kill an adversary, provided the government commands it."

You must have the same conviction about the general call, when you are called to the ministry of teaching: you should consider the voice of the community [31] as the voice of God, and obey. You should not imitate a bungling monk whom the *Historia tripartita* praises as a holy man. When he was called to the office of a bishop, he cut off his ear and then threatened that he would cut off his tongue as well, rather than assume the office of a bishop.[32] When he was given such a command, that foolish and even ungodly fellow refused an office that is most pleasing to God and supremely necessary and profitable for men. Why did he not rather accept the office of minister and say with Paul (1 Cor. 9:16): "Woe to me if I do not preach the Gospel"? So early did superstition make its way into the church.

Let us, therefore, remember this brief statement: "Abraham went, as the Lord had told him," and write it above all the activities that we carry on, whether at home or abroad, whether in war or in peace, whether during a plague or in any other danger. Then it follows that even if we have to die, we may comfort ourselves that we continued steadfast in our obedience to God. Even though the outcome may

[31] We have rendered *Respublica* with "community"; see the note in *Luther's Works*, 13, p. 46, note 6.

[32] The *Historia tripartita* (see also p. 18, note 29) took this story from Sozomen, *Ecclesiastical History*, Book VI, ch. 30.

seem rather sad, it is a great comfort to know that you have obeyed God. Therefore you should expect help from Him and a far greater reward than if the matter had turned out according to your own way of thinking.

Obedience deserves to be praised as obedience only if it proceeds from the promises or from the commands of God. Without these nothing has the right to be called obedience, unless perhaps one would want to call it the obedience of Satan; for not to obey God and His Word is to obey Satan.

Therefore let the Word, or the call, be our chief concern. For this alone produces true obedience and worship that is pleasing to God; and if we render this, we are able not only to defend ourselves with the witness of our conscience but also to look for help from God, whose voice we follow even in real danger.

"The Lord has said" — whoever keeps this phrase in mind in all his actions will always live happily and be full of hope. But Satan, who envies us this happiness, keeps us from this true obedience. He uses an outward show to draw us to the obedience of himself, that is, to an obedience like that of the monks, which does not have the command of God.

As I stated above, the pope insists on obedience in all his decrees because he wants to be the chief priest and the vicar of Christ; and he adds the awe-inspiring threat that if one does not obey, this disobedience will threaten peril to his soul. He also adds the magnificent promises that those who run to the wonder-working power of SS. Peter and Paul will have plenary remission of all their sins. With such promises he embellishes all his works — the worship of the saints, the invocations of the saints, the Masses, etc. — in order to spur the simple on to obedience. And alas, he has indeed found the people too obedient. How many thousands of human beings were plunged into hell by this obedience while they thought that they were going straight to heaven!

Even though the ungodly teachers will experience the awful judgment of God because of these deceptions, the throng that followed them is not excused either. They should have considered whether such mandates contained what Moses says here: "As the Lord told him." Wherever this is absent, there is obedience not of God but of Satan. Thus the pope filled the world with a satanic obedience; for he prescribed, not what God had commanded but what he himself had devised. Hence it came about that his entire religion was not genuine but manufactured and self-chosen, mere hypocrisy.

Let us, therefore, remember the commands in the Apocalypse, where it is stated (Rev. 18:4-5): "Come out of Babylon, My people, lest you take part in her sins, lest you share in her plagues; for her sins are heaped high as heaven, and God has remembered her iniquities." But how shall we come out? No doubt by not permitting ourselves to be led by the nose [33] like a bear. But when some pope commands something, let us not immediately obey. First let us ask and say: "Mr. Pope, I hear that you have prescribed this. But show me the Word and whether the Lord has spoken it; then I shall gladly obey. But if the Lord has not spoken it, and your command is in conflict with the Word of God — as when you declare that ungodly vows have value, or when you prescribe abstention from marriage, from foods, etc. — I will not obey. I have a different command of God; that I will follow."

But he says: "I am the lord of the church, and it is stated (Luke 10:16): 'He who hears you, hears Me.'" We know that the pope seeks to become the lord both of the church and of the world. But Christ clearly forbade him this when He said to the apostles (Luke 22:25-26): "The kings of the Gentiles exercise lordship over them. But not so with you." And Peter says (1 Peter 5:3): "Not as domineering over those in your charge." But let him prove from the Word of God that he is the lord of the church, and we shall believe him.

We know another statement of Christ (Matt. 23:11): "He who is greatest among you, let him be least, and let him serve the others," evidently in order that the entire authority may be, not with men but only and altogether with the Word. The Word must rule in the church. In this instance we have the clear command from heaven (Matt. 17:5): "Listen to Him."

When the pope claims to be lord of the Word, and when he wants to bind and loose (Matt. 16:19) everything at his discretion, that is, prescribe laws and issue commands — for this is how the son of sin falsely interprets the words of Christ — he will surely not be able to get away with this while we are around. A curse on all those who do let him get away with this! For he has not received his power from Christ but impudently and wickedly arrogates it to himself.

[33] On the expression "to lead by the nose as a bear" see the note in W, VII, 637.

How rude this egotist is, that the beast compels even kings to kiss his feet! Now if he asked that this be done out of love, in order to increase the respect for him in the church, one could perhaps put up with it; for we know that contempt for the ministry is a noxious evil. But when he demands this as a matter of right, as an article of faith, and at the peril of damnation — this is altogether in conflict with the Word of Christ.

Similar demands are even more destructive, as when he insists on the effectiveness of the indulgences, the intercession of the saints, and other things as something necessary for the forgiveness of sins. Actually, therefore, we are contending not so much against the pope as against an enemy and adversary of Christ, because he has set up articles that are in conflict with the Gospel of Christ and because he sets faith aside altogether. And he does this solely in order to support his tyranny, not by lying in wait for goods and people, as tyrants usually do, but by destroying souls and consigning them to hell.

Thus the example of the holy patriarch who died so many thousands of years ago serves as a pattern for the church to this day and forewarns it against hypocrisy. Therefore these words should be written with golden letters, not only on walls but in all our statements and deeds: "As the Lord told him." For they teach that true obedience consists in hearing and following the Word of God that is being spoken to you. Where, then, there is no Word, either there is no obedience at all, or it is an obedience of Satan. In one's entire life and in all activities, therefore, one must consider the Word, not only in the church but also in the household and in the government. If you have the Word and follow it, you have obedience also. For they are correlatives; but when one of the correlatives is removed, namely, the Word, obedience is also removed, and there is none.

And Lot went with him.

Behold God's marvelous counsel! The promise pertained to Abraham only, not to Lot. Nevertheless, God attaches Lot, like a proselyte, to Abraham as his companion and moves his heart so that he wants to go into exile with his uncle rather than remain in his native country among the idolaters. This is because the promise given to Abraham stated not only that Abraham would be blessed with his descendants, but also that he himself would be a blessing, that is, that through him others would become partakers of the blessing, even though the promise did not properly pertain to them.

In the Holy Scriptures there are many historical accounts that show similar examples. The king of Egypt did not belong to the holy people; yet when he embraced the religion of Joseph, he was made a partaker of the promise, or the blessing. Because the king of Nineveh adopted the faith of Jonah, he partook of the promise that was given to the people of God, even though he was not one of the people of God. We could add here Job and the kings of Babylon and Persia. Not only was their success extraordinary — for the Lord blessed their rule because of their religion — but through faith they became partakers of the eternal blessing as well.

Today, too, it happens that those who do not have the Gospel, nevertheless share in our blessing and enjoy the peace that the Lord grants His churches because of the Word, because they share our life, that is, because they dwell together with us and we among them. For God is rich in mercy and wants most men to enjoy His gifts. Therefore He adds companions in blessing, just as Ruth, who was a daughter of Lot, says to her mother-in-law (Ruth 1:16): "Your people shall be my people, and your God my God." That is: "Even though I am not of your people, your God will not cast me aside. He will take care of me and will grant that I shall not live as a widow."

Abram was seventy-five years old when he departed from Haran.

This is a definite, clear, and plain statement that Abraham did not depart from Ur but [34] from Haran, when he was seventy-five years old. We must, therefore, assume a twofold departure. The first was when father Terah, with his sons Abraham and Lot, departed from Ur of the Chaldeans. This, too, was a journey undertaken toward the land of Canaan; but when they were prevented by some accident, they stopped at Haran and remained there for some time, as the text above clearly shows. But when father Terah had died there, Abraham moved his habitation a second time and set out from Haran for the land of Canaan.

Earlier I touched on the question whether Abraham was the first-born.[35] Although Lyra stoutly denies this because he does not notice that sixty years are lost in the case of Abraham, I am of the opinion that he was the first-born, because the text clearly asserts

[34] The Weimar text has *se*, but this should undoubtedly be *sed*, the reading given by all the other editions.

[35] See p. 238, note 34.

here that he was seventy-five years old when he departed from Haran. Yet if someone wants to hold a different opinion, I shall not argue with him. If anyone is able to harmonize these seventy-five years with the age of Terah, who lived two hundred and five years, I shall acknowledge him as a master.[36]

It should be noted here that if anyone wants to calculate the time of the giving of the Law after the promise, of which Paul speaks in Gal. 3:17, he must begin from this year, which is the seventy-fifth year of Abraham's life. For from this year it is exactly four hundred and thirty years to the departure of the Children of Israel from Egypt. Up to the time that they went down to Egypt two hundred and fifteen years passed; and the people of Israel lived for the same number of years in Egypt. Therefore if you add these two numbers, there results the number cited by Moses in Ex. 12:40 and by Paul in Gal. 3:17, namely, four hundred and thirty years.

But let the reader take careful note of Paul's statement (Gal. 3:17): "The Law was given four hundred and thirty years after the promise was given to Abraham." Therefore it follows that the Law does not justify, since Abraham was just long before the Law was given, in fact, even before he was circumcised and before he built an altar. This is the incontrovertible conclusion.

But the same passage of Paul proves that the promise was given to Abraham and that Abraham was called and told to set out, not when he lived in Ur but while he was stopping over in Haran. Therefore Scripture states above (Gen. 11:31): "Terah took Abram and Lot, his sons"; but here it says: "Abram took Sarai his wife."

But this statement conflicts with the passage, Acts 7:2; and Stephen's authority must not be minimized. He repeats these very words and states clearly that these words were spoken to Abraham in Mesopotamia. Hence Moses and Stephen contradict each other. How shall we harmonize them? Each of the two is a trustworthy witness, and yet they do not agree with each other.[37]

The customary answer is that Abraham was called twice, once in Ur of the Chaldeans, perhaps by the patriarch Shem, and later on in Haran, but that Moses is satisfied with relating the later call in

---

[36] Thus in 1532 Luther had said at table concerning the difference between St. Paul and the Epistle of James: "To him who can make these two agree I will give my doctor's cap, and I am willing to be called a fool." W, *Tischreden*, IV, 253 (No. 3292a).

[37] See p. 242, note 41.

Haran. Thus these witnesses do not disagree; for Moses relates the later, Stephen the earlier call.

Nevertheless, it seems to me that the accurate account of what happened is given by Moses and not by Stephen, who certainly derived his knowledge of this story from Moses alone. But when we relate something incidentally, it often happens that we do not pay such close attention to all details as do those who are engaged in leaving behind a written account of an event for their descendants. And so Moses is the historian, but Stephen is little concerned about the details; for the account appears in Moses, and Stephen merely aims at having his hearers realize that the father of this people had neither Law nor temple and yet was acceptable to God and pleased Him. The chief point of the matter is this: Stephen emphasizes that God does not disclose Himself on account of the temple or circumcision or the Law; but He justifies, remits sins, and bestows eternal life solely on account of the promised Seed, whom the synagog had previously slain.

5. *And Abram took Sarai his wife, and Lot his brother's son, and all their possessions which they had gathered, and the persons that they had gotten in Haran.*

Moses relates all this in order to emphasize still more the faith of Abraham, which surely was great and admirable. For we shall readily learn from our own example how many inconveniences, dangers, and hardships are involved in a long and difficult journey with so large a household. But the holy man overcomes them all by patience and forbearance. For he believed that however difficult and perilous the undertaking, God would be present with His blessing and in His time would surely fulfill what He had promised.

These facts are intended to comfort us in all temptations, that is, to strengthen our faith, so that when any hardship occurs, we are not immediately discouraged but hopefully pray and wait for help. For perseverance is needed, and it is not enough to have made a good beginning. What you have begun well you must diligently pursue.[38]

Look at Abraham. He leaves Ur of the Chaldeans, where he was born, his home, his possessions, his kindred, and the neighbors with whom he has associated, and goes into exile to Haran and sets up a new household. When he has stayed there for some time, he is

---

[38] The proverbial saying is *Quod bene coeperis, urgendum est gnaviter.*

commanded to migrate from there toward Canaan; and the farther away this was, the greater were the dangers and the hardships he had to undergo.

Now if Abraham had been alone, there would have been less toil and hardship, even though he would not have been out of danger completely. Someone who is alone, not tied to wife and children, even enjoys traveling through various regions; for he has only one stomach to take care of. Therefore if this house or this town does not please him, he looks for another. But our traveler is not alone; he is taking along a large number of souls, among whom are some that are very close and very dear to him — his wife Sarai, his nephew Lot, and Lot's daughters. He likewise is taking along all his substance, that is, his wealth. This consisted, not, as it does today, of gold, silver, and costly household goods but of beasts of burden and cattle. For Mesopotamia was famed for the richness of its pastures and the great number of its cattle and beasts of burden. The region has its name from being situated between two very large rivers, the Tigris and the Euphrates, which encompass Babylon also; and Mesopotamia and Babylonia were nearly always ruled by one king.

Haran, too, is a part of Mesopotamia, although later on its name was changed somewhat to Aram. Furthermore, the care of cattle requires many servants. Therefore Moses says: "And the persons that they had gotten in Haran." He includes here not only the daughters of Lot — I believe that they were born at that time, for from the departure from Haran to the destruction of Sodom there is an interval of twenty-five years — but also the rest of the domestics, the male and female servants, and their children. For the events that follow show that Abraham had a large number of domestics, since he put three hundred of them under arms (Gen. 14:14).

I have often stated that the word נֶפֶשׁ strictly denotes an animate or living body.[39] Such a large multitude this head of a household is taking along into an unknown region, to men who had a different religion and were therefore hostile to this exile. Let no one have any doubt that they faced endless dangers, inconveniences, and hardships. If his wife was exposed to danger so many times, what shall we suppose befell the domestics and the cattle?

In this passage, therefore, Moses wants to set before our eyes an

[39] Cf. *Luther's Works*, 1, p. 51.

extraordinary example of faith; if we compare ourselves with it, we must be ashamed of ourselves. For who will claim that he has experienced even one tenth of these trials and dangers? When we move to another area with our household, we do not go to strangers but to friends; even if they are strangers, they are at least linked with us through language and religion. But far different is the migration of this exile of ours. St. Paul, therefore, calls him "faithful" in Gal. 3:9, because he undertook this journey with so large a company and was supported only by his trust in the mercy of God, who had promised that He would bless him.

But his companions on this journey should not be cheated of their deserved praise either. It is no trifle that Sarai and Lot's wife followed the opinion and plan of their husbands, for women are highly fearful of traveling from one place to another and leave their own people only with the greatest reluctance.

The servants and maids surprise me; for if they had been like ours, they would never have lifted a foot. What was the source of this great obedience, this ready will to comply with the authority of the head of the household? When both the wives and the domestics heard Abraham preaching about God's promise, they no doubt acquiesced in his words and wished that they also might become partakers of the future blessing through Christ.

Therefore we shall call these companions of Abraham not simply his household but the true and holy church, in which Abraham was the high priest. He instructed it concerning God's mercy, which would be revealed through His Son, who would first rule and bless the descendants of Abraham and all who allied themselves with him, and secondly would take on flesh in His time and transfer the wrath and curse from His people to Himself, so that they would be rid of all their sins and escape the punishment of eternal death. Sarai, Lot's wife, Lot's daughters, and the servants of both believed this preaching of Abraham. Therefore they followed the holy head of the household with the utmost joy, preferring to endure want, danger, and all kinds of harm to forfeiting the possession of such great promises — even though the possession was not yet a reality but merely a hope.

In this manner the Lord comforted Abraham himself; for it was indeed a blessing of God that he could find companions for his exile, and such good and godly ones at that, who also held the Word in high esteem and followed it.

Hence the psalm properly praises this pilgrim of ours when it states (39:12): "I am a sojourner, like all my fathers." David is looking at the image of faith. Even though he was a king, yet when he was exposed to a variety of dangers, as Abraham was in the unknown land, he sustained himself with the promise alone, and in it alone he found comfort.

And we, too, must glorify this example for ourselves, not only to strengthen and comfort ourselves but also to remove the luster from the extraordinary works of the saints, of which the pope's church boasts, when in reality they are stinking filth in comparison with the works and faith of our sojourner or exile.

The verb עָשׂוּ, "they had gotten," denotes not only the procreation of children but also the care and training both of children and of cattle.

And they set forth to go to the land of Canaan. When they had come to the land of Canaan. . . .

In this passage one must note that Abraham is commanded to go out and that he has the promise of the blessing, but that the place to which he must go has not yet been revealed to him. Up to now he is uncertain in what part of the earth the Lord wants him to dwell. But that he heads directly for the land of Canaan is not because he knows definitely that the land of Canaan is to be given to his descendants. This promise will follow later on. The reason for going to Canaan is that he is following the patriarch Shem, who was living in Salem. Perhaps Shem had called him out from Ur. Because the promise of the Seed was vested in Shem, Abraham wanted the benefit of either his advice or his comfort until the Lord would indicate the place where he should live.

Hence this journey was made in faith, for he did not yet know the place of his abode. First he migrates from Ur of the Chaldeans, his native country, to Haran; next from Haran to Canaan. There he does not stay in one place but is compelled to move frequently, sometimes by the wickedness of his neighbors and sometimes by the Word of the Lord, until he finally goes to Egypt. From Egypt he again migrates to Canaan. Yet he does not stay in one place. Now Hebron, now Beersheba, now Mount Moriah is his abode. If he had been weak in his faith, he would have been overwhelmed by impatience, would have abandoned the Word, and would have put an end to his roamings. It is, therefore, an admirable example of faith that the holy man does not become weary but continually comforts himself with the Word of the Lord, relies on it, and does not think that what God has once promised is futile. Thus he hangs completely in the clouds, or in heaven, with his hope, and he does not permit it to be taken from him.

6. *Abram passed through the land to the place at Shechem, to the oak of Moreh. At that time the Canaanites were in the land.*

These facts also serve to throw additional light on this story, namely, that Abraham undertook so extensive a journey with so large a host of men and cattle. It is amazing if some of them did not yield to temptation and say impatiently that they were provoked because he did not stay either in Haran or at some other place.

Shechem is familiar from Joshua (20:7). When the Children of Israel crossed the Jordan, they first came by the royal road to Jericho, then to Ai, and finally to Bethel. Shechem lies north of Bethel, not far from the two familiar mountains Ebal and Gerizim, and not far from Jerusalem. In later times, as the historical accounts and the sermons of the prophets show, there lived in these places a people who were very proud because the patriarchs had dwelt there, as the Roman pope is amazingly proud because, as he says, he occupies the see of Peter.

Some translate the word אֵלוֹן with "oak," others with "field" or "plain"; but this is immaterial, for it makes no difference in the meaning. Moreh, however, is the name of a mountain mentioned in Judges 7:1.[40] When Gideon had established his camp toward the south, the Midianites pitched their camp toward the north in a valley near the rock Moreh. But it is uncertain where the place got this name, for מוֹרֶה means "teacher."[41] I am of the opinion that in that place there had been some priest who instructed the neighborhood concerning religion and the worship of God. The same term appears in Ps. 9:20: "Give them a lawgiver." Likewise in Ps. 84:6: "The teacher will be clad with blessings." But in this passage it is a proper noun for the place where Abraham stopped first.

The fact that Moses adds that the Canaanites were in the land serves to remind us of the wretched exile in which the holy patriarch

[40] The original has "Joshua 7."

[41] It appears that Luther is identifying this proper noun with the common noun in passages like Is. 30:20; they are spelled exactly the same in the Hebrew text.

lived. For he dwelt not among friends but in the midst of enemies and among men who were different in their worship and religion. By the will of Noah this region had indeed been assigned to the godly Shem, but the children of Nimrod had poured out of both Arabias and had taken possession of it by force. Thus you see that in all ages the lot of the church is the same: it is the prey of the ungodly, and yet the Lord preserves it in a marvelous manner, even against the gates of hell (Matt. 16:18).

7. *Then the Lord appeared to Abram, and said: To your descendants I will give this land.*

After Abram, the exile, has been annoyed and troubled among the Canaanites long enough and in various ways, he finds great comfort in his trials, to keep him from being overcome by impatience. For it is true that no flesh would be saved (Matt. 24:22) unless at that time the days were shortened and comfort followed. He who perseveres in faith will surely experience in the end that God does not forsake His own. He indeed defers His comfort and strains the sinew to such an extent that you think it is about to tear. But in due time He is at hand; and when we seem to be on the verge of collapse, He supports us with His help. For this reason Ps. 9:9 bestows this title on God, calling Him "a Helper at the appropriate time."

The text does not indicate in what year this revelation was given, but the circumstances suggest that it was when Abraham was almost exhausted by his burdensome exile and endless migrations. When God comforts him before he comes to Shem, this is intended to make the patriarch a profitable example for the church and a source of comfort; from it we, too, can learn that in our trials we must firmly maintain our faith that God will surely be with us and will comfort us.

Now at last a definite place is pointed out where the descendants of Abraham should settle. Note, however, how precisely and logically the Lord puts His words. When these words are spoken by the Lord, Abraham has neither a seed nor a land. Later, when a seed is born to him, he still does not have a land. Indeed, as Stephen says (Acts 7:5), he does not have "even a foot's length." Therefore this promise agrees with the former one, which states that Abraham will have a numerous posterity; for the land is promised not to him but to his seed. With this promise Abraham is satisfied, and he does not complain about his exile as long as he knows that his descendants will not be exiles.

This promise is truly a physical one; for although the saints live by faith and overcome present hardships by their hope for a future life, nevertheless in this life and in the great weakness of their flesh they require a physical consolation to help them recover from their evils and regain the strength that is weakened by their daily hardships.

So he built there an altar to the Lord, who had appeared to him.

Here for the first time you see that though the holy patriarch is an exile and a sojourner, nevertheless, on account of the promise made to his seed, he gives consideration to a definite habitation. Now for the first time he builds an altar to the Lord, who had appeared to him. That is, he appoints a definite place where the church should come together to hear the Word of God, offer prayers, praise God, and bring sacrifices to God; for this is what it means to build an altar.

Abraham builds an altar; that is, he himself is the bishop or priest, and he himself teaches the others and gives them instruction about the true worship of God. This must be the one purpose both of altars and of temples, that those who gather there hear the Word of God, pray, give thanks to God, praise God, and carry out those forms of worship which He has commanded. Where these activities are not present, there altars and temples are nothing but workshops of idolatry, of which the papacy is full; for the true forms of worship are disregarded, and meanwhile the entire worship is devoted to the blasphemous and ungodly sacrifice of the Mass.

But here the question is asked whether Abraham has the right to do this when he does not have a definite command from God. For it is idolatry to establish worship as a result of one's own choosing and not as the result of a command of the Lord. My answer is: Abraham did not arbitrarily select this place for his altar. The Lord Himself, who appeared to Abraham there, selected it; for the Lord is its first founder. He shows Himself there because He wants to be worshiped there and to have His promise proclaimed.

Likewise later, when Jacob had seen the angels ascending and descending on a ladder, he said (Gen. 28:17): "This is none other than the house of God, and this is the gate of heaven." Therefore because the Lord is the first to tarry there and sow His Word, He truly dedicates or consecrates the place, so that it is not secular but sacred and serves sacred purposes; for it is the Word by which all things are consecrated (1 Tim. 4:5). At this place, however, the Word is proclaimed, not by a human being but by God Himself.

Hence the first temple is the one that the patriarch Jacob builds. Of course, it is not one like ours; it is a heap of stones in a field. Here the church gathered to hear the Word of God and to perform the sacred rites. This place gave his worldly descendants the opportunity for countless acts of idolatry, as the sermons of the prophets prove. Among others, it is especially Hosea who prophesies against the kingdom of Israel.[42]

The Samaritan woman in the Gospel account defends her religion with the example of the patriarchs when she says (John 4:20): "Our fathers worshiped on this mountain"; for she is speaking of this very same mountain גְּרִזִּים, which I think either was the rock Moreh or was not far away from it. And reason is indeed caught in this snare and cannot free itself. It hears: "Abraham did this, and the action pleased God"; from this it immediately concludes: "Therefore I shall do the same thing; and I, too, shall please God." But when the prophets denied that this conclusion was valid, they were beaten and slain.

The insolence and pride of the Shechemites was extraordinary. For this reason Sirach calls them "foolish" (Ecclus. 50:26). Because they knew that an altar was built by Abraham on Mt. Moreh, they made it their business to build a splendid temple on Mt. Gerizim at the time of Alexander the Great, with Alexander's permission, as Josephus relates in the eighth chapter of his second book.[43] Since Moses foresaw this wickedness, he once more urges the godly in Deut. 16:5-6 to follow, not the examples of the patriarchs but the Word of God, saying: "You shall not sacrifice in any place whatever, but at the place which the Lord has chosen." This statement he repeats in that same sermon, not once but many times. Because the location of the tabernacle would be changed rather often until at last a temple was built, Moses wants them to respect the place that the Lord points out in His Word, to gather there, and to perform the sacred rites there.

But we see that the holy prophet exhorted them in vain. For the tabernacle and the temple were despised by the idolaters, and other places of worship were sought. Something similar has happened

---

[42] Luther is thinking of passages like Hos. 10.
[43] Josephus, *Antiquities of the Jews*, Book XI, ch. 8.

among us; for we make more of the basilica of Peter in Rome than of all other places where the Word, the sacraments, and the valid use of the keys have been, although it is an established fact that where these are, there God is present and gracious.

8. *Thence he removed to the mountain on the east of Bethel, and pitched his tent, with Bethel on the west and Ai on the east; and there he built an altar to the Lord and called on the name of the Lord.*

This new journey is toward a neighboring place, for Bethel and Jericho are not far from Mt. Moreh and are all located on the royal road. But if you should ask why he did not remain any longer at Moreh, there is nothing we could suggest except the acts of hatred and violence of his neighbors, among whom he lived. These he experienced not only because he was an alien, but because he was the originator of a new religion and had his own separate gatherings and did not follow the idolatry of those among whom he was living.

Just as we mentioned above about Moreh among the Shechemites, so it is clear from the prophets that the idolaters seized this opportunity to erect a temple and altar at Bethel. For Bethel was a venerable name, since it means the house of God. Therefore the idolaters regarded it as suitable for divine worship, as, for example, Jeroboam established his calf worship there (1 Kings 12:28-29). Later (Gen. 28:19) Moses will mention that Bethel was formerly called לוז, but that Jacob named it Bethel because the Lord had appeared to him there.

Here you should note the godliness of the holy patriarch. Even though the people who lived at Moreh were beginning to hate him chiefly on account of his religion, yet this does not cause Abraham to give up his devotion to his religion. On the contrary, he erects an altar on this mountain, which is midway between Bethel and Ai, in order to perform his duty as bishop; that is, he instructs his church concerning the will of God, admonishes them to lead a holy life, strengthens them in their faith, fortifies their hope of future blessing, and prays with them. The Hebrew verb includes all these things.

I have preferred to leave the words as they appear in the Hebrew text and not to follow our translator, who explains them as dealing merely with calling upon God.[44] In this meaning the expression

---

[44] The Vulgate has *et invocavit nomen ejus*.

appears in Joel 2:32: "And it shall come to pass that all who call upon the name of the Lord shall be delivered" or shall escape.

But in this passage Moses is speaking of the entire ministry, just as "calling upon God" itself includes the entire ministry. "How are men to call upon Him in whom they have not believed? And how are they to believe if there is no preacher?" (Rom. 10:14). Hence the meaning is: He cried in the name of the Lord; that is, he instructed his people about the name of the Lord, that they might learn that God is merciful and benevolent toward the human race, since He promises a Seed by whom His wrath is to be removed and the eternal blessing that was lost in Paradise through sin is to be restored. And upon this acknowledgment of God there follows the exhortation that in all dangers we should look to this merciful God, pray for His help, and call upon Him. Now go ask our popes and bishops: "Who anointed Abraham to fill this priestly office among his people?"

9. *And Abram journeyed on, still going toward the Negeb.*

This is his third migration within the land of Canaan. So it is clear what a welcome guest he was to the people of that land. Even though the place is not mentioned by name here, it is likely that it was Hebron. Since this was a royal city, in which there were also priests of the Canaanites, there could be no room there for Abraham. This passage reveals Abraham's amazing courage and his extraordinary perseverance in the faith, that despite the many migrations and the ill will and treachery of men he did not give up. He kept his hope in the promise that had been made to him; and he did not keep silence about the name of his God but preached publicly, although he had often experienced that this one thing gave occasion for endless hatred and acts of violence.

This example of extraordinary faith the Holy Spirit here sets before our eyes. Previously, in our discussion of Cain's sin and punishment, we stated that he had to be a wanderer on the earth.[45] But Abraham is holy through faith. Besides, he has the promise of an excellent blessing. Compare these facts with his lot, and you will realize that he is enduring punishment similar to Cain's. Like one who is cursed, he is wandering about in the land that has been promised to him, and not alone at that, but with his wife, his nephew by his brother, and all his domestics. Thus "the Lord leads His saints in a wonder-

---

[45] *Luther's Works*, 1, 293—295.

ful manner" (Ps. 4:3); and if they persevere in the faith, they ultimately receive what they believe. Let us, therefore, prepare ourselves for such conflicts and steadfastly persevere in the faith. For this is the purpose for which these accounts are written.

10. *Now there was a famine in the land. So Abram went down to Egypt to sojourn there, for the famine was severe in the land.*

There have never been any theologians or other readers whom the passage before us would not have offended, even among the Jews. It is so amazing, so full of questions and offenses, especially if it is correctly understood; for here offenses both of faith and of morals reveal themselves. The land of Canaan was promised to the seed of Abraham. Therefore Abraham undoubtedly held the strong hope that he would remain there. But look at the historical account, and you will say that everything happened and turned out contrary to his faith and the promise. Persistently he clings to the Word and does not allow himself to be turned away from it by the unfavorable outcome. Is this not overcoming hope through hope, or, as Paul expresses it (Rom. 4:18), "without hope to believe in hope"? The same thing happens to Jacob below in chapter thirty-two when he wrestles with the angel.

Abraham roamed about in the land, and nowhere did he find a place at which he could remain for any length of time. Finally came the misfortune that he was compelled to leave this promised land and on account of famine to migrate to Egypt with his entire household. Was this not a severe trial of his faith?

Let us, therefore, learn what sort of dominion our God exercises on earth — obviously a weak and stupid dominion if one follows the judgment of reason. Previously this land abounded with manifold gifts of God; now, just when the holy man comes into it, holding the promise of God in a very strong [46] faith, immediately there arises such a famine that his life would certainly be in danger unless he looked for another place. Similar famines were endured later on by Isaac, Jacob, Joseph, Elijah, Elisha, and other prophets; and by Paul, too, at the time of Claudius (Acts 11:28). And today we hear that everywhere the Gospel is blamed because the grain is more expensive and the harvest less abundant.[47]

[46] Although all the editions contain the reading *infirmissima*, we have read this as two words, *in firmissima*.

[47] Cf. *Luther's Works,* 13, pp. 249—250.

God is wont to act in this way. He governs this life in such a manner that it is full of offenses and vexations, in the eyes not only of the ungodly but also of the godly, although, like holy Abraham, the godly overcome them through faith. When religion flourished and the holy patriarchs, prophets, and apostles were ruling, all sorts of disasters occurred. How do these facts agree with the promises in Ps. 37:19: "In the days of famine they have abundance"; in Ps. 112:7: "He is not afraid of evil tidings"; "The Lord delivers him in the day of trouble" (Ps. 41:1); and "I have not seen the seed of a righteous man seeking bread" (Ps. 37:25)? Or is Abraham not seeking bread when he migrates from Canaan all the way to Egypt, in order to escape the famine?

My answer is: These things happen by a definite counsel of God, in order to test the faith of the saints. But they happen for a time; later there follows not only an earthly compensation, as Abraham became very rich, but also an increase of faith and a deeper sense of God's mercy. Therefore Paul states (Rom. 5:3) that even though the saints sigh, complain, and wail when they are afflicted, they nevertheless also glory in their cross or tribulation, since they are aware of the amazing governance of God.

In this manner Abraham is tested, not to his disadvantage but for his own great good, as the following events will show. For the Lord is putting his faith to a test by this very trial, which surely was not a small one. When he had to migrate from Canaan, he could have thought: "Where is the promise that was given to me concerning this land, which I must leave now unless I want to perish from hunger with my people? Is this the way God does what He promises? Is this the way He concerns Himself about me?"

In the first place, however, the holy man considers the spiritual promise about the eternal kingdom through the Son of God, and with this he comforts himself. In the second place, he does not discard his confidence in the physical promise either; for he knows that if he has to emigrate this year because of the famine, it will be possible to return at another time. Therefore he overcomes this trial by his patient hope for the future blessing.

Let us do the same thing when we experience the same adversities. As I stated above, the masses are complaining now about various misfortunes like high prices, pestilence, wars, etc.; and it is true that these are more numerous and more frequent than they used to be. But in addition to the sins and the great ingratitude, which provoke

God to inflict punishments, let the godly remember that this happens as a trial for those who believe. Let them not follow the stupid and ungodly opinion of the masses, who think that these evils can be corrected if the old wickedness of the pope is restored, if Masses are celebrated for the dead, if indulgences are purchased, and if processions are made around the fields, as the Jews declared about the queen of heaven in Jeremiah (44:17). How much nearer to the truth is it that we are now paying the penalty for that ungodliness, especially since some still persistently advocate it while they despise the Word?

Hence you see here an outstanding example how faith is tried in the saints; and yet holy Abraham does not succumb, as do the ungodly, who are immediately offended at the first sensation of a trial and shrink back. For they discard the Word, without which it is impossible to stand firm. But the godly seize the Word and support themselves against temptation with it as with a staff, lest they be overcome.

The text states that Abraham undertook this seventh and most difficult journey because of the famine. Yet who would not believe that the ungodly Canaanites forced him to it with their impudence, by continuing to declare that this foreigner, who was bringing in a new form of religion, was the cause of this disaster, the man on whose account God had begun to curse the otherwise blessed land? This has always been the world's opinion about the godly. Therefore the pious man voluntarily yields to animosity and exposes himself to danger.

In this instance, moreover, Abraham is guided not entirely by the Word but by his reason as well. He knew for certain that he would not be permitted to return to the place from which he had departed, for he had been commanded by the divine Word to depart from Ur and Haran. Attracted by the fertility of the land, therefore, he sets out for Egypt, in the hope that grain will be cheaper there. In earthly dangers reason has its place; it has the capacity to concern itself with some things and to give advice.

Hence this prudent householder, finding himself in danger, directs his destiny by reason and yet does not discard his faith. Even though he has been compelled by necessity to leave the Promised Land, he still believes that in due time it will be given to his descendants. Meanwhile he goes to Egypt as to a hiding place from which he can return to Canaan at a convenient time. Moses indicates this clearly when he says that he migrated to Egypt לָגוּר שָׁם, "in order to be a sojourner there," and not in order to look for a permanent abode there; for he was compelled to do so by an emergency, which he knew would not last forever but for one or two years.

Perhaps those among the Canaanites who were very kindly gave him the advice to go to Egypt because they thought that at such a time Abraham with his many domestics would be a burden on the rest of the neighbors. But the majority of them hated his religion and considered him the cause of this evil, for they did not realize that God is wont to punish the contempt of His Word and religion with famine and other adversities.

11. *When he was about to enter Egypt, he said to Sarai his wife: I know that you are a woman beautiful to behold;*

12. *and when the Egyptians see you, they will say: This is his wife; then they will kill me, but they will let you live.*

13. *Say you are my sister, that it may go well with me because of you, and that my life may be spared on your account.*

This passage greatly offends the fathers and all the theologians because Abraham himself not only lies, but he urges his wife to lie too. Perhaps the lie can be excused; but this cannot be excused, that willingly and knowingly he exposes his wife to the danger of adultery and by this lie invites the Egyptians to adultery, even though they might have spared a married woman. Now that they hear that she is unmarried, they think they can possess her without sinning.

Thus this passage has given rise not only to many questions but also to a variety of offenses; for Abraham values his own life more highly than the chastity of his wife and the welfare of others. We shall first speak about lying, concerning which Jerome and Augustine engage in an argument.[48] Augustine assumes three kinds of lies: the playful, the obliging, and the deadly.

Playful lies he calls those of poets or of actors on the stage. We know that they are lying when they represent something as actually having been done; yet the lie does no harm and is even pleasing, because it entertains and provokes laughter. This, therefore, can be termed a literary sin.

The second kind of lie is the obliging one, when we lie for the

[48] Augustine, *Reply to Faustus the Manichean*, Book XXII, pars. 33 ff.

sake of someone's good, as Michal lies when she says (1 Sam. 19:17) that David had threatened her with death. Augustine relates the example of a certain bishop who was unwilling to betray someone who had taken refuge with him. Such is the lie of Hushai the Archite (2 Sam. 15:34) and that of the woman at the well of רָגֶל (2 Sam. 17:20). This lie is called "obliging" because it not only serves the advantage of someone else, who would otherwise suffer harm or violence, but also prevents a sin. Therefore it is not proper to call it a lie; for it is rather a virtue and outstanding prudence, by which both the fury of Satan is hindered and the honor, life, and advantages of others are served. For this reason it can be called pious concern for the brethren, or, in Paul's language, zeal for piety.[49] Strictly defined, it is a lie when our neighbor is deceived by us to his ruin and our own advantage. Out of respect for the fathers I am keeping this distinction, even though it is not precise enough.

So far as Abraham's action is concerned, let us maintain that he did not lie; or at least let us say that it was an obliging lie and praiseworthy foresight. The Jews,[50] like those sevenfold asses, the Stoics, interpret this action quite harshly and accuse Abraham of a sin so great that they maintain it was punished among his descendants by the Egyptian captivity. At all events, there was no sin involved in his plan; and so far as he was able, he controlled his misfortune with prudence.

Abraham came into the land of Canaan because of the Lord's call. Then the wickedness and the acts of violence of the neighbors among whom he was living, as well as the difficulty of the times, compel him to change places. But because he was not permitted to return to the place from which he had come, he goes to Egypt, famous for its fertility. It may be that Egypt was already notorious among its neighbors on account of its tyranny, for it had a very powerful king. Where the government is not guided by the Word of God, power is generally misused for tyranny, just as someone has said: "The names of good kings can be inscribed on one ring."[51] All this troubled Abraham's mind so that he feared for himself and gave thought to a way of either counteracting or avoiding the danger.

Someone may say: "What? His faith is not wavering, is it? He

[49] This appears to be a reference to Titus 2:14.
[50] Lyra on Gen. 12, *Additio* iii.
[51] Cf. *Luther's Works*, 13, p. 167, note 34.

does not doubt God's promise that He will preserve him and help him in danger, does he?" I am not denying that his faith struggled somewhat, for we have instances before our eyes that even the most eminent men have fallen. Did not Moses encounter a severe trial at the waters of strife (Num. 20:12)? And David's horrible fall is well known (2 Sam. 11:4).

Thus when Abraham had let the Word get out of his sight and heart and, yielding to his reason, considered the dangers, he began to waver but was not altogether overwhelmed. Indeed, the faith that struggled triumphed in the end; for when he was in the very danger he feared, he did not abandon his faith; but through prayer he received from God what he desired.

When Abraham was tempted by this danger again in the house of Abimelech, he revealed the reason for this plan when he stated in chapter 20:11: "There is no fear of God at all in this place, and they will kill me." Here he truly reveals the grave conflict of his conscience, which is wounded during the exile by this painful shaft, so that he thinks: "See, you are alone. You are a foreigner wherever you go, and you bring with you a religion that is foreign and new. Are you the only one who is holy? Are you the only object of God's concern? And have so many nations and peoples been cast aside by God?"

We have a similar experience today when our opponents bawlingly flaunt before us the lofty title "church" and ask whether all those who preceded us and followed the religion of the pope have been condemned. Abraham was able to defend himself in this struggle because he knew that he had the promise and the Word, but that those heathen were without the Word and for this reason were not the object of God's concern. But the heart is too weak and does not readily give room to this conviction.

Therefore we can declare that amid so many dangers Abraham's faith gave way to some extent and that although this is a sin, it was nevertheless a sin of weakness. And this is the opinion of this action generally held by those who are of a milder disposition and do not rave as the Jews do.[52]

But another thought comes to me, a thought that induces me not only to maintain that Abraham did not sin and that his faith did not waver but to believe that this very plan came from a very strong faith and from the Holy Spirit. Someone will say: "How so?" Even

[52] Lyra on Gen. 12:13, sec. a.

though Abraham, full of faith, is aware of the various dangers, he still looks only at the promise. He knows that it has been given to him and his seed and has, so to speak, been attached to his body. Hence though he maintains that God will do what He has promised even if he should be killed in Egypt, he nevertheless feels that God must not be put to the test. Therefore he looks for every means of safety or self-defense, as though he were saying: "I am not avoiding the death of this body if it thus pleases God; and yet the promise must not be wasted through negligence.[53] If I am able to obtain it and my life, it is well; but if I must surrender my life among this ungodly people, then the Lord, who has given me the promise of the blessing, will easily be able to revive me after I have died. But I must not for this reason overlook some way of saving myself. Therefore, my dear Sarah, do not say that I am your husband; say that I am your brother. Thus I shall remain alive through your favor. But as for you, do not have any doubt. You will experience the help of the Lord, so that nothing dishonorable may befall you; and I shall also help you in this regard as much as I am able, with prayers before the true God, who has promised that He will be merciful."

This opinion is more to my liking, because it is in agreement with Scripture. A similar example is presented below, when Isaac is about to be sacrificed. There, as the Letter to the Hebrews (11:19) bears witness, Abraham also comforts himself with the hope that God is able even to restore the dead to life.

Because Scripture often presents Abraham to us as a believing father and a perfect model of faith, I prefer to decide in favor of the opinion that here, too, his great faith is revealed rather than either that he sinned or that his faith succumbed in the trial.

Although this is human, the account given here does present an extraordinary example, about which we can render the verdict that no saint, in life as well as in death, conducted himself in such a manner as did Abraham. It is the same to him whether he dies or lives, for he clings to God, the Giver of the promise; and yet he does not rashly surrender his life. He exposes his domestics, his possessions, and finally also his wife to danger, in order to keep his life, not indeed on his own account but on account of the promise, which depended on his body; for he had been told: "In you will all the families of the earth be blessed." This word engenders this anxiety and care for preserving his life. Therefore he risks anything rather than his life.

[53] Luther uses a German expression here: *die sol nicht verwarloset werden.*

Consequently, it is no unimportant or small matter that induces Abraham to appear to expose his wife to danger. He does not do this simply in order to keep his earthly life but in order to glorify God, that He may remain truthful in His promise, which the holy man had extolled so often before his domestics and through which he had so often been comforted in sundry dangers. If it is treated in this manner, the passage will offend no one. Whatever is done to the glory of God and to bestow honor and praise on His Word is well done and deserves to be praised.

Let us realize that also in this passage the Holy Spirit wanted to present a most extraordinary example of faith, one that would instruct us to rely firmly on the promise of God and to insist on it. If the entire world were to express its disagreement; if everything seemed to turn out unfavorably; and, finally, if you yourself were to die — there will still come to pass what God has promised you in Baptism, in the Word, in the Lord's Supper, and in absolution, provided only that faith relies on the promise. God cannot lie. Therefore faith, which relies on the Word, cannot lie or deceive either. Sooner would heaven collapse; sooner would stones become bread; and sooner would God raise up children for Abraham from stones (Luke 3:8).

"But Abraham," someone will say, "was the cause of very many offenses. Not everybody understood his plan, but everybody saw that his wife was being led into certain danger. This is surely not in agreement with Paul's rule, who commands (Eph. 5:28) that we should love our wives as we love our own bodies."

My answer is: This has nothing to do with Abraham, for he does right and does not sin. We too, teach the Word of God, and we teach it with particular faithfulness and care; yet many are thereby offended because of this. But how does that concern us? If there are offenses, they are taken, not given.[54] Why, then, should we have conscience scruples as a result of this? Thus Abraham did what he could; and in order that the promise might remain unshaken, he was not disturbed even by the danger to his wife. This is an outstanding faith, and those who give proper consideration to this example are edified by it. But if some are offended, what does this matter to Abraham?

But the faith of Sarah is also extraordinary because she obeyed her husband when he gave her this advice, and she was not disturbed by her own danger. She could have said: "I will not do it. Why should I rashly surrender my modesty? This is an empty pretense.

---

[54] Literally, "they are passive, not active."

You are repudiating me because I am barren, and you are taking advantage of the opportunity to marry someone else." But you hear nothing of the kind from her. She obeys her husband, who is urging her on; and in pure faith both of them commend themselves to the mercy of God. Who would not praise these spouses? Who would not admire them? Who would not wish to imitate their outstanding faith and obedience?

Hence these are outstanding examples and notable accounts. Yet we skim over them with a rather slothful mind as though they were useless. But to him who examines and considers them carefully the heart of the matter finally reveals itself, and the salutary doctrine becomes apparent, which should light the way for the godly throughout their entire life and in all their actions.

How few there are who, when they read these words that Abraham addresses to his wife as he reveals his plan to her, suppose that they can learn anything from them! But since the Holy Spirit wanted this to be committed to writing, the student of the Holy Scriptures will regard nothing as so insignificant that it is not helpful, at least as a guide for our life and conduct.

In this passage the Holy Spirit provides instruction about home life when he relates that Abraham spoke so amicably to Sarah. In the first place, he entreats her; in the second place, he adds those words about her beauty. Here you hear nothing tyrannical, nothing dictatorial; everything is affectionate and lovely, the way it ought to be among those who are well matched. As Solomon says (Ecclus. 4:30): "Do not be like a lion in your home." Of course, the husband does have the rule over the wife. Nevertheless, as Plutarch learnedly advises, it should not be the kind of rule usually exercised over slaves but the kind that the soul has over the body; for the soul is joined to the body in natural amity and is affected by both the comfort and the discomfort of the body.[55]

A third question must also be discussed at this point: whether Abraham can be excused for having such evil suspicions about the Egyptians, whom he did not yet know. Every suspicious person is a slanderer in his heart; therefore, by this way of thinking Abraham slanders the king of the Egyptians and the entire nation. He fancies that they are tyrants given over to lust and ready to kill. If he did not have these fears, he would not devise this plan.

[55] Plutarch, *Conjugal Precepts*, par. 33 in W. W. Goodwin (ed.), *Plutarch's Morals* (Cambridge, Mass., 1874—78), II, 498.

But slander is a great sin, and there is a familiar proverb that says: "It is better to spend one's life among wild beasts than among suspicious human beings."⁵⁶ Paul, too, lists suspicion among the foremost sins in 1 Tim. 6:4. It is the fountain from which proceed slander, disharmony, strife, etc. Christ, therefore, teaches the opposite and commands us not to judge or condemn anybody (Matt. 7:1). Every suspicious person sets himself up as a judge over others and condemns them.

The philosophers have also condemned suspicions as the poison of friendships. There is a learned discourse by Cicero where, in the character of Laelius, he severely criticizes the familiar dictum of Bias: "Love like one who is about to hate."⁵⁷ Cicero truthfully declares that friendships cannot exist where people are given to suspicions. Moreover, suspicion means to maintain that someday you will hate him whom you now love. Closely related to this is Aristotle's designation of truth as the mother of love.⁵⁸ Neither households nor governments can last without mutual trust. How much harm suspicions, even about rather small matters, cause among spouses! Even more serious evils follow when this plague invades the commonwealth.

And yet by his example Abraham teaches us to foster suspicions. What is more, Holy Scripture directs and advises us to be suspicious when it plainly states (Ps. 116:11): "All men are liars." "A man's enemies," says the prophet (Micah 7:6), "are the men of his own house." "Do not trust a friend" (Ecclus. 6:7). "Put not your trust in princes" (Ps. 146:3). "Guard the doors of your mouth from her who lies in your bosom" (Micah 7:5). And Christ says (Matt. 10:34): "I have not come to bring peace, but a sword."

These are clear words of Scripture. And yet what will our life be like if we follow them, if we live with one another in distrust, in suspicions, and in evil thoughts — the wife with the husband, the subjects with the government, and the domestics with the master of the house? Furthermore, what will become of the command of Christ (Matt. 7:1, 3): "Judge not; see not the speck in your brother's eye"? Finally, what will the church be like, which preaches repentance to sinners and urges us not to despair utterly about sinners? Therefore that famous rule of the jurists does not hold in the church: "He who

---

⁵⁶ Perhaps an adaptation of the saying in Prov. 21:19.

⁵⁷ Cicero, *De amicitia*, ch. XVI, par. 59.

⁵⁸ This may be a reference to Aristotle, *Nicomachean Ethics*, Book IV, ch. 7.

is once evil is always assumed to be evil";[59] for Christ wants the brother's offense to be forgiven even seventy times seven times (Matt. 18:22). How shall we reconcile these statements, which are diametrically opposed to each other?

So far as the statement of Bias is concerned, which Cicero criticizes so severely, I am fully convinced that Cicero did not understand what Bias had in mind. The statement of Bias is not what is termed an absolute proposition; it is a conditional one.[60] That is, Bias does not mean to say that one who loves should be certain that he will hate the one he loves, but that it is possible for one who loves now to hate later. Similarly, Augustine says that it often happens in life that one loves someone whom one previously hated.[61] But let us leave the philosophical question to the philosophers to investigate.

Let us consider these theological matters: both what Abraham did and what Scripture forbids to do. It forbids judgment, that is, it forbids us to be suspicious; and yet it commands us not to trust anyone. We shall see how these two statements can be reconciled.

The entire matter hinges on distinguishing between the two statements that the Holy Scriptures make. The first demands that we love both our friends and our enemies. The second demands that we do not put our trust in a human being, for it can happen that he will fail us.

But just as reason does not see the complete reason for the first statement — for it considers it right to assume a hostile attitude toward those by whom we have been offended — so it sees still less the reasons why we should not trust all men to the same extent. It considers the life of individual people; and on the basis of their conduct it considers some good, others evil. Moreover, it thinks that the good deserve love, but that the evil deserve hate. This is the judgment of reason; it cannot rise beyond this. In addition, it maintains that the good deserve not only love but also trust. Hence arises the reliance on human beings, which the Holy Scriptures completely condemn, because it is not only fraught with dangers but is even godless — fraught with dangers because it fails; godless because this reliance is due the Creator, not the creature.

---

[59] The usual form of this epigram is *Qui semel est malus, is semper praesumitur esse.*

[60] The technical term here is *propositio de inesse* as contrasted with a *propositio modalis.*

[61] Perhaps a reference to Augustine, *On Christian Doctrine*, Book I, ch. 29.

Hence the Holy Scriptures declare, in the first place, that we should love all human beings equally and that we should do good to all, not only to the good and to those whom we consider worthy because of their conduct but also to the evil. For this is God's way; He pours out His benefits without distinction, and Christ Himself refers us to this example (Matt. 5:45).

In the second place, they teach a judgment about human beings that is different from the one that can be made on the basis of conduct alone. Because of hypocrisy such judgment is unreliable and subject to error. How often friendships break up! How often someone who is considered pious is caught in an evil design! The writings of the heathen from every age of antiquity praise many pairs of friends. Is not this very fact a sufficiently weighty and clear evidence that our judgment about human beings errs when it is based on their conduct?[62]

Therefore Holy Scripture commands us to consider not simply the conduct of another person but the Word and the fear of God. Where we find these, the people are no doubt pious; yet it can happen that they, too, fall. We all know the weakness of our nature and the power of our enemy, who is striving to draw us away from the truth and rob us of the fear of God. Therefore not even here can there be the unfailing confidence that others will always remain the same. How much less confidence, therefore, should be placed in those who are without the fear of God!

Philosophy is not aware of this source of evil: that our entire nature is corrupt, and that though for a time it simulates love by certain acts of kindness, it is nevertheless not a steadfast love and is very easily destroyed.

But let me return to the matter we had before us. Abraham sets out to go to the Egyptians. He does not hate them, yet he distrusts them. The reason is his awareness not only that nature per se is evil and is addicted to lusts, but also that Egypt is devoid of the Word and the true religion. Why should he not fear danger in these circumstances?

Therefore he commits himself and his life to God. Yet he does not disregard the means by which he was hoping to protect it. Thus he proceeds on the royal road. He hates no one, and yet he trusts

---

[62] The meaning of this rather obscure passage seems to be that true friendship is rare.

no one. If others show him some kindness, he considers this an advantage and delights in it, nevertheless in such a way that if the kindness should cease or some adversity should occur, he would not be provoked or begin to hate another person.

Of such friendships philosophy has no knowledge. Because it has no adequate insight into human nature, it supposes that it is possible to find people so virtuous that they never forget their duty. While it is looking for such friendships, it becomes involved in implacable enmities, which the Greeks call ἀσπόνδους.[63] For these there is no remedy.

But those who are taught by the Holy Scriptures realize what is in man, and for this reason they place complete trust in God and not in a man; yet they love all equally and show kindness to all, even to their enemies. They know that God wants it so.

This, then, is solid friendship and the most steadfast love. It has its source, not in our judgment but in the Holy Spirit, who urges our minds to follow the Word.

Just as a lack of confidence is necessary because everything human is uncertain, so love, on the other hand, as Paul says (1 Cor. 13:4, 7), is not suspicious, but is hopeful even about evil things. For it maintains that both can happen: those whom it considers pious can fall, and those who are evil can improve.

He who does not trust human beings is not for this reason suspicious; nor does he, as the Holy Scriptures express it, judge or condemn his neighbor. This suspicion or judgment has no hope for improvement. But even when love sees something of which it must disapprove, it never ceases to hope. Therefore it is ready to forgive; and it does forgive, not seven times but seventy times seven times (Matt. 18:22). For it knows that both propositions are true. Every human being, so far as lies in him, is a liar, and therefore it puts its trust in no human being. And at the same time God is benevolent; He forgives sins and rejoices at the conversion of the sinner, and it is for this that He has intended His Word, in which the Holy Spirit is present. This is the source of hope, so that love does not despair entirely even of the wicked.

Therefore we must utterly reject philosophical judgment, which decides on the basis of behavior that some are evil and others are good; and we must adhere to this universal statement (Ps. 116:11):

[63] Cf. Rom. 1:31; 2 Tim. 3:3.

"Every man is a liar," and likewise (Ps. 14:2-3): "The Lord looks down from heaven upon the children of men, to see if there are any that act wisely, that seek after God. They have all gone astray, they are all alike corrupt; there is none that does good, no, not one." This is our nature, which we bring with us from our mother's womb and which we keep until the Holy Spirit improves it. Therefore one must trust no human being insofar as he is a human being, even though one finds his conduct beyond reproach. Yet there must be no hate; no matter how evil one considers him, one must not for this reason abandon him or despair of improvement.

Furthermore, we are saying nothing at this point about particular callings that appear to preclude love. For the blows that the head of the family and parents inflict on their children or domestics do not have the appearance of love, and it appears to be anger when the government punishes evildoers with the sword and kills them. But they are commanded to do this, and they would sin if they adjusted their calling to this normal rule about equal love for good and evil, a rule they themselves must obey when they are not engaged in their calling.

The same kind of answer must also be given to the statement of Micah when he advises (7:5): "Guard the doors of your mouth from her who lies in your bosom." The prophet certainly does not want spouses to harbor suspicions, which are always linked with disagreement and quarrels; but he wants the wife to be loved. Paul explains this very command beautifully in the Letter to the Ephesians (5:25).

Among the foremost praises of a wife is this, that her husband's heart trusts her, that is, that her husband loves her dearly, does not bear any ill will toward her, and is convinced that he is being loved and that his interests are being served by his wife.

For this reason Augustine learnedly enumerates three benefits in marriage: trust, children, and its sacramental character.[64] And truly, if there is no trust, hearts will never unite closely; nor will there ever be any true love between them. But this world has nothing more beautiful than this union of hearts between spouses.

Sirach likewise declares (Ecclus. 25:1) "My soul takes pleasure in three things, and they are beautiful in the sight of the Lord and

---

[64] "Therefore the good of marriage throughout all nations and all men stands in the occasion of begetting, and faith of chastity: but so far as pertains unto the People of God, also in the sanctity of the Sacrament." Augustine, *On the Good of Marriage*, ch. 32.

of men: agreement between brothers, friendship between neighbors, and a wife and husband who live in harmony."

Thus the prophet [65] does not want suspicion and hatred to exist between spouses; he wants the utmost love and good will, which cannot exist without mutual trust; and yet he wants a limit to this trust, because it can happen that it is mistaken. For she is a human being; and although she fears God and pays heed to His Word, nevertheless, because she has Satan, the enemy, lying in wait everywhere and because human nature as such is weak, she can fall and disappoint your hope somewhere.

When you foresee this with your mind, you will be readier to forgive, and you will be less distressed if anything happens contrary to what you had hoped. Thus love will remain, and harmony will not be disturbed. For nothing has happened that was not anticipated, and love is readiest to forgive. This is indeed a rare gift; but you, because you are a Christian, should remember that this ought to be your attitude.

How the world is accustomed to act is well known. Harmony, says the poet, is rare even among brothers.[66] And we observe that from the most insignificant matter — or, as we say in German, from pigeon droppings — quarrels arise among neighbors.[67] In these circumstances suspicions and hatred prevail.

But even though the Christian trusts no human being, he does not hate any human being either; and although he maintains that no one is so strong that he cannot be overcome either by his desires or by Satan, he is still very hopeful about everybody, even about evil men. Thus he keeps his love chaste, pure, and strong also toward his friends; but his complete trust he has placed in the goodness of God alone.

We do not learn this from heathen philosophy, which approves of hatred against enemies and assumes that an evil person is always evil. Therefore it avoids and hates him, and breaks the tightest bonds of friendship. But the Holy Scriptures teach otherwise. They dispose of trust, but they demand love. Thus Abraham is afraid of danger from the Egyptians, but this does not cause him to hate them. He is hopeful and reflects that he wants to enjoy the benefit of their

---

[65] That is, Micah 7:5 as quoted four paragraphs earlier.

[66] Ovid, *Metamorphoses*, Book I, l. 145.

[67] This proverb does not appear in the standard collections of either German or Latin proverbs.

good things as much as he can. Yet if something untoward should happen, this is not unexpected, and it does not move him to hatred. Thus the Holy Scriptures teach ethics, or the theory of duties,[68] far better than any Ciceros or Aristotles.

14. *When Abram entered Egypt, the Egyptians saw that the woman was very beautiful.*

15. *And when the princes of Pharaoh saw her, they praised her to Pharaoh. And the woman was taken into Pharaoh's house.*

This is a most amazing account if we consider it more closely. Sarah was only ten years younger than Abraham. But Abraham was seventy-five years old when he left Haran for the land of Canaan, and before this journey into Egypt perhaps ten more years had elapsed. Therefore Sarah was more than seventy years old and was already an aged woman. It seems amazing not only that her beauty is praised, but also that the king falls in love with her and brings her into his house.

As usual, the Jews invent some old wives' tales about Sarah, that she had been enclosed in a box and was found by the tax collectors and brought to the king.[69] But let us disregard these absurd ideas, which befit their Jewish authors. Nor is this explanation enough: that while the Egyptians were dark, the bodies of the Orientals were whiter, and that for this reason Sarah was attractive to the Egyptians. For age deserves more praise than beauty does, and people think favorably of old age even if they do not think favorably of beauty.

Therefore the extraordinary beauty in the aged Sarah may have been a miracle, by which God wanted to dispose the king of Egypt favorably toward Abraham and thus make known among the heathen the promise concerning the future Seed; for Abraham preached everywhere, as Isaiah states about him that he preached righteousness wherever he went.[70] Or, what is more likely, our age has deteriorated to such an extent that at that time a sixty-year-old woman was comparable in both beauty and vigor to one who is thirty years old today.

At the time nature was livelier and hardier than it is now, in the

---

[68] A reference to the *Nicomachean Ethics* of Aristotle and to the treatise *On Duties* of Cicero.

[69] Lyra on Gen. 12:15, sec. b.

[70] As on p. 246, this is an application to Abraham of the words in Is. 41:2: "Who stirred up one from the east?"

old age of the world. For just as there was a gradual increase in wickedness, so there was a decline in the gifts with which God endows the godly. Besides, Sarah was aided by nature in preserving the charm of her beauty; for she was barren. She was not yet worn out by the pains and the travail of childbirth, which greatly impair the beauty and vigor of the body.

Other historical accounts from that era reveal that during these more than three thousand years our life expectancy has declined at least thirty years. For a fifty-year-old woman to give birth among us is almost a miracle. And in his prayer Moses declares (Ps. 90:10): "The years of our life are threescore and ten, or even by reason of strength fourscore; yet their span is but toil and trouble." But if we look at our generation, the vigor of the mind and the strength of the body surely begin to decline after forty years are completed. So much has nature deteriorated because of sin. Discerning men have observed that other creatures are gradually deteriorating too, as Vergil learnedly discourses about seeds.[71]

But what shall we say about Abraham at this point? He suffers a new and very painful affliction when he sees his wife, a chaste and saintly matron and the manager of his entire household, taken away to the royal court. He looked on with great grief, but he comforted himself with the faith that God would not cease to care for him and would protect his wife even among the unbelievers, to keep her from being subjected to anything disgraceful. With this faith he reassures himself; with this hope he soothes his worries and tears, and prays ardently that this hope may not fail him.

Just as the earlier dangers of the diversified and long traveling exercised his faith, so here, too, his faith is exercised, that he may justly be set before the church as a perfect example of faith, as a brave soldier, who conducted himself with valor not in only one battle but in many diverse dangers.

The Jews relate that, according to royal custom, Sarah was not brought to the king immediately but was kept under guard for a time.[72] We read about the Persian king Ahasuerus (Esther 2:2-3) that the maidens whom the king wanted were not brought to the king immediately but were anointed with oil of myrrh for six entire months, then for six more months with other perfumes, and at last

[71] Vergil, *Georgics,* Book I, ll. 193—199.
[72] Lyra on Gen. 12:13, sec. a.

were brought to the bed of the king. But if the Egyptian kings also followed this custom, the restraint of those heathen must have been great, not to be carried away headlong by their violent lust, as is the case among us.

Not only the example of the Persian kings but also the statement of Moses himself induces me to believe that this was the procedure with Sarah. Since a certain plague followed, a short time must necessarily have intervened; yet meanwhile Sarah was not summoned for concubinage with the king.

The sovereigns of the Greeks and the Romans allowed themselves to be carried away completely by their lusts. The morals of the Egyptians were more virtuous, and their decency greater, than among the other nations; for although polygamy was permitted among them, they appear to have lived more chastely than those who observed monogamy. Similarly, King Abimelech of the Palestinians decrees the death penalty, to keep Rebecca from being ravished (Gen. 26:11). These facts prove that although there was polygamy, the decency of those nations was extraordinary.

The Jews prattle that while Sarah was living at the court Abraham taught the Egyptians astronomy; and Josephus goes to great lengths to show that the Jews surpassed all the other nations in their knowledge of the mathematical sciences and governmental affairs.[73]

But he would have done better if he had extolled these ancestors of his people, not because of those gifts, which are theirs by nature, but because of the other greater ones, which come from the Holy Spirit, namely, that Abraham gave instruction to the Egyptians about the will of God, about the true worship of God, and about true prayer. These are more excellent gifts than knowledge about the motion of the stars, the meanings of the stars, and similar things.

Yet I think that these things also were revealed to the fathers by God. The writings of the Gentiles praise the Chaldeans as well as the Egyptians, because they diligently cultivated the study of these sciences.[74] Whether Abraham instructed the Egyptians concerning these sciences, or whether, like Moses, of whom Stephen declares (Acts 7:22) that he was learned in all the wisdom of the Egyptians, he himself learned these matters from the Egyptians, is of no importance.

[73] Lyra on Gen. 12:16, sec. g; Josephus, *Antiquities of the Jews*, Book I, ch. 8.

[74] As Acts 7:22 shows, the Egyptians were almost legendary for their wisdom and learning.

This much, however, is certain: even though this eminent man did not neglect the study of nature, in which it is profitable to contemplate the outstanding works of God, nevertheless he had a greater interest in spreading the knowledge of God and establishing true forms of worship, fear, and trust among the nations. For this is a most excellent work of love, one which all the saints are invited to carry on by the confession of their faith.

16. *And for her sake he dealt well with Abram; and he had sheep, oxen, he-asses, menservants, maidservants, she-asses, and camels.*

This little section is highly necessary; for it serves not only to praise and glorify God, who does not desert those that are His, but also to praise the faith of Abraham. For in this passage you see that those who believe are the object of God's care and are preserved in the most immediate danger. Not only is Abraham in favor with the king because of his sister Sarah — for the king believed that she was his sister — but the Egyptians, too, respect him, although, as will be related below, they had a dislike for shepherds.

Moreover, this passage also reveals the extraordinary kindness of the Egyptian people, who are so obliging and kind to this sojourner. For although the king is kind to Abraham because of Sarah, it is clear that the connection through marriage, which it was assumed would occur, was highly esteemed by the king. But because there is no kingdom in which conditions are so good that there is no tyranny at all, Abraham feared for himself.

Thus this is the outstanding lesson here: to learn that God is the Protector of those who trust in Him and that He does not desert His own even though He permits them to be tried. David likewise deals with this account in a superb manner and enlarges on it in Ps. 105:12-15 as it deserves: "When they were few in number, of little account, and sojourners in that land, wandering from nation to nation, from one kingdom to another people, He allowed no one to oppress them; He rebuked kings on their account, saying: 'Touch not My anointed ones, do My prophets no harm!'"

Observe how the prophet emphasizes each detail, in order to demonstrate to us that God will surely have mercy on and bless those who trust in Him.

This passage is, therefore, a fountain from which there originate those magnificent addresses of the prophets, inviting us to maintain hope and trust in the mercy of God and dispensing the comfort that in the end God will deliver and bless. "Blessed are all who take refuge in Him" (Ps. 2:11). "I sought the Lord, and He answered me, and delivered me from all my fears" (Ps. 34:4). "This poor man cried, and the Lord heard him, and saved him out of all his troubles" (Ps. 34:6). "Call upon Me in the day of trouble; I will deliver you, and you shall glorify Me" (Ps. 50:15). "Many are the afflictions of the righteous; but the Lord delivers him out of them all" (Ps. 34:19). But who is able to remember all similar statements even in the Book of Psalms alone, to say nothing about the rest of the prophets?

Clearly they realized that these events were recorded by the Holy Spirit, not for the sake of Abraham but in order that we might be taught faith by such examples and might not despair in dangers, because in this passage God reveals that He will be the trustworthy Protector of all who believe in Him and put their hope in His mercy.

He does indeed allow His own to be tried, just as this was surely a very great and almost unbearable trial; but He does not forsake them in the trial. He delays His help, but this does not mean that He withdraws it. At His appointed time He is at hand and delivers, without sparing even great kings who are loaded with power and wealth.

We see that when some very learned men saw both the dangers of the pious and the successes of the wicked, they were so offended by this apparent unfairness that they denied that there is any providence or concern of God about human beings, and they maintained that everything happens by chance.

And for reason this is indeed an insurmountable offense, which we observe disturbing even the godly at times. Thus Ps. 73:2-3 says: "My feet had almost stumbled, my steps had well-nigh slipped. For I was envious of the arrogant, when I saw the prosperity of the wicked." For reason is aware only of the categorical assertion that the pious suffer and the wicked prosper; it is not aware of the hypothetical assertion that God delivers the righteous from evil and that His righteous anger slays the wicked.[75]

But the Holy Spirit points out the hypothetical assertion, as they call it in the schools, when He states in Ps. 34:19: "Many are the afflictions of the righteous, but the Lord delivers him out of them all." Therefore when the saints see that they are afflicted, they still do not for this reason depart from the commands of God; but to this minor

[75] The introduction of this distinction between categorical and hypothetical may be due to an editor; see Introduction.

premise they add the conclusion of faith and maintain that they, too, will be delivered from those adversities and dangers.

These are revelations of the Holy Spirit; philosophy is not aware of them. Therefore it is offended; it denies providence and concludes that God does not concern Himself with human affairs, but everything happens by accident and by chance. In his treatises *De finibus* and *De natura deorum* Cicero confronts this very difficulty.[76] He does not venture to say either that God is unjust or that He does not concern Himself with human affairs; yet he does not see any reason why the situation in this life is so unfair that the wicked flourish, while the pious fail even in their most honorable efforts and plans.

What is the reason for this blindness? No doubt it is this: reason looks only at the adversities of the present and is impressed and overwhelmed by them, but of the promise concerning the future it has no knowledge at all. The Holy Spirit, however, commands us to disregard the things of the present and to look at those of the future. He says (Ps. 27:14): "Wait, be strong, and let your heart take courage; yea, wait for the Lord." Thus these passages are intended to teach and strengthen faith and hope, and this foremost doctrine will often be repeated in this historical account of Abraham.

17. *But the Lord afflicted Pharaoh and his house with great plagues because of Sarai, Abraham's wife.*

Here at last is the happy outcome of the trials. Not only is that godly couple delivered out of danger and fear, but the king and his house are overtaken by evils and afflicted. This comfort is impressed on us by the Holy Spirit throughout Scripture, and experience confirms it; yet we, as though we were blind and deaf, do not accept it when we are tried, and we do not believe that it is true.

Consider what usually happens. When we are in dangers, do we not think that there will be no end of the evils and that we must succumb? Similarly, when we see that the wicked flourish, we maintain that their good fortune will be permanent, as though there were no God who either would concern Himself with those who are in distress or would punish those who misuse their prosperity. Thus offense prevails in both instances. But this happens because of original sin, which makes us prone to despair and, contrariwise, slow to faith and hope.

[76] Cf. p. 208.

Therefore the example of Abraham should be carefully considered and imitated. When he was in a very pressing danger, he nevertheless maintained that it was impossible for God to abandon those who believe in Him. Hence he did not give up hope; but the more serious the danger, the more he believed God would speedily deliver him and Sarah. Eventually the outcome bore him out.

The same thing will happen to us if only we do not allow ourselves to be robbed of our faith. Indeed, I myself have experienced this in many grave dangers.

But the flesh usually holds us captive, as Paul complains about himself (Rom. 7:23): "I see in my members another law." The spirit indeed is willing, receives the Word of God, comforts itself in dangers, and wants to be glad and exult even under a cross; but it is overwhelmed by the flesh. The flesh habitually looks only at the things that are present and is influenced and impressed only by them; but it regards as worthless the things that are not present, those which the Word teaches, because it does not see them. Therefore it transgresses under both conditions, when its prospects are bright and when they are unfavorable. When they are bright, it does not keep within the bounds of moderation; for it does not see the threatening evils. When they are unfavorable, it cannot be comforted; for nowhere does it see the deliverance that the Word promises.

And yet in the godly there remains a sighing that has its seat in the innermost heart; and in some measure, although very faintly, it opposes the distrust and despair and impatience that are in the flesh, lest we become blasphemers. This the Lord regards; the rest He forgives.

The great danger of his dear wife worried Abraham too; and without a doubt he felt the emotions of the flesh to the point of despair. Therefore he thought: "What if your wife, who has now been taken away, should never return to you? What if I should lose her forever?" Tears and other sighs followed these thoughts, and I have no doubt that he spent sleepless nights; yet while he is troubled by these thoughts of the flesh — for he is human — the Spirit leads him back to the Word, to cause him to think of the promise given to him. With this he comforts himself in his worries and tears, and he hopes that at His own time God will return his wife and will see to it that she suffers nothing dishonorable. As he hopes, so it happens. For it is true that a hope that relies on God and His Word is not disappointed.

Let us, therefore, keep this account before us, and let us accustom ourselves to foster our hope and to comfort our hearts when we are being tried. "Woe to you," says Sirach (Ecclus. 2:14), "who have lost your endurance!" For what is left but despair when the Word is lost? Therefore Scripture urges everywhere that we should "wait for the Lord." That is, we should not lose courage or abandon hope but should comfort ourselves with the hope of the coming deliverance. Otherwise we may suffer the fate of the unbelieving Israelites in the desert, of whom Ps. 78:33 states: "Its days vanished in emptiness"; that is, they died "without having attained their promises because of their unbelief, and they endured various afflictions through their entire life." And in Ps. 107:11 it is written: "They spurned His counsel"; that is, they did not want to believe and did not want to hope. For this reason they were gradually destroyed.

Let us, therefore, impress these facts on ourselves. If we are Christians, we shall have to endure many adversities. Today we see the great tyranny of the bishops and of some princes. Our heart is fearful, and we wish that the punishments of the ungodly and the deliverance of the church would come quickly. Many become discouraged because of impatience and all but fall away.

But let us wait for the Lord and be patient like Abraham, for He will surely come. Unless we have lost patience, He will hurl down the tyrants; but His church He will preserve. For this is His nature. As we read in Isaiah (54:7-8), He tries His own and for a moment forsakes them; but later on He receives them with great mercy.

But just as the church and the godly should comfort themselves with hope, so those who are flourishing and trouble the church, should fear the punishments; for although the Lord delays, He nevertheless will not delay forever. Nor was the power of any king or monarch ever great enough to save him from eventually paying the penalty for his ungodliness and collapsing. But at what time, in what manner, and at what place this will happen — this the godly, like Abraham, should leave to God.

At this point the question is raised with what sort of disease the Lord afflicted Pharaoh and his house.[77] The text does not reveal this, just as it does not mention how the reason for this plague was revealed to Pharaoh. It is certain that Abraham did not point it out to him; for he had deceived the king when he said that Sarah was his sister

---

[77] Lyra on Gen. 12:17, sec. h.

and not his wife. Furthermore, for this reason the king appears to be guiltless. For he did not take her away as the wife of another, but as a single woman; nor did he want to abuse her as a harlot, but to keep her as his wife.

I dislike the Jews, who concoct the most insipid and most foolish ideas when they carry on a discussion about these uncertain matters. They maintain that the punishment in this passage was a disease which the physicians call gonorrhea, when the semen flows of itself.

Below, when Rebecca was taken away from Isaac by the king of the Philistines,[78] Scripture states that there followed the punishment that the vulvas of all the women were closed, so that they could neither conceive nor give birth.

I think that something of this kind also happened here. Because the king takes a strange woman, he is punished with a punishment that affects women, so that a woman is unable to be a woman, that is, cannot give birth but miscarries and meets with other dangers of childbirth. For usually "one is punished by the very things by which he sins," as it is written in the Book of Wisdom (11:16).

Furthermore, here once more the Egyptians are praised for having some knowledge of God and for realizing that this misfortune is not a casual occurrence or some common malady but a punishment inflicted by God on account of a definite sin. For this misfortune is not a slight one. Among all the various kinds of death I consider it the saddest sight when a mother dies with her unborn child.

Since these occurrences were rather frequent after Sarah had been seized, the king was moved by the influence of the Holy Spirit to wonder about the cause of the evil. And because this sickness came into the court together with Sarah, so that the wives of the king at the court either encountered difficulties in childbirth or died, he addressed Sarah reproachfully and asked who she was. It was then that he realized that she was not the sister of Abraham but his wife, and that she was a married woman. So he let her go. This is my own surmise about the punishment, because the text states that Pharaoh and his house were stricken with great plagues; and thus the punishment is in agreement with the sin.

What we translate with "on account of Sarah" is עַל־דְּבַר in the Hebrew, "on account of the word of Sarai." But it is customary in Hebrew to use the noun דָּבָר in a very wide sense, just as we use

---

[78] Actually, this occurs in the story of Sarah, Gen. 20:18.

the word "thing." For it means not only "word" but also "cause," "business," "act," "matter." Therefore the evangelists in the Gospel account also frequently employ this Hebraism. Thus when they state about Mary (Luke 2:19): "She kept these words in her heart," they are speaking not only of what was said but of the entire occurrence.

In this passage the Jews explain "the word" in an active sense and say that it was an angel who guarded Sarah's body and at Sarah's order smote the Egyptians as often as she gave the command to do so. But who does not realize that here there is a Jewish fabrication? The Jews take advantage of every opportunity to make their ancestors appear glorious and great before the world.

But Sarah was too pious a woman to want to harm people, and I think that this plague occurred without the knowledge of Sarah and Abraham. This much is sure: they placed no hope in the possibility that the Egyptians might be afflicted; but all their hope was placed on the promise of God, because they believed that God would preserve them and direct all things in such a way that it would be clear that He is a God who blesses in accordance with His promise. Let us, therefore, reject this fabrication of the Jews, who distort everything to the glory of their deeds and of their nation; for here we ought rather to praise God's power and mercy, and to consider the trust of the saints in the promise.

Moreover, we must consider here the clear evidence both that the government among the Egyptians was most honorable and that the judgments against adulterers were severe; for the king himself returns Sarah to her husband as soon as he hears that she is the wife of Abraham.

Here the serious question arises why Pharaoh was punished, and with so severe a punishment at that, even before he attempted anything with Sarah; for it is certain that he sinned in ignorance.

The theologians as well as the jurists answer with the distinction that there is a twofold ignorance: one of the law, which excuses no one; the other of the action, which does excuse.[79] But here law must be logically defined as consisting, not of all the opinions of the teachers — for these are countless and usually conflict with one another, since the jurists argue about the fine points of the law and rarely reach agreement — but of the law that has been published among the citizens or has been accepted through use and custom.

[79] The legal maxim is *Ignorantia legis neminem excusat*.

He who does not know what has been publicly proclaimed or has been accepted through use, is not excused; for he could have learned about it from his neighbor. And laws are proclaimed for the purpose of giving light to all in general and in order that those who act contrary to them may know that they are guilty and may expect to be punished.

But not to know what Bartolus or Baldus [80] judges or concludes in a given case should not be called ignorance of the law. For law consists, not of the opinions of the teachers and their questions but of information that has been set forth publicly.

But ignorance of a fact is when I know the law and do not know the fact, as when the head of a household supports a thief in his home but does not know that he is a thief. In this instance he knows the law, namely, that it is forbidden by law to steal; but the fact he does not know. He incurs no danger when he supports a thief of whom he does not know that he is a thief and whom he aids neither with advice nor with help. This distinction is a useful one, and I mention it in order that we may not be deceived by the inept wisdom of some men who, because of their inordinate desire to argue, ridicule sensible and useful pronouncements made for the purpose of teaching.

In their schools the theologians enumerate other kinds of ignorance. The first kind is the one they call "invincible," [81] which was invented to excuse shortcomings, because it cannot be overcome or improved through any effort or perseverance. Thus Cicero's lack of knowledge of God is invincible. When you read his treatises *De natura deorum* and *De finibus bonorum et malorum*, you realize that he has omitted nothing that mankind is able to attain by means of human reason and all its powers; yet he does not know what God's will is and what His attitude is toward us. The reason for this lack of knowledge is that the ability to know God comes, not from our innate reason but from the Spirit of God, who enlightens our minds through the Word. Since Cicero lacked this, he had to struggle with a lack of knowledge that was invincible.

[80] Bartolus de Saxoferrato (1314—57) was a famous jurist at the University of Perugia; Baldus was his pupil.

[81] "If ignorance be such that it is altogether involuntary, either because it is invincible, or because it pertains to that which a man is not obliged to know, then such ignorance completely excuses one from wrongdoing." Thomas Aquinas, *Summa theologica*, I—II, Q. 76, Art. 3.

This very example refutes that famous dictum of the scholastics: "When a man does the best he can, God without fail bestows grace";[82] for Cicero did the best he could, yet he did not obtain grace. Yes, his study hurled him into deeper darkness, so that he actually had doubts about the existence of God. When anybody ponders such lofty matters without the Word and relies solely on the light of reason, his errors inevitably become progressively greater.

The theologians had no reason for thinking up this kind of ignorance; for one must not look for any means of defending sins, as is frequently done in the *Summa angelica* where it deals with the instruction of conscience.[83] The author of this book caused much offense when into theological discussions he introduced statements that concern the government and the management of the home.

When I, as a young theologian, read that book in order to enable me to counsel consciences at confession, I was very often deeply offended; for it treated in a forensic and legal manner matters that belonged to the judgment of God and the church.[84]

In the affairs of government there is room for invincible ignorance, as when someone is at fault because he is encumbered by sickness or is insane. But these ideas should not be carried over into religion and matters of conscience. We are born with the blindness of original sin. That evil is invincible in the sense that it holds even the regenerate captive; but this does not make it excusable, the way the scholastics have declared invincible ignorance excusable, so that it directly excuses from everything — for thus they express themselves — that is, does away with sin entirely. If we maintain that this is true, it will also follow that human beings are saved without Christ if they do the best they can. So great is the blindness in the schools and churches of the pope.

Consider Pharaoh. So far as his conduct is concerned, he is in invincible ignorance; for he does not know that Sarah is Abraham's wife, and he hears directly from Abraham that she is only his sister. Yet God inflicts very severe punishments on him. Do you not see

---

[82] See p. 123, note 44.

[83] This does not refer to the *Summa theologica* of Thomas Aquinas, as the Weimar editors maintain. As Luther indicates, it refers to a manual of casuistry, the *Summa de casibus conscientiae* of the Franciscan theologian Angelo Carletti di Chivasso (1411—95); it was called *Summa angelica* after him.

[84] It will be recalled that the controversy over indulgences arose out of Luther's experiences as a confessor.

in this instance that the famous statement of the scholastics about invincible ignorance, which excuses from everything, is false?

Thus when Christ says (Matt. 11:23-24): "If the mighty works done in you had been done in Sodom, it would have remained until this day. But I tell you that it shall be more tolerable on the Day of Judgment for the land of Sodom than for you," He maintains the ignorance of Sodom in comparison with the people of Capernaum. Nevertheless, He declares that Sodom is not excused from everything for this reason. He says that it is excused to this extent, as they express it in the schools, that its punishment will be milder because of that ignorance.

But why say a great deal? If anyone maintains that this invincible ignorance merits an excuse, he subverts Holy Scripture and deprives the world of Christ, "the Sun of righteousness" (Mal. 4:2), who was revealed for the purpose of removing this ignorance. For it is really nothing else than original sin, and he who maintains that this deserves an excuse grasps none of the sacred teachings.

The second variety of ignorance they call "inert" or "crass" ignorance,[85] such as exists when one hears the Word, which one could learn if one wanted to, with indifference and without enthusiasm. This, they correctly declare, is inexcusable.

The third is "affected" ignorance,[86] when we painstakingly guard against knowing or learning anything. They correctly teach that this deserves a double punishment. An example of it today are those at the courts of bishops and ungodly princes who intentionally keep away from our books and are unwilling to read them, so that when asked by their princes, they can swear without hesitation that they have no knowledge of our doctrine.

Thus the wicked in Job 21:14 say: "We do not desire the knowledge of Thy ways"; and in the Gospel (Luke 19:14): "We do not want this Man to reign over us." This they call affected ignorance.

If you should ask where to place the pope with the papists, either we shall say that they belong in this last group — for they attack and condemn many things they know are good and in harmony

---

[85] Ignorance is said to be "crass" when almost no attempt has been made at self-enlightenment.

[86] Ignorance is said to be "affected" if one purposely neglects the means of finding out what one ought to know. On the various kinds of ignorance cf. Thomas Aquinas, *De malo*, Q. 3, Art. 6—8, *Sancti Thomae Aquinatis . . . opera omnia* (New York, 1948 ff.), VIII, 266—270.

with the Word — or we shall simply classify them among the persecutors and opponents of sound doctrine, as the pope is called Antichrist for this reason.

Then what shall we answer to the question that has been put about Pharaoh? Nothing else than what the account itself presents. His ignorance is well known; yet because God inflicts punishment on him, it follows that his ignorance does not excuse him. Let us, therefore, maintain both: Pharaoh's action is a mistake, and it is a bad mistake; otherwise no punishment would follow.

But if anyone is of the opinion that this punishment was sent, not because Pharaoh intended anything evil but that he might be prevented from the evil that would have followed if the punishment had not intervened, let him see to it that he does not defend sin while he is excusing a mistake. For even if Pharaoh was ignorant, he would have become an adulterer. Adultery is always a sin; and in this instance the distinction between ignorance of the law and of fact, which is valid in court, does not apply.

18. *So Pharaoh called Abram, and said: What is this you have done to me? Why did you not tell me that she was your wife?*

19. *Why did you say: She is my sister, so that I took her for my wife? Now then, here is your wife, take her, and begone.*

In the first place, as I remarked above, let us take note here of the outstanding comfort that God takes care of His own and does not forsake them when they are in danger, provided only that they do not lack faith. Thus Peter, too, dispenses comfort in 1 Peter 5:6-7: "Humble yourselves under the mighty hand of God, that in due time He may exalt you. Cast all your anxieties upon Him, for He cares about you."

In the second place, we should note how wonderfully God plans this opportunity. Just as He promised above (Gen. 12:2-3): "I will make your name great, you shall be blessed, and a blessing," so here the promise is proved in fact. Abraham becomes known at the king's palace. The king learns that he is the object of God's care, and without doubt he himself is also blessed through Abraham; that is, he comes to the knowledge of God. For in this passage the Holy Spirit reveals merely the beginning of the conversation, which surely was somewhat stormy. The king appears to be greatly agitated when he realizes that he has been deceived by a foreigner in this manner.

But when Abraham pointed out the reasons for his plan, he no doubt preached to the king about God, about the promise given to him, and about the future Seed, and thus quieted the king's anger.

These events appear to be the prelude to future occurrences. Just as in this instance a Pharaoh who fears God lets Abraham go in order that he may not suffer additional plagues, so later on in Egypt an entire people was let go by a godless Pharaoh who did not fear God — not in a kindly manner but because of his fear of more serious perils.

Hence these are not gentle words: "What is this you have done to me?" He is laying stress on the circumstances; he points out that he is a king, but that Abraham is a guest. The king no doubt resented very much being deceived by his guest and being exposed with his people to such great misfortunes; and if God had not mercifully intervened, this would have meant Abraham's death. For kings are not inclined to put up with disrespect, and it was easy to interpret this fraud as disrespect.

But the king's wrath is mollified by the speech of Abraham. He points out the reasons for his plan, in order that the king may realize that he himself had provided the occasion for this lie by his tyranny; for if it had been safe to tell the actual situation, Abraham would surely not have lied. But now, when he decides on a white lie for his own safety, he reveals that telling the truth would have involved a definite danger.

It is a common sin of kings that they often become tyrannical and too harsh when they try to strengthen their authority, and many evils in government are the result.

Augustine relates that a certain prefect of Antioch — more in order to frighten the rest of the citizens than because the situation required it — imprisoned a certain citizen and fixed a large sum of money for his release. While the prisoner's wife rushes about anxiously and is worried about getting the money together, she meets a certain very rich citizen. He promises her the sum of money on condition that she will gratify his desire, for she was an exceptionally beautiful woman. Under the pressure of necessity she lays the entire matter before her imprisoned husband; and on his advice and urging — for he was eager to be freed from prison — she accepts the condition. When the rich man has satisfied his lust, he sends the woman away as he gives her a sack filled, not with gold but with sand. When the woman sees that she has been deceived, she discloses the entire affair to the prefect. Then the prefect, highly indignant at the deed, acknowledges that the occasion for this sin was given by his unwarranted verdict when he made too severe a use of his rank; and he says: "This is my sin." He immediately lets the imprisoned husband go without cost and presents to him all the wealth of the rich man who had deceived the poor woman.[87]

That is the way of kings and princes. Because they are accustomed to tyranny, they often sin; but these sins are hidden, since they result from the customary exercise of tyranny. The magistrates neither see them nor pay any attention to them; they suppose that these sins are the rewards of their power. Eventually, however, God brings the sins to light and punishes them severely, as we observe here in the instance of Pharaoh.

Hence this passage helps us to maintain that we all are full of sins, but especially the kings, princes, and other, lower officials. Either they are in the habit of winking at the sins of their subjects and of neglecting their duty, or they misuse their power and act too harshly to safeguard their prestige. Even though God should overlook these public sins for a time, nevertheless, as I have said, He is wont to punish them and bring them to light in the end.

So far as Abraham is concerned, Pharaoh was completely innocent; for the sin he committed, he committed because he was misled by Abraham. But he was not innocent before God. Therefore God punishes him and thus teaches him — yes, even compels him — to fear God and henceforth not to live by his emotions but to do his duty. And it is his duty to frighten the wicked, but to protect the good (Rom. 13:3).

But now he acts in an entirely different way, for he rules in such a manner that Abraham is compelled to fear the utmost danger and does not consider himself safe if he should tell the truth.

Magistrates are commonly guilty of such sins, and God is wont to punish these sins in various ways. Therefore earnest prayers must be offered for the magistrates, that God may not permit them to go astray but may guide them to do their duty. For, if they neglect this, there will be no end to the punishment that God is compelled to inflict, lest their sins become a habit and wicked men make

---

[87] Luther is referring to the case of Septimius Acindynus, as narrated in Augustine's *The Lord's Sermon on the Mount*, Book I, ch. 50.

a virtue out of a vice. Even Seneca states: "Where vices become the custom, there is no remedy." [88]

Such was Rome at that time, and it is the same now; for nothing is regarded as shameful there except theft and beggary.

In the management of the home the heads of the household also sin often, although they are neither evil nor aware of their sins. Spouses encounter various adversities whose cause they do not know. No government is without sin; so great is the weakness of the human hearts. If David and other godly kings and princes frequently sinned in managing public affairs, is it any wonder that those men transgress who are not ruled by the Holy Spirit but yield to their own desires?

Sometimes the profligacy of the subjects is so great that they require strict discipline and severe punishments. King Matthias of Hungary was aware of this; but when he governed his people with a harsh rule, he often lapsed into tyrannical cruelty, although he was both learned and rather humane, and not a bad ruler.[89]

Examples like this teach us that human affairs are such that unless God guides magistrates with extraordinary kindness, they cannot retain their rule without committing serious sins. For this reason sundry and severe punishments afflict governments and commonwealths.

But the fathers enumerate other causes of afflictions.[90] Sometimes God sends punishments, not because He finds in the man a sin that deserves such a punishment but because He wants to test his faith and patience.

Job did not deserve such punishments by his life; for he was God-fearing, guileless, and virtuous. And yet he is most painfully scourged by Satan with the Lord's permission, in order to test his faith and perseverance. For the Lord tells Satan (Job 2:3): "You moved Me against him, to destroy him without cause."

It tends to instruct and comfort us when we learn that God often causes even the innocent to experience the most serious misfortunes and punishments, merely in order to test them. When faint hearts feel the punishments, they immediately think of sin, and believe that these are punishments for sin. But one must maintain that the godly experience many evils, solely in order that they may be tested.

[88] Seneca, *Epistles*, 39.
[89] Cf. *Luther's Works*, 13, p. 172, note 38.
[90] One such discussion is in Augustine, *The City of God*, Book I, chs. 28—29.

Thus the Lord says of His people in Jer. 49:12: "If those who did not deserve to drink the cup must drink it, will you go unpunished?" Even though Daniel and his companions endured the captivity among the heathen, nevertheless they had not deserved the captivity because of their sins, as the others had.

Similarly, in the revolt of the peasants many very fine men perished, not because they were just as guilty as the rebels but because they were among the rebels.[91] For disasters never occur among a people without also affecting the godly. These are being tested, but the others are being judged.

Then, too, the godly are often afflicted, not because their sins deserve it or because they are being tested, but in order that they may be kept humble and may not be puffed up on account of their gifts. Thus Paul says about himself that a thorn in the flesh was given to him to keep him from becoming conceited because of his extraordinary revelations. "An angel of Satan," says he, "beats me with his fist that I may not exalt myself" (2 Cor. 12:7). It is as though he were saying: "Because of my superb gifts I might rate myself above all the other apostles and perhaps look down upon them; but God is curing this evil with that thorn of Satan, to show me that I am nothing and to cause me to humble myself."

This is also the reason why the church, which God has endowed with the most excellent gifts of the forgiveness of sins, the Holy Spirit, and eternal life, experiences such manifold dangers and misfortunes. If it enjoyed these gifts without affliction, it would become proud and boastful.

Thus you may observe that frequently a pious and godly person is afflicted with a variety of perils and misfortunes in quick succession, when, on the other hand, for the wicked and ungodly everything turns out in accordance with their heart's desire.

This inequitable state of affairs often gives rise to resentment in the saints. But if you consider the situation rightly, you are enduring these hardships for your own great good; for if you had no affliction, you would become proud and would be condemned. Now when God ties want, scorn, sickness, a vexatious wife, and disobedient children to your neck like a heavy stone, you are not what the Greeks call ὑπερήφανος or proud; but you take it patiently, and you do not look down upon those who are less gifted than you. These discussions

---

[91] Luther is speaking of the Peasants' War of 1525.

about the causes of misfortunes are profitable, for they supply not only knowledge but comfort as well.

The fourth reason for punishments or misfortunes is this, that we may be cleansed or improved. Thus because Mary Magdalene is leading an impure life, she is afflicted with seven evil spirits (Luke 8:2), in order that she may be compelled to repent and lead a better life. In Prov. 22:15 Solomon states: "Folly is bound up in the heart of a child, but the rod of discipline drives it far from him." And Isaiah (28:19) says: "Trouble produces understanding."

The fifth cause is that amazing procedure by which God does nothing that does not reveal His glory and majesty.

Thus when the apostles raised a question about the man who was born blind (John 9:1), Jesus declares that neither he himself nor his parents had sinned, but that this had happened in order that the glory of God might be revealed, that is, that Christ through this miracle might show Himself to be the Son of God and might invite more men to faith and the knowledge of God.

It would not be out of place to assign the account before us to this category. For it is clear that on the occasion of divinely inflicted punishments the king came to the knowledge of God and of the true religion. But this result is incidental; for the text points out the true reason for these punishments when it says "on account of the affair of Sarai," that is, that God brought on these punishments because the king had taken Sarah away.

In this way the holy fathers, especially Augustine and Bernard, debate about punishments and misfortunes.[92] For they observe that innocent Job is tested, that Paul is turned back and humbled, and that Magdalene is cleansed or invited to repent, but that in the case of the blind man nothing more is involved than that God may manifest His glory.

Even though these are various kinds of trials, they are nevertheless a fatherly chastisement and not a rod of wrath such as we see in the instance of Herod and other wicked men, who are afflicted with horrible punishments, upon which eternal death and damnation still follow later on.

Against this wrath the prophet prays when he says (Ps. 6:1): "O Lord, rebuke me not in Thy anger, nor chasten me in Thy wrath"; as if to say: "Rebuke me, I have no objection; I shall also gladly

---

[92] See note 90 above.

bear it that Thou dost chasten me, provided only that there be no wrath and anger."

Thus Jeremiah prays for himself and for his people (10:24): "Correct me, O Lord, but in just measure; not in Thy anger, lest Thou bring me to nothing." He distinguishes wrath from the judgment by which we are cleansed and improved, but with restraint and for our own good.

More reasons that lead God to visit us could be assembled. We sin continually, and for this reason we foster and nourish original sin, the wages of which is death (Rom. 6:23). But God remits this eternal punishment to those who believe and commutes it into such punishments as I have mentioned, which are part of this present life only and benefit us because they test us or make us humble, improve us, or give luster to the glory of God. Let us, therefore, bear them with patience and even give thanks to the merciful God who is chastising us with good judgment and not in anger, that we may persevere in the fear of God and be saved.

20. *And Pharaoh gave men orders concerning him; and they set him on the way, with his wife and all that he had.*

This sudden dismissal and the added protection prove that Pharaoh was greatly frightened by those plagues. He realizes the likelihood that the foreigner Abraham may be harmed by his people. Moreover, because he realizes that the seizure of Abraham's wife was punished by God, he fears similar punishment if Abraham should be harmed by anyone of his people. Therefore he orders him to leave Egypt with his possessions, and he adds an escort, lest Abraham meet with some mishap on the journey.

Thus you see that God is the protector of those who place their hope in Him. He tests their faith and permits it to be tried, but He does not abandon them; indeed, eventually He gloriously delivers His own, and with great benefit to others.

It was a severe trial for Abraham to be deprived of his wife. But what advantages followed upon this trial! The king is brought to the knowledge of God. Therefore he fears God and humbles himself. Abraham, however, not only suffers no harm but is even sent away with great honor and with a royal escort.

Hence Abraham's faith, which before this had been somewhat troubled, is strengthened. It would have been enough for him if he alone were being sent away unharmed; but now he is sent away well enriched, with all his domestics, and he is provided with a public guard. He would hardly have dared wish for this honor.

But in this way God shows that all those who have their hope fixed on His mercy are the objects of His care. Therefore let us also learn to obey God and to bear patiently whatever He plans for us, with a sure faith and with the hope of a glorious deliverance, which we shall surely experience in the end. For this is why the Holy Spirit has recorded this outstanding account for us, that in patience and hope we may work out our salvation. Amen.

CHAPTER THIRTEEN

1. *And so Abram went up from Egypt, he and his wife, and all that he had, and Lot with him, into the Negeb.*

AT the beginning of this chapter the geography causes some confusion. Abram is in Egypt, and he is returning to the land of Canaan. Therefore the question is asked how it may be said that he set out toward the south,[1] when Canaan is located toward the north. But the answer is easy: Moses is not speaking of the journey; he is speaking of Abraham's abode, namely, that when he returned from Egypt, he stopped in the southern part of the land of Canaan and carefully avoided the places that were rather close to the land from which he had gone out. Consequently, this little section, too, serves as an example of his patience and endurance, or rather of his utterly confident faith in the promise. For the holy man remained unwearied by so many migrations and clung with a firm faith to the promise concerning his descendants, who would possess the land of Canaan.

2. *Now Abram was very rich in cattle, in silver, and in gold.*

Strictly speaking the word כָּבֵד does not mean rich; it means heavy and weighed down with burdens. Moses mentions three kinds of wealth: cattle, silver, and gold. The word מִקְנֶה is derived from the verb קָנָה, which means to acquire, to purchase, to possess. But מִקְנֶה is commonly used for cattle, as below in chapter 46:32, where Joseph instructs his brothers and his father that when the king would inquire about their occupation, they should answer that they were men of מִקְנֶה, cattle. And in Ex. 12:38 occurs: "Sheep, oxen, and small cattle."

Jerome translates this word with "animals of various kinds"[2] and thus makes it a generic term including the smaller quadrupeds, which the Latins usually call a flock.

Here, too, Abraham's great faith is praised. Although he was weighed down with a large number of domestics and had with him

---

[1] Where we have "the Negeb," Luther has "the south."
[2] The Vulgate reads: *Erat autem dives valde in possessione auri et argenti.*

[324]

flocks and cattle, he was nevertheless able to bear so many migrations. No doubt the gold and silver were gifts of the king, with which God, in His marvelous counsel, alleviated his long exile.

Here Moses mentions for the first time that Abraham was very rich and well supplied with gold and silver. This is comforting to exiles and strangers. For sometimes God is wont to pursue such a course and even in the midst of misfortunes to enrich His own with temporal goods.

If there were perpetual struggles and perplexities when trials come, and no intervals of comfort, faith would be shaken. For this reason God sometimes allows us a breathing spell and assuages cares and misery with some comfort, just as we use a potion or spices to revive those who are exhausted by trouble or grief and to keep them from dying.

We should keep this example in mind in our perils, that we may bear patiently the adversities facing us and wait for comfort in faith. God is faithful, and with the trial He provides also an escape (1 Cor. 10:13). Of course, the real deliverance takes place only when we are rid of this flesh and leave this life.

But prior to this perfect deliverance He often comforts our troubled hearts, granting also earthly advantages, which prove both that God does not forget His own and that the rewards of godliness are sure. Just as it was a great trial that Sarah was taken away from Abram by this powerful king, so it is also an extraordinary comfort that nothing untoward happens to Sarah and that Pharaoh sends Abraham away with rich presents and wealth.

The philosophers and the monks have often found fault with this passage and have wondered why the Holy Spirit records that Abraham was rich or greatly encumbered with the possession of cattle, silver, and gold. Both arrive at the opinion that so holy a man should not have had any wealth but should have lived in poverty, as befits someone who has put all his hope in the mercy of the one and only God, especially since he was an exile.

But let us remember that these things were written, not for the sake of Abraham but, as Paul says in Rom. 15:4 and in 2 Tim. 3:16, for our instruction, reproof, and comfort; for the Holy Spirit saw the monstrous thoughts of men about godliness, thoughts which were not only brought into the church in our age by the monks and the Anabaptists but have been there in every age.

The philosophers indeed believed that they would achieve a great reputation if they disposed of their money and called themselves beggars. The monks did the same thing, and they were even more harmful nuisances because they taught that such beggary was an act of worship toward God. The Anabaptists, too, think that those who have any possessions of their own are not Christians.

But the Jews are the greater scoundrels. They misuse these and similar statements of Scripture in defense of their greed and usury, as though Abraham had gained such great wealth among the heathen by exacting interest. And it is not surprising if they misuse the example of the holy patriarch, for from the Messiah Himself they expect nothing else than wealth and power. Thus foolish people err in both directions — some by their excessive abstinence, others by their excessive acquisitiveness.

All this proves the extreme ignorance of the human mind, which lacks the knowledge not only of God but even of creatures. The philosopher Crates discards his wealth, Epictetus goes begging, and the Stoics do not permit wealth to be called a good thing.[3]

Why is this? It is because they observe that through the use of wealth men generally become worse. Therefore they suppose that it would be advisable for them to condemn wealth and refrain from it altogether. It was the same with the monks. Because they saw that many people were occupied with the cares of this world, they considered themselves safe from this evil if they gave up everything, entered monasteries, and refrained from all secular activities.

Moreover, this opinion was strengthened because they used to teach in the churches that man has an upright will; therefore everybody concluded that there was no danger whatever if these stimulants to evil had been removed.

But, as I have said, it is the utmost blindness and the most execrable ignorance that they transferred human faults from man to creatures, which in themselves are good and are gifts of God. One must distinguish between the thing possessed and the possessor. The thing possessed is as God created it, but the possessor is different from the way he was created by God. Hence the fault lies not in the thing but in the possessor. This the stupid people did not see.

They taught that it was chastity if one avoided any association

---

[3] Crates (*ca.* 365—285 B. C.) was a Cynic philosopher; Epictetus (*ca.* A. D. 55—135) was a Stoic philosopher.

with girls and women. Thus they wanted to provide a remedy by depriving themselves of things, and they were misled by the false principle that man is good and that his natural powers are perfect; but they learned from actual experience that they were never less chaste than when they were alone and without women.

I do not think that Francis was an evil man; but the facts prove that he was naive or, to state it more truthfully, foolish.[4] He establishes the law or rule that his followers should live according to the Gospel. But he maintains that it is the most perfect rule of the Gospel to sell everything and give it to the poor. Since he proposes this to others as the heart of the Gospel, shall we not consign him to the foolish philosophers who refused to have wealth rather than let him remain among Christians?

The Gospel gives us instruction about greater things, namely, that we should acknowledge our sins and hope for forgiveness of sins through the merit of Christ. This the good father does not see; and he thinks that the Gospel sets forth a new law, like the one in Plato's *Republic*, about selling things you possess. Yet with what great approval the world accepted his teaching! If the account is true, Francis begged for bread and other necessities of life, and then distributed them among the poor. But look closely at his successors. Did they not look out for themselves and for their kitchen rather well?

John XXIII did not condemn the Franciscans with the intention we have.[5] He decreed by a public edict that those who maintained that Christ and His disciples had no possessions of their own were heretical and obdurate. He raged cruelly against the Paupers of Lyons, who professed that they were imitating the poverty of Christ; and many of them he burned.[6]

He saw that the power and the wealth of the popes would give rise not only to envy and hate but also to a reputation for ungodliness if those people who had no possessions were considered to be living a holy life. And these Paupers of Lyons did publicly censure the popes and declare that it was not fitting for them to keep their wealth.

[4] Luther often spoke this way of Francis; cf. *Luther's Works*, 22, pp. 50—52.

[5] John XXIII was one of the popes at the time of the Council of Constance; he ruled 1410—15 and is usually counted as an antipope today. Probably Luther means Pope John XXII, who had condemned the heresy on poverty in 1323.

[6] A reference to the Waldensians, who were attacked by the Inquisition in the thirteenth century.

John XXIII, therefore, defended the possession of wealth and condemned the mendicants, but with an intention different from ours. He was not concerned with religion, but he did not want to be considered less holy just because he was wealthy.

When he raged against the people of Lyons in such a fashion, the Franciscans recognized their danger. Therefore they did not find fault with the pope's greed; but, as the proverb says, they scratched each other like mules.[7] They praised the popes, and the popes, in turn, praised them.

These stories in Scripture are a useful antidote against errors of this kind. For they teach that the fault does not lie in those things that are good and are truly gifts of God but in the human beings who possess them and make use of them.

Therefore he is not only a philosopher but also a good theologian who does not condemn the things that God has given but condemns their use or control. Thus the psalm states (62:10): "If riches increase, set not your heart on them"; as if to say: "Riches are good; therefore be concerned about your heart that it may not be evil." It is likewise not evil to look at a woman, for woman is a good creature of God; but the fault is in your heart, because it desires a woman who is not yours.

Therefore the monks, who shun the sight of a woman in order to preserve their chastity and who shut themselves up in monasteries, burn with lust even more when they are alone, because they have unclean hearts. It is not a real cure for lust if you avoid the sight of a woman; nor will you cure a vice by refraining from things, but by controlling and using them, as experience teaches. For, when a girl is denied to them, this makes men crazy; but when she is granted to them, they become tired of her.

Strive, therefore, to become pious first and to approach the use of things with a clean heart; in the things themselves there is no fault. But because people do not do this, they are like the moron who did not stand straight in the sunlight and then became very indignant because he saw that his shadow was crooked.

Thus people do not see that the fault lies in themselves. Hence when they try to refrain from the use of things, they become more inflamed than those who have the things and make use of them.

Eyes, feet, and hands are gifts of God; and so, if you become in-

---

[7] *Mutuum muli scabunt* was the title of a satire by Varro.

flamed when you look at a girl, it is not the fault of your eyes; your heart is to blame. Therefore would it not be the utmost folly if you wanted to pluck out your eyes, so that after this you could not look at a girl? For in this manner the heart is not cured but becomes ten times more inflamed. As the poet says: "We strive for what is forbidden, and we always desire what is denied." [8]

Let us, therefore, reject those monkish and foolish ideas. When we are called either to the management of human affairs or to marriage, let us not think that there is anything evil in the management or in the use of things; if there is any fault, it is in the heart. Let us see to it that the heart is right. Then everything will be right.

Great philosophers have considered it a praise of their wisdom if they kept away from holding public office; but Aristotle's conclusion is more correct when he says: "The office reveals the man." [9] The common saying is well known: "A solitary man is either a beast or a god." [10] But the minor premise must be added: He cannot be a god; and the perfect conclusion is that a solitary man must of necessity be a beast.

Thus Paul says in 1 Corinthians,[11] with reference to the enjoyment of things created by God, that they are not to be rejected or shunned, just as in this passage the Holy Spirit declares about Abraham that he was very rich in cattle, silver, and gold.

If it were a virtue to cast possessions away and to be a beggar, Abraham would be praised without deserving it. But now he keeps on managing and using his possessions, and his special effort is to keep his heart pure. He does not become proud because of his wealth and does not gain and preserve it in a greedy manner; but he is generous and hospitable, as the accounts that appear below show.

Thus since he himself is without faults, his use of his possessions is godly, holy, and faithful. You should do the same thing, whether you are in the married state, in public office, or in another situation. Then you will make good use of your possessions — wife, children, prestige, and other things; for they are good in themselves, like your eyes, ears, tongue, and limbs, which were created and given to you by God.

[8] Ovid, *Ars amandi*, III, 4, 17.
[9] Cf. Aristotle, *Politics*, Book I, ch. 2.
[10] The usual form of the proverb is *Homo solus aut deus aut daemon.*
[11] Presumably a reference to 1 Cor. 8.

It was a famous maxim, not only in the schools of the philosophers but also among the theologians: "What is outside us does not concern us." [12] Money and similar things are outside us; hence they do not concern us.

This sophistry sounds good, but it is harmful and ungodly. You must rather say: "The things that are outside us concern us very much." For God said (Gen. 1:28): "Have dominion over the fish of the sea and over the birds of the air and over the earth with everything that it contains." Among these gifts are also gold and silver. Make use of these, but in such a way that your heart is good, that is, without greed and without harm to anyone else.

In the first place, provide for the livelihood of the people of your household, "so that you may not be worse than a heathen" (1 Tim. 5:8). In the second place, use these things for the advantage of others. Be on your guard, as against a plague that is sure to occur, lest, like foolish Crates, you throw your possessions away or, like Epictetus and the Stoics, do not consider them good and useful. Instead, you should recognize that these gifts are not only good but also honorable, and that they were created by God to be delectable and to lessen somewhat the discomforts of the saints, just as we hear about Abram in this passage.

It is objected, however, that this was valid in the Old Testament but that in the New Testament Christ and the apostles taught differently. For Christ says (Matt. 19:21): "Sell what you possess, and give to the poor"; and also (Matt. 5:3, 6): "Blessed are the poor in spirit. Blessed are those who hunger and thirst." And Paul says (2 Cor. 6:10): "As having nothing." These are the arguments of the mendicants and of those who profess poverty. With these arguments they deceive themselves and others; for truly they are empty sophisms, not proofs.

Even though one maintains that Christ was poor, still He had a moneybag, of which Judas had charge; and from this it follows that He had something of His own, and that He made use of His own means.

Furthermore, if this is sure about Christ, who is the Head and Lord of everything, what new thing is poor Francis trying by being so intent on possessing nothing that he forbids his followers even to touch money? Meanwhile, however, he permits the use of other things;

---

[12] *Quae extra nos, nihil ad nos.*

and when an abundance of these is available, it is no great discomfort or inconvenience for us to do without money.

But why say a great deal? Both the foolishness and the hypocrisy of this attitude deserve censure. Someone has said rather wittily, that he wonders what kind of human beings these are who do not touch money; for they are the enemies either of God or of the government or of both — of God, because they refuse to have anything to do with His creature; of the government, because they loathe the likenesses of the princes on the money most of all, since they are not averse to touching golden chalices and silver images. Who does not see this foolish error? And yet they have fooled the entire world with their deceit.

These examples exhort us to hold fast to the Word with even greater zeal, for it is the only way to avoid being taken in by such deception. Why should we prefer Francis to Abraham? Is it because Francis refrains from the use of money? But Abraham, as Moses expresses it, "is weighed down with silver and gold." If silver and gold are things evil in themselves, then those who keep away from them deserve to be praised. But if they are good creatures of God, which we can use both for the needs of our neighbor and for the glory of God, is not a person silly, yes, even unthankful to God, if he refrains from them as though they were evil? For they are not evil, even though they have been subjected to vanity and evil.

As for you, reform your mind, and use these things with a sincere heart. If God has given you wealth, give thanks to God, and see that you make the right use of it; if He has not given it, do not seek it greedily. Have patience, and trust God to give you daily bread; and beware of those pernicious ideas of the monks, lest you judge or condemn those whom God has abundantly blessed. For Christ has not forbidden the use of His creatures; He wants us to control our emotions.

Our teacher is the Spirit; and He Himself [13] also possesses something as His own, as the evangelists bear witness when they state that to Judas was assigned the duty of handling the money. Paul, too, worked with his hands, in order to support himself with his own means and not with someone else's. So away with the false piety of the monks and their foolish hypocrisy!

[13] The syntax of this sentence is unclear, but the thought is clear; the *ipse* here seems to refer to the Holy Spirit, but actually it means Christ.

3. *And he journeyed on from the Negeb as far as Bethel, to the place where his tent had been at the beginning, between Bethel and Ai.*

Moses reveals that Abraham did not remain in the same place, but that he had several encampments. Because at least six or seven patriarchs were living at that time,[14] it is likely that they also had gone to the same area and that Abraham stayed with each for a while. For the Hebrew text indicates that Abraham changed his encampments in quick succession and thus eventually turned aside toward Bethel.

וַיֵּלֶךְ לְמַסָּעָיו: and he went according to or in conformity with his stations; that is, after repeatedly changing his abode he finally came to Bethel. And there is no doubt that on this occasion many of the Canaanites came to a knowledge of God and embraced the true religion.

4. *To the place where he had made an altar at the first; and there Abram preached the name of the Lord.*

In the Hebrew there is a clear difference between these two: to call *on* the name of the Lord and to call *in* the name of the Lord. The first is used for what we express by "to seek something from God," to ask of God through prayer, etc. But in its strict sense to call *in* the name of the Lord is to preach, teach, read, and whatever else there is that pertains to the ministry of teaching. When Moses states here that at this place Abram called *in* the name of the Lord, it is the same as if he said that he erected a public chapel or an altar, at which he preached and taught about the true religion — mainly, of course, to his household but then also to the neighboring Canaanites who came together at this place.

Even though that entire generation in general[15] had been cursed and separated from the godly, nevertheless on repeated occasions there were some who received the Word. Hence Abraham was a priest and prophet of God; he chose a definite place at which to teach, pray, and sacrifice.

These are the proper duties of a priest; by the grace of God we also assume them, in order that among us there may be established a church for God. For these forms of worship must continue

[14] Cf. *Luther the Expositor,* p. 103.
[15] See p. 177.

from the beginning of the world until its end, even though in the perversion of morals toward the end of the world very few will observe them.

So much for the difference between calling *on* the Lord and calling *in the name of* the Lord. If someone should maintain that they mean the same thing, I shall not quarrel with him; for by their nature preaching and prayer are connected with each other. It is impossible to pray unless one has first instructed the people concerning God. In fact, you will never pray successfully in private unless you have preached to yourself either the Creed or some other passage of Scripture that draws your attention to the goodness of God as the One who has not only commanded you to pray but has also added the promise that He will hear you.[16] Through this private sermon, which you direct to yourself, your heart is impelled to pray.

The same thing takes place publicly in our churches. We have no silent forms of worship,[17] but the voice of the Gospel is always heard. Through it men are taught about the will of God. And to the sermons we add prayers or thanksgivings.

Similarly in 1 Cor. 14 [18] Paul desires that the churches should first be taught and exhorted. Then thanksgiving or prayer may properly follow.

Zechariah (12:10) promises that the Lord will pour out the Spirit of grace and of supplication. It is the Spirit of grace who gives instruction concerning the will of God and incites men to faith by praising the mercy of God. The Spirit of prayer follows Him, for those who know that God is reconciled and propitious call upon Him in danger with a firm hope of deliverance. Thus preaching and prayer are always together.

Moreover, Abraham is praised in this passage because he did these things, not in some corner — for fear of the threats or the violence of the heathen — but in a public place, in order that by his own example and that of his people he might lead others to the knowledge of God and to true forms of worship.

Perhaps this altar was near some freestanding oak or on a small hill under the open sky, and was covered with an Arabian tent, with-

---

[16] Cf. p. 16, note 25.

[17] Luther is referring to the *Stillmesse* in the canon of the Mass, against which he had written in 1525 (W, XVIII, 22—36).

[18] Apparently a reference to 1 Cor. 14:13.

out any adornment — a plain church, not a beautiful one if you consider its equipment, but most attractive because of the preaching and the sincere prayer.

Today we see that the churches are royally adorned. But, O God, what kind of preaching goes on in them! What kind of prayer! You hear the doctrine of Satan, not that of Christ. Nothing is proclaimed there except lies, and the prayer is downright blasphemy.

Thus the German proverb is true: *Finstere Kirchen und liechte herzen.* Somber churches and illuminated hearts commonly go together. Such was the church of Abraham, in which was heard the voice of God and true worship. But look at the churches; they are often resplendent, but the hearts are gloomy or even blind.

Thus it is not the stones, the construction, and the gorgeous silver and gold that make a church beautiful and holy; it is the Word of God and sound preaching. For where the goodness of God is commended to men and hearts are encouraged to put their trust in Him and to call upon God in danger, there is truly a holy church. Whether it is a dark nook or a bare hill or a barren tree, it is truthfully and correctly called a house of God and a gate of heaven, even though it is without a roof, under the clouds and the open sky.

Therefore one must pay primary attention to the character of the teaching and prayer, not to the character of the building. What God demands is that people be converted and He be glorified, but this is achieved solely through the Word and prayer.

When Abraham spoke the Word here, he undoubtedly experienced the troubles that accompany it. For Satan, the adversary of Christ, was alive at that time too. Therefore he plagued Abraham with the countless evils that usually follow the Word — persecution, hatred, contempt, antipathy, and countless perils. These rewards of his godliness Abraham surely endured. Even though they are not recorded, we know that the nature of the Word is such that wherever it is taught, the prince of the world is infuriated.

These are the two principal effects the Word brings about: it glorifies God, and it judges and condemns the prince of the world together with the flesh and sin. From the fate of the Word one can easily understand Abraham's experience in his office as bishop. But since he was chosen by God to be a bishop, he had God as his Protector against the raging of Satan and the world.

5. *And Lot, who went with Abram, also had flocks and herds and tents,*

6. *so that the land could not support both of them dwelling together; for their possessions were so great that they could not dwell together,*

7. *and there was strife between the herdsmen of Abram's cattle and the herdsmen of Lot's cattle. At that time the Canaanites and the Perizzites dwelt in the land.*

After the divine worship and the instruction in religion and faith toward God, which must always be the main topic, there follows a second most important topic and a very fine example both of love toward one's neighbor and of patience.

It was no minor matter that in the midst of strange nations Abram is compelled by necessity to separate from a very faithful companion and very dear nephew. A faithful friend is a great boon and a precious treasure in any situation of life, not only because of common dangers in which he can be both an aid and a comfort but also because of spiritual trials.

Even if one's heart is well grounded by the Holy Spirit, it remains a great advantage to have a brother with whom one can converse about religion and from whom one can hear words of comfort.

When Abraham is deprived of his nephew, with whom he has lived in exile among the heathen for so long, and loses one who has shared so many trials and dangers, who would not consider this a heavy cross and a great evil? I for my part consider the loss of all my possessions less important than that of a faithful friend.

When Christ was wrestling with temptation in the garden (Matt. 26:37 ff.), we see Him seeking comfort among His three disciples. When Paul, in Acts 28:15, saw the brethren coming to meet him, he took courage from the sight and experienced comfort. Loneliness distresses a person who is solitary and deprived of his intimate friends. He can exert himself and struggle against it, but he does not overcome it without great difficulty.

Everything is less burdensome if you have a brother with you; for then the promise applies (Matt. 18:20): "Where two or three are gathered in My name, there am I in the midst of them." Therefore solitude should be shunned and the companionship of familiar people sought, especially in spiritual perils.

The text gives three reasons for this separation of Lot and Abram. The first is that because of the large number of sheep and cattle the land was unable to support the two together. By his departure Abram did not want to deprive his nephew of anything but wanted to look out for Lot's advantage.

The second is that the Canaanites and Perizzites dwelt in the land. Since they were in power, the exiles were not permitted to extend their territory to suit their needs but had to be satisfied with the boundaries the masters of that area had defined.

Because of the promise Abram was indeed the real lord of that entire region; but he calmly puts up with the domination of the heathen and waits patiently until God would drive them out. He does not make use of his right; nor does he seize possession by stirring up a rebellion or a war, as someone else would perhaps have done. The holy man calmly puts up with this inequity, tolerates the hostile and unjust domination, and himself remains an exile and sojourner. Let us endeavor to imitate this example.

The third reason is the strife that arose among the herdsmen. Nobody should doubt that both masters often tried to put an end to it. But their efforts were in vain. The servants remain stubborn; and once they have begun to hate, they do not permit that hatred to be sated or blotted out.

This, too, was a just cause for separating. If the mutual hatred of the domestics is such that it cannot be dispelled, it eventually spreads to the masters and affects them; for on the master rests the obligation to defend his people against the violent acts of others.

Thus there were weighty reasons why Abram and Lot separated, and Scripture mentions them to keep us from supposing that this parting of relatives occurred as the result of insignificant events. Nothing sadder could happen to Abram, but he yields to necessity in order to avoid even greater unpleasantness.

But let us also take notice of the law of love and of unity. Abram was Lot's uncle; he was the older; he had greater prestige because of the promise. In addition, he was a priest and prophet of the Lord, and he lacked nothing whatever so far as prestige and authority were concerned. And yet, disregarding all this, he yields his right and puts himself on the same level with his nephew,[19] who was far be-

---

[19] The text of all editions has *avunculo* here, but the obvious intention is *nepoti;* we have translated accordingly.

neath him in age, prestige, influence, and position. Is this not what Christ commands in John 13:15 ff., that he who is the greater should be as the lesser and as the servant of the others? [20]

Abram could have prevailed by reason of his authority and right, and have said: "I am the older. To me the promise has been given and the inheritance of this entire land; to you it has not been given. Even though we are both sojourners now, nevertheless because of the promise I can demand for myself the part I want. Therefore you and your people must look for another place; I and my people shall remain here." It was completely within Abram's right to say this to his nephew and to stay where he was. Abram surely had the right to do this, but he yields his right. Thus he gives us a most profitable example for preserving unity when he avoids the famous dictum: "Extreme justice is extreme injustice." [21] For Moses' account is as follows.

8. *Then Abram said to Lot: Let there be no strife between you and me, and between your herdsmen and my herdsmen; for we are kinsmen.*

9. *Is not the whole land before you? Separate yourself from me. If you take the left hand, then I will go to the right; or if you take the right hand, then I will go to the left.*

What could Abram have said that was more proper and more conducive to peace? He puts himself on the same level with Lot and says: "Behold, we are kinsmen." Next he even lowers himself beneath Lot by letting him have the choice of where he would most like to go. Thus the uncle yields to the nephew, the older to the younger, the prophet and priest of God to the pupil — and all this to keep their love from being destroyed and to avoid giving occasion for strife.

This account is worthy of our careful attention, for it teaches how all laws and rights are to be dealt with. The purpose of all earthly laws is peace, harmony, and quiet, or, as we theologians express it, love. Whoever does not direct the laws to this end, or understands them in a different manner, is greatly in error. Thus we see that today the misuse of the laws is very great.

[20] Despite the reference to John 13 the words quoted are from the Synoptic Gospels, Matt. 20:26-27 and its parallels.

[21] This adage is quoted in Cicero, *On Duties,* Book I, ch. 10.

Because the whole world is engrossed in ambition and is profoundly wise, there is no place for love; jealousies, dissensions, and wars abound everywhere. Even though you do what Abram did for Lot and yield your right, yet peace cannot be maintained, not even if you should bear wrongs and disregard them. So corrupt and wicked is the world! It does not deserve this sacred teaching.

Nevertheless, the pious must be taught and admonished diligently. After they have come to know God and have begun to believe, they must also learn how to conduct themselves toward their brethren, so that, following the example of Abram, they may yield their right. For the purpose of all laws is love and peace. To this end all rights and all laws, of whatever kind they are, must be directed, although, of course, human laws are not to be put on a par with the laws of God in every respect.

God's promise and the Sacraments allow no suspension; for they are deeds and words of God directed toward us. He Himself wants to perform them if we accept them. Therefore it is a sin to dispense with or modify something in them or to change them, as the pope did when he withheld the chalice in the Lord's Supper.

But since the purpose of earthly laws is love, they must be invoked in such a manner that no offense is committed against love and, as Abram says in this passage, that there be no strife. Abram remains Lot's most affectionate uncle; and Lot, in turn, remains Abram's very dear nephew. But where the public peace is in danger, let love be the queen and teacher who moderates the laws and modifies them with a view toward lessening their severity.

This modification calls for courageous and extraordinary men. As we can see, the teachers of the law do not debate according to love; but everywhere they stress the utmost justice and the letter of the law, as they term it. Hence they do not deserve to acquire this godly knowledge. But in the church let hearts be taught not to stress our rights so rigorously, but to moderate the laws in accordance with what appears to be beneficial to the community.

Let me add an example. The Carthusians have a law that they should not eat meat throughout their entire life.[22] Now if one of them became sick, and his physical condition [23] (as the physicians

---

[22] Carthusians are not allowed to eat meat at all, and on Fridays they are forbidden milk products.

[23] The Latin word here is *complexio*.

call it) or his habit of life could not endure the endless eating of fish, and therefore his life were in danger, the monks still insist on this law, without any mildness or dispensation. And even if they could save this wretched fellow's life with one morsel of meat, they would not do it. This is indeed stressing the law without dispensation and forgetting that the purpose of all laws is love. Therefore Gerson and others have correctly disapproved of this severity.[24]

And this is the fault in all the monasteries: even though human bodies are different by nature, they are forced to observe the same law with regard to food and other things, without any consideration either for the state of health or for the person.

As a young man I saw many Carthusians at Erfurt who were excessively pale and walked with a cane, although according to their years they should still have been vigorous.[25] Surprised at this misfortune, I would inquire where they had contracted this trouble. They answered: "From vigils." I asked: "But why don't you sleep?" They used to answer: "It is not allowed."

The religion of the monks is one that knows no mildness and no moderation. Therefore it is most unfair and most unjust; for it gives no consideration to the purpose of the law and has no regard for love; but, as Paul says in Col. 2:23, "it does not spare the body." Hence it is true what Terence says, that extreme justice is extreme injustice.[26] God does not want bodies to be killed; He wants them spared; indeed, He wants them to be nourished and fostered, in order that they may be fit for their calling and for the duties they owe the neighbor.

Foolish lawgivers and reprehensible conformists, who do not recognize the use and purpose of laws! Medicine must serve to protect, aid, and restore health. It has its canons and rules, but they are not to be stressed too rigidly. There must be consideration for the body; if it is somewhat weak, the potency of the medicines must be moderated. Otherwise it is not a medicine, but poison for the body. On the other hand, stronger bodies need more powerful drugs.

Thus in the case of the government the purpose of preserving the peace must always be kept in mind. If a prince were to punish the

[24] The reference is to Jean Gerson (1363—1429).
[25] The city of Erfurt was known as "little Rome," having twenty cloisters.
[26] See p. 337, note 21.

offenses of his people in such a way as to give occasion for uprisings, it would be better to close his eyes to the offenses than to punish them. What good is the law if it fails in its purpose and if everything goes to pieces? But, as I said, this moderation calls for extraordinary judgment.

The emperor, they say, is the living, breathing law.[27] But the theologians maintain that the law is the counsel of an upright man. For after the law has been enacted, it remains for good judgment to moderate it in certain cases. It is impossible for a lawgiver to be aware of all the special and general cases that can occur, for they are countless.

According to the theologians, the concept of law necessarily includes the counsel of a devout man who controls the law as cases develop; thus it does not become harmful, but the purpose of the law is maintained, namely, to be beneficial and to preserve the peace. If a law is in conflict with love, it is no law. Love is the mistress and teacher of the law, who commands a law to keep silence; for in certain cases the law teaches injustice, not justice. It does this if someone should want to follow it without moderation.

Hence the German proverbs about the young doctor of medicine who needs a new cemetery, about the jurist who recently took over a public office and starts wars all over the place, and about the young theologian who fills hell with souls. Because these men lack the practical experience that engenders wisdom, they do everything in accordance with their own canons and rules. This is why they get into difficulties and make mistakes to the great detriment of people and affairs.

Therefore you must learn that peace and love are the moderator and administrator of all virtues and laws, as Aristotle beautifully says about clemency in the fifth book of his *Ethics*.[28] And Augustine's teaching is not at all like that of the silly Carthusians. He says that not everyone is to be clothed, fed, and ruled in the same way, because not everyone is in the same state of health. A very wise saying.

He did not establish monasticism as it is today, but as a kind of learned society of men who contributed from their inheritances into

---

[27] This question of the emperor as *lex viva et animata* had figured in the question of the conflict between the emperor and the law of the empire, as this question was debated by the supporters of the Reformation.

[28] Aristotle, *Nicomachean Ethics*, Book V, ch. 10.

a common treasury and studied together.[29] Among this group he did not maintain the arithmetic proportion, which is the most accurate and divides things equally, but the geometric, which distributes in keeping with the circumstances.[30]

Therefore keep this example in mind and learn to yield your right in order to maintain harmony, just as Abram does not take into consideration his age, his authority, and his prestige but strives to attain the one objective of keeping the peace.

If he had consulted some young jurist or superstitious theologian, this man would have urged him not to yield but to insist on his right; for the promise concerning the land had been given to him, to be held and safeguarded, and so no perpetual servitude should be imposed on his descendants. Indeed, a fair-seeming speech! But because it does not serve peace and harmony, it must be rejected and must be considered most inequitable, however much it may appear to have been drawn from what is really the law.

Thus Abraham acts properly, and in a saintly and godly manner, too, when he yields his right and gives consideration to preserving harmony. Paul exhorts similarly in Eph. 4:32: "Forgiving one another if someone has something against his brother," and in Phil. 4:5: "Let all men know your forbearance."

But moderation really denotes yielding one's right and forgiving something for the sake of maintaining harmony. It is needed throughout life, for extreme justice is extreme disharmony.

Nevertheless, you should realize that this is being said about our laws and this earthly life, not about the laws of God, His promises, or the Sacraments. For there extreme justice should prevail, in accordance with the statement (Matt. 10:37): "He who loves father or mother more than Me is not worthy of Me." But in those things which people command us to do allowance is made for love, the moderator of the law and of all court actions; it is the main thing to be considered and followed. Therefore in order to preserve it, Abram, with extreme sorrow, sends his nephew away. Physically they were separated, but in spirit they were most closely united; this was something greater and more delightful for him than all his wealth.

[29] See, for example, Augustine, *Of Holy Virginity*, chs. 13 ff.
[30] Cf. *Luther's Works*, 13, p. 120, note 68.

10. *And Lot lifted up his eyes, and saw that the Jordan valley was well watered everywhere like the garden of the Lord, like the land of Egypt in the direction of Zoar; this was before the Lord destroyed Sodom and Gomorrah.*

The passage before us seems barren and dull, because it contains nothing but the departure of Lot from his uncle and some geography besides, a description of the region in which Sodom and Gomorrah were located. It calls it a plain, not as though there were no other plains near the Jordan — for it traverses the entire land of Canaan in a winding course — but because among all the other fields this region was the most fruitful and outstanding; here Lot stayed, beyond the Jordan and toward Egypt.

Moses points out the reason for the fruitfulness by saying that it was watered by means of the Jordan before Sodom and Gomorrah were destroyed; for after this punishment the appearance of this land or region was different, something the Lord wants Moses to record with a special design. For he adds that the region in which the five cities were situated was such that one could call it a garden of God, that is, a place where God might dwell and in which He would delight, since it abounded in all the best fruits.

I am familiar with the explanation of the Jews, who maintain that the expressions "garden of God," "cedars of God," and "city of God" are used for reasons of magnificence, as in Jonah 3:3: "Nineveh was a large city of God" (Jerome omits the term God), that is, a magnificent city.[31] And "cedars of God," in Ps. 80:10, the Jews interpret to mean that the plantations of trees and the vines in the land of Judah were so highly prized that they can be compared to large cedars; and in Ps. 104:16-17: "There the birds will build their nests, there are the trees which the Lord has planted," that is, large trees.

The Jews fabricate this interpretation because of their excessive wisdom and their innate pride, namely, that they alone may be called the people of God, and not the Gentiles. Nineveh, they say, cannot be called a city of God, as though God were dwelling there as He did among us in Jerusalem. The reason for this designation is a different one, namely, that it is a large and magnificent city. But this explanation is worthless; for we know that God is also the God of the heathen, even in time.[32] Hence Nineveh is called a city of God

---

[31] Cf. p. 201, note 38.

[32] Apparently this means that God will be God of all men not only in eternity but even in time, *temporaliter.*

because God gave it increase and His blessing, and because He is concerned about it and governs it.

Similarly, trees of God are called those which the Lord made and about which He is concerned, since He supplies rain, sunlight, and winds, from which they derive their increase, even if ungodly men own them. And it is indeed no small comfort that God establishes, maintains, and protects governments, and that they do not, as we generally suppose, either rise or fall by accident. The heathen are not aware of this control; they fancy that governments are established and controlled by their own effort.

Hannibal thinks that he is conquering the Romans by reason of the great courage and the extraordinary diligence he possesses. Alexander has greater gifts, which enable him to be successful in all his undertakings. But these are "masks." [33] They are the only things we see. But God's control, by which governments are either strengthened or overturned, we do not see.

This is what it really means when Nineveh is called a city of God, and likewise when the trees are said to be trees of God; for they are controlled and fostered by God so that they grow. Even if they are helped by human industry and labor as well, these would be vain without God's blessing. And who, I ask you, takes care of the forests and the groves, the trees in the vast uninhabited places?

Christ says (Matt. 5:45): "Your heavenly Father lets His sun rise over the good and the evil." He calls the sun God's sun, which He Himself created to invigorate nature.

Thus what is called a garden of God here is not, as the Jews prattle, a large one; it is one that is cultivated not only by human hands and effort but by God, because the Lord makes it fertile and blesses it.

It is said that traces of this gift are in existence to this day. For near the Dead Sea the most beautiful fruits are produced; but when they are opened, they are full of a vile odor and ashes, obviously, as the poet says, "monuments of an ancient crime." [34]

Therefore I think that this very place was Paradise,[35] and that after the Flood there adhered to it something of the richer blessing;

---

[33] See *Luther's Works*, 14, p. 114, note 9.

[34] Cf. p. 136, note 6.

[35] See p. 204, note 43.

eventually this also perished, because of the wickedness of the inhabitants. Even after Moses' death the region in which Jerusalem and the Dead Sea are located was assigned to the tribe of Judah. And it is very fitting that in the same land where a tree brought ruin to the human race, the offense of the first tree should be expiated on the tree of the cross, and innocence and eternal life should be returned to man through the Son of God.

Accordingly, the plain on both sides of the Jordan was most delightful, a small trace of the former Paradise. Even today there is no other place on earth that produces balsam except two gardens near the Dead Sea in the territory of עֵין גֶּדִי. But עֵין גֶּדִי is in the neighborhood of this plain which Moses calls a garden or Paradise of God, because God gave extraordinary vigor, appearance, and beauty to this garden and its fruits. Other gardens are also beautiful; but compared with the field or the garden near Sodom, they appear to be gardens of men and not of God.

This account deserves to be considered carefully, that we may learn how fearful a thing sin is. We see that this garden of God has been turned into hell itself because of the sins of men. For what else is the Dead Sea than hell? It is a horrible lake of bitumen. Moreover, in it is swallowed up the beautiful river Jordan, which supplied this land with water at the time of Abraham. The historians have no knowledge of this; therefore we are right to rank Moses above all of them. It was not without reason that he added this description to this account.

Moses compares this place to Egypt. It is watered by the Nile and is famous for its extreme fertility, but today without a doubt it has lost much of that blessing because of the sins of the people. These not only obstruct the blessing of a land but do away with it entirely, as we observe today that Thuringia is being turned into stones.[36]

The Holy Spirit has occasionally inserted this description of the land in order to instruct us about the wrath and curse of God that usually follows sin, and to teach us the difference between what this earth was like before sin and what it is like after sin. The proverb is true: "When the people is cursed, the land is cursed."[37] Where

---

[36] Later in these *Lectures on Genesis* Luther states that it now took seven years to produce what used to be produced in three years on the soil of Thuringia (W, XLIV, 658).

[37] *Maledicta gens, maledicta terra.*

God bestows the most blessings, there men curse God most. They misuse His blessing and abundance; not only do they abandon themselves to lazy indolence but by doing nothing they gradually learn to do evil.

This is the fault of original sin. Hearts infected by it will endure evils of every sort more readily than a blessing. For this reason Moses, too, laments in Deut. 32:15: "Jeshurun waxed fat, and kicked; then he forsook God who made him, and scoffed at the Rock of his salvation"; thus the passage before us also bears witness that in the most excellent part of the world there were the worst people.

11. *So Lot chose for himself all the Jordan valley, and Lot journeyed east; thus they separated from each other.*

12. *Abram dwelt in the land of Canaan, while Lot dwelt among the cities of the valley and moved his tent as far as Sodom.*

Since his uncle gives him the choice, Lot takes the better place, near the Jordan. But Abram stays toward the right, in the neighborhood of בֵּיתְאֵל and עַי, which are some miles distant from the Jordan, near whose banks Sodom was located.

But one must not understand this passage to mean that Lot occupied the entire region. Moses is referring to the choice, namely, that Lot chose that land for himself because in it he wanted to look for a dwelling place and was still uncertain which part would become his.

It is likely that this very holy man journeyed through the five cities and was not able to pitch his tent permanently anywhere except in the neighborhood of Sodom. But Abram remained in the land of Canaan because it had been promised to him. The five cities that were to be destroyed are separated from the land of Canaan, but the land of Canaan was to remain.

13. *Now the men of Sodom were wicked, great sinners against the Lord.*

Beautiful indeed was the praise of this excellent land. Moses called it the Paradise of the Lord and compared it to Egypt. But who are the people who inhabit it? Wicked men and great sinners. Thus in God's Paradise there live the sons of the devil, and the richest places contain the most detestable men in the entire world.

Why is this? No doubt in order that you may learn that it is God's custom to give the best to the worst. This is a most serious offense; by it the patience even of the saints is troubled, not to mention the wise men of the world and the philosophers. It is for this reason that Ps. 73:3-6 states: "I was envious of the arrogant, when I saw the prosperity of the wicked. For they have no pangs; their bodies are sound and sleek. They are not in trouble as other men are; they are not stricken like other men. Therefore pride is their necklace." "But all the day long I have been stricken, chastened every morning" (Ps. 73:14).

Thus God gave the rule of the world to Alexander and the Greeks, the worst of men. After the Greeks He gave it to the Romans, who were Epicureans. Similarly, we see that the Turks are most successful. After the Epicurean Romans were punished, there are nations in Europe which inhabit the richest region, truly a garden of God, although they surpass all the others in the worst vices — pride, envy, and cruelty.[38] Thereby God causes great consternation for human reason. As a result it concludes that human affairs are of no concern to God.

Yet we must not maintain that these situations come about by chance or without a reason. It is the will of God; by these means He makes the world foolish, so that it debates whether the things that are good, profitable, and delightful are actually good. The Stoics deny that they are good, although they teach that they are preferable to evil. Even though the Peripatetics assert that these things are good, they are offended because they are bestowed on the worst people.

Reason cannot cope with the offense of such extreme disparity. Since it is a fact that this place is a garden of God, reason is of the opinion that the Sodomites should not be put into it, but honorable and very good men. It considers it unfair that the wicked are shown favor by God, and it leans toward the opinion that these good things are not actually good.

But let us maintain not only that these gifts must be given a place among the things that are good and are declared to be such, but also that they are good things from God. For who is there to deny that the well-known gardens of Spain and of Italy are excellent gifts of God?

But why are they given to the worst people to enjoy? The psalm

[38] This seems to be aimed against Italy and perhaps against Spain.

quoted above makes it clear that this question is beyond our comprehension, and it directs us to keep the end in mind. Even though the ungodly fare well for a while, they finally go down into eternal doom. And even though the godly are afflicted, the Lord nevertheless leads us according to His own plan and in the end receives us into glory.

In this connection the extreme blindness of our minds becomes apparent. When we reflect on this amazing guidance of God, we are truly, as the psalm (73:22) states, "like a fool and a beast." If our reason were sound by nature, our judgments would be sounder; but since it is corrupt and depraved by nature, we arrive at such silly opinions that we regard as evil those things of which we make an evil use, and we deny that the good, delightful, and profitable things are really good.

O Stoic, it must not come to this! Your judgment will be better and sounder if you employ the abuse of things to appraise your own mind and not the things themselves. Because your heart misuses the things that are good by their nature, what else will you conclude than that your heart is evil and that by nature your will is not only not good but truly evil? Otherwise it would become good through the good things, whether they be useful or delightful.[39] Now, since you are evil, you are made worse through the use of the good things.

We see how many people are depraved by their affluence, but this is not the fault of the blessing of God. A harlot adorns herself with gold and jewels; yet the gold and jewels are good gifts of God, and it is a mistake to attribute the shame of the harlot to them. This is the general rule by which we must judge about the things or creatures of God, because the entire fault lies with your lust and your depraved will and reason.

A woman is beautiful. Very well, this is a gift of the Lord and Creator. But I am inflamed with desire. Does this make beauty an evil thing? Not at all! It is you who are evil because you are unable to make good use of a good thing. Thus the good things which are called useful and delightful convict us of the corruption of our nature, because neither the will nor the intellect is right; otherwise we would make good use of good things.

Crates is extolled among the philosophers because he threw a large amount of gold into the sea and thereafter supported himself

[39] On this distinction cf. Augustine, *On Christian Doctrine*, Book I, chs. 3—4.

by begging.⁴⁰ But does he not thereby convict himself of having a corrupt heart, since he declares that he is unable to make the right use of his gold?

Furthermore, what good, I ask you, did he achieve? Hollow ambition took the place of the greed he had seemingly driven away; that is, after one devil had been driven out, seven others, who were worse, took his place (Matt. 12:45).

Let us, therefore, learn what Holy Scripture asserts: that this region near the Jordan was very fertile. Hence there was at that place a superabundance of useful and delightful good things, given by God for men to enjoy and not for committing sin. But nature, which is corrupted by original sin, is unable to enjoy without abuse the things created and given by God, not because this is the nature of created things but because the heart of him who uses them is evil. But if the heart has been reformed by the Spirit, it makes use of both the useful and the delightful things in a holy manner and with thanksgiving.

Paul similarly states (Rom. 14:6, 8): "He who eats, eats in honor of the Lord. He who marries, marries to the Lord. Whether we live or whether we die, we are the Lord's." For he who believes, has everything and is lord of all; he can make use of all things in a holy manner.

Therefore it is an error when the philosophers condemn things because of their abuse. For it is obvious that as natural reason has no knowledge of God, it also has no knowledge of God's creation. The thought of the heathen poet is more correct. Things, he says, are like the heart of him who uses them.⁴¹ Thus there is a difference among human beings: one has plenty, another is in want. But if the one who is in want has an upright heart, he is wealthier than the rich man; for he is satisfied with a little and gives thanks to God for the most important possessions, that is, the knowledge of God and the grace revealed in Christ. But the rich man, as the tragic poet says,⁴² is poor among his accumulated gold; and in the midst of the greatest abundance he feels want.

Where does this difference come from? Obviously not from the

---

⁴⁰ See p. 326, note 3.
⁴¹ Terence, *Heautontimorumenos*, I, 2, 21.
⁴² Seneca, *Hercules*, 168.

nature of the things we use but from a difference in the heart, as St. Paul states in Phil. 4:12: "We know how to be abased, and we know how to abound."

So much about this account, which presents to us this general truth that the ungodly spend their lives in the uninterrupted misuse of the best things, while those who live in righteousness and faith make good use even of evil things, and whatever they do is good.

The Holy Spirit fails to say anything about Lot's activity in prayer, fasting, alms, and other works that strike the eye and evoke admiration. He informs us solely about matters concerning the household. These the masses consider unimportant and of no great benefit. "What does it matter," they say, "that Lot and Abram separate, and that Lot chooses the best part of the land for himself?"

But the learned theologian does not look at the bare works. He considers the person and the heart; and if the heart is full of faith, he concludes that everything he does in faith, even though in outward appearance it is most unimportant — such as the natural activities of sleeping, being awake, eating, and drinking, which seem to have no godliness connected with them — is a holy work that pleases God.

All godly people have some definite times at which they pray, meditate on holy things, and teach and instruct their people in religion; nevertheless, even when they are not doing these things and are attending either to their own affairs or to those of the community in accordance with their calling, they remain in good standing and have this glory before God, that even their seemingly secular works are a worship of God and an obedience well pleasing to God.

Thus in this passage the Holy Spirit gives a description of Lot's management of his household, which has no appearance of sanctity; and yet these very works in connection with the household are more desirable than all the works of all the monks and nuns, be they ever so laborious and impressive. Lot's wife milks the cows; the servants carry the hay and lead them to water.

God praises these works, and Scripture calls them works of the righteous. Thus it is stated in this passage: "Lot chose the plain of Jordan"; for it was left to his wish and will to choose which place he wanted.

Scripture does not state in this passage whether he did a good or an evil work; but because he was walking in the faith in which he had left Ur of the Chaldeans together with Abraham, this was a true work of righteousness, although it was a childish act and one that pertained to the household.

But these facts are related in order that everyone may have a sure comfort in his calling and may know that "the works of the body" must be done too, and that one must not always devote oneself to "spiritual works," as the monks taught. The body must be given time to rest and to refresh itself with food and drink.

Even though these works do not have the appearance of sanctity, one remains in good standing even when one does these things. For we observe that God did not consider it beneath His dignity to have these seemingly unimportant and paltry works recorded in His book. Whatever the godly do, even if it is a work that is not commanded, is pleasing to God and acceptable on account of faith. But if it is a work that God commands, there is that much less doubt that the obedience receives God's approval.

Everyone knows the statement of Ecclesiasticus (15:14-17): "It was He who created man in the beginning, and He left him in the power of his own inclination. If you will, you can keep the commandments, and to act faithfully is a matter of your own choice. He has placed before you fire and water: stretch out your hand for whichever you wish. Before a man are life and death."

And the statement of Augustine agrees with this, if you understand it properly: that God so governs the things He has created that He nevertheless lets them act on their own impulse.[43]

Hence man does not have such freedom that if God has commanded something, he can do it or not do it. So far as the commands of *God* [44] are concerned, man is not free; he must obey the voice of God, or he will endure the sentence of death. His freedom pertains to things about which God has given no command, as, for example, outward actions. At table one is at liberty to take either pears or apples, to drink either beer or wine, to dress either in white or in black, and to go either to the one friend or to the other. In such matters man has a choice, and it is certain that even these optional works become a worship of God and please God if you walk in the faith and abide by the commands of God or have a good conscience. People need to be taught such things.

[43] Cf. p. 76, note 86.
[44] The original has capital letters where we have italics.

14. *The Lord said to Abram, after Lot had separated from him: Lift up your eyes, and look from the place where you are, northward and southward and eastward and westward;*

15. *for all the land which you see I will give to you and to your descendants forever.*

So far Moses has told about Lot's departure from Abraham to the garden of Paradise and the excellent land in which, however, the worst of all men were living. That is God's way: He permits His own to be afflicted in various ways; but the ungodly He makes fat, corpulent, and broad. This seeming unfairness offends the godly. But they must cling to the comfort of which Ps. 73 speaks. Jeremiah (12:3) also says that the ungodly are being fattened for the day of slaughter. And Job 21:13, 17 says: "They spend their days in prosperity, and in peace go down to hell. The lamp of the ungodly will be put out, and a flood will come over them." Those who keep this end in mind will easily overcome this offense.

Now comes the third passage [45] in which it is written: "The Lord spoke with Abraham." I have often exhorted that in the accounts, or, as the masses call them, the legends of the saints, this chief feature of the account must be particularly observed, namely, the Word of God. In all ages God has done great things and wonderful works through His saints. These works are impressive and strike the eye; but for us who teach as well as learn the Holy Scriptures, God's own utterance must be especially resplendent. This, above all, adorns the legends of the saints and distinguishes them from the accounts of the heathen. They are called "sacred" accounts because the Word of God shines in them.

Even though the achievements of monarchs like Alexander are marvelous and grand, and even though learned men have described them very beautifully in words, nevertheless, compared with the sacred accounts, they are mere shadows; for they lack the light and are truly like a picture that has been well painted but has been placed in a dark corner so that it cannot be seen. They are like a body without a head and like flesh without a spirit.

Therefore the account of Abraham is most excellent because it is replete with the Word of God, with which everything that he did is embellished. Everywhere he is led by the Word of God, who prom-

---

[45] The first two passages are Gen. 12:1 and Gen. 12:7.

ises, commands, comforts, and admonishes, so that it is evident that Abraham is an extraordinary friend and intimate of God.

These facts are great and worthy of admiration. For, I ask you, what are the glorious victories and triumphs of kings in comparison with this friendship that Abraham has with the Divine Majesty — that he has God close by, to converse with him, direct him, love him, and preserve him?

If you examine the accounts of the holy fathers in this way and appraise this excellent gift rightly, they will no longer seem unimportant and insignificant; but they will excel all the accounts of all the monarchs, however great the outward appearance of their achievements may be. They do indeed strike the eyes with their seeming importance, but the heart that is properly instructed looks at the Word of God and sees that the holy patriarchs heard God and that God graciously guided and protected them. It prefers this gift to all the wealth of the world.

Let us, therefore, look with admiration at this holy father Abraham, who does not go about in gold and silk but is adorned, surrounded, crowned, and clothed with the divine light, the Word of God. Therefore his story must be preferred to all the accounts of the world. At their best these merely spread some clouds of works, which are pleasant in appearance but without any true fruit, and are generally even sad and full of fear. For they are devoid of the Word of God, which alone is the true light that gladdens and teaches the heart; and God's judgment and wrath are more noticeable in them than are His mercy and grace.

Therefore we Christians are truly blessed if, as Vergil says about farmers, we recognize our benefits.[46] The heathen have countless volumes of their achievements, written in all languages; but we have the sacred accounts, authenticated by the Word of God. We hear God speaking intimately with human beings; we see God governing human affairs in a wonderful manner and preserving His own in the midst of dangers. If the Jews had appraised these gifts as they should be appraised, would you not say that they are blessed? It is as the psalm (33:12) says: "Blessed is the nation whose God is the Lord!" And again (Ps. 144:15): "Happy the people whose God is the Lord!"

The Persians, the Greeks, and the Romans may be great. But since they do not have this gift of the Word, they surely are not happy. For not only do they not have this God, but they do not even

[46] Vergil, *Georgics,* Book II, l. 458.

know Him. The Lord does not speak with them, even though He blesses their governments for a time.

Therefore David is right when he says (Ps. 60:6): "With exultation I will divide up Shechem"; that is, I shall be pleasing to my God, and I shall rejoice in His gifts, because "God has spoken in His sanctuary." This is the main thing, and in it he glories and rejoices, as if he were saying: "This is our prerogative, that we have a sanctuary in which God speaks. Even though other kings are more powerful than we, still they do not have this gift in which we glory, that we hear God speak with us through His prophets."

Moses bestows grand praise on this same gift in Deut. 4:6 ff.: "Behold, a wise and understanding people. There is no other nation so great that it has gods drawing near to it the way our God is present at all our entreaties; for what other nation is there so famed that it has ceremonies and righteous judgments and a law affecting all?" They realized that this was a great gift of God.

Now if we Christians also realized this great gift of ours, we would truly be blessed, as Christ says in Luke 10:23-24: "Blessed are the eyes which see what you see! Many kings desired to see what you see, and did not see it."

Indeed, I would go even further and say that just as we now praise Abraham because of this gift, so he would praise us in the New Testament even more; for he saw the day of Christ, as John 8:56 states. But he saw it only in faith and in the spirit.

But we see this glory face to face. We hear God speaking with us and promising forgiveness of sins in Baptism, in the Supper of His Son, and in the true use of the keys. These Abraham did not have, but he saw in the spirit and believed.

Therefore our glory is greater; but because we do not take care of it or thank God enough for such great gifts of grace, our studious concern for power and pleasure is greater. Consequently, the Turk, the pope, and countless other devils must come from Italy, Spain, and all the corners of the earth, to vex, afflict, and kill us because of our unspeakable and disgraceful contempt.

Thus the church is the pupil of Christ. It sits at His feet and listens to His Word, that it may know how to judge everything — how to serve in one's vocation and to fill civil offices, yes, how to eat, drink, and sleep — so that there is no doubt about any area of life, but that we, surrounded on all sides by the rays of the Word, may continually walk in joy and in the most beautiful light.

But alas, we are not aware of our gifts. Only those who are spiritual rejoice and give thanks to God. Because the rest are carnal, ungrateful, greedy, and proud, they will be deprived even of what they have; and the punishment will befall them that they will listen to Satan instead of Christ and to heretics instead of the apostles, namely, to men who seek in the Word their own wisdom and glory and everything else except the joy and the heavenly blessings the Word brings us.

This wretched situation should grieve all Christians, that in the great light and glory of the Word the majority remains blind and loves the darkness more than the light (John 3:19). They see that this is the source of all the misfortunes of the people — that the Turk makes an invasion; that heresies increase; that the pope is intent on maintaining his sovereignty, which is founded on the invocation of the saints, on countless exchanges and sales and good works, and on other things through which he has led wretched souls away from the Word. People toiled and struggled at these things to such an extent that some dressed in a coat of mail and went on foot to the farthermost parts of Spain, to St. Iago's.[47] But when they returned, the simpletons did not know what they had either done or experienced! This was a just judgment of God.

These things, or some that are even sadder, will happen to our people later, after we have passed away, because they do not care for that grace which Abraham desired to see, although Abraham had barely a few droplets of the riches of which we possess a vast sea.

But this is the usual lot of the church: the more abundantly the Word is revealed, the greater is the ingratitude of the people; for they misuse it to their own glory and to cover their sins. Therefore God sends strong delusions (2 Thess. 2:11), as is evident from the example of the pope, who, in place of the Word, forced upon the church his own decrees, decretals, legends of the saints, and other trumpery. The world wants to be deceived.

Let us, therefore, learn in all the legends to admire this chief glory of God's Word, which, like the sun in the midst of the sky, shines in these accounts of the holy fathers. Those who do this will make their way through the countless tumults and monstrosities of human works, which are the only things reason admires; for they will be intent on this one thing alone, whether the Lord is speaking and what He says.

[47] See *Luther's Works*, 23, p. 24, note 22.

We read about Hilarion that throughout seventy-three years he tasted neither meat nor butter nor milk.[48] This appears to be a magnificent work; it practically stuns our reason. But if you ask whether Hilarion did this at the command of God or of his own accord, then this self-elected work, because it lacks the light of the Word of God, becomes utterly worthless and is truly a work of darkness, especially if, as usual, some spiritual pride was connected with it.

Because God is merciful, perhaps He did not count against the good man this silly practice of religion with which he tortured his body; but if someone wanted to set up this work as an example and make a worship of God out of it, he ought to be completely condemned, whether he be Jerome or Hilarion or Anthony. For they admired and were zealously devoted to such superstitions.

We must appeal to our touchstone and look at the Word of God. We must not simply give our tacit approval to such hideous sanctity, but we must ask whether God has commanded such a thing.

If you see a baptized person walking in his baptismal faith and in the confession of the Word and performing the works of his calling, these works, however ordinary, are truly holy and admirable works of God, even though they are not impressive in the eyes of men.

Therefore we must distinguish carefully between the glory of the Word of God, which alone is the true light and the highest adornment, and those prodigious and fair-seeming works. For God is pleased with those works which we undertake at His command.

Saul seems to be doing the right thing (1 Sam. 15) when he does not kill all the cattle of the Amalekites but keeps the choicer animals for worship. But because God had clearly given the command that all had to be killed, this deed provokes Him to extreme anger. Therefore the fair-seeming work is nothing but an abomination, because it was undertaken against the Word of God.

Hence Scripture uses the ominous terms "divination" or "idolatry" when one does not listen to the Word of God, or when one undertakes something without, or contrary to, the Word of God. This is surely an awful statement and definition, especially if you consider how common and fashionable this practice is in the world.

Therefore Paul warns the Colossians (2:18) to be on their guard against those who walk in arbitrary worship, even though in appearance this may seem to be the religion of angels. These are, he says,

[48] Cf. *Luther's Works*, 23, p. 76, note 59.

the commands of men; that is, they do not have that sun and glory, the Word of God. Hence they must be shunned and not be regarded as forms of worship.

I am too prolix in my comments on this text; but since I was taught by my own peril, I know how necessary this admonition and teaching is. Scripture everywhere commands us to be humble and to guard against pride as a fountain from which the wrath of God flows. But it is not pride to hold the Word of God in high esteem and to glory in it.

Age, sex, and callings differ greatly in this life. One teaches the church; another serves the government; still another instructs the youth; a mother busies herself with the care and upbringing of children; and the husband is concerned with providing an honest living. In the opinion of the world these are not very grand and impressive works. But if you look at the Word, that heavenly adornment and divine glory, why should you not act proudly over against Satan, and why should you not give thanks to God for such great gifts? For these are not bare works; they are adorned with the Word of God, since they have been enjoined on you by God. On the other hand, those superstitious works in the world are, as Paul calls them (Col. 2:23), arbitrary worship without the Word of God, and, as the same Paul calls them (Eph. 5:11), "unfruitful works."

"Nevertheless," some say, "the pope and the church have commanded them." The pope is none of our concern, and the church is none of our concern! Besides, it is not the church if it draws away from the Word, if through self-chosen forms of worship it increases idolatry and offenses and furthers the destruction of souls and not the glory of God.

For the church is the pupil of Christ; and although it teaches, it does not teach anything except what has been entrusted to it by Christ. Even the Spirit of God does the same thing (John 16:14): "He will take what is Mine."

Therefore if we want to practice godliness, let us not do so by means of unfruitful works but by means of fruitful ones. That is, let us first receive the Word of God, and let us believe in Christ. Then let us walk in our simple calling: Let the husband support his family; let the maid obey her mistress; let the mother wash, dress, and teach the children.

Because these works are done in one's calling and in faith in the

Son of *God*,[49] they shine in the sight of God, of the angels, and of the entire church of God. For they are clothed in the heavenly light, the Word of God, even though in the sight of the pope's church they are despised for being ordinary and common.

As I have said, it is not without cause that I am emphasizing this, but because it is so necessary; for human nature is fickle and is easily swayed, and our flesh is very foolish. Therefore it is easily taken in by amazing and unusual works.

I admit that the saints of God did things that were similar in outward appearance. Thus John refrained from wine, ate locusts, and wore a camel's hide. But you are altogether blind if you are not aware of the vast difference. He did these things because he was commanded to do them, for we know that he was a Nazarite and was called by God into the desert.

Abraham and Lot actually separate from each other, as we see in this account of Abraham. This separation, it is true, was not commanded by a special Word; yet God approves of it. For He continues to speak with Abraham. Indeed, He speaks with him in a most friendly manner, so that it is clear that God is not only not provoked by this change of place but even approves of it. Does God, then, approve of works that are undertaken without His Word?

No. For although the saints do not always have a particular or special Word, they nevertheless do not sin against the general Word. Indeed, because they do what they do in faith in the Son of God, their action is altogether right. Thus Lot was at liberty to go in whatever direction he desired.

We are at liberty to eat either meat or fish, to drink either water or wine, provided we give consideration to our well-being and make use with thanksgiving of the things that were created for our use. God has given no commands that are against this. The pope does give commands to the contrary, namely, that we should abstain from meat on Friday and Saturday. But he who acknowledges the pope as his teacher has no part with Christ.

Thus in this passage the Lord approves of the separation of relatives and ratifies it, inasmuch as He converses with Abraham in such a friendly manner. But this blessing must not be extolled in the case of Abraham alone; for, as I stated above,[50] in this respect we are better off than Abraham. What happened to Abraham several times

[49] Here again we have used italics where the original has capital letters.
[50] See p. 353.

happens to us every day: that God converses with us, not about earthly blessings but about eternal ones.

But, someone will say, how did God speak to Abraham? From heaven, as Christ converses with Paul near Damascus? My own opinion is this: He did so through the patriarch Shem and through the human ministry. Paul, too, similarly states in 1 Thess. 2:13: "You accepted the Word from us, not as the word of men but as what it really is, the Word of God, which is at work in you believers." Similarly, Christ says (Luke 10:16): "He who hears you hears Me."

Thus we have been overwhelmed with the riches of divine mercy by having this light so abundantly, because God presents Himself to us everywhere through the ministry of men and converses with us. For this blessing we ought to thank God and rejoice sincerely. It proves that we are the friends of God and that God cares for us, whether we live or die. If Cicero, Plato, and others could have attained this great good, do you think that they would have sat still and would not rather have gone to the remotest parts of the earth? Therefore our danger is so much the greater if we have been ungrateful for this great gift. For the wrath of God will not cease; even now it is threatening us through the Turk and the popes, men who are well-nigh demons so far as their hatred and cruelty are concerned.

At the outset, therefore, one must take note of this saying: "The Lord said." To hear Him is the greatest glory and the utmost blessing. But as I said above, I think that the Lord did not appear to Abraham here, but that He spoke to him through Shem or Melchizedek.

Hence it is a great virtue that Abraham permits himself to be guided by the Word in this manner, and that he receives the divine utterance, which he hears from his father Shem.

One must note, however, that even though the region into which Lot wandered adjoined the land of Canaan, in this passage the Lord separates it from the land of Canaan and does not include it in the promise He gave to Abraham. The reason for this is that He knows it must be utterly destroyed because of sin. Therefore Lot, too, is a guest there only for a time. As the sequel shows, it was first harassed by wars because of sin; later on it was completely laid waste by fire which fell from heaven, when the people continued to be indifferent about their repentance.

The promise given to Abraham in this passage speaks especially of a physical blessing, just as the one in the twelfth chapter above speaks of a spiritual blessing. Therefore it is easily understood and does not require a lengthier explanation, so long as one notices what an amazing situation this is: through the promise Abraham is the lord of this entire land, and yet actually he does not have or possess a footbreadth of it (Acts 7:5)! Those who learn from his example to rely on the Word will eventually experience that they have not believed in vain.

16. *I will make your descendants as the dust of the earth; so that if one can count the dust of the earth, your descendants also can be counted.*

Note must be taken of this little section because below, where the second part of the first spiritual promise will be explained, Moses expresses himself differently and commands Abraham to count the stars (Gen. 15:5). There he compares the descendants of Abraham to the stars and luminaries of heaven, but here to the dust of the earth.

These comparisons indicate the twofold posterity of Abraham: the one, earthly and physical; the other, heavenly, spiritual, and eternal. The promise before us is entirely material; it deals with the possession of the land of Canaan and the growth of physical Israel. It is for this reason that Moses likens it to the dust of the earth. But later on, in connection with the eternal promise about Isaac and about the heavenly Seed, Christ and the church, Abraham is commanded to count the stars.

From this passage the prophets no doubt learned to call the people of God "heaven" and "the host of the heavens," and to call the godly teachers "stars." Thus Daniel (8:10) states that Antiochus would cast down stars from heaven to earth. This usage must be carefully noted by students of the Sacred Scriptures.

This passage reminds us to direct our discussion, in the first place, toward the strengthening of our own faith and, in the second place, against the stubborn Jews. The text states clearly here that the descendants of Abraham according to the flesh should have possession of this land forever. But for one thousand five hundred years the Jews have not had possession of this land; hence it follows clearly either that Moses is lying or that God has cast aside and forsaken the Jews, His people, so that they are no longer the people of God.

What answer will you give to this, you circumcised fellow? It will be difficult to say that Moses is lying; yet the actual situation indicates clearly that your nation has lost possession of the land of Canaan.

If you say that this happened because of the sins of your people, is not God giving these promises to Abraham himself before he had any descendants and before they sinned?

Furthermore, if you maintain that this is punishment for their sins, come, did not your ancestors sin before the Babylonian captivity? They killed the prophets, and they sacrificed their sons and daughters to demons and poured out the blood of the godly like water. Yet even though God was incensed against them and cast them aside for a time, He did not forsake them completely. He gave them teachers and prophets, and in the end He even restored them to the land of Canaan. And during the captivity itself, though they were exiles according to their bodies, nevertheless with their hearts they held fast to Canaan and remained in Canaan, which they knew would have to be restored to them after seventy years.

Compare the present situation with this. You have no promise, nothing sure to wait for, and no clearly defined time of your exile. What, then, has come of this promise? Does it not follow either that God has lied or that the Jews are no longer the people of God? But it is impossible for God to lie; hence this leaves the conclusion that the Jews have been cast aside by God and have ceased to be the people of God.

Nor will any Jew be clever enough to parry the argument that after being driven out without any definite limitation of time, they have now been living outside their land for one thousand five hundred years, without prophets and without promises, whereas the prisoners in Babylon had both of these and knew that they would return to Jerusalem.

It was the same when Jacob was commanded to migrate to Egypt. Even though his descendants remained there for four hundred years, still he had the promise that they would return to the land of Canaan after the fourth generation.

But under the monarchy of the Romans the Jews are entirely without any promise; the prophets, too, threaten them with eventual destruction.[51] Thus this passage demonstrates that the Jews are no longer the people of God, but that they have been cast aside by God because they denied Christ.

Therefore Moses' statement, "I will give this land to your descendants forever," must be understood as "that is, up to the time of

---

[51] Luther is thinking of passages like Is. 51:19.

Christ." They should have received Him and listened to Him. They had been appointed heirs of this land until this King of theirs would come; and if they had received Him and listened to Him, they would have kept the Promised Land.

But because, according to John 11:48, they try to keep their land after they have destroyed Him, the opposite takes place; and they themselves perish without any hope of help.

Therefore one must observe that the word עוֹלָם does not denote unlimited or eternal time, but an uncertain length of time or a long time without any definite termination.

Thus Ex. 21:6 [52] says about the slave whose ear has been pierced as a sign of his perpetual slavery: "He will be a slave forever," that is, as long as he lives. And thereafter, throughout the entire Pentateuch, this word עוֹלָם recurs with the meaning of a time that is indefinite but limited; for example (Num. 18:23): "It shall be a statute among your generations forever," that is, until the time of Christ.

Thus the Jews must confess that they are no longer the people of God; for if they were the people of God, they would have that land. Now that they have been driven out of it, who will believe that they are the descendants of Abraham?

In our time there arose in Moravia a foolish kind of people, the Sabbatarians, who maintain that the Sabbath must be observed after the fashion of the Jews. Perhaps they will insist on circumcision too, for a like reason.[53] Our churches, in which the Word of God is heard, know nothing of such nuisances; but in those places where the Gospel is excluded because of the rabid attitude of the prince, everything is full of them.[54]

Unlearned and foolish people are beguiled by this one word that Moses uses in this passage: that the Jews had to preserve these ceremonies and forms of worship "forever." Hence, they say, the Sabbath, circumcision, and the other ceremonies should not have been abolished entirely but should be preserved.

But as for you, confront them with this passage, "To you and to your descendants I will give this land forever," and beset the Jews

[52] The original has "Ex. 23."

[53] For more details cf. Luther's statement at table in the spring of 1537 (W, *Tischreden*, III, 442 [No. 3597]).

[54] Sometimes Luther made this claim that the left wing of the Reformation arose only in territories that had not followed him, but at other times he was willing to admit that it had actually arisen in Lutheran territories as well.

as well as their apes, the Sabbatarians, by asking where the land is that was given to them to possess. If they do not have a land, how can they insist on the sacrifices and other things commanded in the Law?

These commandments were expressly addressed to those descendants who had the promise and the possession of the land of Canaan. Therefore when the land ceases to be and is lost, the Law also ceases; so do the kingdom, the priesthood, the Sabbath, circumcision, etc.

It is surely most amazing that human beings can be led into such a great error by such silly reasoning. Even though this is of minor importance, it is nevertheless necessary to point out that the word עוֹלָם does not denote infinite time; it denotes finite time.

17. *Arise, walk through the length and the breadth of the land, for I will give it to you.*

You observe that Abraham, who, according to the promise, is the lord of the land of Canaan, is merely a guest and has no definite place to come to rest with his people; for he is commanded to migrate from one place to another. And this is the reason why the fathers regarded also their material promises with a spiritual understanding. Thus the Letter to the Hebrews (11:9-10) states very beautifully: "By faith Abraham sojourned in the Land of the Promise, as in a foreign land, living in tents with Isaac and Jacob, heirs with him of the same promise. For he looked forward to the city which has foundations, whose Builder and Maker is God." Through this faith Abraham overcame a long and troublesome exile; nor did it offend him that Lot had an abode that was both definite and very comfortable.

18. *So Abram moved his tent, and came and dwelt by the oaks of Mamre, which are at Hebron; and there he built an altar to the Lord.*

Mamre is the proper name of a man, as is clear from the following chapter, in which Moses states that he was an Amorite. The word אֵלוֹנֵי some explain as a grove, others as a plain. Be that as it may — and we leave these matters to the philologians — Mamre, like the nobility among us, lived in the country near the famous city of Hebron, which had in its neighborhood אֵלוֹנִים, that is, a wood or an oak grove, just as cities commonly have woods in their neighborhood, both because of the pasture and also because of the convenience of getting wood. At Mamre's place Abram was hospitably received with his entire house.

Moses takes special care to mention that there he built an altar to the Lord; that is, as I stated above, Abraham preached at that place and gave instruction about the true worship of God.

But this is no small comfort, that God gathers remnants from the heathen and lets them partake of the blessing of Abraham. Unless Mamre had been a godly and pious man and, like Abraham, had believed in the true God and had heard His Word from Abraham, he would not have received Abraham hospitably; nor would Abraham have gone to him.

Even at that time, therefore, God had His worshipers among the heathen, worshipers whom He called in a marvelous manner through the holy patriarch, in accordance with the promise given him above in chapter 12:3: "You will be a blessing"; that is, "The blessing is so inherent in you that wherever you may come, others will also receive a blessing through your ministry."

Christ also sends out His disciples in the same way (Matt. 10:13): "If the house is worthy, let your peace come upon it."

Mamre received Abraham hospitably with all his household; and that brought him this benefit, that he heard Abraham teaching his people about God and true worship. This doctrine Mamre receives, and from a wild and barren branch he becomes a fruitful root and tree. He becomes a sharer in the faith and the blessing. So closely does he join the holy patriarch that with his two brothers he even aids Abraham in the war against the heathen and for God.

Therefore this passage must be noted against the Jews; for the blessing through holy Abraham extends also to the heathen, who actually had no claim on the promise.

For it is the opinion of the Jews that they alone are the people of God, but that all heathen have been cast aside by God, although Scripture is full of such accounts of how heathen also have been called to share the promise through the holy prophets.

The holy patriarchs were especially zealous in endeavoring to bring as many as possible to the knowledge of God. Therefore Abraham not only takes care of his household, but he also builds an altar. There he teaches the true religion; there he calls upon God; there he publicly practices the outward forms of worship. The Amorite Mamre and his brothers join him, and so a large church is established.

CHAPTER FOURTEEN

1. *In the days of Amraphel king of Shinar, Arioch king of Ellasar, Ched-or-laomer king of Elam, and Tidal king of nations,*

2. *these kings made war with Bera, king of Sodom, Birsha king of Gomorrah, Shinab king of Admah, Shemeber king of Zeboiim, and the king of Bela (that is, Zoar).*

THIS passage seems to be altogether barren, yet Moses is very prolix in his description of the time and the place. It has, however, been corrupted in various ways through the carelessness or bungling of the scribes.[1]

First of all, one must realize that "by anticipation," as Lyra calls it,[2] Moses is employing words of his own time, words which were unknown when these events took place; for these names were given to these places in later times.

The Jews think that King Amraphel is Nimrod, with whom we dealt above. I do not know whether this claim is correct or not, for there is no evidence on which we could rely with certainty. Let us, therefore, let the Holy Spirit exercise His function as teacher in this passage; He wanted these matters recorded in this way, and let us be content that this Amraphel was the king of Babylon or Shinar.

Now it is known from the sacred record that the first kingdom after the Flood or after the division of languages was Babylon, a most fertile place. This kingdom was established by Nimrod, Ham's grandson, to whom Africa was assigned. His son Cush had possession of Egypt. But Ham's grandson Nimrod was dissatisfied with the paternal boundaries. He attacked the holy generation in the east, and through tyranny he took possession of the land of Shinar and built Babylon, as Moses related previously, in the eleventh chapter.[3] Babylon was

[1] In his treatise *On the Shem Hamphoras* (1543) Luther even suggested that Christian students of the Old Testament publish a Hebrew text purged of these corruptions (W, LIII, 646).

[2] Lyra on Gen. 14:7, sec. r.

[3] Apparently this is a reference to Gen. 10:10-11.

destroyed rather frequently. First the kingdom was turned over to Assyria; then, after the defeat of the Assyrians, again to Babylon; and later on to the Persians and Medes, etc.

The second king is Arioch. Our translator makes him the king of Pontus,[4] but Moses states that he was the king of Ellasar. Here one must guess what Ellasar is. But the similarity of the name persuades me that as Babylon is toward the east, so Ellasar is toward the north, in other words, that it is Assyria.

The third king is Ched-or-laomer, king of Elam, that is, Persia, a great and vast region toward the south.

The fourth king is Tidal, king of nations. Here one must take note of the expression of Holy Scripture, which calls "nations" those peoples whose shores are washed by our Mediterranean Sea. Thus Paul is called "the apostle to the nations" because he was sent especially to the nations dwelling along the Mediterranean Sea toward the east. Hence this king was master of Cilicia and the neighboring regions.

These men were the monarchs or Caesars at that time. With a common plan they started a war against the kings of the five cities. This may have been because they were provoked by these kings. Moses explains a little later that they had revolted against Ched-or-laomer; because that part of the earth was very highly cultivated and very rich, they were unwilling to bear his yoke and became bold. Or it may have been because they were attracted by the hope of getting a better land for themselves.

"As it was in the beginning, so it is now and ever shall be, world without end."[5] Princes who are not satisfied with what they have endeavor to get the possessions of others if they are better. As a German proverb says, "Everybody grabs for what is good." If Milan had not been located on such fertile soil, kings would never have engaged in such great conflicts about it. This may have been the cause also of this first war of which Scripture makes mention.

Zoar, which Moses mentions last, was one of those five cities; but it was the smallest, and Lot took refuge in it. Its location is still extant. Thus the power of those cities was not great, even though their land was very highly cultivated and very fertile.

---

[4] The Douay Version follows this when it renders this phrase with "Arioch king of Pontus."

[5] A quotation from the *Gloria Patri*.

3. *And all these joined forces in the Valley of Siddim (that is, the Salt Sea).*

I stated above that Moses is using the names current in his own time, for then the Salt Sea was not yet in existence. But in Scripture the name Salt Sea is given to the Lacus Asphaltites or the Dead Sea, of which we spoke a little while ago. Thus at Moses' time that entire land or field was a bituminous lake; but when the war was waged here, it was the valley of שָׂדִים that is, of fields, a very highly cultivated and very fertile place, which the Jordan watered like a garden.

4. *Twelve years they had served Ched-or-laomer, but in the thirteenth year they rebelled.*

5. *In the fourteenth year Ched-or-laomer and the kings who were with him came and subdued the Rephaim in Ashteroth-karnaim, the Zuzim in Ham, the Emim in Shaveh-kiriathaim,*

6. *and the Horites in their Mt. Seir as far as Elparan on the border of the wilderness.*

Because of the words whose meaning has been lost this verse is like a hedge of thorns. Yet we must make our way through it. It mentions the reason for the expedition and its outcome. The people are called Rephaim, from רָפָא, "to heal," as though one called them saviors of the land or fathers of the fatherland. This was the name for kings at that time.

Similarly, the Saxons call their nobles "Goodman," for noblemen should strive after virtue and be of benefit to their people. It is for this reason that they have wealth, and rank in prestige above the masses, who look for nothing but their own advantage and therefore cater to their lusts.

But the nobility should display a loftier spirit. They should be busy with state affairs; they should defend their people bravely and by their own example encourage them to virtue. They should not, as is now their habit, revel, rob, plunder, and despoil their own people.

It is, therefore, an admirable term for the government to call them Rephaim, saviors or healers, who cure the abscesses and ailments of the body, put thieves and robbers to death, and defend their people against acts of violence.

But what happens now also happened then: power makes men

arrogant and tyrannical. Our flesh is so weak that glory and power do not agree well with it. Consequently, this most pleasing name fell into disrepute, and because of the deteriorating nobility the name Rephaim was given to giants and tyrants. Therefore God incited these four kings to punish those Rephaim who had forgotten their office and were not healers and saviors but oppressors of liberty and of the commonwealth.

Ashteroth-karnaim seems to designate a kingdom that was called Og Bashan later on, beyond Jordan in the neighborhood of these five cities.

Joshua (12:4) also mentions that some of these Rephaim were left, for they were smitten but not destroyed. Later on the Ammonites and the Moabites occupied these places.

I do not know what Ham is. The text says that the Zuzim were there. But the context shows that they were neighbors of the Rephaim in Ashteroth.

The Emim are famous from the Pentateuch (Deut. 2:10-11); later on the Edomites inhabited those places. Today the name Arabia Petraea is used.

Thus it appears that these four kings from the east proceeded toward the south. But all these are honorable names with which people honored the government.

זוּזִים denotes "robust men," as we say in German, "the great heroes." [6] They disregard danger and are ready to give up their life for the fatherland.

אֵימִים denotes such as are to be respected, to be regarded with trembling and fear, whom the masses must honor and respect.

The Horites are also Edomites, a part of Arabia Petraea. The Edomites drove them out.

The desert Paran is familiar from the writings of Moses;[7] it adjoins the tribe of Judah on the south.

7. *Then they turned back and came to Enmishpat (that is, Kadesh), and subdued all the country of the Amalekites, and also the Amorites who dwelt in Hazazon-tamar.*

The fountain of Mishpat, or of judgment, is a place that is familiar from the Book of Numbers.[8] The Amalekites lived between Egypt

[6] The phrase is *die tewren Helden.*
[7] So especially in Num. 13.
[8] In the Book of Numbers it is called Kadesh.

and the Holy Land. Hazazon-tamar is another name for Engedi, the best place in the world and very near to the five cities, a remnant of Paradise.

Thus it is clear that these four kings first conquered the Edomites, the Amalekites, the Ishmaelites, the Midianites, and the neighboring regions round about, and that then they attacked the five cities, which were now deprived of the protection of their neighbors.

8. *Then the king of Sodom, the king of Gomorrah, the king of Admah, the king of Zeboiim, and the king of Bela (that is, Zoar) went out, and they joined battle in the Valley of Siddim*

9. *with Ched-or-laomer king of Elam, Tidal king of nations, Amraphel king of Shinar, and Arioch king of Ellasar, four kings against five.*

10. *Now the Valley of Siddim was full of bitumen wells; and as the kings of Sodom and Gomorrah fled, some fell into them, and the rest fled to the mountain.*

11. *So the enemy took all the goods of Sodom and Gomorrah, and all their provisions, and went their way.*

The explanations of the wells of bitumen differ. Some think that they were pits from which either white clay or material for plaster was dug; others think that they are wells, as Moses calls them. But whatever it was, it was some special gift that was useful and necessary for building. Thus the historical accounts about Alexander relate that he dug wells of bitumen at Babylon.[9]

Perhaps Moses mentions these wells because a frightened soldier fell into them and perished when he sought safety in flight.

If we compute the time, barely thirty years had passed since the death of Noah when this war began. At that time Shem and six other patriarchs were still living; and while these most holy men are ruling and teaching the world, such great disturbances arise.

This is an awful example, that men so quickly forgot the Flood and the division of the languages, that they devoted themselves to tyranny and disturbed the world with wars. The holy patriarchs watched this with the utmost grief, but they were unable to remedy these great evils.

You have here a description of the way the world looks when it

[9] Alexander captured Babylon during the campaign of 331—330 B. C.

not only forgets the Word of God but even despises it. Therefore it incurs the punishments it deserves.

The same thing will happen to Germany when I am dead; for even while I am still alive, I am compelled to hear and see many shameful things that will not escape severe punishment.

And this is the reason why Moses gives such a careful description of this war, namely, that we may see the reign of the devil and of reason. God wants governments to exist; He wants evildoers to be condemned and the godly defended. But Satan corrupts the hearts so that the authorities degenerate into tyrants. Then follow wars and uprisings, the punishment of sins. These affect the godly too, as we shall hear now about Lot. But the Lord knows how to rescue the righteous man in the evil day.

12. *They also took Lot, the son of Abram's brother, who dwelt in Sodom, and his goods, and departed.*

13. *Then one who had escaped came, and told Abram the Hebrew, who was living by the oaks of Mamre the Amorite, brother of Eshcol and of Aner; these were allies of Abram.*

Here Moses reveals his true reason for presenting such a detailed account of this war, namely, in order to impress on us the great miracle that follows, Abraham's glorious victory.

This passage is too rich and too lofty for me to be able to explain all its sections as they deserve. The main point and chief content of the lesson is to have you see this: God places His own under the cross; and although He delays their deliverance, nevertheless in the end He gloriously snatches them out of their dangers and makes them victors, but only after they have first been greatly vexed and have been wearied to despair by sundry conflicts.

To be aware of this divine procedure with which God rules us is profitable and necessary. Thus we learn to show patience in adversity, to trust in God's goodness, and to hope for salvation, but in prosperity to humble ourselves and give the glory to God. For it is His custom to do both: to bring down to hell and to bring back, to afflict and to comfort, to kill and to make alive.

This is the game, with its continual changes, that He plays with His saints. For there is no perfect joy in this life, as there will be in the life to come. Sometimes, like an angry father, He inflicts punishments; sometimes, like an affectionate father, He fosters and comforts His children.

We must learn this carefully in order to be ready for every event, as Paul says about himself in Phil. 4:11-13: "I have learned, in whatever state I am, to be content. I know how to be abased, and I know how to abound. I can do all things in Him who strengthens me."

Thus this account was written not for the sake of those five kings but for our sakes, so that when we are in a trial we may be strong, but when we are not in a trial we may be humble and grateful.

He who can remain on this road, which is truly the royal road, is blessed. He is cheered by hope and does not become discouraged in adverse circumstances; on the other hand, when everything is serene, he does not exalt himself or become arrogant. Someone has rightly said: "The blessed have maintained a middle course." [10] The human heart is very weak in both directions and — something that is very difficult to believe — perseveres more readily in adversity.

In this passage the word הַפָּלִיט must be noted. It denotes one who has been rescued, and, as we are accustomed to express it, the remnants of some defeat, those who have escaped. This is, moreover, an appropriate term for the saints. God permits them to sink so deeply in perils that they appear lost. Yet in the end they are delivered in a wonderful manner. Thus when the entire world is condemned, we who confess Christ and put our trust in His death will be saved like remnants.

The Jews have various foolish comments about this man who escaped.[11] Since they disregard the passages that teach faith, hope, and patience, they look eagerly for foolish ideas of this sort. But it is not altogether useless to be acquainted with the foolish and silly ideas of such stupid people. Everyone knows that these are the punishments for their stubborn disbelief or lack of trust.

Thus they falsely allege that the messenger of this defeat was King Og, because he belonged to the descendants of the Rephaim, even though the historical account reveals that Og was killed more than four hundred years later by Moses when he had set out from Egypt. To be sure, thereby the ungodly Jews are proving to us their learning and their doctrine.

How much more profitable it would be to do without a discussion

---

[10] The Latin proverb is *Medium tenuere beati*.
[11] Cf. Lyra on Gen. 14:13, sec. c.

about his person — for, after all, of what concern is it to us who that messenger was and what his name was? — and to give consideration to what all the circumstances point out and prove! There was a godly and holy man who held the patriarch Abraham in high esteem and came to him with sure hope of the deliverance that would be granted by God through him.

Why, then, does he bring this message to Abraham in preference to everyone else? Why does he not return to his own home, content with his own safety? In the first place, he is distressed by the defeat of his brothers; in the second place, he has the hope that through Abraham, as His beloved deliverer, God will set the captives free and restrain the arrogance of the heathen. One can reflect on this intention of his with profit, but whether one knows his name or not is of no concern at all.

Here for the first time Abraham is called a Hebrew, and there are extensive discussions about this name. Augustine (although he retracts this opinion later on) and Burgensis maintain that the Hebrews got their name from Abraham; but this is erroneous.[12] Above, in chapter ten, we heard praise for the house of Eber, who was the father of all the sons of Eber (Gen. 10:25 ff.). From him Abram receives this surname and is called a Hebrew because he adhered to the faith and confession of Eber.

When all the rest forsook the sound doctrine and the true worship of God and joined various sects at the time of the hideous division of languages, Eber retained the true worship, resisted the idolatry of the Babylonians, and overcame the awful offense caused by Nimrod and his followers. For this reason it was only right that all his descendants, that is, the church itself up to the time of Christ, were called Hebrews.

Since Abram was his follower, he is called a Hebrew, not so much because of blood relationship as on account of the religion he had received from Eber.

Hence wherever this name appears in the Scriptures, we must understand the Hebrews to mean the followers of the pure religion and the true church.

Thus Abram is expressed called a Hebrew here, that is, one of the pure and true saints who did not deteriorate like the others from the house of Shem and of the other holy fathers.

[12] This material comes from Lyra on Gen. 14:13, sec. d.

So far as its true meaning is concerned, עֵבֶר is an adverb and means "across" or "beyond." The Hebrew language makes no distinction between "on this side" and "on the other side"; therefore עִבְרִי is a passer, one who is across.

Perhaps this name was given to Eber by his father through the Holy Spirit because he would separate from the idolaters and would not live with them.

When Abraham hears the messenger, he is not perturbed by the plight of the five cities and their kings. But he is worried about his kinsman Lot. Therefore he takes counsel with the brothers Mamre, Aner, and Eshcol, and urges them to bring aid. The text also states that there was an alliance among them.

They deserve praise not only for their kindheartedness in receiving the sojourner Abraham hospitably but also for their saintliness and godliness. For if they had not had the true knowledge of God and, having given up the practice of idolatry, had not actually learned to worship God aright, Abram would never have allied himself with them by a covenant.

But their faith becomes especially apparent in this: the risk does not induce them to refuse their help, but they unite with Abram, certain that God will be with him and will grant victory.

But anyone who has given consideration to the glorious victories of the four kings and their power will easily estimate how difficult it was to believe this. What is Abraham with his allies in comparison with these?

But these holy Amorites, who had been made participants of the divine blessing through Abraham, comfort themselves with the sure hope of God's help. They know that Abraham is dear to God. Therefore they fear no danger and ally themselves with him. It is for this reason that the Holy Spirit wanted to give special praise to their godliness by revealing that they were united with Abram in an alliance and that they brought him aid.

14. *When Abram heard that his kinsman had been taken captive, he led forth his trained men, born in his house, three hundred and eighteen of them, and went in pursuit as far as Dan.*

Here is an outstanding example of brotherly love. Without a doubt Abram heard about the rout of the five kings and the sack of their cities. But he does not arm himself for their sakes; for he knows, as Scripture states, that they are the worst of all men. He does not interefere with God's just judgment. So far as they are concerned, he lets the punishment run its course.

But the situation of his kinsman was different: he knew God, he called upon and worshiped God, and the ungodliness of his fellow citizens distressed him. Therefore Abraham considers him worthy to be freed, and he gets his servants ready; that is, he equips and arms them.

The verb רִיק actually means to bring out or draw a sword. So in the psalm (35:3): "Draw the spear against my enemies," where our translation has "pour out." [13] But in this passage one may correctly translate it "to arm."

Where the Latin has "servants," the Hebrew is חֲנִיכִים. This is derived from the verb חָנַךְ, which means to dedicate or consecrate. Thus they say "to dedicate a vineyard, a house, or a bride," in the sense of to take possession of, or as we say in German, to take charge of and occupy. Thus a house is dedicated when it is lived in. Therefore those are called חֲנִיכִים who have been brought up and trained by someone in his household.

From this one may estimate the wealth and power of Abram, who had so many domestics that had been brought up in his house and were fit for war.

Among these were many husbands, who themselves had numerous children. If you count the children, the mothers, and the maids, I believe that Abram's household amounted to at least a thousand persons. He himself supported them all.

For where there are three hundred and eighteen men who are fit for war and, as Scripture calls them, חֲנִיכִים, born and brought up in the house, there necessarily are many brothers, sisters, daughters, and mothers. Thus God played strangely with this holy patriarch by giving him such a large household, yet not even a footbreadth of ground (Acts 7:5).

Consider, by contrast, our present-day customs: a husband and wife away from their own country can hardly find a place to stay, even for themselves.

Therefore these must have been people of outstanding kindness and godliness, to receive a householder who was encumbered with such a large number of persons. But without a doubt there was greater frugality at that time, and people did not waste the necessities of life so shockingly, as we are in the habit of doing today.

[13] The Vulgate has *Effunde frameam*.

Some have compared this number of Abraham's army to the Council of Nicaea, at which three hundred and eighteen bishops dealt a blow to Arius;[14] but this has nothing to do with the subject matter, even though the allusion is rather pretty.

15. *And he divided his forces against them by night, he and his servants, and routed them and pursued them to Hobah, north of Damascus.*

This is an outstanding miracle. The Holy Spirit wanted all posterity to become aware of it. That is why He first described the four monarchs or kings, as well as their outstanding and glorious victory when they defeated the Rephaim, the Zuzim, and the Emim, and sacked the five cities after their kings had been defeated.

For who would not marvel at the bold undertaking, that all by himself, with a mere three hundred and eighteen household slaves who had not been trained for war but were tending cattle and had now been armed for the first time, Abraham pursues these four victorious kings and their army and has the courage to attack them? Is this not an impossible and unbelievable situation?

Let us consider what sort of man Abraham was. Earlier he was so apprehensive that out of fear for his life he denied that Sarah was his wife; but now he is so brave and daring, and so strengthened by the Holy Spirit, that with a few men, not trained for war at that, he has the courage to pursue the four monarchs. What is there in the historical accounts of all the heathen to match this courage?

The Alexanders, the Hannibals, and the Scipios vie among themselves over supremacy in the glory of achievement, but I place Abraham ahead of them all.

He faces the enemy, not with a blind attack or with reckless daring but in faith; and so he is victorious. He had an insight that neither Alexander nor Scipio could have: through the Holy Spirit he brings along from home into battle the conviction that he would be victorious and that he would release his brother Lot. This is what is most admirable in his victory; and this is why it surpasses all the victories of all the heathen, be they ever so brilliant.

Aside from this, Abraham is a poor foreigner in the land of Canaan, for he does not own a footbreadth of ground. Moreover, he is so

---

[14] There were considerably fewer than three hundred eighteen bishops at Nicaea, but the number was soon changed in the light of this passage in the Book of Genesis; cf. the *Ad Afros epistola synodica* (*ca.* 369), par. 2.

fainthearted that in Egypt, because of his fear of death, he denies that Sarah is his wife. But here he is given such courage by the Holy Spirit that he promises himself the victory over the four monarchs, and there is no doubt that through this faith he would have overcome the forces of the entire world.

Moreover, how great his self-restraint is! He reverts to a peaceful life after he has defeated these monarchs, and he lays down his arms when he could, with the sword, take possession of the land of Canaan, which was promised to him by God!

But he does not do this; he remains a sojourner and a guest, and acquires nothing by force of arms. He draws the sword against these kings, not because he is actuated by some covetousness but in order to free his kinsman, whom he saw innocently involved in the misfortunes of the community.

Let us remember that he is not set before us as an example that we should imitate, as Münzer and the rebellious peasants did. They wanted to fight in accordance with Abraham's example, although they did not have Abraham's spirit.[15] For Abraham resorts to the sword and arms his men, not recklessly but at the command of the Holy Spirit; otherwise he would have sinned.

We must distinguish between a miracle and examples. The latter we should imitate, but the former we cannot imitate without presumption. Indeed, it would be useless and dangerous to imitate it.

Thus in all actions you must first be certain of the command of God. If you are not sure, forbear, or you will come to grief.

The extraordinary prompting of the Holy Spirit is described in this passage for our comfort. We should know how wonderfully God deals with His saints, that we may learn to have hope in trials, but to restrain our rash impulses when we are not being tried. After Abram has set his brother free, he lays down his arms. He does not become arrogant because of his victory; nor does he by force of arms take possession of a place where he may dwell with his people, although he could very easily do so. The distinguished victor is satisfied with his lot and does not give up his exile, to which he knows he has been called. These facts are worthy of note.

Samson also performed many very great and almost unbelievable feats, but Abraham's victory is far more glorious. We are right to extol his outstanding faith, for he is not dismayed by the small number of his own people or by the large number of the enemy; he simply

[15] See p. 320.

concludes that the victory will be his, not because of some rash impulse but as a result of his sure hope of the divine aid promised by the Holy Spirit.

Yet Abram does not undervalue the ordinary means. With prudence and with a definite plan he undertakes the attack, and at night he falls upon the unsuspecting men in their sleep. Roused by their danger, the enemies are frightened by the angel of the Lord and take to flight; for they do not realize that there are so few against them.

Similarly, we heard above that Pharaoh was frightened (Gen. 12:18). In faith Abraham foresaw this outcome, that through His angel God would put the enemy to flight. Hence it was not the swords and the weapons but the faith of Abraham that routed the enemy.

For God's grace responds to faith; where it is present, the victory is already won, and only then are plans and arms granted success.

Abraham makes use of a military stratagem both when he attacks the enemy at night and when he attacks with a divided army, not in one place but in many. And so the enemy, thrown into disorder by fear and danger, suppose that a countless multitude is present and turn to flight. The weapons frighten them, but it is actually the faith of Abraham and of his people that defeats them and puts them to flight.

Gideon is called by God and is strengthened even by miracles, yet he is afraid. Abraham attacks such powerful enemies without such a call, without an army, and without signs and wonders. Was this not outstanding faith and truly heroic courage?

Dan lies within the borders of the land of Canaan. Moses states that Hobah is to the left of Damascus, but what sort of place it was we do not know. Since the camp and all the booty had been left behind, Abraham seized the possessions of the enemy without any risk and with utmost safety.

Let us, therefore, learn how God takes care of His own and how wonderfully He guides them, and in trials let us comfort ourselves with examples of this kind. God permits His own to be tried in various ways and to be vexed to the point of despair, but in the end He gloriously delivers them and magnificently exalts them. Abram did not dare hope for such a great blessing. It would have been enough for him if he could free his kinsman. But now other advantages are added, for Moses relates the following.

16. *Then he brought back all the goods, and also brought back his kinsman Lot with his goods, and the women and the people.*

Thus one man who is loved by God is the occasion and cause for many blessings upon others. The people in the five cities were very wicked. For this reason God visited them with war, yet on Abraham's account many are set free. Hence he was truly, as was stated above, "a blessing even for the evil." Similarly, on the other hand, an entire nation often suffers for the offense of one person when God is angry.

Let us, therefore, maintain not only that Abraham was a heroic man, but that he was also full of faith and spirit. For this reason he was not only successful, but he also took a very modest advantage of his victory and behaved very humbly, as the following events will show. As I said before, he could have taken possession of the entire land of Canaan after this victory; but he did not understand his promises as dealing with a material blessing only. For he endured being an exile in the land of Canaan and looked at the spiritual blessing, as Christ states (John 8:56): "Abraham saw My day and was glad." Therefore he deserves to be praised and preferred above all the monarchs of the world.

The text makes mention of the captive women whom Abram brought back. It is the mischief of war that the weaker sex is the spoil, and that in their lust ungodly soldiers mistreat girls and matrons. And this is generally the saddest aspect of warfare, that it disrupts marriages and carries off children. But God wants these punishments of sin to be apparent, in order that we may learn to resist the desires of the flesh and to obey His voice.

But He mitigates His wrath with His marvelous goodness, and this on account of one righteous person whom the same punishment had carried away. The Sodomites and their neighbors were very wicked men; therefore God visited them with war, and the wrath of God rested heavily on them. Yet these villainous and ungrateful people receive this outstanding benefit through Abraham because of pious Lot. Their wives, children, and possessions are restored to them.

Thus God honors His own, and often, because of one or two persons, He preserves the most wicked and most ungrateful people. There is no doubt that the entire world would go to ruin in one moment if some holy men were not standing in the way of God's wrath and were placating God with their prayers.

The ancient poets had the excellent idea — no doubt on the basis of the discourses of the fathers — that Atlas carried the heavens on his shoulders; for there are always people on earth who bear the wrath of the Lord and on whose account God spares the world.

Jerusalem could not be captured and destroyed as long as the apostles lived and taught there. But when the time of its capture was at hand, they were commanded to flee to the mountainous regions and to withdraw to Galilee.

Christ says in the Gospel (Matt. 22:7) that the army sent by the king destroyed the murderers; and below the angel says to Lot (Gen. 19:22): "Go to Zoar, and save yourself there; for I can do nothing till you arrive there."

Hence both statements are true: God spares the wicked because of the pious; and when He punishes, He punishes the wicked.

But the world neither believes nor understands this. Look, for instance, at the Turk, who has unbelievable successes and magnificent victories over us. Is he not so puffed up by them that with this one argument he wants to prove that he is more pious and more righteous than we are? Actually, if it were not for this church of the saints, God would utterly destroy not only the Turk but the entire world.

Just as many people were saved through Abram and because of Lot, people who, after suffering a defeat, got back their native land and their possessions — something they would never have ventured to wish for — so it still happens that whatever good thing the world has, it has solely thanks to the saints on earth and because of them.

Hence when you see God's blessing, you would be doing the right thing if you encouraged yourself and reflected that there is still a church on earth and that the holy seed has not perished altogether, even though it is small in number, and that because of it God shows kindness to all the rest of the world.

The ungodly do the opposite. They assume that they are the cause of the blessing, and they attribute everything to their own wisdom and righteousness. Therefore they smugly give themselves up to their pleasures; they revel and are arrogant, just like the Sodomites. Eventually they are punished, but the godly are preserved.

But this account also serves to make you see how the pious are always being trained by their own adversities, that they may be cleansed more and more and daily become more pious. For the elect all things work together for good (Rom. 8:28), even the rod and the cross. The flesh is mortified, faith is strengthened, and the gift of the Holy Spirit is increased.

On the other hand, when the ungodly are burdened with a cross, they become worse; for the German proverb holds good, that after a sickness people rarely become better. For the time being they indeed repent and suffer torment, like the Egyptian Pharaoh; but later on they slip back into their former tracks and become even worse. This is the nature of the ungodly. This lashing should have taught the Sodomites to come to their senses, but they become worse and do not cease until they are utterly destroyed.

The perverseness of the human heart is surely great. In misfortunes and dangers there is nothing more fearful and nothing more dejected than an ungodly person. The world seems to narrow for him;[16] and if he could, he would force his way through mountains of bronze. But when the storm subsides, all fear is shaken off, and he reverts to type.

For example, a story is told about a sailor who was overtaken by a storm and made vows to St. Nicholas, the alleged patron of seafarers, that if he were saved, he would set up a silver statue for him; but when he had been saved, he did not set up even a wooden one.

Hence the proverb is true, that after long journeys and extended illnesses men become worse. For those who are not truly mortified are humbled only outwardly. Thus the comic poet represents the young slaves as seemingly faithful and obedient to their masters; but if the masters turn their backs, the slaves immediately revert to type.[17]

Let us, therefore, remember that God sends a scourge with the intention that after we have been humbled, we should repent and improve. But those who return to their vomit (2 Peter 2:22) will, like the Sodomites, bring an even more serious evil upon themselves.

17. *After his return from the defeat of Ched-or-laomer and the kings who were with him, the king of Sodom went out to meet him at the Valley of Shaveh (that is, the King's Valley).*

You observe that the king of the Sodomites has also been humbled for the time being. He goes out to meet Abraham, whom previously he perhaps had not even considered worth looking at. And you should not imagine that he came alone to meet him; he brought with him

---

[16] Cf. *Luther's Works*, 14, p. 37, note 40.

[17] This was a theme of several Latin comedies.

his royal retinue; and when they all prostrated themselves at the feet of the holy patriarch, they appeared to acknowledge that it was God who had given the victory.

Now if Moses had recorded the words of those who expressed their congratulations and the happy shouts of welcome — for they acknowledged and praised him as truly the father of the fatherland and worthy of a royal scepter, because he had achieved such great things with such success — you would say that the Sodomites, who had been the worst possible people, had become the holiest. But how long does this last? Abram was about eighty-six years old. Isaac is born when Abram is a hundred years of age, but by then Sodom lies there destroyed.

Thus they enjoy the grace and mercy that belonged to Abraham, and they become sharers of someone else's faith and love. They should have been reminded by this lashing, as well as by this blessing, that they ought to refrain from sin and live a holy life. And the beginnings were indeed favorable; they go to meet Abraham and express their gratitude with extraordinary respect. But after a few years the peace and quiet drive them crazy; they revert to type and forget the disaster. Moreover, they no longer acknowledge Abraham as the originator of their blessing, but they ascribe it to their own effort that they dwell in the Paradise of God and in the best part of the world.

Therefore they smugly indulge in sins, and by their ingratitude they heap up other sins. Not only the holy men but even God Himself receives no honor at all among them.

Therefore just as the godly are improved by the lash of God, so after disasters the ungodly become worse and drive God to the extreme punishment of utterly destroying them. Thus in our time Greece has been laid waste and destroyed by the Turk.[18] The same thing will happen to the Germans; they will not be protected by the virtue of their princes.

The philologians argue much about the King's Valley. Lyra, who follows the Targum, maintains that it was a plain in which the king trained his soldiers and horses for war, and also one in which he was in the habit of walking about.[19]

To me it seems likely that this was the name of a certain place,

[18] The Turkish conquest of Greece had been going on for a century, since before the fall of Constantinople in 1453; but the island of Rhodes, for example, did not fall until 1523.

[19] Lyra on Gen. 14:17, sec. o.

just as we call "royal" a valley near Saalfeld because it is a very deep valley; likewise we call a mountain in Franconia "royal" because of its excellent grapes; likewise *Fürstenfeld*.

Thus it was called the "King's Valley" because it was vast. Toward it there hastened from all the neighboring places those who had lost either wives or slaves or their possessions. I have no doubt that it was in the neighborhood of Jerusalem, outside the territory of the king of Sodom.

Abraham, marching home from Damascus to Hebron with his men, kept Sodom on his left. Perhaps he wanted to go to Jerusalem to Melchizedek, the high priest, and intended to give thanks to God there and to tell him about the great blessing of God and about the glorious victory that God had granted.

But after Melchizedek has learned about the victory through rumors, he and his men meet Abraham as he is distributing the booty. This was a very beautiful gathering of the church from all nations. And so Melchizedek, the priest and king, delivers an excellent sermon, in which he first bestows high praise on the kindness of God, who had blessed Abraham. He wants this outstanding gift to be recognized and thanks given to God for it. In the second place, he adds a prayer, as is customary in sermons, and blesses Abraham.

18. *And Melchizedek king of Salem brought out bread and wine; he was priest of God Most High.*

At this point it is customary to discuss, in the first place, who Melchizedek was, since it is written in the seventh chapter of the Letter to the Hebrews (v. 3) that he was without a father, without a mother, without a genealogy, without a beginning or an end. Therefore he is a type of our Priest Christ, who is the eternal Priest.

It is true that Melchizedek is mentioned in this passage very abruptly. Moses simply states that he was the king of Salem; but he does not mention his family, the time at which he began to rule, or those who succeeded him in the kingdom. The Epistle to the Hebrews is right in applying this to the eternal kingdom of Christ.

On the basis of the general conviction of the Hebrews it is assumed that this Melchizedek is Noah's son Shem.[20] Even though not much depends on whether their conviction is right or wrong, I gladly agree with their opinion; for the computation of the times

[20] Lyra on Gen. 12:6, sec. q.

based on the historical accounts proves not only that Shem was living at that time, but that he even survived Abraham, and that he died not long before Jacob's entry into Egypt.

Consider, therefore, what kind of ruler Abraham had, namely, the holy survivor of the first world and of the Flood. Without a doubt Shem often brought this sad example of God's wrath to the attention of his people.

It is awful to think that in so short a time the world deteriorated so much; for a little later, Shem, who saw the Flood, saw the Tower of Babel built by the ungodly and the languages confused, the most serious misfortune that could happen to the church if you consider the ministry of the Word. And so the entire Orient departs from the true worship. Abram and Lot are rescued from idolatry by God. Later there arise the wars of the kings; Lot is carried off; and Sodom and its entire vicinity are destroyed by fire from heaven because of their sins.

In this manner Scripture covertly indicates how great the wickedness of the world was at that time, and how awful the contempt of the Word; and further, how extraordinary the godliness and virtue of Abraham was. He overcomes all these offenses with a strong faith and accepts and honors the despised Shem as the only minister or priest of the true God.

Such examples comfort us if they are properly considered; for if it happened to those outstanding men that they found so few disciples, is it any wonder that today there is such a great multitude of the ungodly, while the church is so isolated and so small?

Thus I am pleased with the general opinion that Melchizedek is Shem, because there was no greater patriarch at that time, especially in spiritual matters. By common consent the churches and the people honored him with this name and called him מַלְכִּי־צֶדֶק, which means righteous king, because of the office he held.

He held both offices, that of king and that of priest. And although he did nothing inordinate in the government but managed all affairs righteously, he gained a reputation for righteousness because of his service in the church; for he taught the forgiveness of sins through the future Seed of the woman.

Since the world either had no knowledge of this doctrine or considered it worthless and persecuted it, Shem alone was called a righteous king. This holy and venerable old man the people of Salem chose to be their king.

In the neighborhood were the kings of Sodom and Gomorrah, and others, who far surpassed him in wealth and prestige. Without a doubt they despised this poor but righteous king; but in his own church and among his own people Shem is [21] Melchizedek, that is, a righteous king.

The others are tyrants, servants of idols, originators of offenses, and kings of unrighteousness; and the wrath of God, war, and the sword overtake them. But Shem is king in Salem; that is, he is a king of peace.

Because he inculcates the true doctrine about the Son of God, preserves the churches, the worship, and the discipline, not only the peace of the world but also the peace of God comes upon him.

This is the reason why he loses his own name and, with the consent of the fathers and of the godly, is called Melchizedek because of his office, and king of Salem because of the place. Thus Peter calls the patriarch Noah a preacher of righteousness (2 Peter 2:5) because he taught how we are justified before God.

Therefore we shall maintain that in those times Shem was the high priest. Scripture honors him with true and very beautiful praise when it gives him the name "righteousness."

What is our Roman pontiff, who insolently boasts that he is the head of the church, in comparison with Shem? His praises and the eulogies of his virtues stand out in 2 Thess. 2:3-4, where it is said that he is the king of ἀνομία and the enemy of righteousness.

But here another question arises, about the bread and the wine that were brought out. The papists know that Melchizedek is a type of Christ. Moreover, because it is stated that he brought out bread and wine, they force this into an analogy and declare it to be a type of the sacrifice of the Mass, in which, following the example of Melchizedek, what is seemingly bread and wine but is actually the body and blood of Christ is offered for the blessing of him who offers it and of others.

As a result, the account before us is celebrated in public hymns and is solemnly sung. And Lyra, who is surely a theologian not to be despised, defends this opinion very strenuously.[22]

But the good man is mistaken and does not note what part of the analogy the Letter to the Hebrews stresses most.

[21] The Weimar edition has *et* here; but we have followed the other editions, which read *est*.

[22] Lyra on Gen. 14:18, sec. b.

About the bringing out or the offering of the bread and the wine the author of the Letter to Hebrews says absolutely nothing.

For in this there is no suggestion of an analogy. What contributes toward an analogy is this, that this king has the name "righteousness" and that he is a priest too, a priest who blesses. This is not done according to the order of Levi, from whom, in the person of Abraham, a tithe is taken here, and who has a father and a genealogy; but Melchizedek is without a father, without a mother, and ἀγενεαλόγητος.

The analogy, therefore, lies in these features, and especially in the statement that He is an eternal Priest, not mortal like the Levites but the eternal Son of God. He lives forever and forever rules His church. As a Priest, He teaches, reconciles, prays, is not temporal, and is not united with sinners. And even though He bore all the infirmities of our flesh, He nevertheless dies no more.

This analogy the author of the Letter to the Hebrews notes; but about the bread and the wine, as a historical detail, he is not concerned at all.

What is the purpose of this sacrifice, even if we should grant that it is a sacrifice? Surely, one should not compare it to the sacrifice of Christ, which is everlasting and, after it has once been made, is valid forever. For this Priest "entered once for all into the Holy Place . . . and by a single offering He has perfected those who are sanctified." [23]

But the sacrifice of the papists differs in no wise from that of the Levites; for it is repeated daily. Therefore, as the Letter to the Hebrews states, it must be considered an imperfect sacrifice.

One must, therefore, hold fast to the statement of the psalm (110:4): "Thou art a Priest forever." The Levites had their sacrifices and their priests; but they were temporal, where one followed the other. Our Priest, however, is both without an end and without a successor. Indeed, He is even without a beginning; for He is from eternity and lives eternally, and He also has an eternal sacrifice, by which we who live from the beginning of the world until the end of the world have been redeemed.

This is what the Letter to the Hebrews wants considered, not the offering of bread and wine or the offering of the blood and body of Christ about which the papists are dreaming.

Lyra is very much incensed against the Jews because they explain

---

[23] A conflation of Heb. 9:12 and Heb. 10:14; cf. *Luther the Expositor*, pp. 237—254.

the verb הוֹצִיא, "he brought out," as though he had set a table for refreshing the tired men and the prisoners, although the text clearly states that the enemy had left behind enough booty for them to eat. Therefore he maintains that it must be understood as referring to an offering.

I believe that Melchizedek brought out bread and wine; that is, he arranged a festive meal, as is customary for guests and friends who are just arriving, and that thus he gave thanks to God for the victory given to Abraham.

It was the custom, as appears from the books of Moses, that those who joyfully brought thanks banqueted before the Lord. The Levites kept their own part of the sacrifice, but those who brought the sacrifice would eat what remained in a solemn feast.

Thus, first of all, Melchizedek teaches and gives thanks to God; then, in order that there may be some evidence of the people's joy, he arranges a feast and in this manner congratulates Abraham on his victory and calls upon the rest of the church to give thanks.

This is the simplest meaning, and it is in harmony with Scripture; for when it speaks of daily and plain food, it expresses itself somewhat like this: "And he placed before him bread and water." But in this passage it speaks of the wine that was set before them, in order to express that it was a festive meal, just as we, too, live more luxuriously on festive days than when we perform our ordinary tasks.

But if someone should maintain that bread and wine were sacrificed by Melchizedek, I shall not object vehemently, provided that he grants me this, which is the point at issue, that in the Supper Christ did not sacrifice bread and wine but distributed it. For the text does not say that He sacrificed bread, but that He gave it to His disciples. And no sane person is so impudent as to maintain that the apostles were commanded to sacrifice bread and wine.

But when the papists make this assertion, they clearly betray a sickly mind and extraordinary lack of sense. Thus Faber cites evidence from Theocritus and Vergil to prove that in 1 Cor. 11:24-25 Christ used the word "to do" in the sense of "to sacrifice." [24]

But this prattle does not deserve to be refuted. For what does the fact that Melchizedek brings out bread and wine have to do with the Mass? Whoever tries to prove the sacrifice of the Mass from this

---

[24] Vergil, *Bucolics*, Ecl. III, l. 77.

could just as well prove purgatory, the primacy of Peter, and indulgences from the same passage!

Perhaps someone could contrive out of this the allegory that just as Melchizedek brings out bread and wine, so Christ brings out the bread of life and the wine of joy, that is, the Holy Spirit with His gifts. But allegories of this sort prove nothing, and it is better to teach these things at their proper places; for it is hazardous to change meanings in this way and to depart so far from the literal meaning.

Therefore I advise that the simple and sound meaning should be accepted, which the very character of the words and the circumstances suggest: that after Melchizedek had preached and had given thanks to God for the outstanding victory, they arranged a joyous and sumptuous feast, like that on a holiday, in order to urge others also to give thanks.

But when the papists depart from this simple meaning and are intent on confirming and adding support to their sacrifice, which is private and not public, they even shamelessly pervert the text; for they insert in the passage a causal conjunction, although it is not in the text.[25]

They read thus: "Melchizedek, the king of Salem, brought out bread and wine, for he was the priest of the most high God" — obviously in order that their argument may have force: because he was a priest, he sacrificed when he brought out bread and wine.

But even if we grant them this, what follows? What does this have to do with Christ, who did not sacrifice bread and wine but distributed it to His disciples? What does it have to do with the church, which, in conformity with Christ's example, does not sacrifice bread and wine but distributes it to the believers? Yes, what does it have to do with you, you priest? You are not going to sacrifice bread and wine, are you? If so, what great feat are you performing? Or if, as you dream, you sacrifice the body and blood of Christ, what does this have to do with the sacrifice of Melchizedek? Will you not finally open your eyes and learn the truth? You are not the one who offers the body and blood of Christ, are you? For Christ did this Himself.

But this sacrifice of Christ is eternal, according to this statement (Heb. 10:14): "By a single offering He has perfected those who are sanctified." If, then, the sacrifice that Christ once offered has been perfectly made, what is left for you to do? Are you going to add

---

[25] The Vulgate has *erat enim Sacerdos Dei altissimi*.

something to its perfection? If, as you hope, you are adding something, the sacrifice of Christ is no longer perfect but is imperfect, inasmuch as it needs your sacrifice.

This desecration alone, by which the sacrifice of Christ is blasphemed, is reason enough for us to separate from the church of the pope. Why should we give up Christ's sacrifice and accept a human being's sacrifice, for which there is no command anywhere in the Word of God?

Christ says (1 Cor. 11:24-25): "Do this in remembrance of Me"; that is, "Take, eat, and drink this bread and cup, and proclaim My death." He does not say: "Sacrifice the bread and the wine." Where, then, will they get proof for their own sacrifice?

Thus we read in this passage about Melchizedek that he brought out bread and wine; or, as the Hebrew has it, he caused bread and wine to be brought out, or had them brought out, as one ordinarily does from a pantry.

About the sacrifice of the New Testament absolutely nothing is said. But if Melchizedek is a type of Christ, it will not immediately follow that Christ, too, must bring out bread and wine. And it is fully certain from the Letter to the Hebrews and from Ps. 110:4 why Christ is called a Priest according to the order of Melchizedek, namely, not because He offers bread and wine, but because He is an eternal Priest and bestows blessings.

This perversion of Scripture shows how in every age Satan has used God's name and Scripture for blasphemies, and how the descendants gradually strayed from the faith of their fathers.

The psalm, as I have stated, makes mention of the priesthood of Melchizedek, and the Letter to the Hebrews has masterfully elucidated the entire discussion. But what has the pope done? Disregarding the facts which the Holy Spirit wanted considered especially, he is concerned with this alone, that bread and wine are sacrificed by Melchizedek; and out of this he invents the sacrifice of the Mass, which is the utmost desecration and abomination.

Thus he keeps the name of our Savior and the sacraments; but since he has lost the Spirit, he misuses these for blasphemies only and takes the name of the Lord in vain. Out of the sacraments he makes a human work, for to the promises of the forgiveness of sins he adds the condition of worthiness and satisfaction. Thus he turns everything into misuse.

Let us, therefore, give thanks to God for our deliverance from these nuisances and for our true knowledge of religion and the real meaning of Scripture.

We know that it is a historical fact when this passage speaks about bringing out bread and wine. But that Melchizedek blesses Abraham and that Abraham gives him tithes — this we know is the main point the Holy Spirit wanted to emphasize, in order to signify the priestly office of Christ, which is eternal and which consists solely in bestowing blessings, as He forgives sins and frees from death all who believe in Him. He deserves the name "Righteous King," and He is the King of שָׁלֵם, or of peace.

But here it must also be noted that in this passage Moses calls God by a new name. He states that Melchizedek was a priest לְאֵל עֶלְיוֹן, of God Most High. The psalms rather frequently employ this name;[26] I believe it is derived from the word עַל, which means "over" or "upward," to indicate the difference of the forms of worship in existence at that time.

The king of Sodom, the king of Gomorrah, the Rephaim, the Babylonians, and others had their own particular gods and forms of worship; for the world has always been full of various kinds of sects. But the holy fathers and the descendants of Eber worshiped God עֶלְיוֹן, that is, the Most High, who above all others is the one and eternal God.

Hence the angels also sing (Luke 2:14): "Glory to God in the highest," while Satan and his condemned angels fly about in the air. But the true God has a higher abode, which Satan is unable to reach.

By this name the holy fathers wanted to exclude the various gods and forms of worship and condemn them, for they worshiped Him alone who is the supreme and the Most High.

Paul says in 1 Cor. 8:5-6: "There are many gods" (that is, the world has various forms of worship); "but for us there is one God" (that is, we adhere to the One who gave His Son for us and who through His Spirit gathers for Himself a church on earth).

Hence this is the meaning of this passage: Melchizedek was a priest, prophet, and preacher who continued pure in the knowledge of that God who is the true and Most High God. This name includes the repudiation of all other gods and forms of worship. At that time the world had other priests as well, but Melchizedek was the chief priest of the supreme God. Happy over the victory granted to Abraham by God, he arranged a festive meal.

[26] See, for example, Ps. 7:17; 9:2; 18:13, etc.

19. *And he blessed him and said: Blessed be Abram by God Most High, Maker of heaven and earth.*

Here again the text separates the worship and profession of Abraham from the forms of worship of all the heathen; and it confirms what was said above in chapter 12:3, that not only Abraham himself was blessed, but that he would be a blessing also for others. For through him had come rescue and blessing for his adversaries, who were under the curse and wrath of God and were paying the deserved penalties for their sins by a harsh captivity.

All this serves to comfort Abraham and to strengthen him in faith and patience. Abram had given glory to God among the heathen when he professed the true doctrine publicly. Therefore, God exalts him in turn, in the sight of the heathen by this glorious victory. And now there comes the preacher, the holy patriarch, who did not end this address in so bald a manner as Moses relates but without a doubt added dialectical arguments and all sorts of rhetorical embellishments.

He said: "What are your [27] gods, whom you have worshiped thus far? My God alone is the Most High God. He has given this victory to His faithful servant and has performed this miracle which you have seen.

"Is it not a miracle that this one man with a few allies routed and put to flight so many powerful kings — and dreaded ones at that because of their great victories? Rid yourselves of your vile idols, who have turned you over to your enemies to be plundered, and accept our God, 'who alone does wonders' (Ps. 136:4)."

Melchizedek did not finish this sermon in a single hour; and even if one should assume that he finished it in one hour, later on it reached the neighboring heathen and various places. And thus through this wonderful work the true church was signally strengthened in the midst of very great difficulties.

Previously Abram had been a despised person, and his church was held in the utmost contempt in the eyes of the heathen. It is for this reason that he is compelled to move so often from place to place and to seek new abodes. But now, prompted by such an outstanding victory, all come running in large numbers and eagerly desire to see this foreigner, whom God in the highest has helped this way.

The Letter to the Hebrews gives a lengthy treatment of this passage, which states that Melchizedek blessed Abraham. And we must

---

[27] The "you" here is plural, for this is addressed to kings.

take note of the expression he uses; he calls him blessed by God Most High.

Before the world, as the account shows, Abraham was despised and unimportant; and without a doubt many cursed him. But for the Most High God he was one who was blessed, who was an heir of the blessing that the woman's Seed would bring. This blessing was not temporal; it was a real and eternal blessing of God.

The world admires earthly blessings, such as those in Ps. 144: 12-15: "May our sons in their youth be like plants full grown, our daughters like corner pillars cut for the structure of a palace; may our garners be full; may our sheep bring forth thousands; may our cattle be heavy. Happy the people to whom such blessing fall!" [28] Melchizedek is not speaking of such a blessing in this passage; he is speaking of the eternal and spiritual blessing, which deals with eternal life, about which the aforementioned psalm states (144:15): "Happy the people whose God is the Lord!" In this blessing Abraham finds comfort, but the temporal blessing he commits to God.

Now if he had given attention to the temporal blessing only, it would have been just as easy for him to take possession of the land of Canaan during this disturbance as it had been for him to rout these four kings. But he waits patiently for this blessing and comforts himself with a blessing that is God's real blessing, which carries with it the promise of spiritual and eternal benefits, namely, the forgiveness of sins through the blessed Seed and life eternal.

Through this sermon of Melchizedek Abraham is set apart from all the other fathers, and his house or family is marked with this most glorious distinction: that the blessing of God must surely be expected from it, and that there is no church anywhere except in the house of Abraham and among those who ally themselves with Abraham.

If the pope had such a promise, he could truthfully glory in the name "church." For the church is placed in the house of Abraham, as on a high and prominent mountain, so that people may see where God wants to dwell and whence the blessing of God and eternal life must be expected.

Therefore Abraham is called one who is blessed in the Most High God. Angels, princes of the world, and judges are also called gods, because they hold a divine office;[29] but God is called עֶלְיוֹן, the Most

---

[28] Ps. 144:12-13 was a favorite passage of Luther's as a denunciation of materialism; cf. *Luther's Works*, 22, p. 193.

[29] Notably in Ps. 82:6; cf. John 10:34.

High or the Highest, because He is the sole and only One above all things.

In this sermon therefore, Melchizedek presents Abraham to the entire world and declares that only with him, in his house and family, are the church, the kingdom of heaven, salvation, forgiveness of sins, and the divine blessing.

The occasion for this outstanding discourse was given by the miraculous victory. Thus not only were the bodies of the captives set free, but also countless souls were saved from eternal death after they had learned to know the true God on the basis of the obvious miracle and of the enlightening sermon. Truly, this victory was not unfruitful; it was glorious and remarkably effective, if you consider it carefully.

I remember reading about this as a young man; but because I was an inexperienced theologian and no competent teacher had happened along, I read about it without any admiration, as though it had been one of Livy's historical accounts. I was not aware that Abraham was being praised to us this way because he had the blessing of God, that is, the forgiveness of sins and eternal life, since he alone has the promise of the Seed and is called the blessed of the Lord.

Furthermore, the name of God is explained more fully by what the text adds about the Possessor of heaven and earth. The verb קָנָה means "to possess." From it comes the name קִנְיָן "possession." It points out the God who has heaven and earth under His control as His property and possesion. In this way, therefore, it excludes all false gods, yes, even angels, kings, the holy fathers, etc.

To this one Most High it ascribes being the Head of the family, whose abode is the heaven and the earth, and who, like the head of a household, directs and rules whatever there is anywhere — angels, devils, human beings, tyrants, slaves, saints, and wicked men. All these are in the household of God and are forced to acknowledge Him as the Head of the household and to obey His will.

"Abraham," says Melchizedek, "has a God who alone is the true God. If anyone does not believe this, let him consider this recent miracle, that with three hundred domestic slaves and eighteen confederates he overthrew the four most powerful kings. He will indeed agree that in the hand of this God are all the tyrants, indeed even all angels and devils."

A somewhat similar description of God is found in the Book of Daniel, when Daniel says to King Belshazzar (5:23): "The God in whose hand is your breath, and whose are all your ways, you have not honored." The breath and the air, says Daniel, without which no one can do for a moment — God owns them; we do not.

Melchizedek praises the Divine Majesty as the only and supreme God, who has everything in His hand and controls it with power and dispatch; for He gave the four kings into the hands of Abraham, a beggar and sojourner. "Why, then, do you deceive yourselves and worship stones and wood, the works of your own hands? Why do you not turn to the God of Abraham, who has revealed to you so clearly that He alone controls and possesses the heaven and the earth?"

He praises the God who bestows blessings, and at the same time he instructs the church and calls the heathen away from their idolatry to the true knowledge of God.

Now, just as we are in the habit of doing, he adds thanksgiving to this sermon, in order to carry out fully his duty as a priest. He strengthens Abraham in his faith, teaches the people about the true God, calls them away from idolatry, and gives thanks to this merciful God for His Word and His other gifts.

20. *Blessed be the God Most High, who has delivered your enemies into your hand!*

Here the philologists are at odds about the husks of the words. But let us adhere to the simple and true meaning. Melchizedek attributes the entire achievement to its true Performer, God, as though he were saying: "Abram, you have done great things; but God did them through you. This victory must be ascribed, not to you but to God, the Possessor of heaven and earth."

Abram gladly heard that the glory of this achievement was being transferred from him to its true Author. For him it was enough that he was blessed in the Most High God and that his house was destined to be the abode of the true church. The glory he gratefully leaves to God, and he himself was satisfied with peace on earth and the good will of men (Luke 2:14).

Scripture directs us to this humility so that we may not become proud because of our gifts but may maintain that they are not ours but God's; then we shall praise God with one accord and give thanks to him.

You notice that this is a rather short sermon if you count the words; but if one were to explain it more fully and elaborate on it according to the rules of the rhetoricians, he will see that it is very long and that it contains whatever can be discussed about religion. It gives instruction about the true God; it refutes the worship of idols; and it exhorts to humility and thanksgiving, because everything we have is ours solely as a favor and gift of God.

And he gave him a tenth of everything.

The Jews explain this passage in various ways, because the words sound as though Melchizedek had given tithes to Abraham. But there is, in the first place, the clear testimony of the Letter to the Hebrews (7:2), which not only declares that Abraham gave the tithes but also concludes from this that the priesthood of Melchizedek was something far greater than the Levitical priesthood, as the blessing also proves. For the lesser does not bless the greater, but the greater the lesser.

But the addition that he gave tithes of everything must in no wise be applied to the booty. A little later the text states clearly that Abraham was unwilling to accept of the booty even a thread or a shoelace offered him by the kings.

Thus the phrase "of everything" must not be applied to the booty, which Abraham restored to its owners, but to the possessions of Abraham. This was not the first time that he gave tithes of these to the priest Melchizedek; he did so every year.

Even before that victory Abraham conducted himself humbly, acknowledged Shem as a priest of the Most High, and gave him tithes, as did Lot and the other fathers who lived at that time. All these honored Melchizedek as the oldest and as one who through his ministry revealed a shadow of the future kingdom of Christ on earth.

The author of the Letter to the Hebrews carries on a most ingenious and learned discussion about the tithes that were given by Abraham; and the sure witness of the Holy Spirit is in it, for no one could have seen those things which he sees.

In the first place, he takes from the psalm (110:4) the statement that Christ is a Priest according to the order of Melchizedek. He ingeniously maintains these contrasts: therefore he is not a priest according to the order of Levi, and therefore He will not be, as Aaron was, a temporal priest; He will be an eternal one. For Melchizedek was without a father and without a mother, and had neither a beginning nor an end.

It also follows that the Levitical priesthood would come to an end completely, and that the spiritual priesthood would supersede the temporal. All this is learnedly thought out and can in no wise be refuted.

In the second place, he discusses the tithes: Abraham is the father of Levi; therefore if Abraham gives tithes to Melchizedek, who will deny that Melchizedek is far above Levi? Who will not agree that his priesthood is greater, more distinguished, and more excellent than the Aaronic priesthood? But Christ is a Priest according to the order of Melchizedek. Therefore let Aaron yield, and let the worship under the Law give way as a shadow gives way to the body.

Thus he concludes most emphatically that the priesthood under the Law must come to an end, because there is promised a Priest according to the order of Melchizedek. Before him Abraham, the father of Levi, humbled himself, and to him he gave tithes when Levi was still in his loins. But let the studious reader learn these matters from the author himself. We shall go on to the rest of the account.

21. *And the king of Sodom said to Abram: Give me the persons, but take the goods for yourself.*

22. *But Abram said to the king of Sodom: I have sworn to the Lord God Most High, Maker of heaven and earth,*

23. *that I would not take a thread or a sandal-thong or anything that is yours, lest you should say: I have made Abram rich.*

24. *I will take nothing but what the young men have eaten, and the share of the men who went with me; let Aner, Eshcol, and Mamre take their share.*

Thus far we have heard the outstanding sermon delivered in the royal valley at a gathering which included not only the king of Sodom himself but also the king of Salem, the priest of the supreme God, and without a doubt the other neighboring cities and nations. They congratulated Abraham on his outstanding victory and gave thanks to God for His splendid gift.

Certainly the king of Sodom acts as though he were converted and instructed by this sermon of the king of Salem and by the miraculous victory of Abraham. He converses in a most friendly manner with Abraham, whom he had previously despised as a beggar and sojourner and as one who had nothing that was his own in that land. And he not only congratulates him on such an outstanding victory, but as a reward for his victory he even offers him the entire booty and is more than satisfied if he receives the people as a gift.

We must not suppose that this wealth was small, for those four kings had plundered everything far and wide. Such great wealth he offers to Abraham with the utmost good will and asks that the souls — that is, the wives, sisters, daughters, citizens, young men, children, etc. — be given to him; for this is the meaning of נֶפֶשׁ. But the word רְכוּשׁ, which we render "goods," denotes every kind of wealth and possessions except human beings. All this — beasts of burden, herds, garments, gold, silver, and whatever else there is — he leaves to Abraham to take possession of it as a victor; he asks that the persons only, or the souls of the human beings, be restored to him.

But just as the king of Sodom deserves to be praised for his generosity in acknowledging Abraham worthy of such rewards, so Abraham likewise, who achieved this victory with his danger, efforts, and expenses, is set before the entire world, but especially before the entire church, as an exceptional pattern of all virtues. For he generously turns down the offer made to him and restores everything to its former owners. For himself he leaves not even a thread or a shoelace of all the booty.

Do you not observe in him a heart that is free of ambition, cupidity, greed, and the other vices by which even great men are commonly affected? How different the conduct of our centaurs is, who rightly or wrongly seize for themselves whatever they can! If princes add even one village to their domain, they at once demand that their titles and coats of arms be inscribed and amplified. They do not have even a trace of this generous disposition; but they look for glory, prestige, and advantage in everything they undertake.

But Abraham is concerned solely about the welfare of his neighbor. He does not want to be enriched and does not want even a thread added to his possessions.

This expression is unfamiliar to us, but it is a highly meaningful statement. The meaning of חוּט is "thread"; but this is an instance of synecdoche, as when one says "iron" for "sword."

Thus we read in Joshua (2:18) about a scarlet thread suspended from a window. This was not what we call a thread in German; but the raw material stands for the finished product, and thread denotes something made of thread, or something woven, a scarlet cord.

Thus in the Song of Solomon (4:3): "Your lips are like a scarlet thread," that is, like a scarlet cord.[30] So one should realize that in this passage the meaning is: "I not only do not want cattle, oxen, and asses, to say nothing of persons or prisoners; I not only do not want your garments, coats, and shoes; but I do not want even a cord with which to lace either shoes or bodices."

It was doubtless a common expression, just as when we say: "I wouldn't want a tag for myself." [31]

And so John says about Christ (Mark 1:7): "I am not worthy to untie His shoelace." This indicates his great humility. In the instance of attendants we notice that the servants touch the arms, the sides, and the feet of their masters when they are about to assist them. "This," says John, "I do not presume to do; for I am unworthy to unloose a lace of His footgear."

These figures of speech are very delightful and amazingly meaningful if we correctly understand the way these people expressed themselves.

But someone will say: "Why does Abraham act so proudly, and so rudely reject the generous offer of a neighboring king? Surely it was proper to demand back the costs of the war. He did not gain this victory without a huge effort and great danger. Why, then, does he refuse what as a victor he could claim as his own in full justice, since now the king even presents it to him?"

My answer is: This is manifest evidence to make one realize how Abraham understood the promises of God.

The Jews are still of the opinion that the promises of Holy Scripture deal with the wretched and troublesome life on this earth. But Abraham, who indeed had the material promise concerning the land of Canaan in his hand, voluntarily foregoes his divine right as victor to take possession of all those goods, as well as the gift of the king. He has knowledge of another greater and more lasting possession, namely, the blessed Seed. With this he is content; the other things he leaves to the will of the Lord and does not seize them by force when the opportunity presents itself but waits until the Lord Himself will put them into his hands.

Abraham is aware of the dispositions of people. In true humility — lest he be ungrateful to Abraham — the king of Sodom offers him

---

[30] The German phrase is *ein rote schnur*.

[31] Here again Luther breaks into German: *Ich wolt mir nit ein nestelstefft begeren.*

the possession of everything except the prisoners. But what would have happened if Abraham had accepted the proffered gift? Without fail the heathen would say that Abraham was enriched through their generosity and nobleheartedness, but this would completely obscure and cover up the immeasurably great and eternal promises given to Abraham.

Therefore he does the right thing when he declines this offer and does not accept even a thread. Thus it will be clear to everybody that whatever happens to Abraham later on, will happen solely as a result of the Lord's blessing, not as a result of any human favor.

Because Abraham is sure of the Lord's benevolence and certain that because of His blessing he would have more lands and wealth than the king of Sodom or anyone else could give him, he does the right thing when he declines this gift.

"Do not," he says, "cause me this disgrace, and do not impose this ignominy on me, that you, the king of Sodom, made me rich, and that if Abraham had not had you, he would have nothing. Take your booty and go, but do not impair my glorying in the only God, the kindly One who gives promises. He is the Possessor of heaven and earth, while you are only the possessor of Sodom. I shall hold fast to that Giver, Blesser, and Savior. You and your people, as human beings who yourselves need your possessions — you I shall let go."

Thus you see that the holy patriarch Abraham is endowed with all virtues. For the sake of his nephew Lot he serves in utmost love those who were unworthy of his kindnesses. When he has achieved the victory, he is not eager to increase his wealth and power but has a heart that is free of ambition, greed, and other lusts; and he clings only to the promise of eternal life and to the Possessor of heaven and earth.

This the blind Jews should consider in their father Abraham, of whom they boast in this passage. On this basis they should appraise the kingdom of the Messiah, to whom alone Abraham clings after disregarding the land of Canaan and all its wealth. He was promised to Abraham, not in order to grant him a kingdom in Sodom or the land of Canaan, and to make him similar to other kings, but to be God Most High, who can give more than the king of Sodom, who indeed could have made Abraham rich but could not have protected him against sin and death.

How much different the ungodly descendants are from their father! Abraham is content with eternal and spiritual benefits, and those that are material he proudly disdains; but they neither expect nor seek anything but what is material. They are so little concerned about the spiritual benefits that they even persecute and hate the preaching of the Gospel, because it is a doctrine that gives no instruction about wealth and power but only about the forgiveness of sins.

Thus Abraham is described to us here as full of faith and of hope concerning eternal life. He makes use of this earthly victory as of a field or any other thing that serves only to exercise the body but does not give the heart cause for worry. His heart he keeps attached to the mercy of God and to the promise of the future Seed, in accordance with the statement of the psalm (62:10): "If riches increase, set not your heart on them."

He has a wife, servants, and maids; but he has all these as though he did not have them. He is a true monk; for he truly despises the pleasures, glories, and riches of the world, and with his whole heart he is engaged in waiting for the promise concerning Christ. For this alone he longs and wishes, but other things he rates far below this and almost disregards in comparison with this superb gift.

The men who bring these accounts or legends to the attention of the people are right in their efforts and serve their churches well. Except for the prophets and the apostles, what are all the saints in comparison with Abraham? Although he took part in earthly affairs and managed the state as well as his household, nevertheless with a noble heart and a firm grasp on the divine and eternal promises, he despises and disregards those things. Without fear of the kings of the world or of the opinions of other people, he wants to keep unimpaired and inviolate his praise for God, the Possessor of heaven and earth.

But he is so concerned about his neighbor that while he disregards his own right, he wants the rights of others to remain unimpaired and inviolate. He does not want to be so faultless and perfect that he harms others. Therefore he wants Aner, Eshcol, and Mamre to have their full and complete share, and he does not pass judgment on them by his example.

This fairness is also an outstanding virtue. For you may observe many people who are pious in a perverted way and want to force others to follow their example. This is an obvious unfairness and should by no means be tolerated. But among Abraham's domestics there is outstanding piety as well as obedience.

At their own risk these men had been Abraham's companions in the battle, and they seem to have had the right to demand the booty they had obtained through their hard work. But Abraham gives them none of the booty except food and drink; and the godly servants are not offended, nor do they murmur. They want to show that they are like their master, and they gladly follow in the path of his godliness and his courtesy.

These examples are the sources on the basis of which laws, ordinances, and decrees ought to be drawn up. For God gave this age a man of unqualified rectitude, in comparison with whom Aeneas, Achilles, Agamemnon, etc., those heroes to whom the heathen give much praise, are nothing.

Here you see an inimitable example of great faith toward God and of perfect justice and love toward men.

Here you hear nothing, as in the prattle of the popes, about fasting, about a particular choice of food, about shaving the head, and about a special form of clothing. Abraham eats and drinks with his people what the season offers, but he practices faith and love with the utmost zeal.

And God did not kindle this light in those times without result. Through this courtesy many of the heathen were undoubtedly induced to accept the God of Abraham.

But if some were not moved by this excellent example, they deserved to be given over to their reprobate mind (Rom. 1:28); and God will eventually punish the ungrateful, as the following account about Sodom will show.

Let us, therefore, keep this outstanding example in mind, and let us set it before us to imitate as long as we live. The calling of the apostles and of the prophets was extraordinary. Moreover, Christ and John the Baptist are beyond comparison. But all these had a short span of life. Abraham, however, lived for a long time and did many wonderful deeds besides. Therefore he is rightly considered the chief of all the saints.

Index

By WALTER A. HANSEN

A baculo ad angulum 271 fn.
Aaron 17, 242, 393, 394
Abel 89, 116, 140, 197, 233
Abimelech 293, 305
Abiram 58
Abraham ix, x, 12, 25, 50, 72, 83, 99, 113, 114, 176, 197, 201, 205, 230, 234, 235, 238, 239, 240, 242, 243, 244, 245, 246, 247, 248, 249, 250, 251, 253, 255, 266, 267, 270, 272, 275, 276, 277, 279, 281, 282, 285, 286, 289, 290, 292, 295, 296, 297, 298, 299, 302, 304, 305, 307, 308, 309, 311, 312, 314, 316, 317, 325, 326, 329, 331, 333, 335, 341, 344, 349, 351, 353, 354, 357, 358, 360, 362, 363, 372, 373, 374, 377, 379, 380, 382, 384, 385, 388, 389, 390, 391, 392, 393, 394, 395, 396, 397
   almost swallowed up by church of Nimrod 231
   builds an altar 284
   called a Hebrew 371
   children of 179
   church of 334
   considered chief of all the saints 399
   descendants of 236, 237, 254, 257, 259, 260, 261, 265, 271, 280, 283, 359, 361
   exposes his wife to danger of adultery 291
   extraordinary friend and intimate of God 352
   faith of 278, 306, 322, 324, 276
   glorious victory of 369, 375, 381
   had very great wealth 252
   holy through faith 287
   knowledge of 222
   marriage of 241, 254, 256
   obedience of 268, 269
   perfect model of faith 294
   preached righteousness wherever he went 303
   preaching of 280
   seed of 257, 258, 260, 261, 262, 264, 265, 288, 294
   twofold posterity of 359
   was a priest and prophet of God 332, 336
Abram 201, 228, 237, 238, 240, 245, 250, 277, 283, 324, 325, 330, 332, 335, 336, 337, 341, 345, 349, 363, 371, 372, 373, 375, 376, 377, 378, 380, 382, 389, 392
Absalom 91
   fomented rebellion against his father David 168
Absolution 46, 48, 295
Abstinence 134 fn., 326
Academic degrees 220 fn.
Accad 199, 200
Achilles 399
Acquisitiveness 326
Acts of the Apostles 241
Ad Afros epistola synodica 374 fn.
Adam 7, 10, 28, 31, 52, 57, 71, 80, 82, 98, 114, 121 fn., 134, 140, 149, 209, 210, 219, 221, 222, 223, 224, 233, 235, 245
   second 26
Addis Ababa 195 fn.
Address to the Clergy to Preach Against Usury, by Luther 263 fn.
Adolescence 119
Adulterer(s) 59, 79, 122, 167, 312, 316
Adultery 6, 84, 141, 169, 203, 214, 291, 316
Aeneas 399
Aeolians 191
Aesop 159, 160
Affliction(s) 17, 24, 50, 61, 62, 93, 104, 105, 156, 195, 204, 226, 304, 307, 310, 319, 320

Africa 187, 194, 203, 364
Africans 194
Agamemnon 399
ἀγενεαλόγητος 384
Ahab 20
Ahasuerus 264, 304
Ai 282, 286
Air 94, 115, 147, 330, 388
Albert, Bishop of Mainz 199 fn.
Alexander 191, 285, 343, 346, 351, 368, 374
Allegory x, 68, 108, 144, 150, 151, 153, 154, 155, 156, 157, 160, 161, 162, 164, 386
  Augustine's, about creation of man and woman 152
  concerning church 109
  theological 158
  zeal for 150
Alms 263, 349
Alps 108
Altar(s) 112, 113, 114, 138, 192, 277, 284, 286, 332, 333, 363
Amalekites 78, 79, 355, 367, 368
Ambition 119, 125, 127, 171, 214, 338, 348, 395, 397
Ambrose 55, 154 fn.
ἀμετανόητα 43
Ammonites 189, 367
Amorite(s) 204, 362, 363, 372
Amos 190
Amphictyones 202
Amraphel 364
Anabaptists 18, 43, 83, 87, 150, 162, 243, 325, 326
Anakim 36
Analysis, grammatical and historical x
Andreas 73
Andria, by Terence 127 fn.
Aner 372, 398
Angel(s) 3, 38, 82, 130, 145, 151, 169, 202, 211, 212, 213, 240, 261, 265, 284, 288, 312, 355, 356, 378, 388, 390, 391
  appear in human form 46
  likeness of 227
  of Satan 105, 320, 388
  of the Lord 376
  who fell 4
Angelo Carletti di Chivasso 314 fn.
Anger 13, 19, 44, 119, 141, 215, 301, 307, 321, 322, 355
  God's 14, 17, 26
Animal(s) 52, 58, 59, 66, 70, 76, 77, 88, 90, 93, 96, 97, 106, 109, 116, 132, 136, 138, 139, 141, 142, 143, 324, 355
  clean 67, 89, 112, 114, 134
  domestic 69
  dumb 74, 75, 104, 115, 134, 144
  forest 133
  impure 160
  tame and manageable 69
  unclean 67, 68, 134, 135
  wild 69, 74, 75, 135, 137
Anniversaries 161
ἀνομία 383
Anselm 270
Anthony 355
Anthropomorphites 45
Antichrist 34, 38, 61, 101, 181, 213, 229, 316
Antinomians 18
Antioch 204, 317
Antiochus 359
Antiquities of the Jews, by Josephus 108 fn., 285 fn., 305 fn.
Apelles 150
Aphaca 18 fn.
Apis 18
Apocalypse 274
Apollonia 205
Apology of the Augsburg Confession 266 fn.
Apostasy 199, 212, 214
Apostate(s) 198, 213, 234
Apostle(s) 17, 40, 57, 76, 85, 86, 88, 192, 274, 289, 320, 321, 330, 354, 365, 378, 385, 398, 399
  foretold that Antichrist would be a respecter of persons 101
  occasionally employed allegories 151
Apostles' Creed 16 fn.
Apostolic succession 102
Apple(s) 136, 269, 350
  of Sodom 136 fn.
April 92
Aquinas, Thomas 44 fn., 313 fn., 314 fn., 315 fn.
Arabia 195, 283
Arabia Felix 195
Arabia Petraea 189, 367
Arabs 217
Aram 206, 279
Ararat 107, 108, 117, 207
Arbaces 206
Arguere a coniugatis 4 fn.
Arioch 365
Aristophanes 161 fn.
Aristotle 93 fn., 121, 124, 126, 146, 147, 159, 160, 162 fn., 190 fn., 199, 207, 208, 271 fn., 297, 303, 329, 340
Arius 374
Ark 28, 46, 58, 66, 69, 70, 72, 73, 75, 76, 77, 85, 89, 90, 91, 96, 97, 98, 103, 104, 105, 107, 109, 110, 111, 112, 114, 115, 116, 120, 152, 153, 156, 158, 159, 160, 162, 163, 174, 182, 192
  extraordinary structure of 81

INDEX

form and bulk of 67
  geometrical shape and proportion of 155
  remnants of 108
Armenia 107, 108, 189, 206
Arpachshad 197, 205, 206, 232
Arrogance 119, 225, 226, 371
Ars amandi, by Ovid 329 fn.
Ashdod 191
Ashes 136, 269, 343
Ashkenaz 109, 193
Ashteroth 367
Ashteroth-karnaim 367
Asia 108, 175, 185, 187, 193, 205
Asia Minor 108, 189
"Asinists" 151
Asphalt, lake of 269
Asshur 200, 201, 202, 205, 206, 214, 232, 247
Assumption of Mary 21 fn.
Assyria 202, 232, 365
Assyrians 98, 200, 206, 365
Astronomy 305
ἀταξία 30 fn.
Atlas 378
Augustine, St. 11, 14, 39, 45, 55, 68, 76, 86, 121, 125, 148, 151, 152, 164, 238, 249, 251, 253, 298, 317, 318 fn., 319 fn., 321, 340, 341 fn., 347 fn., 350, 371
  assumes three kinds of lies 291
  enumerates three benefits in marriage 301
  makes frequent use of allegories 150
Authors, classical ix
Avarice 119
Azotus 205

Babel 196, 199, 200, 211 fn., 217, 227

Babylon 17, 175, 180, 199, 201, 202, 203, 204, 213, 217, 225, 240, 247, 250, 251, 274, 279, 360, 365, 368
  built by Nimrod 200
  king of 62, 364
  kingdom of 232
  punishment of 216
Babylonia 279
Babylonian(s) 98, 99, 157, 200, 371, 388
Baldus 313 fn.
Balsam 344
Baptism 44, 46, 47, 48, 68, 151, 153, 155, 269, 270, 295, 353
  of blood 270 fn.
Barley 157, 161
Bartolus de Saxoferrato 313 fn.
Basilius 39
Bautzen 202 fn.
Bear(s) 66, 69, 74, 116, 135, 136, 274
Beast(s) 58, 116, 132, 136, 329, 347
  flesh of 133
  of burden 279, 395
  savage 70
  wild 74, 75, 139, 199, 297
Beer 350
Beersheba 281
Beggar(s) 175, 326, 329, 394
Belgians 188
Believers 12, 76, 153, 157, 358, 386
Bellum Iugurthinum, by Sallust 227 fn.
Belshazzar 17, 391
Benedict 113, 270
Benjamin 257
Bernard 55, 164, 268, 269, 321
Berosus 32
Bethel 244, 282, 286, 332
Bias 297, 298
Bible 35, 91, 104, 209; see also Holy Scripture(s), Sacred

Scriptures, Scripture(s), Word of God
Latin 122
Bileam 191
Bird(s) 58, 67, 69, 74, 92, 96, 109, 115 fn., 134, 160, 162, 214, 236, 330, 342
  flesh of 133
Bishop(s) 5, 7, 12, 21, 38, 84, 88, 102, 152, 181, 202, 256, 284, 286, 287, 292, 310, 374
  courts of 315
  Eastern 226 fn.
  of Ephesus 226 fn.
  of Mainz 199
  office of 165, 272, 334
Bitumen 66, 67, 217, 344
  wells of 368
Blasphemy 28, 43, 53, 60, 62, 214, 224, 262, 334, 387
Blessed Virgin 4, 54, 114; see also Virgin Mary
Blood relationship 10
Bloodshed 7, 60, 197
Boars 135, 197
Boethius 266 fn.
Bohemian crown 202 fn.
Bondage of the Will, by Luther 39 fn., 44 fn.
Book of Concord 266 fn.
Book of Daniel 258 fn., 391
Book of Ezra 188 fn.
Book of Genesis 374 fn.
Book of Numbers 367
Book of Psalms 307
Book of Wisdom 33, 311
Books of Kings 217
Bow 145, 146, 147, 148
Boxwood 93
Bread 46, 161, 243, 244, 289, 295, 327, 331, 383, 384, 385, 387, 388
  black 270
  of life 386
  of sorrow 49
Briefe, by Luther 21 fn.

Brigands 36
Bruges 137
Brutality 60
Bucolics, by Vergil 385 fn.
Burgensis ix, 71, 234, 371
Burghers 6, 24
Butcher 133
Butcher shop 133

Caesarea 205
Caesarea Philippi 205
Caesars 365
Caiaphas 218, 221
Cain 10, 116, 140, 141, 181, 185, 196, 197, 200, 210, 219, 221, 223, 287
  church of 10
  curse of 180
  descendants of 3, 6, 27, 177
  family of 28
Cainites 10, 26, 27, 29, 98
  had no part in true church 30
Calah 201, 202
Calf 214, 286
Calneh 199, 200
Camel 357
Camenz 202 fn.
Campanus, John 18
Canaan 21, 174, 176, 178, 182, 204, 206, 217, 237, 247, 276, 279, 281, 287, 288, 289, 290, 292, 303, 342, 345, 358, 359, 360, 362, 374, 375, 376, 377, 390, 396, 397
  means merchant 194
Canaanites 9, 10, 176, 204, 282, 283, 287, 290, 291, 332, 336
Canonists 151
Capernaum 315
Caphtorim 203
Cappadocians 189
Captivity 26, 320, 389
  Babylonian 229, 360

Egyptian 292
  of Jews 101, 262, 264
  of law of sin 127
Cardinals 38, 102, 152, 202, 256
Carlstadt 220
Carnivores 74
Carrion 158, 160, 161
Carthage 194
Carthusians 338 fn., 339, 340
Casluhim 203
Caspians 189
Castor 147
Cato 159, 160
Cats 116
Cattle 74, 79, 88, 92, 104, 133, 135, 142, 279, 281, 282, 324, 325, 329, 336, 355, 374, 390, 396
Caucasus 108
Cause
  depraved 126
  efficient 126
  final 125, 126, 148
  formal 126, 148
  material 148, 149
Cedar(s) 66, 93, 342
Celibacy 25
Cellar 134
Cemetery 340
Centaurs 395
Cerberus 222
Ceremonies 47, 92, 159, 197, 226, 255, 257, 353, 361
Chaff 24
Chaldea 239, 243
Chaldeans 192, 201, 242, 243, 244, 248, 249, 268, 269, 276, 277, 278, 281, 305, 349
Chalice(s) 331, 338
Chants 164
Chapel 332
Charitableness 19
Chastity 19, 270 fn., 291, 301 fn., 326, 328
  Noah's 13, 165
Ched-or-laomer 365
Chickens 116, 133

Chicks 138
Childbirth
  dangers of 311
  travail of 304
Children 9, 25, 27, 28, 37, 42, 52, 57, 58, 66, 78, 79, 83, 86, 87, 101, 104, 111, 112, 115, 120, 127, 136, 140, 141, 145, 165, 167, 173, 192, 195, 204, 223, 231, 233, 243, 249, 252, 257, 268, 271, 272, 279, 281, 295, 301, 329, 356, 373, 377, 395
  are gift of God 132
  blind or crippled 11
  disobedient 320
  of Abraham 179
  of devil 37
  of God 6, 370
  of Satan 220
  of world 64
  of wrath 121
Children of Israel 154, 194, 277, 282
Christ
  church of 230, 248, 256
  compares Gospel to a supper 163
  death of 153, 215, 269, 370
  did not beget sons according to the flesh 229
  eternal Priest 381
  is gradually weakening power of pope 177
  joins and unites all into one faith 215
  kingdom of 61, 69, 157, 179, 261, 381, 393
  knowledge of 229
  lineage of ancestors of 228
  occasionally employed allegories 151
  priestly office of 388

INDEX

promise concerning 209, 219, 229, 231, 234, 236, 257, 398
resurrection of 151
sacrifice of 163, 387
warms us with His Spirit 144
will raise and revive us on Last Day 144 et passim
Christian(s) 60, 125, 155, 213, 263, 302, 310, 326, 327, 352, 353, 354
virtues of 125
Christianity 269
Chronology 82 fn., 230
Church(es) ix, x, 6, 10, 15, 16, 20, 21, 23, 26, 28, 30, 32, 33, 35, 36, 37, 38, 55, 56, 57, 60, 64, 68, 78, 79, 83, 84, 87, 99, 100, 112, 113, 128, 131, 134, 152, 154, 156, 164, 167, 169, 170, 171, 172, 173, 175, 177, 178, 180, 183, 185, 192, 193, 195, 197, 198, 199, 200, 202, 211, 212, 215, 216, 218, 225, 227, 229, 236, 237, 243, 258, 266, 272, 274, 275, 276, 283, 284, 285, 286, 293, 297, 304, 310, 320, 325, 326, 332, 333, 338, 353, 354, 356, 359, 361, 363, 381, 382, 383, 384, 386, 388, 390, 391, 395, 398
allegory concerning 109
always a wall against wrath of God 51
ancient 270 fn.
comfort of 221, 222
enemies of 223
Eastern 226
false 31, 214, 224
fellowship of 179
first 235
godly 220
government of 165
heavenly 213
of Abraham 334
of Adam 10
of Cain 10
of Christ 230, 248, 256
of Gentiles 179
of God 27, 177, 234, 357
of Jews 179, 184
of Nimrod 231
of saints 378
of Satan 27, 52, 53, 101, 176, 213, 224, 240, 247
of ungodly 246
one, holy, catholic 228
pope's 176, 281, 314, 357, 387
rebirth of 245
Roman 12
seedbed of 71
true 12, 27, 29, 30, 31, 50, 102, 168, 181, 194, 210, 213, 214, 219, 224, 235, 257, 259, 280, 371, 389, 392
Western 226
Cicero 124, 159, 160, 207, 208, 255, 297, 298, 303, 308, 313, 314, 337 fn., 358
Cilicia 191, 365
Cimmerian Bosporus 188
Cimmerians 189
Circumcision 12, 44, 146, 163, 192, 278, 361, 362
law of 116
City of God, by St. Augustine 11 fn., 125 fn., 319 fn.
Claudius 288
Clemency 340
Clement, St. 77
Clergyman 83, 84
Cloisters 339 fn.
Cloud(s) 94, 95, 105, 129, 146, 147, 152, 282, 334
pillars of 46
Cohabitation 11, 32
Cold 129, 136
Colossians 355
Comet 147
Comfort 104, 112, 118, 131, 145, 146, 148, 151, 155, 157, 166, 167, 169, 170, 185, 196, 219, 225, 229, 248, 254, 273, 281, 283, 296, 306, 308, 316, 321, 325, 335, 343, 350, 351, 363, 375, 390
of church 221, 222
Commoners 19
Communes 199
Compassion 65, 134, 145, 146
Computation of the Years of the World, by Luther 82 fn.
Concubinage 305
Concubines 10
Concupiscence 30
Condemnation 16, 41, 51, 122
Carlstadt's, of academic degrees 220 fn.
Condignity 123, 124
Confession 166, 314
Confessions, by St. Augustine 14 fn.
Confusion 216
of languages 225, 227, 234
of tongues 200
political as well as economic 215
Congruity 123
Conjugal Precepts, by Plutarch 296 fn.
Conscience(s) 55, 89, 115, 133, 145, 151, 158, 161, 219, 220, 221, 222, 248, 251, 273, 293, 295, 314
good 350
peace of 160
Consolation of Philosophy, by Boethius 266 fn.

Constantine the Great 18
Constantinople 262
  fall of 380 fn.
Continence 165
Continent 136 fn.
Corinthians 152
Corposant 147 fn.
Council 21, 41
Council of Constance
  21 fn., 327 fn.
Council of Nicaea 374
Courts 140
  of bishops and
    ungodly princes 315
Covetousness 30, 375
Cow(s) 349
Cowl 114
Crates 326, 330, 347
Creation 100, 117, 128,
  131, 348
  of man and woman
    152
Creator 146, 207, 209,
  227, 255, 298, 347
Creed 86, 228, 333
Creeping things 74
Crime(s) 127, 140, 169,
  175, 343
Cross-bearers 37
Croton 189 fn.
Cruelty 70, 346, 358
Crystal 69
Curse(s) 136, 137, 175,
  176, 181, 182, 183,
  186, 195, 261, 265,
  274, 280, 344, 389
  of Cain 180
  of God 180
  spiritual and eternal
    180
  temporal 180
Cush 194, 196, 364
Cyclopes 34, 37, 41, 138
Cyrenaica 194
Cyrus 100, 128, 205,
  258, 259

Da demonstrandi! 159 fn.
Damascus 262, 358, 376,
  381
Damnation 17, 71, 246,
  247, 249, 275, 321
Dan 205, 376

Danes 189
Daniel 36, 45, 58, 181,
  200, 206, 229, 254,
  258, 320, 359, 391,
  392
Darius 188, 258, 259
Dathan 58
David 47, 59, 72, 91,
  162, 168, 169, 224,
  250, 252, 258, 264,
  281, 291, 306, 319,
  353
  horrible fall of 293
Day of Judgment 315;
  see also Day of the
  Lord, Last Day,
  Last Judgment
Day of the Lord 84
De amicitia, by Cicero
  297 fn.
De caelo, by Aristotle
  93 fn.
De catechizandis rudibus,
  by St. Augustine
  45 fn.
De finibus, by Cicero
  308, 313
De Genesi ad litteram,
  by St. Augustine
  86 fn., 148 fn.
De malo, by Thomas
  Aquinas 315 fn.
De natura deorum, by
  Cicero 208 fn., 308,
  313
De Trinitate, by
  St. Augustine, 76 fn.
Dead Sea 343, 344, 366
Death 7, 19, 21, 22, 48,
  49, 53, 77, 92, 132,
  140, 141, 142, 143,
  156, 161, 181, 196,
  231, 246, 247, 249,
  259, 261, 264, 292,
  294, 311, 317, 322,
  350, 375, 388, 397
  engulfs and swallows
    up entire human
    race 153
  eternal 71, 157, 174,
    248, 280, 321, 391
  in fire 149

  is most immediate
    escape from death
    155
  ministers of 158
  ministry of 158, 160
  of Christ 153, 215,
    269, 370
  of saints 154
  of sinners 154
  of ungodly 93
  terrors of 145
Decalog, Luther's
  catechetical
  explanations of 6 fn.
Decency 18, 32, 34, 305
*Decline and Fall of the
  Roman Empire,* by
  Edward Gibbon
  213 fn.
Deer 66, 74, 197
Defamation 171
Deluge 131 fn., 154, 166;
  see also Flood
Demons 11, 119, 147,
  358, 360
Demosthenes 255
Depredation 60
Despotism 142, 219
Deucalion 131, 211
Deuteronomy 135
Deutsche Bibel 242 fn.
Devil(s) 4, 11, 19, 30,
  47, 48, 57, 99, 121,
  156, 157, 165, 197,
  202, 212, 218, 267,
  345, 348, 353, 369,
  391; *see also* Satan
  children of 37
  envy of 143
  language of 265
  may happen to be
    either a succubus or
    an incubus 11
  sons of 12
  tyranny of 261
Dialectician(s) 4, 126,
  271
Dietrich, Veit x
Dioscuri 147 fn.
Disciples 161, 163, 263,
  327, 335, 363, 385
Discipline 30, 126, 127,
  128, 321, 383

INDEX

Discovery, voyages of 207 fn.
Disobedience 12, 30, 141, 175, 273
Displeasure 13, 23
Disticha 159 fn.
Divination 271, 355
Divine Being 45
Divine Majesty 44, 47, 49, 54, 94, 247, 352, 392
Division of languages 214, 215, 216, 228, 364, 368, 371
Doctor(s) 5, 21, 220
  of medicine 340
Doctrine(s) 45, 55, 78, 84, 158, 212, 243, 250, 267, 296, 308, 315, 363, 370, 382, 398
  basic 229
  blasphemous 60
  false 59, 160, 214
  godless 65
  Luther's, of justification 159 fn.
  of free will 41
  of Gospel 163, 181, 184
  of grace 246
  of Law 253
  of pope 251
  of Satan 334
  of works 159
  pure 54
  purity of 18
  scholastic, of merit and grace 123 fn.
  should be conformable to the faith 151
  sound 13, 17, 23, 33, 40, 88, 172, 199, 229, 234, 235, 240, 256, 316, 371
  true 6, 176, 388, 389
Dodanim 191
Dodona 191
Dogmas 218
Dogs 74, 75, 116
Dominic 113, 249, 251, 268, 269

Donum superadditum 121 fn.
Dormice 135
Douay Version 109 fn., 365 fn.
Dove(s) 45, 46, 92, 109, 110, 111, 157, 159, 160, 163, 164
  figure of holy prophets 162
  ten characteristics of 161
Dragons, flying 147
Drought 107, 136
Drunkenness 166, 167, 169
Dung 5, 7

Earth 32, 49, 53, 59, 62, 63, 64, 70, 74, 75, 89, 93, 94, 95, 96, 97, 98, 100, 101, 102, 103, 106, 107, 109, 110, 111, 112, 113, 115, 117, 118, 129, 131, 135, 142, 143, 145, 147, 148, 155, 157, 162, 177, 179, 195, 196, 197, 207, 208, 210, 211, 214, 225, 288, 330, 344, 353, 358, 359, 365, 378, 388, 391, 392, 393, 396, 397, 398
  dregs of 5
  families of 260, 261, 264, 265, 294
  filled with acts of violence 61, 65
  first 52
  fruits of 133
  produce of 76
  saltiness of 66
Easter 226
Ebal 282
Eber 205, 206, 209, 215, 234, 247, 371, 372, 388
Ecclesiastical History
  by Socrates Scholasticus 18 fn.
  by Sozomen 272 fn.

Ecclesiasticus 350
Ecclesiola 37 fn.
Eclipses 129
Eclogues, by Vergil 15
Edomites 189, 367, 368
Egypt 21, 194, 259, 277, 281, 288, 289, 290, 291, 292, 294, 299, 317, 322, 324, 342, 344, 345, 360, 364, 367, 370, 375, 382
  exodus from 155
  king of 276, 303
  kingdom of 231
Egyptians 18, 176, 203, 257, 299, 302, 303, 306, 311
  government among 312
  king of 296
  morals of 305
  wisdom of 305
Elam 205, 232, 247
  king of 365
Elders 170, 173
Election 72, 73
Elephants 135
Elijah 20, 76, 162, 242, 288
Elisha 288
Elishah 191
Ellasar 365
Emim 367, 374
Engedi 368
England 136 fn.
English sweat 136
Enoch 7, 28, 56, 180, 196, 200, 232
Enos 28, 114
Enthusiasts 162
Envy 127, 210, 327, 346
  devil's 143
Epictetus 326, 330
Epicureans 158, 346
Epistle of James 277 fn.
Epistles
  by Horace 22 fn.
  by Seneca 319 fn.
Equinox
  autumnal 92, 93
  vernal 92
Equity 60
Erasmus 44 fn., 125, 158

Erech 199, 200
Erfurt 339
Erhalt uns, Herr 181 fn.
Eris 227
Error(s) 12, 13, 45, 47, 54, 55, 60, 68, 78, 121, 125, 156, 209, 229, 239, 240, 244, 261, 262, 264, 299, 314, 328, 337, 348, 362
   casual 242 fn.
   Manichaean 14
Esarhaddon 202
Esau 230, 231
Eshcol 372, 398
ἐθελοθρησκεῖαι 59
Ethics 303
Ethics, by Aristotle 340
Ethiopian(s) 187, 194, 195, 259
Etruscans 188 fn.
Eunuchus, by Terence 149 fn.
Euphrates 234, 279
Europe 67, 185, 187, 201, 346
Eusebius 190
Evangelists 312, 331
Eve 30, 31, 57, 78, 80, 98, 185, 233
Evil spirits 11 fn., 321
Evildoers 10, 301, 369
Evilmerodach 259
Excommunication 60, 140
Exegesis
   Anabaptist 150 fn.
   rationalistic 13 fn.
Exegetes ix, 164
Exodus 46, 92, 107
Exultet 154 fn.
Ezekiel 51, 74, 188, 191, 194, 201, 218
Ezra 150, 188 fn.

Faber 385
Faith 27, 28, 30, 31, 38, 41, 47, 49, 52, 54, 55, 56, 59, 70, 71, 81, 82, 84, 87, 90, 97, 98, 99, 103, 104, 105, 107, 114, 117, 118, 130, 148, 154, 156, 165, 175, 176, 177, 179, 180, 182, 192, 197, 210, 215, 221, 226, 228, 233, 234, 235, 239, 240, 241, 242, 243, 244, 246, 248, 250, 251, 252, 253, 254, 256, 257, 264, 268, 269, 275, 280, 281, 283, 284, 286, 287, 288, 289, 290, 292, 293, 294, 295, 296, 304, 307, 308, 309, 316, 319, 321, 323, 325, 333, 335, 349, 350, 353, 355, 356, 357, 359, 362, 363, 370, 372, 374, 375, 377, 380, 382, 387, 389, 392, 397, 399
   analogy of 16, 151, 152, 164
   cannot be separated from Word 113
   changes heart and mind 267
   dead 77
   defection from 101
   in the Seed 120
   is a vigorous and powerful thing 266
   knowledge of 152
   living and active 77
   of Abraham 278, 306, 322, 324, 376
   of Jonah 276
Fall 4, 7, 65 fn., 74, 121, 148
Family 166, 253, 260, 261, 264, 265, 270, 294, 301, 356, 381, 390, 391
   of Cain 28
   of Japheth 184
Famine 17, 70, 288, 289, 290, 291
Fanatics 12, 46 fn., 83
Farmers 39, 200, 201, 352
Fasting(s) 113, 123, 134 fn., 161, 349, 399
Faustus 68
Fear of God 5, 11, 55, 72, 96, 148, 167, 171, 196, 210, 230, 239, 240, 250, 299, 322
Feasts 87, 92
Felix culpa 154 fn.
Fides
   generalis 228 fn.
   specialis 228 fn.
Fifth Commandment 139
Fighting 127
Figure(s) of speech 43, 104, 156 fn., 396
Finis 125 fn.
Fir 66, 93
Fire 66, 98, 128, 147, 192, 195, 223, 239, 242, 243, 244, 248, 249, 350, 358, 382
   death in 149
   of hell 127
   of lust 104
   pillars of 46
   St. Elmo's 147 fn.
   unquenchable 24
First Commandment 6 fn.
First fruits 22
First Principles, by John Reuchlin 34 fn.
First Table 6, 8, 9, 12, 30, 55, 58, 59, 61, 65, 86, 87, 89, 159, 212, 250
First-born 3, 237, 238, 239, 276
   of Japheth 190
   sin of 4
Fish 70, 236, 330, 339, 357
   flesh of 133
Flames 147
Flanders 137
Flood ix, 3, 5, 10, 11, 12, 14, 23, 25, 27, 28, 30, 32, 36, 38, 39, 40, 43, 48, 52, 53, 54, 55, 57, 58, 64, 65, 66, 70, 74, 75,

INDEX 409

76, 81, 82, 86, 89, 92, 93, 95, 98, 99, 100, 101, 104, 106, 110, 111, 112, 115, 119, 128, 129, 131, 133, 140, 141, 148, 149, 150, 151, 153, 154, 155, 156, 162, 163, 165, 167, 170, 175, 178, 182, 186, 187, 196, 197, 199, 204, 208, 210, 211, 212, 213, 216, 217, 219, 223, 224, 228, 230, 232, 236, 343, 364, 368, 382; *see also* Deluge
Folk apocalyptic 129 fn.
Folklore, medieval 211 fn.
Food(s) 76, 77, 109, 132, 133, 134, 142, 231, 253, 270, 339, 350, 385, 399
Forgiveness of sin(s) 19, 41, 63, 162, 163, 177, 184, 248, 249, 261, 275, 320, 327, 353, 382, 387, 390, 391, 398; *see also* Remission of sins
Fornication 84, 214
Fortuna 255 fn.
Fox 74
France 191
Francis 113, 249, 251, 268, 269, 327, 330, 331
Franciscans 327, 328
Franconia 381
Free will 39, 40, 42, 121, 122
  doctrine of 41
French 190
Frenchman 214
Funeral 160
Fürstenfeld 160

Gabriel 54
Galatians 187
Galilee 378
Gambling 127
Gaza 205
Geese 133
Gems 195
Genesis ix, 3, 208
Gentiles 91, 93, 98, 99, 178, 184, 185, 190, 212, 227, 229, 254, 257, 305, 342
  church of 179
  kings of 274
Geography 324, 342
Geology 108 fn.
Geometry 67
Georgians 189
Georgics, by Vergil 304 fn., 352 fn.
Gerizim, Mt. 282, 285
German(s) 94, 119, 161, 187, 189, 190, 214, 215, 226, 302, 367, 373, 380, 395
Germany 18, 20, 65, 137 fn., 175, 186, 193, 227, 231 fn., 242, 369
Gerson, Jean 339 fn.
Giants 5, 23, 28, 32, 33, 34, 36, 38, 71, 211, 367
Gibbon, Edward 213 fn.
Gibeonites 177
Gideon 258, 282, 376
Girgashites 204
Gloria Patri 365 fn.
Gluttony 231
Goats 74, 88, 116
  leaping 147
God
  always remembers those that are His 106
  business of 56
  cannot forget His saints 104
  careful architect 68
  changes even the plans of His holy men 185
  children of 6, 370
  church of 27, 177, 234
  comfort from 104
  contempt of 8
  delays both punishments and rewards 176
  dialectician who convicts by association 4
  does not forsake His own 283
  fear of 5, 11, 55, 72, 96, 148, 167, 171, 196, 210, 230, 239, 240, 250, 299, 322
  foresaw that there would always be a great abundance of evil men 141
  fosters and comforts His children 270
  gifts of 5, 6
  has amazing ways with His saints 170
  hatred of 43
  ignorance of 46
  image of 51, 141, 142
  immutable and unchanging in His counsel from eternity 45
  kindness of 98
  kingdom of 62, 63, 194
  knowledge of 12, 42, 43, 121, 123, 124, 125, 126, 206, 250
  likeness of 227
  long-suffering and patient 89
  love of 141
  patience of 85, 86
  permits His own to be afflicted in various ways 351
  places His own under cross 369
  plurality of Persons in 228
  presence of 130
  providence of 76, 93
  sets Himself up as a butcher 133
  sons of, in first world 5
  twofold will of 44
  unveiled 47
  wisdom of 79, 80, 130 et passim

Godliness 6, 12, 16, 32, 59, 60, 61, 69, 170, 192, 193, 205, 210, 213, 251, 286, 325, 334, 349, 356, 372, 373, 382, 399
  pretense of 62, 78
Godly 8, 25, 27, 30, 31, 33, 44, 50, 61, 62, 66, 82, 104, 149, 153, 154, 166, 169, 170, 172, 177, 180, 192, 196, 197, 198, 204, 213, 218, 219, 220, 221, 222, 223, 226, 229, 230, 235, 236, 239, 289, 296, 304, 307, 309, 310, 319, 320, 332, 347, 350, 351, 360, 369, 378, 380, 383
  life of 176
  must beware of all opportunities for stumbling 29
  oppressed by ungodly 176
Gog 188
Gold 195, 268, 279, 317, 324, 329, 330, 331, 334, 347, 348, 352, 395
Gomer 187, 188
Gomorrah 342, 383, 388
Gonorrhea 311
Goodwin, W. W. 296 fn.
Görlitz 202 fn.
Gospel 24, 36, 38, 40, 48, 58, 67, 78, 84, 161, 177, 179, 185, 186, 193, 215, 225, 250, 253, 260, 271, 275, 276, 285, 288, 312, 315, 327, 333, 361, 378, 398
  doctrine of 163, 181, 184
  knowledge of 190
  persecution of 137
  promise of 163
Goths 190, 191
Government(s) 32, 35, 36, 38, 42, 79, 84, 141, 142, 172, 175, 197, 212, 216, 219, 226, 227, 258, 272, 275, 292, 297, 301, 314, 317, 319, 331, 339, 343, 353, 356, 366, 367, 369, 382
  among Egyptians 312
  Christian 263
  of church 165, 261
Grace 4, 19, 39, 40, 41, 53, 72, 73, 82, 87, 103, 105, 106, 111, 117, 118, 120, 121 fn., 122, 123, 124, 149, 155, 156, 169, 184, 213, 240, 250, 314, 332, 333. 348, 352, 353, 354, 376, 380
  doctrine of 246
  era of 162
  irregular 177, 178, 179
  ministers of 163
  ministry of 162
  sign of 147
  suspension of 104
  tokens of 197
  will of 48
  wrath of 223
Grain 24, 161, 162, 288, 290
Grammar 15, 104, 139
  Hebrew 34 fn.
Grammarian(s) 15, 104
Granary 24
Grasshoppers 33
Gratia caritate formata 122 fn.
Gratia gratum faciens 122 fn.
Greater Armenia 189
Greece 108, 191, 193, 380
Greed 17, 19, 65, 127, 246, 326, 330, 348, 395, 397
  pope's 328
Greek 15
Greeks 190, 202, 206, 208, 227, 300, 320, 346, 352
  sovereigns of 305

Gregory I 198 fn.
Grief 141, 145, 217, 225, 226, 304, 325, 368
Griffins 190
Gulf of Cilicia 189

Habakkuk 176
Halle 94, 95 fn.
Ham 25, 58, 72, 120, 169, 171, 172, 176, 177, 178, 181, 185, 194, 195, 196, 200, 204, 210, 222, 230, 364, 367
  appeared wise and holy to himself 168
  born when Noah was five hundred years old 167
  cursed three times 174
  descendants of 186, 211, 213, 214, 216, 219, 220, 221, 223, 228
  established extensive kingdoms 175
  excluded from kingdom of God 177
  extraordinary malice of 173
  generation of 193, 201
  had one or two children 167
  sin of 182, 212
  ungodliness of 180
  wickedness of 170
Hamath 204
Hannibal 343, 374
Haran 238, 239, 241, 242, 244, 276, 277, 278, 281, 282, 290, 303
Hares 133, 197
Harland, J. Penrose 136 fn.
Harlot 196, 259, 311, 347
Harvest 129, 136, 288
Hatred 20, 35, 36, 37, 57, 102, 168, 171, 172, 173, 174, 213, 214, 286, 287, 302, 303, 334, 336, 358

INDEX   411

for Christ and for His church 248
of God 43
Haughtiness 8, 36, 248
Havilah 195
Hawk 138
Hay 74
Hazazon-tamar 368
Health 77
Heat 129, 136
Heathen 12, 17, 18, 42, 52, 114, 116, 127, 132, 133, 147, 152, 160, 178, 196, 242, 248, 255, 258, 260, 264, 265, 270, 293, 299, 305, 320, 330, 333, 335, 336, 342, 343, 351, 352, 363, 371, 374, 389, 397, 399
 virtues of 125, 126
Heautontimorumenos, by Terence 97 fn., 348 fn.
Heaven(s) 5, 6, 12, 16, 40, 45, 52, 58, 61, 70, 76, 82, 83, 88, 94, 103, 127, 146, 147, 148, 151, 152 fn., 155, 167, 211, 213, 224, 225, 236, 242, 256, 257, 269, 273, 274, 282, 284, 301, 334, 359, 378, 382, 392, 397, 398
 days of 129
 floodgates of 107
 kingdom of 21, 177, 391
 queen of 290
 third 86
 windows of 89, 93, 95, 106
Hebraism 312
Hebraists 14
Hebrew 16, 22, 37, 68, 108, 117, 122, 137, 234, 250, 311, 332, 371, 373, 387
Hebron 200, 281, 287, 362, 381

Helen 29
Hell 6, 48, 64, 155, 196, 220, 235, 241, 260, 261, 273, 275, 283, 340, 344, 351, 369
 Christ's descent into 85 fn., 86
 fire of 127
Herbage 74, 75
Hercules, by Seneca 348 fn.
Hercynian
 Alps 108 fn.
 forest 108
Heresy 45, 84, 87, 230, 240, 327 fn., 354
Heretic(s) 18, 37, 38, 60, 88, 108, 167, 182, 213, 354
Hermit 103
Herod 32, 321
Herodotus 188 fn.
Hexapolis 202
Hezekiah 258
Hilarion 355
Himalaya 108 fn.
Historia animalium, by Aristotle 162 fn.
Historia tripartita 18, 272
Historians 91, 34
History 176, 188, 190, 200, 215, 236, 265, 266
 of first church 235
 of first world 234
Hittites 204
Hobah 376
Holewind 106
Holiness 60, 79
 appearance of 172
 pretense of 63
Holy Land 368
Holy Saturday 154 fn.
Holy Scripture(s) 13, 14, 16, 22, 29, 40, 44, 59, 93, 95, 123, 128, 156, 175, 185, 187, 190, 191, 194, 209, 223, 245, 247, 253, 265, 276, 296, 297, 298, 299, 300, 302, 315, 348, 351, 365, 396; *see also* Bible,

Sacred Scriptures, Scripture(s), Word of God
 mysteries of 86
 teach ethics, or theory of duties 303
Holy Spirit 5, 7, 13, 17, 19, 20, 23, 25, 26, 28, 33, 34, 37, 38, 39, 40, 41, 43, 44, 47, 49, 50, 51, 52, 54, 57, 59, 64, 82, 83, 103, 104, 112, 120, 124, 128, 130, 141, 153, 156, 163, 165, 166, 169, 174, 176, 177, 179, 182, 184, 186, 193, 198, 215, 219, 224, 225, 231, 235, 239, 241, 245, 250, 252, 254, 255, 261, 267, 287, 293, 295, 296, 300, 301, 305, 307, 308, 311, 316, 319, 320, 323, 325, 329, 311 fn., 335, 344, 349, 364, 372, 374, 375, 376, 379, 386, 387, 388, 393
 appeared in form of a dove 45, 162
 office of 40
 proceeds from Father and Son 227
 prolix, but not without purpose 143
 repeats nothing in vain 91
Holy water 161
Home 32, 83, 140, 165, 169, 216, 228, 251, 252, 253, 267, 268, 270, 272, 296, 314, 319, 371
Homer 42 fn., 192 fn., 227 fn.
Homicide 142
Horace 22 fn.
Horites 367
Horn gewinnen 220 fn.
Horse(s) 66, 75, 135, 147, 244, 380

Hosea 107, 221, 243, 285
House Postil, by Luther 147 fn.
Household(s) 64, 65, 79, 81, 83, 84, 137, 165, 167, 172, 215 fn., 227, 228, 242, 251, 253, 254, 259, 268, 275, 278, 280, 288, 297, 304, 313, 319, 330, 332, 349, 350, 363, 391, 398
Hunter 197, 198, 199
Hus, John 21, 87, 184 fn.
Hushai the Archite 292
Hypocrisy 59, 172, 218, 251, 270, 274, 275, 299, 331
Hypocrite(s) 59, 160, 161, 168, 214, 224, 251

Iago, St. 354
Idleness 126
Idolaters 60, 192, 205, 240, 242, 246, 248, 249, 250, 252, 275, 285, 286, 372
Idolatry 12, 19, 20, 24, 28, 30, 33, 63, 84, 99, 125, 137, 172, 186, 192, 201, 202, 214, 215, 223, 230, 232, 240, 243, 244, 246, 248, 249, 250, 251, 253, 285, 286, 355, 356, 371, 372, 382
workshops of 284
Ignorance 326
affected 315
crass 315
inert 315
invincible 313, 314, 315
involuntary 313 fn.
of a fact 313, 316
of law 312, 313, 316
twofold 312
Iliad, by Homer 192 fn., 227 fn.
Illyricum 185

Image of God 51, 141, 142
Imaus 108, 207
Immortality 130, 232
Impenitence 38, 39, 49
Impressiones 147 fn.
Incarnation 261
Incest 9, 10
Incubi 11
India 108, 207
Indian Gulf 195
Indulgences 275, 290, 314 fn., 386
Industry 5, 160, 343
Infancy 126
Infants, hideous 11
Ingratitude 289, 354, 380
Injustice 7, 8, 34, 142, 340
extreme 337, 339
Innocence 74
Innocent III 152 fn.
Inquisition 327 fn.
Intellect 123, 151
Interest 263
Interpretation 16, 45, 47, 121, 188 fn., 342
Münzer's, of "This is My body" 150 fn.
Interpreters 13, 15, 71, 93, 137, 164, 182
Intolerance 104
Ionians 188
Ir 202
Isaac 25, 176, 230, 256, 257, 288, 294, 311, 359, 362, 380
Isaiah 35, 45, 98, 142, 162, 163, 203, 229, 245, 246, 303, 310, 321
Iscah 240, 241
Ishmaelites 368
Israel ix, 20, 29, 50, 51, 77, 101, 110, 136, 152, 153, 154, 160, 176, 177, 178, 257, 277, 285, 359
Israelites 152, 310
Italians 188, 190, 215
Italy 189, 191, 193, 346, 353

Jacob 20, 176, 230, 231, 256, 257, 284, 285, 286, 288, 360, 362, 382
Janiculum 188
Janus 188
Japetus 189
Japheth 25, 58, 120, 170, 175, 176, 178, 179, 180, 182, 183, 185, 186, 187, 189, 195, 201, 205, 236
descendants of 192
family of 184
first-born of 190
generation of 194
Jared 28
Javan 188, 189, 192
Jealousy 119, 338
Jebusites 204
Jeremiah 17, 20, 26, 35, 62, 100, 190, 229, 259, 290, 322, 351
Jericho 282, 286
Jeroboam 286
Jerome, St. 13, 23, 25, 36, 37, 109, 119 fn., 150, 151, 164, 187 fn., 189, 190 fn., 191, 253, 291, 324, 342, 355
Jerome of Prague 21, 87
Jerusalem 50, 99, 100, 175, 179, 184, 225, 243, 244, 255, 258, 282, 342, 344, 360, 378, 381
Jeshurun 345
Jesse 72
Jews 10, 13, 14, 17, 40, 42, 46, 52, 53, 69, 71, 77, 82, 92, 93, 98, 100, 107, 109, 110, 112, 129, 137, 160, 170, 174, 178, 182, 185, 190, 201, 203, 205, 226, 227, 228, 237, 238, 240, 243, 244, 248, 250, 256, 257, 260, 261, 263, 264, 265, 266, 288, 290, 292, 293, 304, 305, 311, 312,

INDEX 413

326, 342, 343, 352, 359, 360, 361, 363, 364, 370, 384, 393, 396
captivity of 101
church of 179, 184
cling stubbornly to promise that they are people of God 99
not true seed of Abraham 262
silly ideas of 12
Jezebel 29
Job 178, 206, 259, 276, 319, 321
John 357, 396
John Frederick, Elector 21 fn.
John the Baptist 399
John XXIII 327, 328
Jonah 24, 26, 77, 90, 201, 202
faith of 276
Joppa 205
Jordan 282, 342, 344, 345, 348, 349, 366
Joseph 258, 288, 324
religion of 276
Josephus 32 fn., 108, 285, 305
Joshua 34, 239, 240, 243, 245, 246, 249, 258, 282, 367, 395
Jove 116
Judah 175, 257, 344, 367
kingdom of 203
Judas 330, 331
Judea 187, 189
Judges 258
Judgment 7, 20, 32, 47, 51, 52, 53, 61, 101, 126, 140, 141, 167, 169, 198, 208, 220, 224, 237, 266, 298, 299, 312, 322, 340, 347, 352, 353, 354, 367, 398
God's 4, 21, 100, 266, 273, 314, 373
eternal, of death in fire 149
of church 102, 314
of reason 288

on dogmas of pope 218
sober 168
Julian the Apostate 213 fn.
Junge Engel, alte Teufel 128 fn.
Jupiter 192, 211
Jurist(s) 5, 297, 312, 340, 341
Justice 6, 62, 126, 177, 338, 396, 399
extreme 337, 339, 341
Justification 159 fn.
Juvenal 116 fn., 155 fn.

Kadesh 367
Kedar 189
Kenan 28
Keys 286, 353
King(s) 3, 4, 5, 7, 29, 35, 50, 58, 60, 98, 184, 192, 200, 202, 220, 250, 252, 258, 275, 279, 281, 292, 306, 307, 308, 310, 312, 316, 317, 318, 321, 322, 324, 325, 352, 353, 361, 366, 367, 368, 370, 372, 374, 375, 378, 382, 383, 388, 389, 390, 391, 392, 393, 395, 396, 397, 398
Books of 217
godly 319
of Babylon 62, 257, 259, 276, 363
of Egypt 276, 296, 303, 305
of Elam 365
of Ellasar 365
of Gentiles 274
of Nineveh 259
of Philistines 311
of Pontus 365
of Salem 381, 386, 394
of Shinar 364
of Sodomites 379
Persian 243, 259, 276, 304, 305
King's Valley 380, 381
Kingdom(s) 35, 37, 52, 118, 170, 175, 185,
187, 190, 192, 193, 194, 210, 225, 226, 227, 254, 258, 263, 306, 362, 364, 365, 367
Assyrian 202, 259
Babylonian 200, 202, 255, 259
earthly 264
eternal 196, 289
Greek 255, 259
of Babylon 232
of Christ 61, 69, 157, 179, 261, 381, 393
of Egypt 231
of God 62, 63, 177, 194
of heaven 21, 177, 391
of Israel 29, 101, 257, 285
of Judah 203
of Messiah 397
of Nimrod 199
of world 177
Persian 255
Roman 255, 259
temporal 367
Kingship 169
Kitchen 134, 327
Kittim 191
Knights 200
Knowledge 15, 16, 85, 86, 96, 133, 148, 149, 160, 177, 189, 209, 218, 219, 233, 235, 239, 254, 255, 270, 271, 278, 300, 308, 312, 315, 321, 322, 326, 338, 344, 382
lack of 313
of Abraham 222
of Blessed Seed 164
of Christ 229
of faith 152
of God 12, 42, 43, 121, 123, 124, 125, 126, 206, 250, 306, 311, 332, 333, 348, 363, 372, 392
of Gospel 190
of mathematical sciences and governmental affairs 305

of our corrupt nature 120
of religion 269, 388
of Scripture 5
of sin 41
Korah 58
Koran 262 fn.

Lacus Asphaltites 366
Ladner, Gerhart B. 144 fn.
Laelius 297
Laestrygones 138
Laity 152
Lamech 7, 8, 10, 16, 17, 22, 23, 27, 28, 33, 38, 44, 49, 51, 82, 141
Lampsacus 18 fn.
Land of Promise 246, 362; *see also* Promised Land
Lasha 205
Last Day 11, 12, 49, 63, 128, 129, 144, 153, 177, 239, 256; *see also* Day of Judgment, Day of the Lord, Last Judgment
Last Judgment 26, 63; *see also* Day of Judgment, Day of the Lord, Last Day
Latin 15, 185, 373
Lauban 202 fn.
Laurel 93
Lauterbach, Anton 262 fn.
Law(s) 34, 60, 65, 71, 99, 123, 124, 133, 134, 163, 165, 175, 185, 192, 223, 227, 229, 242, 250, 257, 261, 262, 267, 274, 277, 278, 309, 327, 339, 341, 362, 394, 399
  about sacrifices 116
  civil 140
  doctrine of 253
  earthly 337, 338
  era of 162
  general 147

ignorance of 312, 313, 316
marriage 10
ministry of 158
mistress and teacher of 340
natural and positive 9
of circumcision 116
of First Table 58
of love and unity 336
of nations 140
of Second Table 58
of sin 127
righteousness of 160
Roman 139
teachers of 158, 161
teaching of 159
Lawlessness 119
Lazarus 196
Lebanon 108
Lectures on Genesis, by Luther 85 fn., 204 fn., 344 fn.
Lectures on the Minor Prophets, by Luther 240 fn.
Lehabim 203
Leopards 75
Letter to the Ephesians 301
Letter to the Hebrews 113, 114, 246, 252, 294, 362, 381, 383, 384, 387, 389, 393
Levi 384, 393, 394
Levies 263
Levites 384, 385
Leviticus 74
Lex viva et animata 340 fn.
Libanus, Mt. 18 fn.
Libations 166
Liber hebraicarum quaestionum in Genesim 13 fn., 23 fn., 119 fn., 187 fn., 190 fn.
Liberty 262
  editorial x
Libyans 194, 203
Lichtenberg 242
Lichtenfels 242
Lichtenstein 242

Lie(s)
  deadly 291
  obliging 291
  playful 291
  white 317
Life 155, 156, 164, 168, 172, 175, 177, 204, 215, 217, 227, 235, 247, 253, 263, 267, 268, 271, 275, 276, 289, 292, 294, 296, 297, 298, 299, 304, 308, 310, 319, 320, 325, 335, 338, 339, 369, 374, 375, 396
  bread of 386
  earthly 181, 259, 295, 341
  eternal 151, 153, 154, 160, 181, 184, 237, 256, 261, 278, 344, 390, 391, 397, 398
  everlasting 151
  expectancy of, in Germany of Luther's day 231 fn.
  future 232, 284
  godly 249
  holy 286, 327, 380
  impure 321
  monastic 76, 270
  necessities of 373
  of godly 176
  physical 254
  present 180, 322
  uncertainty of 257
Likeness
  of angels 227
  of God 227
Lion(s) 69, 74, 75, 116, 135, 296
Liturgy for Holy Saturday 154 fn.
Livy 379
Löbau 202 fn.
Locusts 136, 357
Logic, medieval 4 fn.
Lord's Supper 46, 47, 48, 295, 338; *see also* Sacrament of the Altar, Supper of His Son

INDEX   415

Lot 7, 8, 17, 25, 28, 217,
    253, 275, 276, 277,
    336, 337, 338, 342,
    345, 349, 351, 357,
    358, 362, 365, 369,
    372, 374, 378, 382,
    393
  daughters of 279, 280
  wife of 280
Love 50, 65, 91, 122,
    176, 257, 275, 297,
    298, 299, 300, 301,
    302, 337, 338, 341,
    380, 397
  brotherly 372
  for creatures 124
  law of 336
  mistress and teacher of
    law 340
  of one's neighbor 126,
    159, 335
  purpose of all laws 339
  toward fatherland 42,
    125
  toward parents and
    children 42
Lucian 116
Lucifer 12
Lud 206
Ludim 203, 206
Luke 241, 242 fn.
Lust(s) 7, 8, 9, 10, 13,
    14, 17, 19, 20, 24,
    28, 30, 32, 38, 105,
    115, 119, 127, 131,
    222, 241, 246, 296,
    299, 305, 317, 328,
    347, 366, 397
  fire of 104
Luther ix, x, 4 fn., 6 fn.,
    9 fn., 11 fn., 13 fn.,
    14 fn., 16 fn., 18 fn.,
    21 fn., 24 fn., 30 fn.,
    33 fn., 34 fn., 37 fn.,
    38 fn., 39 fn., 42 fn.,
    43 fn., 44 fn., 45 fn.,
    50 fn., 63 fn., 65 fn.,
    68 fn., 72 fn., 82 fn.,
    83 fn., 85 fn., 93 fn.,
    94 fn., 104 fn.,
    106 fn., 107 fn.,
    115 fn., 116 fn.,
    121 fn., 123 fn.,

125 fn., 126 fn.,
128 fn., 129 fn.,
131 fn., 134 fn.,
136 fn., 137 fn.,
147 fn., 148 fn.,
150 fn., 156 fn.,
159 fn., 164 fn.,
180 fn., 181 fn.,
184 fn., 188 fn.,
191 fn., 195 fn.,
198 fn., 202 fn.,
204 fn., 207 fn.,
215 fn., 226 fn.,
228 fn., 231 fn., 235,
240 fn., 242 fn.,
245 fn., 246 fn.,
248 fn., 255 fn.,
262 fn., 263 fn.,
267 fn., 270 fn.,
271 fn., 277 fn.,
282 fn., 285 fn.,
294 fn., 318 fn.,
320 fn., 324 fn.,
327 fn., 333 fn.,
344 fn., 360 fn.,
361 fn., 364 fn.,
390 fn., 396 fn.
Luther the Expositor, by
  Jaroslav Pelikan
  4 fn., 10 fn., 13 fn.,
  15 fn., 47 fn., 82 fn.,
  99 fn., 112 fn.,
  231 fn., 240 fn.,
  332 fn., 384 fn.
Luther's Works ix, x,
  7 fn., 8 fn., 11 fn.,
  14 fn., 34 fn., 45 fn.,
  56 fn., 57 fn., 58 fn.,
  65 fn., 82 fn., 93 fn.,
  112 fn., 113 fn.,
  114 fn., 119 fn.,
  121 fn., 123 fn.,
  134 fn., 140 fn.,
  141 fn., 142 fn.,
  144 fn., 146 fn.,
  148 fn., 150 fn.,
  152 fn., 159 fn.,
  160 fn., 174 fn.,
  177 fn., 180 fn.,
  185 fn., 189 fn.,
  193 fn., 196 fn.,
  199 fn., 200 fn.,
  204 fn., 207 fn.,

217 fn., 222 fn.,
226 fn., 227 fn.,
231 fn., 233 fn.,
244 fn., 246 fn.,
258 fn., 262 fn.,
269 fn., 272 fn.,
279 fn., 287 fn.,
288 fn., 292 fn.,
319 fn., 327 fn.,
341 fn., 343 fn.,
354 fn., 355 fn.,
379 fn., 390 fn.
Luxury 12, 29, 252
Lydians 203, 206
Lyons 327, 328
Lyra ix, 10 fn., 11, 13 fn.,
    14, 33 fn., 38, 52,
    58, 67 fn., 69 fn., 71,
    73, 82 fn., 92,
    104 fn., 107 fn.,
    109 fn., 115, 129,
    138, 164, 166,
    179 fn., 182 fn.,
    189 fn., 190 fn.,
    194 fn., 201 fn.,
    203 fn., 211, 227 fn.,
    232 fn., 234, 237 fn.,
    238, 239, 248 fn.,
    264 fn., 276, 292 fn.,
    293 fn., 303 fn.,
    304 fn., 305 fn.,
    310 fn., 364, 370 fn.,
    371 fn., 380, 381 fn.,
    383, 384

Macedon 191
Macedonia 191
Madai 188
Maeotis 188
Magis passio quam actio
    267 fn.
Magistrate(s) 19, 127,
    173, 175, 318, 319
Magna Graecia 188 fn.,
    189
Magog 188
Mahaleel 28
Mainz 199
Malice 161, 163, 173
  of Satan 174
Mamre 362, 363, 372,
    398
Manasseh 172

Manichaeans 14, 39 fn.
Manure 67
Marburg Colloquy 18 fn.
Marcus Attilius Regulus 125
Mariners 69
Marriage(s) 8, 9, 10, 18, 30, 36, 38, 55, 57, 76, 92, 131, 240, 306, 329, 377; *see also* Matrimony
  abstention from 274
  incestuous 10, 32
  Noah's 25
  of Abraham 241, 254, 256
  three benefits in 301
Martyr(s) 7, 8, 12, 21, 217, 230
Martyrdom 270 fn.
Mary 35, 72, 118, 217, 312
Mary Magdalene 321
Mask(s) 79, 343
Mass(es) 65, 86, 273, 284, 290, 333 fn., 383, 385, 387
Materialism 390 fn.
Mathematics 67
Matrimony 30; *see also* Marriage(s)
Matthias of Hungary 319
Mauritania 194
Mauritanians 203
Maximilian 137
Meat 76, 134, 137, 141, 231, 338, 339, 355
Medea 219
Medes 188, 189, 365
Media 206 fn.
Mediator 215
Medicinal potion 156
Medicine 77, 170, 339
  doctor of 340
Mediterranean Sea 187, 189, 194, 205, 365
Melanchthon 207 fn., 242 fn.
Melchizedek 358, 381, 384, 385, 386, 388, 389, 390, 391, 392, 394
  priesthood of 387, 393

thought to be Shem 382
  type of Christ 383
Melons 65
Mendicants 328, 330
Merchant(s) 124, 194
Mercy 4, 16, 47, 51, 66, 71, 103, 118, 120, 149, 153, 162, 163, 170, 172, 175, 185, 186, 202, 228, 229, 240, 241, 245, 246, 247, 248, 260, 263, 269, 276, 280, 289, 296, 306, 307, 310, 312, 323, 325, 333, 352, 358, 380, 398
Merit
  of condignity 123, 124
  of congruity 123
  of works 122
Merom, waters of 34
Meshech 189
Mesopotamia 206, 240, 241, 277, 279
Messiah 264, 326; *see also* Christ, Savior, Son of God, Son of Man
  kingdom of 397
Metamorphoses, by Ovid 131 fn., 220 fn., 302 fn.
Metaphor 220 fn.
Metaphysics, by Aristotle 208 fn.
Meteorologica, by Aristotle 146, 147 fn.
Methuselah 7, 16, 17, 22, 23, 27, 28, 38, 44, 49, 51, 82, 83, 87, 228
Micah 17, 53, 243, 301
Mice 135
Michael 181
Michal 292
Middle Ages 129 fn.
Midianites 282, 368
Milan 365
Milcah 241
Minister(s) 19, 20, 21, 37, 44, 45, 171, 175, 382

of death and sin 158
  of Gospel 163
  office of 272
Ministry 19, 20, 36, 44, 46, 56, 82, 83, 84, 164, 165, 168, 171, 215, 231, 236, 249, 250, 287, 363, 382, 393
  contempt for 275
  human 358
  of death 158, 160
  of grace 162
  of Law 158
  of papacy 161
  of sin 160
  of teaching 272, 332
  office of 175
Miracle(s) 27, 56, 75, 76, 97, 157, 215, 241, 255, 259, 303, 304, 321, 374, 375, 376, 389, 391
Mishpat 367
Moabites 189, 367
Moderation 16, 309, 339, 341
Mohammed 267
Monogamy 305
Monastery 252, 269, 270, 326, 328, 339
Monasticism 269, 340
Money 161, 263, 317, 326, 330, 331
Monk(s) 21, 78, 86, 104, 113, 114, 115, 150, 152, 160, 249, 251, 252, 253, 268, 269, 270, 271, 273, 325, 326, 328, 331, 349, 350
  Carthusian 103
  Franciscan 124
  religion of 339
Monkeys 113
Moon 92, 147, 152, 156
Moralists 158
Morality 152
Morals 152, 158, 159, 160, 247, 288
  deterioration of 175
  of Egyptians 305
  perversion of 333

INDEX 417

Moravia 361
Moreh, Mt. 282, 285, 286
Moriah, Mt. 281
Mortality 144
Moses 3, 6, 8, 9, 10, 12, 17, 27, 29, 30, 31, 32, 33, 36, 37, 41, 42, 43, 44, 47, 50, 51, 56, 58, 59, 61, 62, 67, 69, 70, 74, 76, 77, 82, 83, 84, 85, 86, 88, 90, 91, 92, 94, 95, 96, 97, 103, 104, 105, 106, 109, 110, 115, 117, 119, 121, 122, 123, 128, 132, 134, 150, 152, 158, 160, 161, 165, 166, 170, 172, 173, 179, 182, 187, 192, 193, 196, 198, 199, 204, 205, 207, 208, 210, 212, 214, 223, 224, 232, 234, 240, 241, 242, 243, 245, 246, 249, 258, 260, 266, 268, 271, 273, 277, 278, 279, 282, 285, 286, 287, 290, 293, 304, 305, 324, 325, 331, 332, 337, 342, 344, 345, 351, 353, 359, 360, 361, 362, 364, 365, 366, 367, 368, 369, 370, 376, 380, 381, 388, 389
  books of 385
  describes Noah as a supreme pontiff and priest 13
  did not inaugurate sacrifices 116
  praises Noah's obedience 80
  reveals plurality of Persons in God 228
Mother 145, 311, 356
Mount of Olives 110
Mules 328
Münzer 150, 375
Murder(s) 6, 9, 55, 60, 127, 138, 139, 143, 161, 167, 169, 171, 197, 214, 226
Murderer(s) 59, 139, 140, 172, 196, 197, 248, 378
Muscovites 189
Music of chants 164
Mutig werden 220 fn.
Mysticism, medieval 104 fn.

Naaman the Syrian 178, 258
Nahor 240, 243
Nathan 72
Natural History, by Pliny 192 fn., 199 fn.
Nebuchadnezzar 203, 258, 259
Negeb 324 fn.
Nero 153
New Testament 12, 16, 46, 105, 162, 163, 215, 228, 229, 330, 353, 387
Nicaea 374 fn.
Nicholas, St. 379
Nicomachean Ethics, by Aristotle 297 fn., 303 fn., 340 fn.
Nile 344
Nimrod 196, 197, 198, 200, 203, 205, 206, 210, 212, 214, 219, 224, 230, 232, 240, 246, 247, 364, 371
  children of 283
  church of 231
  disturbed church of God 234
  kingdom of 199
Nimrodites 247
Nineveh 200, 201, 202, 214, 225, 232, 342, 343
  king of 259, 276
Ninevites 24, 26, 43, 178
Nisan 226 fn.
Noah ix, x, 8, 10, 12, 16, 17, 22, 23, 25, 27, 28, 33, 37, 38, 40, 47, 49, 50, 51, 52, 53 57, 58, 61, 62, 63, 64, 66, 67, 71, 73, 75, 76, 82, 83, 84, 85, 86, 89, 91, 92, 96, 97, 98, 101, 102, 103, 104, 105, 106, 109, 110, 111, 112, 113, 114, 115, 117, 119 fn., 129, 131, 132, 133, 135, 143, 145, 148, 153, 154, 155, 156, 157, 158, 159, 162, 163, 167, 173, 175, 177, 178, 179, 180, 182, 183, 184, 186, 187, 189 fn., 193, 194, 196, 197, 204, 209, 214, 216, 219, 220, 221, 222, 225, 228, 235, 236, 245, 249, 283, 368, 381, 383
  became drunk 166
  began to plant a vineyard 166
  declared "perfect" in relation to Second Table 55
  declared "righteous" in relation to First Table 55
  endowed with many outstanding qualities 172
  filled office of bishop 165
  found favor 70
  generations of 54
  gifted with marvelous steadfastness 56
  godly descendants of 210
  had no daughters 7
  herald of righteousness 24
  holy, righteous, gentle, and compassionate man 81
  illustrious and grand example of faith 87
  just and perfect 165

lay naked in his tent 166
lived three hundred and fifty years after Flood 230
mouthpiece of Holy Spirit 44
obedience of 80, 90
order of sons of 174
saintliness and chastity of 13
stays on royal road 77
treated and regarded as stupid and worthless person 59
Noblemen 5, 6, 24, 366
Nobles 19
Non necessitat 121 fn.
Notes on Ecclesiastes, by Luther 271 fn.
Numbers 34
Numidia 194
Numidians 203
Nuns 349

O sancta simplicitas! 184 fn.
Oakum 66
Oath 246
Obedience 36, 77, 78, 126, 193, 251, 252, 271, 272, 273, 275, 280, 296, 349, 398
highest form of 173
inward 270
of Abraham 268, 269
outward 270
Noah's 80, 90
Obstinacy 17
Ocean 94, 95, 107, 245
October 92
Odor(s) 117, 136, 269, 343
of pleasantness 116
of rest 116, 117
Odor suavissimus 116 fn.
Odyssey, by Homer 42 fn., 192 fn.
Oecolampadius 243
Oeconomia 215 fn.
Of Holy Virginity, by St. Augustine 341 fn.

Offering 116, 117, 385
of bread and wine 384
Office(s) 19, 20, 102, 229, 329, 340, 353, 367, 382, 383
divine 390
of bishop 165, 272, 334
of Christ 388
of Holy Spirit 40
of minister 272
of ministry 175
priestly 114, 287
Og 259, 370
Og Bashan 367
Old Testament x, 58, 228, 237, 330, 364 fn.
liturgical divisions of text of 54 fn.
Olive 93
branch 92, 93, 110, 157, 160, 162, 163
leaf 110
oil 162
tree 110, 157, 162, 163, 185
On Baptism, by Tertullian 270 fn.
On Christian Doctrine, by St. Augustine 164 fn., 298 fn., 347 fn.
On Duties, by Cicero 303 fn., 337 fn.
On the Abuse of the Mass, by Luther 137 fn.
On the Good of Marriage, by St. Augustine 301 fn.
On the Shem Hamphoras, by Luther 364 fn.
Oppression 12, 19, 34, 119, 222
Oppressors 36
Opus alienum 134 fn.
Oranges 65
Orient 382
Origen 14, 150, 151, 158, 164
had better sense than popes 152
Orientals 303
Orimasda 243

Orphans 99
Ovid 131 fn., 219, 220 fn., 302 fn., 329 fn.
Ox(en) 74, 137, 138, 324, 396
Oxford Classical Dictionary 189 fn.

Palestine 187, 204
Palestinians 305
Palm 93
Palus Maeotis 188 fn.
Papacy 61, 86, 113, 164, 198, 271, 284
ministry of 161
Papists 22, 24, 33, 36, 51, 55, 64, 79, 99, 100, 101, 102, 103, 160, 161, 168, 170, 220, 222, 243, 251, 315, 383, 384, 385, 386
boast of name of God in vain 53
maintain that they are the church 52
Paradise 3, 52, 57, 74, 86, 110, 136, 154, 178, 194, 195, 219, 222, 287, 343, 344, 345, 351, 368, 380
serpent in 157
Paran 367
Parents 9, 10, 12, 29, 30, 31, 32, 42, 78, 83, 120, 127, 128, 167, 169, 173, 174, 175, 192, 251, 252, 270, 271, 272, 301, 321
first 163
Pastors 84; *see also* Minister(s)
Pathros 203
Pathrusim 203
Patience 19, 57, 105, 217, 278, 322, 323, 324, 331, 335, 346, 369, 370, 389
God's 85, 86
Patriarch(s) x, 3, 7, 10, 12, 18, 22, 23, 27, 28, 30, 31, 37, 53, 54, 55, 100, 132,

INDEX

166, 175, 179, 184, 187, 206, 210, 212, 235, 236, 240, 242, 245, 247, 249, 251, 252, 254, 260, 261, 268, 269, 275, 277, 281, 282, 283, 284, 285, 289, 326, 332, 352, 358, 363, 368, 371, 373, 380, 382, 383, 389, 397
  age of earlier 8
Patricians 200
Paul, St. 16, 17, 23, 40, 41, 44, 48, 50, 59, 72, 73, 77, 86, 88, 99, 105, 121, 122, 152, 153, 157, 160, 168, 171, 177, 178, 179, 184, 185, 191, 230, 237, 247, 272, 273, 277, 280, 288, 289, 291, 295, 297, 300, 301, 309, 320, 321, 325, 329, 330, 331, 333, 335, 339, 341, 348, 349, 355, 356, 358, 365, 370, 388
  enjoins that prophecy or doctrine should be conformable to the faith 151
Paupers of Lyons 327
Pears 65, 350
Peas 157
Peasants 6, 19, 24
  rebellious 375
Peasants' War 320 fn.
πείθω 183
Pelagians 39
Peleg 205, 216
Penitence 63
Pentateuch 246 fn., 361, 367
Perfidy 65
Peripatetics 346
Perizzites 336
Perjury 8, 141
Persecution 16, 214, 334
  of Gospel 137
Persia 187, 365
Persian Gulf 195

Persians 205, 232, 243, 352, 365
Pestilence 17, 143, 210, 289
Peter, St. 3, 8, 28, 60, 64, 81, 84, 85, 86, 89, 90, 99, 151, 153, 155, 156, 252, 273, 274, 282, 286, 316, 383
  calls Noah "herald" of righteousness 13
  praises first world 10
  primacy of 386
Pharaoh 17, 152, 153, 154, 259, 310, 311, 312, 314, 316, 317, 318, 322, 325, 376, 379
Pharisee(s) 42, 161
Philanthropy 42
Philip 32, 49
Philistines 203
  king of 311
Philo 68
Philologians 362, 380
  crosses of 237
Philologists 182, 392
Philology 15
Philosopher(s) 14, 123, 133, 146, 147, 152, 155, 160, 207, 297, 298, 325, 326, 327, 328, 329, 330, 346, 347, 348
  have clever discussions about God 43
Philosophy 124, 127, 148, 160, 207, 299, 300, 302, 308
Phoenicia 18, 206
Phrygians 191
Physicians 117, 311, 338
Piety 6, 18, 59, 152, 170, 398
  false 331
  zeal for 292
Pilate 37
Pilgrimages 123
Pine 66, 93
Pitch 66, 67, 136
Plague(s) 70, 75, 77, 136, 143, 226, 227, 272,

274, 297, 305, 310, 311, 312, 317, 322, 330
Plato 43, 142, 160, 207, 327, 358
Play 126
Pleasure(s) 29, 34, 51, 126, 353, 378
  carnal 158
  physical 267
  sensual 12
Plebeians 200
Pliny 192, 199
Plurality of Persons in God 228
Plutarch 296
Plutarch's Morals, W. W. Goodwin (ed.) 296 fn.
Poet(s) 91, 127, 131, 149, 150, 189, 222, 291, 302, 329, 343, 348, 378, 379
Poland 136
Poles 189
Politics, by Aristotle 126 fn., 199 fn., 329 fn.
Pollux 147
Polycrates, Bishop of Ephesus 226 fn.
Polygamy 305
Pomegranates 65
Pontiff 24, 234
  Roman 7, 383
Pontus 365
Pope(s) 5, 12, 17, 20, 21, 38, 41, 61, 63, 84, 87, 88, 89, 99, 100, 134, 137 fn., 152, 156, 176, 177, 196, 197, 213, 223, 224, 229, 244, 256, 267, 270, 275, 282, 287, 290, 315, 316, 327, 338, 353, 354, 356, 390, 399
  boast that they are vicars of Christ, successors of Peter 60
  boasts that he is the church 102

church(es) of 176, 281, 314, 357, 387
doctrine of 251
greed of 328
His Most Execrable Lordship 151
judgment on dogmas of 218
makes sheer angels of his saints 240
misuses his power for support of idolatry 33
regarded and condemned as very Antichrist 181
religion of 293
seeks to become lord of church and world 274
tyranny of 220
wants to be head of church 198
wants to be vicar of Christ 273
Poverty 270 fn., 325, 330
of Christ 327
Prayer(s) 19, 42, 51, 77, 84, 123, 171, 184, 222, 223, 284, 293, 294, 304, 305, 318, 332, 333, 334, 349, 377
Preacher(s) 22, 24, 26, 40, 56, 249, 287, 388, 389
of righteousness 383
Preaching 16, 20, 22, 24, 25, 26, 27, 56, 84, 202, 333, 334, 398
Noah's 98
of Abraham 280
of Christ 17
Turkish 249
Predestinarianism 104
Predestination 50
Prelates 152
Prestige 172, 199, 238, 247, 262, 318, 329, 336, 337, 341, 366, 383, 395
Pretense 59, 268, 295
of godliness 62, 63, 78

of holiness and wisdom 63
Priapus 18
Pride 6, 71, 127, 212, 248, 253, 342, 346, 355, 356
of Schechemites 285
Priest(s) 19, 21, 22, 24, 98, 114, 116, 117, 160, 197, 198, 202, 247, 280, 282, 284, 332, 336, 337, 381, 382, 383, 384, 386, 388, 393, 394
Priesthood 32, 185, 197, 362
Aaronic 394
Levitical 393, 394
of Melchizedek 387, 393
physical succession to 229
spiritual 394
temporal 394
under the Law 394
Primogeniture 183
prerogatives of 190
Prince(s) 5, 19, 34, 35, 38, 63, 84, 198, 199, 202, 220, 310, 318, 331, 339, 361, 365, 380, 395
Christian 262
godly 319
of world 88, 334, 390
ungodly 315
Procreation 9, 57, 115, 132, 241, 281
Promise(s) 26, 40, 48, 51, 54, 56, 57, 72, 77, 98, 100, 101, 103, 105, 107, 114, 131, 143, 145, 146, 147, 153, 155, 156, 170, 176, 177, 178, 183, 185, 186, 211, 250, 254, 256, 258, 260, 261, 264, 267, 269, 273, 275, 276, 277, 280, 284, 287, 288, 289, 293, 294, 295, 308, 309, 310, 312, 317, 324, 333, 335,

336, 337, 338, 341, 358, 359, 360, 362, 363, 377, 390, 396, 397
concerning Christ 209, 219, 229, 231, 234, 236, 257, 398
God's ix, 266
of Gospel 163
of Satan 266, 268
of Seed 10, 31, 52, 53, 55, 63, 64, 71, 144, 179, 180, 235, 236, 281, 303, 391, 398
that a universal flood is no longer to be feared 129
Promised Land 361; see also Land of Promise
Propagation 132
Prophecy 26, 84, 152, 157, 174, 175, 176, 177, 178, 184, 186, 218, 219, 222, 263
should be conformable to the faith 151
Prophet(s) 26, 40, 43, 45, 51, 52, 57, 70, 83, 85, 94, 98, 114, 136, 143, 155, 157, 162, 171, 184, 197, 200, 219, 220, 221, 243, 245, 255, 258, 259, 261, 262, 265, 282, 285, 286, 288, 289, 297, 301, 302, 306, 307, 321, 332, 336, 337, 353, 359, 360, 363, 388, 398, 399
false 161
Proselyte 275
Prostitutes 18
Psalms 61, 104, 180, 222, 388
Ptolemais 205
Ptolemy 208 fn., 188 fn.
Punishment(s) 3, 9, 11, 18, 20, 22, 23, 25, 35, 43, 58, 60, 61, 62, 65, 66, 71, 81, 84, 85, 86, 117, 124, 131, 136, 145, 148, 158, 175, 176, 182,

INDEX

212, 215, 219, 220, 221, 223, 224, 226, 261, 280, 287, 290, 310, 311, 312, 314, 315, 316, 318, 319, 321, 342, 354, 360, 369, 370, 373, 377, 380
  by fire 149
  eternal 196, 322
  of Babylon 216
  of sins after this life 139
  novel kind of 70
  sevenfold 140
  universal 26
Pura naturalia 121 fn.
Purgatory 86, 161, 386
Put 194
Pyrrha 131 fn.
Phythagoras 189

Quadrupeds 324
Quarelling 127
Quarrels 302
Queen of heaven, in Jeremiah 290

Raamah 195
Rabbi David 14
Rabbi Solomon 14, 234, 238
Rabbis 15, 33, 34, 58, 67, 104, 107, 138
Rahab 259
Rain(s) 69, 89, 92, 93, 95, 105, 106, 129, 142, 343
Rainbow 66, 71, 147, 148, 149, 163
  color of 146
  curvature of 146
Rainfall 136
Rama 195
Raven(s) 108, 109, 135, 147, 158, 159, 160, 161, 162, 163
Reason 13, 41, 43, 46, 64, 65, 67, 78, 88, 119, 123, 125, 126, 127, 128, 135, 152, 160, 166, 173, 176,

180, 184, 207, 208, 236, 242, 243, 246, 250, 254, 263, 267, 268, 290, 293, 298, 308, 313, 314, 346, 347, 348, 354, 369
entirely devoid of any knowledge of God 42
  judgment of 288
  lower part of 121
  upper part of 121
Rebecca 231, 305, 311
Rebellion 168, 271, 336
Red Sea 77, 107, 153, 154, 155, 259
Redemption 17
Reformation 63, 340
  left wing of 361 fn.
Rehoboth 202
Relatives 139, 251, 252, 254, 268, 336, 357
Religion(s) 6, 52, 60, 61, 65, 87, 165, 170, 186, 192, 197, 198, 202, 208, 210, 213, 214, 215, 216, 219, 227, 229, 250, 264, 279, 280, 282, 283, 285, 286, 289, 290, 291, 314, 328, 335, 349, 355, 393
  Babylonian 247
  false 63
  knowledge of 269, 388
  manufactured 270, 274
  of Joseph 276
  of monks 339
  of pope 293
  papistic 251
  pure 235, 242, 371
  true 201, 206, 212, 234, 245, 262, 269, 321, 332, 363
Remission of sins 120, 273; *see also* Forgiveness of sin(s)
Repentance 23, 26, 27, 40, 51, 52, 176, 223, 297, 358
Rephaim 366, 367, 370, 374, 388

Reply to Faustus the Manichean, by St. Augustine 68 fn., 291 fn.
Reptiles 74
Republic, by Plato 327
Resen 201
Respublica 272 fn.
Resurrection 232
  of Christ 151
  of flesh 155
Reuchlin, John 34 fn.
Revelation(s) 83, 86, 162, 163, 164, 174, 249, 283, 320
Revelation of John 150
Revelry 127
Rhetoric, medieval 4 fn.
Rhetoricians 393
Rhipaeans 190
Rhodes 380 fn.
Riches 9, 64, 87, 102, 124, 181, 247, 263, 328, 354
  of divine mercy 358
Ridicule 71
Righteous 3, 12, 84, 100, 197, 307, 349
Righteousness 3, 12, 18, 28, 41, 43, 62, 135, 161, 171, 246, 249, 250, 267, 269, 270, 303, 349, 350, 378, 382, 384
  appearance of 60, 61
  God's 56
  herald of 13, 24, 84
  lost 8
  man's 56
  Noah's, in contrast with his contemporaries 119 fn.
  of Law 160
  of works 158, 159
  preacher of 383
  pretense of 63
  Sun of 383
Riphath 190
Rites 116, 255, 285
Robbery 60, 214
Roman Empire 177, 194 fn., 195

Romans 17, 179, 205, 208, 221, 229, 343, 346, 352, 360
sovereigns of 305
Rome 192, 200, 217, 220, 225, 243, 286, 319
little 339 fn.
Rosary 114
Rose 168, 169
Rose, H. J. 189 fn.
Royal road 77, 78, 282, 286, 299, 370
Ruth 276

Saalfeld 381
Sabbatarians 362
Sabbath 129, 214, 361, 362
Sacrament(s) 72, 84, 197, 286, 301 fn., 338, 341
Sacrament of the Altar 47; *see also* Lord's Supper, Supper of His Son
Sacramentarians 15, 18, 87, 243
Sacred Scriptures x, 126, 237, 359; *see also* Bible, Holy Scripture(s), Scripture(s), Word of God
Sacrifice(s) 73, 80, 88, 114, 117, 118, 132, 138, 139, 142, 166, 173, 197, 242, 272, 284, 362, 386
imperfect 384
law about 116
of Christ 163, 387
of Mass 383, 385, 387
Sailors 106, 181
Saints 8, 21, 31, 44, 61, 81, 104, 112, 113, 120, 136, 145, 167, 169, 170, 171, 172, 178, 199, 216, 217, 240, 243, 245, 247, 249, 267, 268, 287, 289, 290, 294, 306, 307, 312, 320, 330, 346, 357, 369, 370,
371, 375, 391, 398, 399
church of 378
communion of 179
death of 154
fellowship of 181
intercession of 275
invocation(s) of 273, 354
legends of 35, 354
remain steadfast only with difficulty 128
works of 281
worship of 273
Saintliness 12, 59, 60, 135, 188, 372
Noah's 13
Salem 247, 281, 382, 383
king of 381, 386, 394
Sallust 227
Salt Sea 366
Salt wells 94
Salvation 24, 39, 40, 41, 43, 72, 112, 153, 155, 178, 249, 261, 267, 323, 345, 369, 391
Samaritan woman 285
Samson 258, 375
Samuel 19, 50, 91, 102, 270
Sanctity 349, 350, 355
Sanhedrin 248 fn.
Santes Pagninus 14 fn.
Sarah 238, 251, 252, 253, 254, 294, 295, 296, 303, 304, 305, 306, 309, 310, 311, 312, 314, 321, 325, 374, 375
barrenness of 241
Sarai 240, 241, 277, 279, 280, 321
Sardanapalus 206
Satan 8, 11, 17, 115, 128, 157, 168, 169, 184, 197, 218, 219, 222, 228, 236, 258, 259, 273, 275, 292, 302, 319, 354, 356, 369, 387, 388; *see also* Devil(s)

angel of 105, 320
assaults of 154, 235
children of 220
church of 27, 52, 53, 101, 176, 213, 224, 240, 247
darts of 217
doctrine of 334
is a liar and a murderer 172
malice of 174
promises of 266, 268
rage and blows of 230
service to 216
slave(s) of 21, 102
temptations of 48
thorn of 320
transforms himself into an angel of light 213
tries every means to obstruct Word of God 18
wants superstition regarded as religion 213
Satires, by Juvenal 116 fn., 155 fn.
Saul 50, 78, 79, 80, 91, 355
Savior 114, 248; *see also* Christ, Messiah, Son of God, Son of Man
Saxons 188, 366
Scipio 374
Scholarship x
humanistic 33 fn.
Scholastics 13 fn., 43, 46, 47, 48, 121 fn., 314, 315
patrons of free will 39
Scoffers 62
Scotus 124
Scripture(s) ix, 15, 16, 17, 24, 34, 35, 37, 43, 45, 46, 49, 74, 77, 94, 117, 119, 122, 132, 153, 155, 156, 157, 158, 162, 164, 187, 189, 198, 202, 222, 227, 239 fn., 240, 241,

INDEX 423

253, 257, 263, 277, 294, 297, 298, 308, 310, 311, 326, 328, 333, 336, 349, 355, 356, 363, 365, 366, 372, 373, 382, 383, 387, 388, 392; *see also* Bible, Holy Scripture(s), Sacred Scriptures, Word of God
  does not lie 233
  heart and core of 150
  knowledge of 5
  trustworthiness of 233
Scythia
  extra Imaum 108 fn.
  intra Imaum 108 fn.
Scythians 188, 189
Sea of Azov 188 fn.
Seafarers 207
Seasons 129, 136, 208
Seba 195
Second Table 6, 9, 12, 30, 42, 55, 58, 59, 61, 65, 86, 87, 89, 141, 159, 212, 248
Sects 18, 269, 388
Seculum 36
Seed 27, 53, 56, 57, 66, 97, 100, 103, 104, 120, 265, 283, 284, 287, 304, 378
  Blessed 10, 12, 162, 164, 247, 396
  future 23, 317, 382
  heavenly 359
  of Abraham 186, 257, 258, 260, 261, 264, 265
  of Satan 213
  of woman 178, 390
  promise of 31, 52, 55, 63, 64, 71, 144, 179, 180, 235, 236, 281, 303, 391, 398
  Promised 178, 278
Seedtime 136
Seleucia 200, 202
Seleucus 200
Semen 311
Senate 200
Seneca 319, 348 fn.
Senility 169
Sennacherib 202
Sephar, Mt. 207
September 92
Septimius Acindynus 318 fn.
Serpent(s) 27, 71, 135, 151, 204, 229, 265
  brazen 113
  fiery 136
  in Paradise 157
  wise as 163
Servant(s) 176, 252, 279, 280, 336, 337, 349, 373, 389, 396, 399
  of idols 383
  of servants 198
Servetus, Michael 18
Servitude 174, 176, 186, 264, 341
Servus servorum Dei 198 fn.
Seth 28, 29, 114, 178, 180, 209, 228, 235
Sex 29, 30, 31, 356
  weaker 377
Sexual intercourse 11 fn., 115
Sexuality 18 fn.
Sheba 195
Shechem 244, 282, 353
Shechemites 285, 286
Sheep 66, 74, 88, 116, 137, 138, 144, 324, 336, 390
Shelah 247
Shem 25, 58, 71, 170, 175, 176, 178, 179, 180, 181, 183, 184, 185, 186, 187, 193, 195, 196, 197, 198, 201, 202, 204, 206, 209, 217, 219, 225, 228, 229, 231, 232, 234, 235, 236, 240, 242, 247, 249, 250, 251, 277, 281, 283, 358, 368, 371, 381, 383, 393
  generation of 194, 208
  godly descendants of 212
  outlived Abraham by thirty-five years 230
Shepherd(s) 34, 215, 306
Shinar 199, 200, 205, 217
  king of 364
Ship(s) 66, 68
  flames on 147
Short Confession on the Blessed Sacrament, by Luther 43 fn.
Sickness 118, 314, 320, 379
  sweating 136 fn.
Sicut universitatis Conditor, by Innocent III 152 fn.
Sidon 194, 204, 205
Sign(s) 144, 146, 148, 149, 255, 259, 376
  of grace 147
  of terror 147
  of the bow 145
Sihon 259
Silesia 136, 202
Silvae, by Statius 150 fn.
Silver 279, 324, 325, 329, 330, 331, 334, 395
Simeon 217
Sin(s) ix, 8, 13, 14, 16, 21, 22, 26, 30, 31, 32, 33, 39, 40, 42, 43, 48, 49, 52, 53, 55, 58, 60, 65, 70, 74, 85, 95, 100, 113, 123, 128, 131, 133, 134, 135, 136, 137, 141, 142, 143, 154, 157, 161, 167, 170, 172, 173, 194, 205, 209, 212, 216, 219, 220, 222, 223, 224, 227, 237, 241, 247, 250, 253, 263, 264, 269, 274, 278, 280, 287, 289, 292, 293, 297, 300, 311, 316, 319, 334, 344, 354, 358, 360, 369, 377, 380, 382, 397
  against First Table 6, 59

against Second Table 6
forgiveness of 19, 41, 63, 162, 163, 177, 184, 248, 249, 261, 275, 320, 322, 327, 382, 387, 390, 391, 398
Ham's 182
law of 127
makes us all guilty before God 140
ministers of 158
ministry of 160
of apostasy 214
of builders of Tower of Babel 210, 211
of divination 271
of first world 10
of flesh 6
original 4, 5, 6, 9, 118, 119, 121 fn., 127, 149, 167, 168, 171, 308, 314, 315, 345, 348, 353
punishment of, after this life 139
remission of 120, 273
Sinner(s) 41, 43, 49, 53, 66, 87, 100, 167, 172, 182, 221, 297, 300, 345, 384
death of 154
obdurate and callous 96
Savior of 248
Sirach 6, 285, 310
σκύβαλα 7
Slander 168, 297
Slave(s) 247, 296, 361, 374, 379, 381, 391
of Satan 21, 102
of slaves 176, 177
Slavery 361
Smugness 23, 24, 26, 28, 38, 50, 51, 53, 58, 64, 73, 119, 175, 181, 212, 223, 225, 240, 256
Society 83
Socrates 43, 125
Socrates Scholasticus 18 fn.

Sodom 7, 17, 28, 48, 50, 61, 205, 269, 279, 315, 342, 344, 345, 380, 381, 382, 383, 388, 394, 395, 396, 397, 399
"Sodom and Gomorrah II. The Destruction of the Cities of the Plain," by J. Penrose Harland 136 fn.
Sodomites 9, 136, 217, 224, 346, 378, 380
king of 379
Solomon 29, 39, 93, 117, 143, 148, 154, 157, 218, 264, 296, 321
Solstices 92
Son of God 28, 48, 49, 154, 181, 184, 195, 248, 253, 260, 265, 269, 289, 321, 344, 356, 357, 383, 384; *see also* Christ, Messiah, Savior, Son of Man
Son of Man 21, 84; *see also* Christ, Messiah, Savior, Son of God
Song of Solomon 396
Song of Songs 157
Sons of God 5, 9, 11, 12, 20, 21, 27, 29, 30, 31, 32, 33, 37, 54, 180, 195, 224
Sophists 42, 72, 121, 122, 123, 266
Sorceresses 11
Soul(s) 14, 37, 58, 73, 85, 86, 98, 100, 101, 131, 138, 144, 161, 207, 208, 217, 222, 262, 273, 275, 279, 296, 301, 340, 354, 391, 395
destruction of 356
Sowing 129
Sozomen 272 fn.
Spain 189, 191, 346, 353, 354
Spaniards 189, 190
Sparrow 96

Spears 147
Spengler, Lazarus 154 fn.
Spices 65, 195, 231, 325
Spider 168
Spirits
evil 11 fn., 321
misguided 83
Springtime 93
St. Elmo's fire 147 fn.
Stars 192, 256, 257, 305, 359
State(s) 32, 33, 36, 37, 38, 64, 65, 79, 83, 119, 131, 137, 165, 167, 169, 170, 171, 172, 193, 197, 198, 199, 253, 263, 398
Statius 150 fn.
Stephen 241, 242, 277, 278, 283, 305
Stillmesse 333 fn.
Stoics 292, 326, 330, 346, 347
Stomach 231, 279
Strait of Gibraltar 187
Strength 174, 181, 304
physical 9
Succubi 11
Suicide 138
Summa angelica 314
Summa de casibus conscientiae, by Angelo Carletti di Chivasso 314 fn.
Summa theologica, by Thomas Aquinas 44 fn., 313 fn., 314 fn.
Summer 129
Sun 92, 107, 148, 152, 156, 192, 236, 343, 354, 356
of righteousness 315
Sunshine 142
Superstition 192, 213, 215, 244, 247, 250, 272, 355
Supper of His Son 353; *see also* Lord's Supper, Sacrament of the Altar
Supreme Majesty 45

INDEX

Suspensio gratiae 104 fn.
Suspicion(s) 297, 300, 301, 302
Sweating sickness 136 fn.
Swine 36, 109, 116, 169, 270
Swiss 202
Synagog 265, 278
Synecdoche 395
Synoptic Gospels 337 fn.
Syria 108, 204, 206, 258
Syrians 257
Syrup 156

Tabernacle 46, 67, 179, 255, 285
Tapinosis 156 fn.
Targum 380
Tarshish 191
Tarsus 191
Tartars 188, 189, 190, 191
Taurus 108
Tautology 91
Tax collector(s) 42, 303
Taxes 263
Teacher(s) 19, 22, 39, 78, 83, 122, 128, 159, 167, 186, 259, 272, 282, 312, 313, 338, 360, 364, 391
  fanatical 162
  godly 18, 32, 84
  Jewish 138
  of Law 158, 161
  new 243
  perverse 243
  ungodly 251, 273
Teaching(s) 18, 23, 87, 112, 122, 161, 166, 192, 199, 210, 229, 235, 313, 327, 334, 338, 340
  Christ's 86
  ministry of 272, 332
  of Law 159
  ungodly 86
Temple(s) 67, 71, 98, 99, 100, 112, 179, 202 fn., 255, 278, 285, 286
  of Jupiter 192

Temptation(s) 7, 48, 104, 106, 165, 216, 278, 282, 290, 335
Ten Commandments 47, 48
Terah 238, 239, 240, 242, 243, 249, 276, 277
Terence 15, 97 fn., 127 fn., 149 fn., 339, 348 fn.
Tertullian 270 fn.
Testimony, false 9
Tetrapolis 200, 201, 202
Thanksgiving 76, 77, 178, 333, 348, 357, 392, 393
The Idea of Reform. Its Impact on Christian Thought and Action in the Age of the Fathers, by Gerhart B. Ladner 144 fn.
The Lord's Sermon on the Mount, by St. Augustine 318 fn.
The Ten Commandments Preached to the People of Wittenberg, by Luther 11 fn.
Theaters 139
Theft 6, 127, 141, 319
Themistocles 125
Theocritus 385
Theologian(s) 5, 86, 119, 124, 125, 148, 150, 159, 288, 291, 313, 328, 330, 337, 340, 341, 349, 383, 391
  scholastic 119 fn., 125
Theologists 151
Theology 42, 148, 164
  doctors of 220
  scholastic 121 fn., 122 fn., 124
Thief 59, 313
Thomas, doubting 21
Thracians 189
Thuringia 344
Tiber 188 fn.
Tidal 365
Tigers 69, 75, 135
Tigranes 191

Tigris 279
Timaeus, by Plato 207 fn.
Tiras 189, 190
Tischreden, by Luther 277 fn., 361 fn.
Tithe(s) 22, 384, 388, 393, 394
Togarmah 191
Tolls 263
Topics, by Aristotle 271 fn.
Torgau 85 fn.
Tortures 123
Tower of Babel ix, 180, 205, 210, 216, 382
Tradition(s) 161
  patriarchal 116 fn.
Tragedies, Greek 8
Trajan 77
Treachery 127, 199
Trinity 18 fn., 227, 228
Troy 189
Truth 125, 126, 147, 158, 184, 241, 243, 269, 290, 299, 317, 318, 349, 386
  mother of love 297
Tubal 189
Turk(s) 12, 52, 53, 60, 137 fn., 188, 191, 195, 196, 197, 213, 223, 224, 226, 256, 262, 263, 266, 346, 353, 354, 358, 378, 380
  practiced circumcision 192
  regarded and condemned as very Antichrist 181
Turnips 65
Twins 233
Tyranny 7, 8, 20, 30, 32, 33, 34, 37, 61, 62, 84, 197, 198, 210, 212, 214, 219, 275, 292, 306, 310, 317, 318, 364, 368
  of devil 261
  of popes 220
  of Satan 48
Tyrant(s) 5, 23, 30, 32, 36, 38, 53, 59, 85,

132, 177, 198, 199, 224, 260, 275, 296, 310, 367, 369, 383, 391
Tyre 191, 194, 205

Unbelief 119, 176, 254, 264, 310
Unbelievers 24, 261, 304
Understatement 156 fn.
Ungodliness 23, 25, 27, 28, 30, 44, 55, 59, 61, 62, 71, 84, 204, 209, 211, 214, 220, 224, 225, 229, 244, 245, 248, 262, 290, 310, 327, 373
  horrible stench of 117
  of Ham 180
Ungodly 4, 7, 8, 20, 26, 30, 35, 38, 42, 44, 51, 55, 56, 57, 62, 70, 76, 82, 84, 89, 127, 133, 153, 154, 170, 172, 176, 177, 180, 192, 195, 196, 198, 204, 212, 214, 218, 219, 220, 221, 222, 224, 225, 226, 227, 230, 235, 241, 248, 251, 283, 289, 290, 310, 320, 347, 349, 351, 378, 379, 382
  church of 246
  death of 93
  insolence of 182
  smugness of 53, 223
  sown in midst of church 194
University of Perugia 313 fn.
Unrighteousness 28, 383
ὑπερήφανος 320
Ur 242, 248, 249, 268, 269, 276, 277, 278, 281, 290, 340
Usury 263, 326
Uz 206

Vacuum 207
Vaga gratia 177 fn.
Vainglory 119

Vandals 189
Vapor 147
Varro 328 fn.
Venice 137
Venom 163
Venti urentes 106 fn.
Venus 18 fn.
Vergil 15, 106, 304 fn., 352, 385
Victor I, pope 226 fn.
Vigils 161, 339
Vindictiveness 104
Vine 134
Vineyard(s) 166, 188, 373
Virgin(s) 7, 18, 72, 97
Virgin Mary 28, 48, 72 fn., 265; *see also* Blessed Virgin
Vitae patrum 11 fn.
Voluntas
  beneplaciti 44 fn.
  signi 44 fn.
Voluptuousness 60
Vomiting 157
Vow(s) 79, 379
  monastic, of poverty, chastity, and obedience 270 fn.
Voyages of discovery 207 fn.
Vulgate 158 fn., 185 fn., 190 fn., 286 fn., 324 fn., 373 fn., 386 fn.
Vulvas 311

Waldensians 327 fn.
Wantonness 62, 126, 141
War(s) 60, 70, 142, 198, 215, 216, 225, 226, 272, 289, 336, 338, 358, 363, 366, 368, 369, 373, 374, 377, 380, 382, 396
  against kings of five cities 365
Warts 108
Wasps, by Aristophanes 161 fn.
Water(s) 64, 66, 67, 70, 71, 74, 85, 89, 93, 94, 95, 96, 97, 98,

102, 103, 105, 107, 110, 111, 112, 129, 149, 154, 155, 157, 158, 162, 231, 266, 267, 269, 344, 349, 350, 357, 360, 385
  holy 161
  of Merom 34
  of strife 293
  salty 76
Wealth 6, 36, 37, 59, 60, 61, 65, 172, 181, 182, 186, 252, 255, 257, 262, 263, 279, 307, 318, 324, 325, 326, 327, 328, 331, 341, 352, 366, 373, 383, 395, 397, 398
Weather 136, 211
  stormy 146
Weimar
  edition ix, 383 fn.
  editors 18 fn., 95 fn., 154 fn., 202 fn., 246 fn., 314 fn.
  text 232 fn., 276 fn.
Whale 77, 90
Wheat 24, 157
Wickedness 6, 8, 14, 17, 22, 24, 25, 28, 32, 39, 41, 44, 45, 47, 52, 61, 62, 63, 65, 84, 113, 120, 127, 128, 134, 173, 201, 210, 217, 219, 220, 221, 229, 248, 281, 285, 290, 292, 304, 344, 382
  Ham's 170
Will 123, 125, 326
  change of 118
  free 39, 40, 41, 42, 121, 122
  God's 112, 124, 125, 142, 143, 145, 173, 251, 255, 286, 305, 313, 333, 346
  good 302, 392, 395
  of grace 48
  of His good pleasure 44, 46, 47, 48, 49
  of His sign 44, 46, 47, 48, 49

of man 270
right, toward God 126
Wine 46, 167, 173, 230, 231, 243, 350, 357, 383, 384, 385, 387, 388
  effect of 166
  of joy 386
Winter 92, 129
Wisdom 3, 4, 5, 6, 9, 12, 15, 18, 46, 65, 78, 119, 160, 171, 208, 258, 329, 340, 342, 354, 378
  divine 120, 170, 266
  inept, of some men 313
  of Egyptians 305
  of God 79, 80, 130
  pretense of 63
Wiseacres 172
Wittenberg 137 fn., 147
Wolf 74, 75, 116, 135, 138
Word of God 30, 32, 33, 35, 40, 41, 47, 82, 104, 112, 132, 133, 146, 171, 173, 209, 218, 222, 236, 248, 250, 271, 274, 275, 285, 292, 295, 309, 334, 351, 352, 355, 356, 357, 358, 361, 369, 387; see also Bible, Holy Scripture(s), Sacred Scriptures, Scripture(s)
Wordiness 88, 96
Work(s) 103, 124, 222, 241, 246, 249, 269, 271, 273, 315, 351, 352, 355, 392
  alien 134
  amazing and unusual 357
  diverse 113
  doctrine of 159
  God's 111, 112, 147, 148, 149, 306
  good 119, 159, 165, 268, 354

holy and life-giving 184
human 149, 387
merit of 122
of Holy Spirit 267
of saints 281
optional 350
righteousness of 158, 159
secular 349
spiritual 350
unfruitful 356
World 8, 23, 27, 30, 36, 37, 38, 43, 49, 55, 56, 57, 59, 60, 61, 62, 65, 68, 82, 86, 87, 89, 92, 97, 99, 102, 140, 142, 143, 144, 148, 149, 153, 154, 163, 167, 168, 169, 170, 172, 173, 175, 176, 180, 184, 186, 191, 193, 194, 195, 196, 198, 200, 204, 208, 211, 212, 216, 218, 219, 223, 224, 226, 228, 229, 230, 235, 237, 244, 245, 247, 253, 254, 257, 258, 260, 261, 265, 268, 273, 274, 290, 295, 302, 304, 312, 326, 327, 331, 333, 338, 345, 346, 352, 355, 356, 368, 370, 375, 377, 378, 379, 380, 382, 383, 384, 390, 391, 395, 398
  after Flood 187
  better 66
  children of 64
  creation of 131
  despises Word and admires what is new 243
  does not understand counsels of God 58
  end of 16
  everlasting 3
  first 10, 19, 24, 40, 52, 63, 64, 66, 70, 81, 209, 232, 234, 236

full of various kinds of sects 388
history of ix
intolerant of sound doctrine 13
kingdom of 177
original 3, 4, 5, 6, 26, 32, 53, 81, 83, 84, 89, 165
power of 181
primitive 3, 114
prince of 88, 334
realms of 177
regarded Noah as exceedingly stupid 71
smug and ungodly 25
smugness of 28
unbelieving 81, 85
ungodly 7, 84
ungrateful 22
unrepentant 20
years of 239
wants to be deceived 354
wickedness of 17, 217
Worldlings 37
Worship 6, 18, 29, 40, 42, 52, 53, 55, 60, 71, 112, 113, 128, 160, 165, 170, 176, 192, 197, 201, 205, 213, 214, 219, 235, 242, 243, 244, 246, 256, 257, 258, 263, 269, 282, 283, 285, 286, 305, 306, 326, 333, 334, 335, 349, 355, 356, 361, 363, 371, 383, 388, 389, 393, 394
  highest form of 173
  idolatrous and ungodly forms of 32, 99, 199, 251
  new forms of 198, 230
  of saints 273
  true 12, 19, 31, 54, 56, 57, 59, 63, 240, 247, 250, 284, 334, 382
Wrath 4, 5, 21, 22, 23, 30, 47, 49, 50, 51, 52, 53, 54, 57, 60, 64, 65, 66, 70, 72,

75, 81, 82, 85, 86, 89, 91, 96, 99, 103, 111, 117, 118, 120, 122, 123, 131, 143, 145, 148, 149, 150, 153, 155, 157, 158, 176, 186, 210, 211, 216, 224, 229, 248, 252, 265, 266, 280, 287, 317, 321, 322, 344, 352, 356, 358, 377, 378, 382, 383, 389
children of 121
era of 163

is truly God's alien work 134
of grace 223
Writers
  Christian ix, 116 fn.
  Jewish 116 fn.
  secular 237

Xenophon 43, 160

Year(s) 93, 208, 304
  civil 92
  sacred 92
  of world 239

Zacharias 178
Zarephath 178, 259
Zeal 125, 171, 185, 331, 399
  for allegories 150
  for piety 292
Zechariah 19, 191, 333
Zemarite 204
Zion, Mt. 101
Zittau 202 fn.
Zoar 265, 378
Zuzim 367, 374
Zwingli 43 fn., 243
Zwyn 137 fn.

INDEX TO SCRIPTURE PASSAGES

Genesis
  1:20 — 74
  1:24 — 74
  1:27 — 121
  1:28 — 64, 236, 330
  1:31 — 51, 64
  2:11 — 195
  3:15 — 64, 178, 229, 265
  3:16 — 49
  4:1 — 185
  4:4, 5 — 116
  4:10 — 61
  4:15 — 140
  4:17 — 196, 200
  6:1, 2 — 10
  6:2, 3 — 224
  6:5 — 120, 122, 127
  6:6 — 117
  6:8 — 26
  6:9 — 245
  6:12 — 55
  7:2 — 134
  7:11 — 89
  7:21 — 74
  8:4 — 116
  8:21 — 39, 145
  9:1 — 115
  10:10 — 202, 217
  10:10, 11 — 364
  10:11 — 214
  10:21 — 234
  10:22 — 201, 232
  10:25 ff. — 371
  11:28 — 248
  11:31 — 277
  12:1 — 242, 351
  12:2, 3 — 316
  12:3 — 363, 389
  12:4 — 271
  12:6 — 381
  12:7 — 351
  12:18 — 376
  14:7 — 364
  14:14 — 279
  14:18 — 247
  15:5 — 359
  17:17 — 238
  18:2 — 249
  18:20, 21 — 61
  18:23-32 — 50
  19:22 — 378
  20:11 — 293
  20:12 — 29
  20:18 — 311
  22:12 — 222
  22:17 — 256, 257
  24:3 — 10
  25:22 — 231
  26:9 — 45
  26:11 — 305
  28:17 — 284
  28:19 — 286
  46:32 — 324

Exodus
  1:20 — 259
  12:2 — 92
  12:38 — 324
  12:40 — 277
  14:21 — 107
  14:28 — 259
  20:13 — 139
  21:6 — 361
  22:15 — 182
  28:30 — 242
  29:18 — 116
  32:32 — 50
  33:20 — 46

Leviticus
  1:13 — 116
  6:12 — 242
  11 — 74
  19:32 — 175

Numbers
  13 — 367
  13:34 — 33
  16:32 — 58
  18:23 — 361
  20:12 — 293
  21:6 — 136
  24:24 — 191

Deuteronomy
  2:10, 11 — 367
  2:33 — 259
  3:3 — 259
  4:6, 7 — 258
  4:6 ff. — 353
  4:7 — 255
  4:24 — 7
  16:5, 6 — 285
  20:17 — 10
  29:13 — 246
  29:19 — 243
  31:29 — 59
  32:15 — 345
  32:21 — 170
  32:24 — 135

Joshua
  2:18 — 395
  6:25 — 259
  11:7 — 34
  12:4 — 367
  20:7 — 282
  24:2 — 239, 243, 246, 249
  24:12 — 246

Judges
  7:1 — 282
  11:29-40 — 113

Ruth
  1:16 — 276

1 Samuel
  9:15 ff. — 79
  12:23 — 19
  15 — 355
  15:9 — 78
  15:22 — 272
  15:22, 23 — **270**
  15:35 — 91
  16:1 — 50
  16:7 — 102
  19:17 — 292

2 Samuel
  11:4 — 293
  15:34 — 292
  17:20 — 292
  18:33 — 91

1 Kings
  4:30 — 217
  11:1-8 — 29
  12:28, 29 — **286**
  16:31-33 — 29

16:34 — 113
17:8-24 — 259
18:17 — 20
18:38 — 242
19:18 — 101

2 Kings

2:24 — 136
5:17 — 258
16:3 — 113

Ezra

1:2 — 128, 258

Esther

2:2, 3 — 304
8:10 — 264

Job

1:1 — 206
2:3 — 319
21:13 — 351
21:14 — 315
21:17 — 351
26:7 ff. — 94
38:11 — 93

Psalms

1:2 — 21
1:3 — 163
2:1, 2 — 35
2:4 — 224
2:5 — 224
2:9 — 3
2:11 — 307
4:1 — 185
4:3 — 288
4:6 — 121
5:9 — 158
6:1 — 321
7:6 — 61
7:17 — 388
9:2 — 388
9:9 — 283
9:13 — 61
9:20 — 282
10:9 — 34
10:11 — 61, 221
10:12 — 222
12:4 — 33
13:1 — 222
13:2 — 61

14:1, 2 — 83
14:2 — 167, 171
14:2, 3 — 40, 83, 301
14:3 — 59
18:13 — 388
27:14 — 308
30:5 — 143, 223
33:12 — 352
34:4 — 307
34:6 — 307
34:19 — 307
35:3 — 373
37:19 — 289
37:25 — 289
39:12 — 252, 281
41:1 — 289
44:23 — 222
45:3 — 182
45:10 — 250
45:11 — 250
50:15 — 307
54:7 — 9
60:6 — 353
62:10 — 328, 398
68:13 — 157
68:20 — 156
73 — 351
73:2, 3 — 307
73:3-6 — 346
73:4 ff. — 33
73:11 — 222
73:14 — 196, 346
73:22 — 347
78:33 — 310
78:68, 69 — 101
80:10 — 342
81:12 — 26, 38
82:6 — 390
84:6 — 282
89:30, 32 — 223
89:30-33 — 257
90:10 — 304
92:7 — 196
92:11 — 9
94:3 — 180
98:9 — 62
101 — 226
104:16, 17 — 342
105:12-15 — 306
107:11 — 310
109:4 — 50
109:11 — 262
110:4 — 384, 387, 393

110:6 — 16
110:7 — 156
112:7 — 289
116:11 — 40, 297, **300**
116:15 — 154
120:5 — 189
127:2 — 49
127:3 — 132
132:14 — 98, 100
136:4 — 389
139:22 — 174
144:12, 13 — 390
144:12-15 — 390
144:15 — 352, 390
146:3 — 297

Proverbs

1:10 — 182
8:27 — 93
10:24 — 218
18:3 — 39
18:22 — 143
21:19 — 297
22:15 — 321
27:9 — 117

Ecclesiastes

1:9 — 148
2:16 — 153, 154

Song of Solomon

1:14 — 157
2:10 — 157
4:3 — 396

Isaiah

1:8, 9 — 229
3:5 — 175
4:6 — 48
10:20 — 229
11:1 — 72
11:11 — 203
14:12 — 12
23:1 — 191
25:2 — 35
28:19 — 321
28:21 — 134
30:20 — 282
31:9 — 98, 255
37:21 ff. — 202
41:2 — 246, 303
44:28 — 34

INDEX

45:18 — 142
48:4 — 220
49:4 — 24
51:19 — 360
54:7, 8 — 310
55:6 — 18
55:8 — 5
57:1 — 24
57:4 — 262
60:3 ff. — 245
60:8 — 157, 163

Jeremiah

10:24 — 322
12 — 62
12:1 — 35
12:3 — 35, 351
15:10 — 17
20 — 62
20:2 — 20
20:7 — 182
20:14, 15 — 20
25:15 — 157
29:10 — 100
38:7-13 — 259
44:17 — 290
49:12 — 320
51:9 — 17
51:27 — 190

Ezekiel

1:5 — 74
6:12 — 70
11:8, 9 — 218
13:5 — 51
13:19 — 161
26:17 — 194
27:7 — 191
27:14 — 191
31:9 — 201
33:11 — 22
38:2 — 188
38:2, 3 — 189
38:6 — 188

Daniel

2:21 — 190, 254
4:31 ff. — 258
5:23 — 391
6:24 — 58
6:26 — 258
8:10 — 359
10:13 — 181

Hosea

2:14 — 183
4:14 — 13
7:12 — 221
10 — 285
10:5 — 243
12:1 — 106
13:15 — 107

Joel

2:32 — 287

Amos

9:8 — 190

Jonah

1:2 — 43
3:3 — 201, 342
3:4, 5 — 24
3:10 — 43

Micah

1:11 — 243
2:6 — 20
2:7 — 53
7:5 — 297, 301, 302
7:6 — 297

Habakkuk

2:3 — 176

Zechariah

12:10 — 19, 333

Malachi

3:8 — 22
4:2 — 315

Matthew

3:12 — 24
3:16 — 45
3:17 — 48
5:3, 6 — 330
5:6 — 41
5:45 — 299, 343
7:1 — 297
7:1, 3 — 297
7:20, 21 — 21
10:13 — 363
10:16 — 163
10:21 — 271
10:34 — 297
10:37 — 341
11:23, 24 — 315
12:45 — 348
12:50 — 48
16:18 — 64, 260, 283
16:19 — 274
17:5 — 274
18:7 — 230
18:20 — 335
18:22 — 298, 300
18:25 — 58
19:21 — 330
19:30 — 194
20:26, 27 — 337
22:2 — 163
22:7 — 378
23:10 — 220
23:11 — 274
23:37-39 — 50
24:13 — 105, 176
24:22 — 229, 283
24:37 — 25, 37
24:38 — 58, 92
26:37 ff. — 335
28:20 — 99

Mark

1:7 — 395
2:4 — 67
6:17 — 32
10:39 — 153
12:25 — 130
13:32 — 26
16:15, 16 — 260

Luke

1:30 — 54
1:51 — 4
1:51-53 — 35
1:52 — 118
1:68 — 178
2:14 — 388, 392
2:19 — 312
2:35 — 217
3:8 — 295
6:35 — 263
8:2 — 321
10:7 — 76
10:16 — 175, 250, 274, 358
10:23, 24 — 353
10:28 — 159

11:17 — 225
12:50 — 153
14:16 — 163
16:21 — 196
16:29 — 83
17:10 — 160
18:8 — 84
18:11 — 42
19:14 — 315
22:25, 26 — 274
22:32 — 99
24:39 — 45

John

3:14 — 151
3:19 — 354
4:20 — 285
4:22 — 178
5:17 — 148
6:40 — 48
8:36 — 123
8:44 — 172, 197
8:56 — 260, 261, 353, 377
9:1 — 321
10:15 — 138
10:16 — 215
10:34 — 390
11:48 — 221, 361
11:49-51 — 218
13:15 ff. — 337
14:9 — 49
14:18 — 99
15:5 — 40
16:8 — 19, 40
16:14 — 356
16:32 — 88
18:36 — 37

Acts

2 — 215
7:2 — 277
7:2, 3 — 241
7:5 — 283, 359, 373
7:22 — 305
11:28 — 288
28:15 — 335

Romans

1:28 — 399
1:31 — 300
2:5 — 43

2:15 — 160
2:17 — 99
3:10 — 40
3:10-12 — 83
4:15 — 158
4:18 — 288
5:3 — 157, 289
5:12 — 121
5:20 — 158
6:3 — 153
6:23 — 322
7:18 — 41
7:22 — 127
7:23 — 309
8:7 — 14
8:28 — 378
9:3 — 50
9:6 — 179
9:16 — 248
9:31 — 160
10:14 — 287
11:11 — 178
11:17 — 185
11:32 — 40
12:2 — 48
12:3 — 168
12:6 — 151
13:1 — 272
13:3 — 318
14:4 — 171
14:6, 8 — 348
14:23 — 113
15:4 — 225, 325
15:19 — 184

1 Corinthians

1:19 — 3
2:5 — 102
2:15 — 61
3:12-15 — 164
4:13 — 177
7:31 — 253
8 — 329
8:5, 6 — 388
9:16 — 272
9:24-26 — 115
10:2 — 152
10:4 — 151
10:12 — 72, 171
10:13 — 325
11:19 — 230
11:24, 25 — 385, 387
11:29 — 47

13:4, 7 — 300
14:13 — 333

2 Corinthians

3:6 — 158, 164
4:7 — 73
5:14 — 16
6:10 — 330
11:14 — 213
12:2, 3 — 86
12:7 — 105, 320
12:9 — 174

Galatians

1:10 — 184
3:1 — 184
3:7 — 179
3:9 — 280
3:17 — 277

Ephesians

2:3 — 121
2:14 — 215
3:8 — 247
4:30 — 17, 44
4:32 — 341
5:11 — 356
5:25 — 30, 301
5:28 — 295
6:16 — 88, 217

Philippians

3:8 — 7
3:13 — 73
3:18 — 50
4:5 — 341
4:11-13 — 370
4:12 — 349

Colossians

2:18 — 355
2:23 — 59, 339, 356

1 Thessalonians

2:13 — 358
5:3 — 93

2 Thessalonians

2:3, 4 — 383
2:3-12 — 101
2:11 — 354

INDEX

1 Timothy
- 1:4 — 237
- 4:3, 4 — 77
- 4:4, 5 — 77
- 4:5 — 285
- 5:8 — 330
- 6:4 — 297
- 6:16 — 46

2 Timothy
- 3:3 — 300
- 3:16 — 325
- 4:2 — 23

Titus
- 2:14 — 292

Hebrews
- 7:2 — 393
- 7:3 — 381
- 9:12 — 384
- 10:14 — 384, 386
- 11:2 — 113, 114
- 11:8, 9 — 246
- 11:9, 10 — 362
- 11:19 — 294

James
- 1:22 — 159

1 Peter
- 3:6 — 252
- 3:18-20 — 85
- 3:21 — 155
- 3:21, 22 — 151
- 5:3 — 274
- 5:5 — 4
- 5:6, 7 — 316

2 Peter
- 1:19 — 81
- 2:5 — 3, 10, 13, 24, 56, 83, 84, 89, 383
- 2:7 — 217
- 2:8 — 8, 17, 28
- 2:22 — 379
- 3:5, 6 — 64

1 John
- 1:5 — 247
- 5:16 — 19

Revelation
- 18:4, 5 — 274

APOCRYPHA

Wisdom of Solomon
- 2:11 — 33
- 2:24 — 143
- 11:16 — 311

Ecclesiasticus
- 2:14 — 310
- 4:30 — 296
- 6:7 — 297
- 10:13 — 6
- 15:14-17 — 350
- 25:1 — 301
- 50:26 — 285

Prayer of Manasses
- 5 — 172

Luther   51749

MERRIMACK COLLEGE LIBRARY
North Andover, Massachusetts

DISCARD

DEMCO